Pop Cinema

Pop Cinema

Edited by Glyn Davis and Tom Day

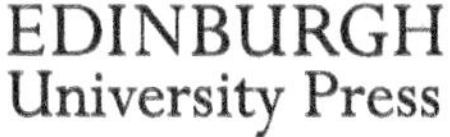

EDINBURGH
University Press

Edinburgh University Press is one of the leading university presses in the UK. We publish academic books and journals in our selected subject areas across the humanities and social sciences, combining cutting-edge scholarship with high editorial and production values to produce academic works of lasting importance. For more information visit our website: edinburghuniversitypress.com

Grateful acknowledgement is made to the sources listed in the List of Illustrations for permission to reproduce material previously published elsewhere. Every effort has been made to trace the copyright holders, but if any have been inadvertently overlooked, the publisher will be pleased to make the necessary arrangements at the first opportunity.

Edinburgh University Press Ltd
13 Infirmary Street
Edinburgh EH1 1LT

First published in hardback by Edinburgh University Press 2024

Typeset in 12 on 14pt Arno Pro and Myriad Pro by
Cheshire Typesetting Ltd, Cuddington, Cheshire, and
printed and bound by CPI Group (UK) Ltd, Croydon, CR0 4YY

A CIP record for this book is available from the British Library

ISBN 978 1 4744 9790 9 (hardback)
ISBN 978 1 4744 9791 6 (paperback)
ISBN 978 1 4744 9792 3 (webready PDF)
ISBN 978 1 4744 9793 0 (epub)

Contents

Illustrations

Figures

Note on Contributors

Kara Carmack is the Assistant Director of Exhibitions and Public Programmes at the New York Studio School. She received her PhD in art history from the University of Texas at Austin and specialises in modern and contemporary art and visual culture, with an emphasis on creative communities, gender and sexuality, and archives. Her current book project, *Marginal Centers: Parties on, off, and through Manhattan Public Access Television, 1972–1983*, focuses on public access television shows produced by Anton Perich, Glenn O'Brien and Andy Warhol. Her research has recently been supported by the American Association of University Women and the Association of Historians of American Art. She has contributed to numerous exhibition catalogues and journals, including *Journal of Visual Culture*.

David Crowley teaches at the National College of Art and Design, Dublin. He is a historian and curator with an interest in Eastern Europe under communist rule. He has curated various exhibitions, including *Cold War Modern* at the Victoria and Albert Museum in 2008–9 (co-curated with Jane Pavitt); *Sounding the Body Electric: Experimental Art and Music in Eastern Europe* at Muzeum Sztuki, Łódź, 2012, and Calvert 22, London, 2013; and *Notes from the Underground: Music and Alternative Art in Eastern Europe, 1968–1994* at Muzeum Sztuki, Łódź, 2017, and Akademie der Künste in Berlin, 2018 (both co-curated with Daniel Muzyczuk). His exhibition *Henryk Stażewski: Late Style* was mounted at Muzeum Sztuki, Łódź, in 2023.

Jon Davies is a curator and writer from Montreal, Canada. He received his PhD in Art History from Stanford University, with a dissertation on the close intertwining of artistic and sexual experimentation in the San Francisco Bay Area. Previously, he worked as Assistant Curator at The Power Plant Contemporary Art Gallery in Toronto and as Associate Curator at Oakville Galleries. His writing on contemporary art, film and culture has been published widely, including in exhibition catalogues, magazines, academic journals and anthologies. His book on Andy Warhol and Paul Morrissey's film *Trash* was published in 2009 and his anthology *More Voice-Over: Colin Campbell Writings* in 2021. He co-edited issues #5 and #6 of *Little Joe* magazine – 'about queers and cinema, mostly' – with Sam Ashby. He was recently co-curator of the 68th Robert Flaherty Film Seminar, 'Queer World-Mending', with Steve Reinke.

Glyn Davis is Professor of Film Studies at the University of St Andrews. Amongst other publications, he is the co-author of *Film Studies: A Global Introduction* (2015), as well as a co-editor of *Queer Print in Europe* (2022, with Laura Guy) and *The Richard Dyer Reader* (2023, with Jaap Kooijman). From 2016 to 2019, Glyn was the Project Leader of the HERA-funded project 'Cruising the Seventies: Unearthing Pre-HIV/AIDS Queer Sexual Cultures'; from 2023 to 2025, he is leading the JPICH-funded project 'Perverse Collections: Building Europe's Queer and Trans Archives'.

Tom Day is Executive Director of the New American Cinema Group/The Film-Makers' Cooperative in New York City. He has previously held teaching and research positions at The Courtauld Institute of Art, University of London and the University of Edinburgh. His writings on film, video and media art have appeared or are forthcoming in *Panorama, Oxford Art Journal, Art History, Short Film Studies* and numerous edited volumes. He is currently writing a monograph on the relationship between television, art and politics in the 1980s, titled *TV Generation: Art and The Political Imaginary of Television on The Lower East Side*.

Clint Enns is a writer and visual artist living in Montréal.

Ed Halter is a writer and curator living in Brooklyn. He is the author of *From Sun Tzu to Xbox: War and Videogames* (2006), as well as the co-editor of *Mass Effect: Art and the Internet in the Twenty-First Century* (2015, with Lauren Cornell) and *From the Third Eye: The Evergreen Review Reader* (2018, with Barney Rosset). His criticism has been published by 4Columns, *Artforum*, the Criterion Collection, the *New Yorker*, the *Village Voice* and elsewhere, and he has curated screenings and exhibitions for the Whitney

Biennial, the Walker Art Center, the Flaherty Film Seminar and more. He runs Light Industry, a venue for cinema in all its forms in New York, and he teaches as Critic in Residence at Bard College.

Juan Carlos Guerrero-Hernández is Assistant Professor at the University of Nevada at Reno. His interdisciplinary research on decoloniality, memory, violence, performance, moving image and photography has been published in journals such as *TDR The Drama Review, Photographies, Cinergie – Il Cinema e le altre Arti, Revista Chilena de Literatura* and *Revista de Estudios Sociales,* as well as in edited books such as *Ventriloquism, Performance, and Contemporary Art* (2023, edited by Jennie Hirsch and Isabelle Loring Wallace) and *Fallen Monuments and Contested Memorials* (2024, edited by Juilee Decker). Guerrero-Hernández has been awarded the National Prize in Art Criticism, merit-based Research Grants in Dance and in Visual Arts from the Ministry of Culture and a merit-based travel grant from the Jack, Joseph and Morton Mandel Center, among others.

William Kaizen is an independent scholar and curator. His research focuses on the history and politics of new media, from video art to video games. He is the author of *Against Immediacy: Video Art and Media Populism* (2016) and has curated exhibitions on the work of pop artist Derek Boshier and the history of pop art on film in the United States and United Kingdom.

Kimberly Lamm is Associate Professor of Gender, Sexuality and Feminist Studies and Art, Art History and Visual Studies at Duke University. She is currently a Research Associate with VIAD (Visual Identities in Art and Design) at the University of Johannesburg. Her scholarship brings together Anglophone literature, contemporary art and the feminist engagement with psychoanalysis. Lamm is the author of *Addressing the Other Woman: Textual Correspondences in Feminist Art and Writing* (2017) and has published work in *Women's Studies Quarterly, Oxford Art Journal, Australian Feminist Studies, Cultural Critique* and *Feminist Theory.* Lamm's forthcoming work includes *Writing in the Kitchen with Martha Rosler and Carrie Mae Weems: From Reproductive Labor to the Affective Labor of the Image* (2024), *Laura Mulvey: Feminist Legacies* (with Laura Mulvey and Anna Backman Rogers, 2024) and *Riddles of the Sphinx* (2024).

Justin Remes is Associate Professor of Film Studies at Iowa State University. He is the author of *Motion(less) Pictures: The Cinema of Stasis* (2015) and

Absence in Cinema: The Art of Showing Nothing (2020). He has also written articles for *JCMS: The Journal of Cinema and Media Studies, Cinema Journal* and *Screen*. His current book project is a work of experimental scholarship titled *Found Footage Films.*

Gillian Sneed is Assistant Professor and Area Coordinator of Art History in The School of Art and Design at San Diego State University. She received her PhD in art history from the Graduate Center at The City University of New York. Her research examines twentieth- and twenty-first-century feminist art histories of the Americas. She explores the intersecting genres of video, performance, conceptual and socially engaged art, and the gendered, sexual and racial politics at play in these practices. Her writing has appeared in *Art in America, The Brooklyn Rail, Flash Art International, Texte zur Kunst* and *Women's Art Journal.* Her most recent publication is the edited volume *The Letters of Rosemary and Bernadette Mayer, 1976–1980* (2022, co-edited with Marie Warsh).

Acknowledgements

We would like to thank the following for their help in bringing this collection to completion: Sam Johnson, Gillian Leslie and Kelly O'Brien at Edinburgh University Press; Nina Macaraig for her diligent copy-editing; Jonathan Flatley; Juan Antonio Suárez; James Boaden for offering helpful suggestions at the proposal stage; Lucy Coslett for research assistance; and Sairaa Bains for help with indexing, rights approval and other editorial demands.

Introduction: Towards a Pop Cinema

Glyn Davis and Tom Day

Between precisely 19:45 and 21:55 on the evening of 9 September 1967 at the Galerie Dorothea Loehr in Frankfurt, the advertising creative, curator and soon to be prominent gallerist Paul Maenz staged a prescient group exhibition named after its opening hours: *19:45–21:55*. Various works displayed on that early autumn evening would eventually be recognised as significant bellwethers in the emergence of conceptual art, land art and post-minimalist sculpture; contributors to the show included such figures as Jan Dibbets, Richard Long and Charlotte Posenenske.[1] An outlier in the group was Peter Roehr, a twenty-three-year-old German artist: unlike those of his fellow invitees, Roehr's contribution was not ephemeral, sculptural or conceptual. Roehr's short film work *Ringer* (*Wrestlers*, 1965) was staged in two parts, both of which were shown away from the Galerie's rooms: the film was projected outside on the façade of the Galerie, and it was accompanied by a large, illustrated billboard that advertised the work in a manner not dissimilar to that of a major Hollywood film (Figure I.1). Such a reference to the American film industry was deeply incongruous in the context of the wider exhibition. However, *Ringer* and its accompanying hoarding illuminate some of the main themes and interests that underpinned Roehr's artistic practice – a practice that emblematises what this collection of essays terms 'Pop cinema'.

There is a notable discrepancy between Roehr's use of a conventional form of advertising, the film billboard and the experimental format of *Ringer*. The film depicts, in grainy appropriated footage, two men, dressed only in trunks, engaged in a Greco-Roman wrestling match. Shot from a low angle, their bodies are framed by intense sunlight as it peeks through an intermittently clouded sky. The footage is in slow motion, which enhances the balletic qualities of the men's tangled embraces. In its entirety the wrestling

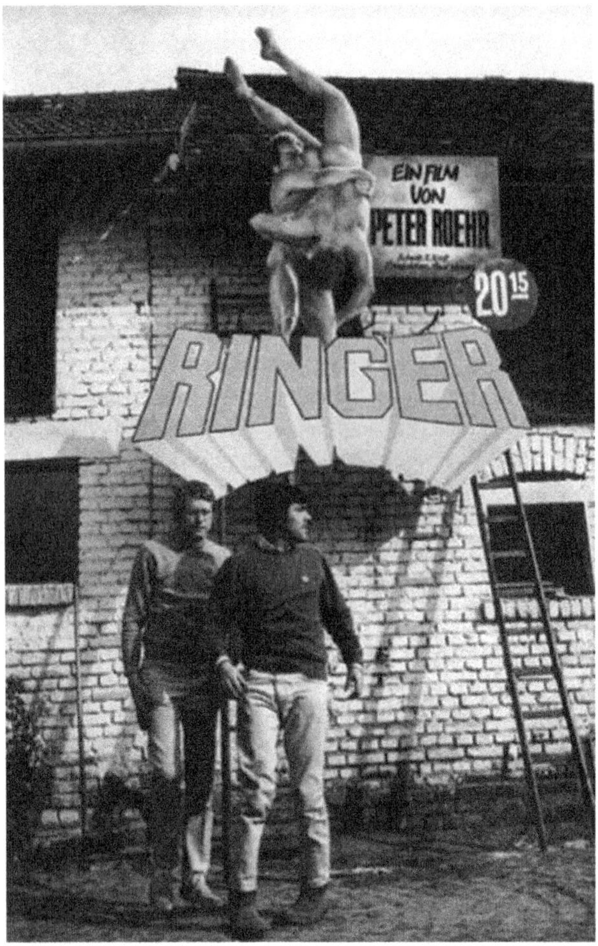

Figure I.1 Peter Roehr (left) and Paul Maenz installing a billboard-style advertisement for Roehr's film *Ringer* (1965) in preparation for the exhibition *19:45–21:55* at the Galerie Dorothea Loehr, Frankfurt, September 1967. Source: Archiv Peter Roehr, Museum für Moderne Kunst, Frankfurt am Main.

sequence lasts for five seconds, but *Ringer* has a duration of fifty-six seconds, as it consists of the scene repeated nine times over. *Ringer* is plotless and guided by a formal conceit that underpins all of Roehr's film works – one based on the principle of serial repetition, in which sequences are seen over and over again, without change or variation. Some weeks after showing *Ringer* at *19:45–21:55*, Roehr wrote in a journal entry:

> [I]n commercial or conventional film the meaning of the content arises in large part through the stringing together and comparison of different facts […] [I]n my films a simple sentence represents the narrative.

> Either: a woman is drying her hair. Or: 2 Cars drive into a tunnel. Through the repetition of this element, something that was initially only noticeable begins to resolve and expand.[2]

Roehr was sincere when he stated that his work was 'simple': that its purpose was not to look outside itself or be hindered by complex narratives. He outlined his working methodology as a basic strategy of collection (or, more accurately, appropriation) and display, as evidenced by two particular statements: 'I assemble things of the same kind together [...] I use no organic objects, but only constructed, preferably industrially-produced things'; and 'I alter material by organising it unchanged. Each work is an organised area of identical elements. Neither successive or additive, there is no result or sum.'[3] He called the art objects that resulted out of this process 'Montages'.

Roehr was keenly aware of other artists working with seriality and repetition, including Minimalists such as Frank Stella, Robert Morris, Donald Judd and Carl Andre; his own work combined their fascination with form with overtly Pop content, primarily drawn from print advertising and television commercials. Indeed, *Ringer*'s use of a repetitive cinematic syntax needs to be explored in relation to its depicted, looped content, as well as its advertising hoarding, which announces the film with the kind of bold, declamatory typography expected of a sword-and-sandal epic. The billboard's promise is not fulfilled by the film itself, which instead presents a truncated and tantalising incomplete moment taken from a film trailer, reiterated multiple times. And yet the relationship between the film and the hoarding is knotty: both engage with the spectacle of popular entertainment, both move facets of commercial culture into (or almost into) the 'high art' space of the gallery, and both reveal a fascination with the affective or erotic charge of the lowbrow. The two components of the work clearly evidence Roehr's position as an art-maker who bridged Pop art and Minimalism, and as a queer artist who excavated latent meanings from given common cultural materials (the '69' position of the bodies of the two wrestlers above the title on the billboard promises a form of deliciously filthy sexual content that the finished film fails to materialise).[4]

Roehr's films can be considered archetypal expressions of what, in this volume, we are terming 'Pop cinema'. His 'Montages' draw on pre-existing moving image materials, appropriating and sampling brief sequences from them. The looped snatches of film – a woman drying her hair with a towel; a spinning Gulf petrol logo; suds draining down a plughole; sunlight illuminating a city-block of skyscrapers – echo and evoke audiences' repeated exposure to the same banal advertisements, over and over again,

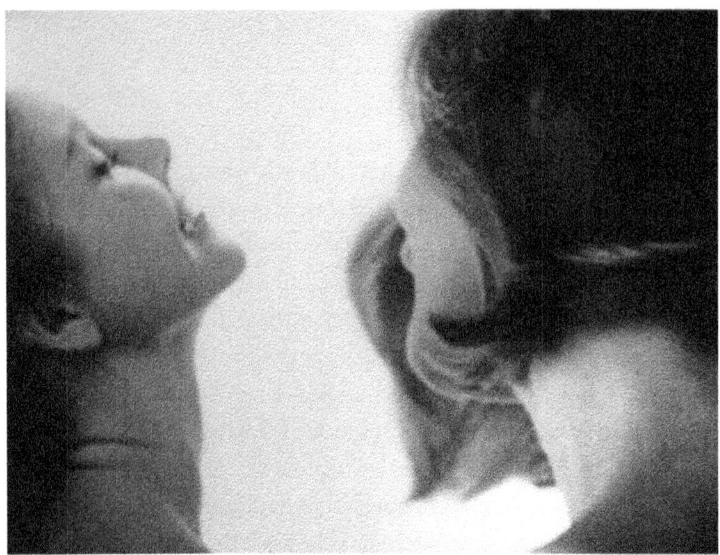

Figure I.2 Peter Roehr, *Haare 14x*, from *Filmmontagen I*, 1965. Source: Archiv Peter Roehr, Museum für Moderne Kunst, Frankfurt am Main. © DACS 2023.

whilst also drawing attention to the repetitive rhetoric of advertising as a form (Figure I.2). The artist's use of quotations, with only minor formal shaping – a sampling, a looping – highlights the mechanical form of his practice, raising questions about the amount of input he had: where exactly is the trace of the filmmaker's hand, his voice? Further, Roehr's films (and, indeed, the idiosyncratic, spectacle-like display of the hoarding advertising *Ringer* at the Frankfurt exhibition) reveal the muddied relationship between experimental film and dominant filmmaking (at once enamoured, critical and playful) that marks much Pop cinema. And if Roehr's films are not 'pure' Pop, his works combining Pop materials and concerns with Minimalist forms, in this he is again typical; as the essays in this book reveal, many 'Pop' films also draw in their form and content on aspects of other art movements.

Pop Cinema is the first book devoted to moving image works which centrally engage with key thematics and concerns of Pop art. All of the essays in this collection examine how principal interests and topics associated with Pop – the repetitions of mass manufacturing, the ambivalent appeal of consumer objects, the collision of affects and imagery in advertising, the widespread adoption of post-war mechanisation, the persistence of delimited and stereotypical gendered forms of representation – have found expression in the work of an array of experimental filmmakers (and some art cinema directors) around the globe. They also explore the ways in which the characteristic aesthetics of Pop – bold, flat planes of colour; repetitive use of images; appropriation of popular culture content (movie stills, comic book panels, newspaper photographs, print advertisements and so on) – were either adapted for the screen, or combined with (or even jettisoned for) alternative formulations. This book has a central and provocative aim: to recalibrate historical and theoretical understandings of Pop, expanding the field to include the moving image. Although Pop has always been a transmedial art movement – finding its expression in paintings, screen prints, sculptures, installations and other forms – cinema has very rarely been considered by historians and theorists as a medium through which Pop could and did manifest. This book begins to rectify that omission. Simultaneously, writing from a contemporary vantage point in which Pop tropes and aesthetics bloom in manifold permutations across moving image culture, this collection's contributors dig out foundational works of the 1960s and 1970s, exploring the varied root sources of this present-day flowering.

Pop is an immediately recognizable art movement to many around the world, due to the striking and widely disseminated work of artists such as Andy Warhol and Roy Lichtenstein. Some of Pop's canonical figures – including Warhol, Lichtenstein and Ed Ruscha – made films. Warhol was a prolific filmmaker, producing hundreds of works (ranging from three-minute-long portrait reels to an eight-hour film of the Empire State Building) within a short span of years, from 1963 to 1968; Lichtenstein made only one film, a three-screen installation commissioned by the Los Angeles County Museum of Art, in 1970, titled *Three Landscapes*; in the late 1960s and 1970s, Ruscha created a number of films, including *Premium* (1970) and *Miracle* (1975).[5] Although there are references to canonical figures such as these in this volume, we have prioritised a broader, global frame on our topic; the essays included here explore the ways in which artists and filmmakers in various countries around the world have used experimental forms of practice to explore Pop preoccupations, sometimes through geopolitically localised inflections. In order to set the stage for the contributions to the book, this introduction sets out some key historical and critical contexts, drawing attention to the foundational ways in which the interrelationships between Pop and the moving image have previously been articulated and understood. Specifically, we consider two key framings: of Pop cinema as 'popular' cinema, and of Pop cinema as connected to underground filmmaking.

Pop Cinema/Popular Cinema

The first wave of critical discourse considering cinema in relationship to Pop focused centrally on narrative film and television, and on works which were *popular* in terms of their appeal to and success with mass audiences. The English critic and curator Lawrence Alloway wrote several pieces for magazines and journals throughout the 1950s and 1960s, in which he outlined his theories of cinema as a Pop art.[6] The culmination of this exploration was a selection of films co-curated with artists Toby Mussman and Robert Smithson for The Museum of Modern Art in New York, and an accompanying catalogue; the programme was titled *Violent America: The Movies 1946–1964*. The catalogue – single-authored by Alloway – contained essays which explored the industrial context of filmmaking in Hollywood, as well as the themes of expendability, iconography and violence.[7] The selection of films which he considered Pop is decidedly popular and generic, including works by major auteurs such as Samuel Fuller, Anthony Mann and Douglas Sirk. Alloway's curatorial and catalogue project was to take film on its own terms, a position that he thought was not being adopted sufficiently by mainstream newspaper critics, whom he saw as beholden to a small number of internationally recognised arthouse filmmakers. As he remarked in a 1964 essay titled 'Critics in the Dark', '[f]ew critics reveal the slightest interest in the cinema's specific kind of communication (high impact, strong participation, hard to remember), or in the technology and organisation through which movies reach us'.[8] Alloway emphasised the ephemeral, disposable quality of the filmgoing experience, along with the industrial context in which mass cultural products are produced.

A bitter fallout occurred after the publication of Alloway's 'Critics in the Dark' essay. Both Pauline Kael and Andrew Sarris were deeply dismissive of Alloway's call for critics to abandon their snobbish affection for serious art films and embrace what he called 'pop movies'. In the closing remarks of the introduction to her first book, Kael wrote that Alloway's position amounted to a 'condescending approach to movies as a pop art'.[9] Sarris went further: 'This is not the attitude of the true movie addict who is too experienced to like everything he sees, but more the rationale of condescending content awareness without any deep commitment to formal excellence'.[10] Sarris saw a pandering shallowness in Alloway's argument, which only considered certain movies worthy of the label 'Pop': 'Even if movies have finally made the scene', he argued, 'their constituencies are still much too large to be adequately represented in the rotten boroughs of pop art'.[11] The charge against Alloway was that, because he was limiting the Pop label to a coterie of genre films, he was unable to take the rest of cinema seriously. In a riposte to the curator, Sarris closed his essay by stating: 'I like pop films as well as anyone. Some of the best ones I know are directed by Jean Renoir and Carl Dreyer'.[12]

Despite his snub of Alloway, Sarris did sometimes allude to Pop in his 1960s reviews of arthouse cinema. Other reviewers, writing in the same decade, drew on Pop as context or reference in their accounts of popular films and TV serials. Indeed, 'Pop' was used regularly in the 1960s as an adjective in a variety of journalistic and broadcast discussions of cultural objects, from fashion to cinema. Widespread use of the word, however, prevented clear-cut understandings of what it meant. As British cultural theorist Dick Hebdige wrote in 1988, Pop became a byword in the 1960s for that which was hip and of the moment, but, at the same time, the word was unmoored from any universally accepted definition:

> By the mid-1960s, the word 'pop', like its sister words 'mod', 'beat' and 'permissive' had become so thoroughly devalued by over-usage that it tended to serve as a kind of loose, linguistic genuflexion made ritualistically by members of the press toward work which was vaguely contemporary in tone and/or figurative in manner, which leant heavily towards the primary end of the colour range and which could be linked – however tenuously – to the 'swinging' milieu.[13]

Hebdige's comments are applicable to critical and journalistic writings about Pop and film authored in the 1960s. In these texts, aesthetic considerations of Pop and cinema align the art movement with the surface of the image, as well as with a preference for lightness and immediacy. Reyner Banham, for instance – a key member of the Independent Group in London, which occupies a significant role in the history of British Pop art – championed the film *Barbarella* (Roger Vadim, 1968), noting its chromatic intensity.[14] Colour is often a crucial point of reference for critics writing about Pop and cinema: for instance, Andrew Sarris identified a use of 'Pop firehouse red' pervading Michelangelo Antonioni's *Il Deserto Rosso* (*The Red Desert*, 1964).[15] In journalistic explorations of Pop and mainstream cinema, Pop is regularly not seen as a serious undertaking, in contrast to most of the critical responses to its fine art incarnations. The term is instead a way to describe the look of something, a way of communicating a work's basic style and accessibility.

An exception to this surface rendering of Pop in narrative cinema can be found in later writings on the films of Jean-Luc Godard. Since the early 2000s, a number of theoretical texts have read the French New Wave director as being in conversation with Pop. Often these writings concentrate on the transmedial, reflexive and intertextual nature of Godard's mise-en-scène:

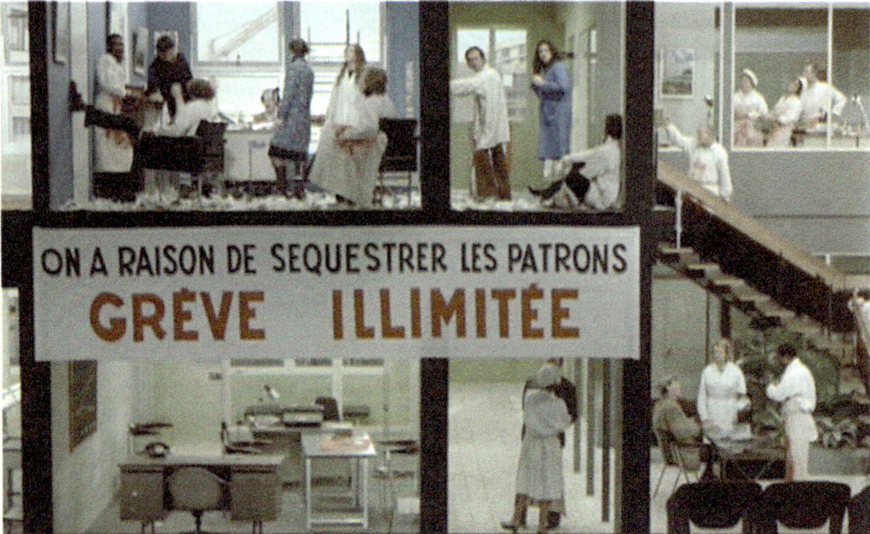

Figure I.3 *Tout va bien* (Jean-Luc Godard, 1972).

for instance, framing devices which align his images with the look of comic book pages, as in *Tout va bien* (1972; see Figure I.3). The 2013 New York Film Festival revival of trailers authored by Godard, predominantly for his own films, saw the filmmaker recognised by some commentators as a Pop artist. The trailers themselves were often composed of quicksilver montages, accompanied by an aural bombardment of post-bop jazz, resulting in a Pop art version of the spectacles associated with what Tom Gunning termed the 'cinema of attractions' – or, as J. Hoberman termed Godard's efforts, a 'cinema of coming attractions'.[16] Beyond these trailers, however, as Ed Halter notes, a number of Godard's narrative feature films demonstrate 'how the graphic sensibilities of Pop could be applied to more serious endeavours', deployed as more than mere style.[17]

Pop/Underground

In contrast to the popular, mainstream and narrative films framed and discussed as Pop, the use of the term 'Pop' as a descriptor for non-narrative and experimental filmmaking has historically been predominantly associated with American underground cinema. This country-wide cinematic practice emerged in the late 1950s, particularly around the urban centres of New York and San Francisco. Underground films were extremely low budget and formally inventive. A heterogeneous and diffuse movement, underground cinema was characterised by style and content that varied widely, from the impressionistic, phenomenologically-informed lyricism of Stan Brakhage to the poverty-row-aping ruin lust of Jack Smith. The content of underground films was often satirical, confrontational, or both. Transgression, of expectations of competency, of style and of socially acceptable content with regard to the display of sexual activity and gender presentation, was a common feature. As Jonas Mekas – filmmaker, impresario of the underground film movement and long-time champion of the cinematic avant-garde – wrote in 1959: 'Every breaking away from the conventional, dead, official cinema is a healthy sign [...] There is no other way to break the frozen cinematic conventions than through a complete derangement of the official cinematic senses'.[18]

Unlike their European avant-garde forebears of the 1920s and 1930s, underground filmmakers were for the most part not aligned with specific art movements. Mekas, along with a raft of fellow filmmakers, attempted to group this motley array of artists under a broad umbrella: The New American Cinema.[19] Broadly speaking, however, there has conventionally been a split perceived in this group of filmmakers between the modernist faction and what we can call the Pop wing. In the former we can locate practitioners such as Brakhage, Harry Smith, Tony Conrad and Mekas himself. In the latter are figures such as Ron Rice, Andy Warhol, Jack Smith, Bruce Conner, the brothers George and Mike Kuchar, and Kenneth Anger. The former group have been characterised as enacting an exploration of personal narratives through poetic forms of film and as destabilising the medium specificity of cinema. Juan Suárez has noted that this camp of the New American Cinema cultivated a 'difficult art for art's sake cinema in stark opposition to commercial Hollywood product'.[20] The Pop grouping, in contrast, was less oppositional towards Hollywood; these filmmakers incorporated explicit references to mainstream cinema in their work, revelling, according to Janet Staiger, in a combination of 'camp satire and popular culture'.[21] Suárez goes further, suggesting that they 'flaunted their immersion in Hollywood myths and showed little preoccupation with the poetry of dreams or the intricacies of subjectivity'.[22] These directors freely borrowed from Hollywood films and commercial culture more generally, 'turning their productions into a mixture of parody and of homage to popular icons and myths'.[23] The inclusion of references to Hollywood and mainstream genre filmmaking led to a perception of this second grouping of underground filmmakers as Pop artists. This was apparent in both the marketing of underground films in alternative newspapers, and in the critical discourse on underground cinema that took shape across the 1960s.

The mainstream and alternative press of the 1960s often connected Pop art with underground filmmaking, with the films of Andy Warhol and Jack Smith repeatedly singled out. Mekas was the first to use the word 'Pop' to describe an underground film, calling Warhol's *Sleep* (1963) a potential, even ultimate, 'extension of Pop Art'.[24] One of a number of minimal, durational works by Warhol, *Sleep*, and other titles including *Eat* (1964) and *Empire* (1964) have been considered Pop art because of their ability to be conveyed conceptually and summarily in a way which is fully comprehensible to viewers, without the need to see the film itself.[25] The framing of such works of (now canonical) avant-garde filmmaking as accessible to a wider audience is reflected in the deployment of the phrase 'Pop' in a variety of contemporaneous advertisements for screenings of films by Warhol, Conner and the Kuchar brothers. Here, it is useful to recall Hebdige's understanding of 'Pop' as a mutable signifier which is employed to connote a cultural object's timeliness, or relative 'hipness'.[26] To give examples: in advertisements in the *Village Voice* from the mid-1960s, the term is used to lure viewers to showings of Conner's *COSMIC RAY* (1961), with the Bridge Theater on St Mark's Place describing the collage film as a 'Pop Art Masterpiece', and to a programme of 'Andy Warhol "Shorties": *Vinyl* [1965] and *Poor Little Rich Girl* [1965]' which are dubbed 'Pop style experiments in cinema vérite, only about 70 mins each!'[27]

By 1966, 'Pop' was being used as an umbrella term under which to gather a wide variety of underground filmmakers. The first and only 'P. U. F. F.' or 'Pop Underground Film Festival' was held in Los Angeles in the summer of that year. The festival brought together a disparate array of underground practitioners, with the organisers slipping in their programming between the groupings of modernist and Pop filmmakers, combining the works of Conner, Warhol and the Kuchars with formalist experiments in abstraction by West Coast filmmakers such as Hy Hirsh and New Yorker Storm de Hirsch. Works such as Hy Hirsh's *Come Closer* (1951) and Storm de Hirsch's *Peyote Queen* (1965) were indicative of the event's bias towards animation, with a number of films from Robert Breer, Stan VanDerBeek and Larry Jordan also featured in the programme. Overall, the selection represented another example of the vague deployment of Pop as a term which seemed stitched into the moment. Within a West Coast context, this meant intermingling Pop with a dose of psychedelia, as seen in the scheduling of films such as *Peyote Queen*, a piece of visual music in the vein of Len Lye's *Free Radicals* (1958), with the beat-caper *Babo 73* (Robert Downey, 1964). In a 5 August *Los Angeles Free Press* advertisement promoting the festival, the link between Pop and recreational drug use was made explicit, the ad leading with the question 'Are you ready to try the first P. U. F. F.?'[28]

Expanding on Mekas' somewhat hazy deployment of the term 'Pop', Parker Tyler, in his 1969 book on underground cinema, proposed that Pop art 'came on the scene almost in step with the reawakening of the avant-garde film in the late fifties'.[29] This observation is paired with a recognition of the diffusion of a Pop aesthetic within mainstream cinema, to which Tyler sees underground cinema as a response:

> Pop Art, with its reliance on photographic processes for its plastic effects, has been very close in spirit to the popular fiction films according to that film type's own ambiguous yet deep affinity with the comic strip. This kinship, in the shape of the rough, robust satire which is more and more prevalent, has come to the fore during the same decade – the sixties – that the avant-garde film has acquired its underground personality.[30]

Tyler's perspective, reading Pop as a current connecting the mainstream and the underground, is presaged in a short essay titled 'The Camera as a God' and written in 1963 for *Film Culture* by Charles Boultenhouse (who was also Tyler's partner). Boultenhouse critiqued the notion 'that commercial film is a natural kind of Pop Art': if we are to 'consider movies as Pop Art', then, '[s]aid without sneers, this means that Hollywood is the Original Pop Art and is *GREAT* because *IT IS* what *IT IS*. Gorgeous flesh and mostly terrible acting! Divine! Campy dialogue and preposterous plots! Divine! Sexy fantasy and unorgasmic tedium! Divine!'[31] Rather than attributing an authenticity to Hollywood – to which underground filmmakers might respond, in adulatory or dismissive ways – Boultenhouse lambasted the mainstream for its trickery: '[t]he teenagers of all ages who worship its fetishes will never be satisfied'.[32]

What Tyler and Boultenhouse's writings highlight are the aesthetic and affective ties connecting mainstream American cinema to underground forms of film. Ronald Tavel, a key collaborator and screenwriter on Warhol's films of the mid-1960s, argued in 1966 that Hollywood was the 'background and material for the *art* of the New American Cinema, much as […] Greek mythology was the subject matter-at-hand for the art of Homer and Sophocles'.[33] Tavel's comparison is both lofty and slyly camp in its arch-seriousness, but highlights the key point that many underground films were crafted as a conscious reaction to the cultural domination of Hollywood cinema. The resulting works were not simply 'home movies of the pop underworld', as a commentator in *Life* magazine had once dismissively assessed them; rather, their makers were wrestling with the iconography and generic expectations handed down to them by Hollywood and its affiliates in b- and poverty-row pictures.[34] Pop underground filmmakers were taking these conventions and forging something distinct, forms of cinema that could potentially stand in opposition to the Hollywood norm of 'Debbie Reynolds or Doris Day, sailing into a saccharine sunset'.[35] Many of the films of Andy Warhol and the Kuchar brothers need to be framed through this optic. When collage and found-footage filmmakers like Conner are added into the mix, it becomes clear that 'Pop' underground directors found inspiration in all manner of moving image materials, from advertising and cartoons to educational and industrial films. Indeed, a filmmaker such as Conner could arguably be viewed as the creator of a type of pure Pop cinema, his work in alignment with Lawrence Alloway's statement that it is the entire ecology of media images which forms Pop's content: 'The communications system of the twentieth century is, in a special sense, the subject of Pop Art'.[36]

Overview of Contents

The essays assembled in *Pop Cinema* largely concentrate on artists whose moving image work is more closely aligned with the experimental or underground formulation of Pop. Mainstream cinema's uses of Pop aesthetics are briefly considered (see Halter's essay, in particular); arthouse examples of narrative film are explored (see especially Crowley's contribution). In order to provide a coherence to the collection, however, the editors have prioritised sustained examinations of a raft of more experimental works from the 1960s and 1970s; this has facilitated the emergence of links and conversations between essays across the book. (An edited collection of essays on mainstream, narrative Pop cinema is a project for a different editorial team to take on in the future.) Such a prioritisation also reflects our personal investments, interests and political affiliations as editors – as does our decision to decentre canonical Pop artists and their films, in favour of other works and filmmakers equally worthy of critical attention. In particular, the selection of material for this collection is influenced by recent turns in curatorial approaches to, and art historical accounts of, Pop art which have drawn attention to women's contributions to the movement, to Pop's temporal elasticity beyond the bounds of the 1960s and to Pop's dissemination and deployment as a style and set of themes and strategies by artists around the globe.[37]

Pop Cinema is divided into three parts. The first and shortest – 'Framing Pop Cinema' – provides further historical context for the rest of the collection through two seminal texts, presented here as one reprint and one reworking. William Kaizen's 'Notes on Pop Cinema' and Ed Halter's 'Pop and Cinema: Three Tendencies' are often identified as landmark essays in thinking through the moving image's relationship to Pop art – as foundational interrogations of the forms and central preoccupations of a Pop cinema. Kaizen has rewritten and updated his piece for this collection; Halter's essay is reproduced in its original version.

Towards the end of April 2011, International House Philadelphia staged a three-day film programme, 'Pop Cinema: Art and Film in the US and UK, 1950s–1970s'. The short season was curated by Kaizen; he also authored the sole text in the catalogue and co-authored its filmography with curator Jesse Pires. In addition to screening the films, the gallery staged a symposium on Pop and film with contributions from critic Jacob Proctor, historian and theorist Kalliopi Minioudaki and artist Derek Boshier. In his catalogue essay, Kaizen outlined a potential categorisation of Pop cinema, arguing that there are 'three main types', 'all of them aligned with the avant-garde'. These are: 'documentary films on the consumption of popular culture and the effects of this consumption on everyday life, shot using avant-garde techniques'; 'collage films made of readymade images taken from the world of pop culture'; and 'sub-z movies that take the genres of commercial film as readymades and then recast them'. In his reworked version of the essay for this volume, Kaizen maintains this typology, but brings his expansive conception of Pop cinema right up to date, suggesting that appropriation-based online video mash-ups and meme culture are indebted to the innovations of Pop film.

Kaizen's essay explored Pop film within particular geographical parameters, focusing on examples from the United Kingdom and United States. In contrast, Ed Halter's essay addresses a broader landscape. 'Pop and Cinema: Three Tendencies' appeared in the catalogue that accompanied the exhibition *International Pop*, which was staged at the Walker Art Center in Minneapolis in 2015. Curated by Darsie Alexander and Bartholomew Ryan, the exhibition included around 140 works from fourteen countries; in adopting a global perspective on Pop, it put canonical examples from the US and UK into conversation with examples from France, Germany, Brazil, Argentina, Japan and elsewhere. (It is hoped that *Pop Cinema* works in a similar manner.) Halter's essay, like Kaizen's, offers a tripartite approach: he identifies three leanings or affinities in Pop's relationship to cinema. These are: 'the movies' foundational influence on the development of Pop and its visual vocabulary'; the attempt by 'a new generation of international filmmakers', from Eduardo Paolozzi to Yoko Ono, to 'reshape [film] along more visionary and personal terms', and in whose work Pop and cinema 'converged'; and the use of Pop aesthetics and dynamics by a range of artists and filmmakers to explore, through the moving image, political materials and themes.

The second part of *Pop Cinema* brings together five original essays dedicated to exploring 'Pop Cinema's Parameters'; each contribution examines the ways in which particular artists and individual examples of films have pushed the limits (temporal, geographical, political, formal) of standard understandings of Pop. Tom Day unpacks photographer and filmmaker William Klein's *Broadway by Light* (1958), a work described by its maker as 'the first Pop film'. Drawing centrally on Kracauer's writings on the mass ornament, Day positions the film in relation to the genre of the City Symphony, as well as a 1956 book of photographs by Klein, titled *Life is Good and Good for You in New York: Trance, Witness, Revels*, a collection that was in part the inspiration for *Broadway by Light*. Day explores at length the relationships between stillness and movement across Klein's photographs and films, pinpointing the artist's evocation of dynamism in his stills and the place of stasis in his moving images.

In his contribution, Juan Carlos Guerrero-Hernández contemplates the intersections between Pop, palette and architecture in Luis Ernesto Arocha's film *Las ventanas de Salcedo* (1966). A collaboration between the filmmaker and the architect Bernardo Salcedo, *Las ventanas* was shot in Salcedo's studio in Colombia and 'enters into a dialogue with Salcedo's emerging work to develop a Pop commentary on society and politics'. Intentionally conceived of as Pop, the short-but-dense black-and-white film gives a central role to a series of humorous box-like assemblages constructed by Salcedo, using animation to bring them to life as 'para-cinematic stages of a drama of light and shadow'. Situating the film within the political context of Colombia in the 1960s, Guerrero-Hernández argues that its use of black-and-white 'allows the director to avoid what Lawrence Alloway identifies as the reigning colourful Pop "aesthetics of plenty"'.

Clint Enns, in his essay, focuses his attention on the films of Japanese graphic designer and filmmaker Tadanori Yokoo, an artist whose aesthetic predilections have earned him the reductive moniker of the 'Japanese Warhol'. Enns discusses all three of Yokoo's animated films – *Anthology No.1* (1964), *KISS KISS KISS* (1964) and *Kachi Kachi Yama Meoto no Sujimichi* (1965) – focusing in depth on the last of these. Enns positions Yokoo's films in relation to his Pop-psychedelic graphic design work, as well as the social and cultural context of Japan in the 1960s, arguing that his animations 'advocate for political change through expanding consciousness and through everyday actions rather than explicit political action'.

Justin Remes' contribution to this volume is a work of experimental scholarship. It focuses on Bruce Conner's found footage film *MARILYN TIMES FIVE* (1968–73), which repeats images of a Marilyn Monroe look-alike named Arline Hunter, posing provocatively with an apple and a bottle of Coca-Cola. In his essay, Remes argues that Conner's film was profoundly shaped by the conceptual art of Marcel Duchamp and the Pop art of Andy Warhol, and that it foregrounds the difficulty of distinguishing between an original and a copy. Just as *MARILYN TIMES FIVE* was constructed from excerpts of a pre-existing film, Remes' essay was assembled from quotations of pre-existing texts. Quotations that appear aligned to the left of the page accurately represent the argument made by the authors being cited. Those that are indented, however, are 'remixes' of their source material and may reinforce, revise, or refute the original quotations. This writing tactic offers a sophisticated commentary on Pop's preoccupation with appropriation and (minor) manipulation, applying a Pop method to scholarly interrogation. The author's own voice is dampened, arguably largely absent, thus inviting the reader to scrutinise and reflect on how criticality is constructed in academic discourse.

Part Two of the book closes with Kimberly Lamm's essay on Niki de Saint Phalle and Peter Whitehead's *Daddy* (1973), a film described by Alissa Clarke as a 'sexually explicit surrealist pop-art Freudian rape revenge fantasy'. Whitehead – as Kaizen identifies in his contribution – was a key figure in the history of British Pop, whereas Saint Phalle was a French-American artist who worked with sculpture, illustration, performance and film; their collaboration resulted in a pseudo-fictional biopic that interrogated the psychic interconnections between Saint Phalle, her childhood experiences of abuse and her art. For Lamm, *Daddy* offers a riposte to Pop's typical reiteration and reification of women's association with consumerism and passivity. Drawing on Martha Rosler's identification of the political potential that Pop can hold for women, Lamm argues that *Daddy* 'refutes the association between femininity and passivity and the entrenched idea that girls and women should relinquish their drives'; using ideas drawn from psychoanalysis, she explores how the film 'writes a feminist fantasy of revealing and dismantling the deeply repressive power wielded through the white patriarchal family'.

Part Three of this collection – 'Pop Cinema, Mass Production and the Politics of Consumption' – examines, from a variety of angles, what many theorists identify as some of Pop's central thematics: its ambivalent relationship to consumer culture, and its engagement with tactics of mass production. Glyn Davis focuses his attention on the work of the Scottish-Italian sculptor, collage artist and filmmaker Eduardo Paolozzi, in particular the

1962 short film *The History of Nothing* that Paolozzi made with support from Denis Postle. Davis highlights Paolozzi's preoccupation with vehicular disaster, especially the car crash, and uses this topic to situate the film in relation to other works by the artist, as well as materials in Paolozzi's collections and archive. Connections outward are also made: to writings and installations by J. G. Ballard, a friend of Paolozzi, and to Pop's broader concern with crashed cars – expressed, in particular, in works by Andy Warhol and Bruce Conner. Drawing on Thomas Crow's writings on Warhol's 'Death and Disaster' series, Davis argues that Paolozzi's film provides an alternative route into considering Pop's engagement with the darker underside of the consumerist dream.

Kara Carmack's essay explores Wynn Chamberlain's film *Brand X* (1970) and its disruption of both the banal, repetitive dynamics of advertising and the quotidian gloss of marketing. The film, Carmack argues, 'deploys the titular marketing strategy of "Brand X" to denounce nearly all aspects of American culture that', by the time of the film's making, 'had become increasingly codified, commercialised, and branded'. 'Brand X' was a marketing term developed in the middle of the twentieth century to refer to an unnamed, unappealing product that 'always fails to perform as well as a comparable name-brand product'; Chamberlain flips this evaluation and revels in the anonymity and low-grade position that X occupies. Indeed, the filmmaker saw 'Brand X' as 'propaganda for the politics of joy and disorder'. Carmack situates the film within the broader media landscape of the time, as well as in relation to an array of revolutionary political currents. In contrast to Pop works that wallow in a widespread culture of consumption, however ambivalently, she argues that *Brand X* 'eschews the brand in favour of its disparaged inverse', offering up a critical position that elevates the degraded and inferior.

David Crowley examines three films produced in Eastern European countries that can be framed and understood as Pop cinema: *Personal Search* (*Rewizja Osobista*, Andrzej Kostenko and Witold Leszczyński, Poland, 1973); *Daisies* (*Sedmikrásky*, Věra Chytilová, Czechia, 1967); and *WR: Mysteries of the Organism* (*W. R. – Misterije organizma*, Dušan Makavejev, Yugoslavia, 1971). All three adopt playful quasi-narrative forms to explore their concerns; all 'address popular culture using its own symbols and techniques'; all 'demonstrate an interest in the media, in celebrity and in consumerism'. A guiding influence in relation to all three is Jean-Luc Godard (as we have already seen, a key figure for Pop cinema) – in particular, the mid-1960s phase of his career, which was viewed and reviewed widely in Eastern European countries.

For her contribution to the collection, Gillian Sneed examines the ways in which a number of female Brazilian artists critiqued the gendered dynamics of television and the domestic in moving image works produced in the 1970s. Although Pop art was a contested term in Brazil, where it was seen as 'negatively associated with the Global North and US cultural interventionist policies', and although 'feminism was not broadly accepted in the Brazilian art world of the time', Sneed argues that works by these artists need to be situated in relation to international Pop art trends, and as 'an alternative to the typically masculinist iterations of Pop cinema across the Americas and in Europe'. Sneed discusses a short experimental documentary from 1972 about the artist Wanda Pimentel, Lygia Pape's films *Wampirou* (1973) and *Eat Me* (1975), and two untitled video works by Sonia Andrade, concluding not only that Brazilian women were 'at the forefront of pioneering Pop cinema', but that 'Brazilian Pop cinema was more political than its counterparts in the Global North'.

Finally, Jon Davies scrutinises Pop's repetitive engagement with the destruction of consumer products through a reading of the late Michael Snow's film *Breakfast (Table Top Dolly)* (1976). Connecting in productive ways with Davis' interrogation of the smashed car and Carmack's exploration of Brand X, Davies looks at the demolition of perishable food products in Snow's film, aligning *Breakfast* with 'a Pop inflected with practices of defilement', but also situating it in relation to other works of art centrally preoccupied with destruction. Cinema, Davies argues, 'has a privileged relationship to destruction due to the medium's capacity to repeat'; wary of destruction's potential associations with masculinity, aggression and power, however, he uses Snow's film to work through 'how creation and destruction, activity and passivity in Pop are shaped by gender, desire and power'.

Taken as a whole, the essays in *Pop Cinema* examine in detail and depth the complex relationships between the moving image and Pop's pivotal preoccupations. However, they offer only a sampling of potential routes in; we hope that these essays will serve as spurs for further exploration, for close attention being focused on other works and practitioners. There is considerable room for further scholarship on Pop cinema, in both its mainstream and narrative forms, and its more avant-garde incarnations. To that end, this collection closes with a final provocation: an appendix that takes the form of a speculative filmography of Pop cinema works. The filmography includes titles that have been included on screening programmes shown as part of Pop gallery exhibitions around the world, an array of titles referenced in the extant literature on Pop and cinema, as well as examples that we as editors felt deserved scrutiny, attention, investigation. Recognition of the variety of these titles, and acknowledgement of their legitimate place in the Pop art pantheon, can only enrich historical and theoretical understandings of Pop as a world-spanning movement.

Notes

1 Suzaan Boettger, 'The Lost Contingent: Paul Maenz's Prophetic 1967 Event and the Ambiguities of Historical Priority', *Art Journal*, 62:1 (Spring 2003), pp. 34–47.

2 Peter Roehr, 'Der Film ohne Story [The Film Without a Story], Dated 28.09.67', Peter Roehr Archive, Museum für Moderne Kunst, Frankfurt, Germany, Inventory Number: 2015/12.19v. All translations from the Roehr archive are by Tom Day.

3 Peter Roehr, 'Notes on Montages I', in *Peter Roehr*, Oxford: Museum of Modern Art, 1978, p. 4; Roehr, 'Notes from the Estate', in *Peter Roehr*, op. cit., p. 8.

4 The Californian artist William E. Jones has written about the *Film Montages* and made a video artwork in tribute to Roehr, which excavates the latent homoerotic coupling found in the bodies of the two male wrestlers at the centre of *Ringer*. Jones' piece, *Film Montages (For Peter Roehr)* (2006), draws on an archive of hardcore gay pornography, manipulating various VHS copies of unnamed films by cutting them into discrete short shots that are repeated and looped a number of times.

5 For more on the films of these artists, see, for instance: John Hanhardt (ed.), *The Films of Andy Warhol: Catalogue Raisonné*, New Haven: Yale University Press, 2021; Douglas Crimp, *'Our Kind of Movie': The Films of Andy Warhol*, Cambridge, MA: MIT Press, 2012; Glyn Davis and Gary Needham (eds), *Warhol in Ten Takes*, London: BFI, 2013; Chris Chang, 'Sky's the Limit: Roy Lichtenstein: Eternal Auteur?', *Film Comment*, 48:1 (Jan/Feb 2012), p. 17; Alexandra Schwartz, *Ed Ruscha's Los Angeles*, Cambridge, MA: MIT Press, 2010, pp. 93–97.

6 See Peter Stanfield, 'Maximum Movies: Lawrence Alloway's Pop Art Film Criticism', *Screen*, 49:2 (Summer, 2008), pp. 179–93.

7 Lawrence Alloway, *Violent America: The Movies 1946–1964*, New York: Museum of Modern Art, 1971.

8 Lawrence Alloway, 'Critics in the Dark', *Encounter*, February 1964, p. 55.

9 Pauline Kael, *I Lost It at the Movies*, Boston: Atlantic Monthly Press, 1965, p. 27.

10 Andrew Sarris, 'Pop Go the Movies!' (1964), in Andrew Sarris, *The Primal Screen: Essays on Film and Related Subjects*, New York: Simon and Schuster, 1973, p. 69.

11 Ibid.

12 Ibid., p. 80.

13 Dick Hebdige, 'Towards a Cartography of Taste, 1935–1962', in Bernard Waites, Tony Bennett and Graham Martin (eds), *Popular Culture: Past and Present*, London and New York: Routledge, 1988, p. 121.

14 Reyner Banham, 'Triumph of Software' (1968), in Reyner Banham, *Design by Choice*, London: Academy Editions, 1981, pp. 133–36.

15 Andrew Sarris, 'Films', *The Village Voice*, 11 February 1965, p. 14.

16 Tom Gunning, 'The Cinema of Attraction: Early Film, its Spectator and the Avant-Garde', *Wide Angle*, 8:3–4 (1986), pp. 63–70; J. Hoberman, 'Advertisements for Himself', *Artforum*, 52:5 (January 2014), p. 57.

17 Ed Halter, 'Pop and Cinema: Three Tendencies', in Darsie Alexander and Bartholomew Ryan (eds), *International Pop*, Minneapolis: Walker Art Center, 2015, p. 190.

18 Jonas Mekas, 'Movie Journal', *Village Voice*, 4 February 1959, p. 6. For introductions to American underground cinema, see Sheldon Renan, *An Introduction to American Underground Film*, New York: E. P. Dutton, 1967; Parker Tyler, *Underground Film: A Critical History*, Boston: Da Capo Press, 1969; and J. Hoberman and Jonathan Rosenbaum, *Midnight Movies*, New York: Harper and Row, 1983. For studies which explore the place of transgression in the movement, see Carel Rowe, *The Baudelairean Cinema: A Trend within the American Avant-Garde Film*, Ann Arbor: University of Michigan Press, 1982, and Ara Osterweil, *Flesh Cinema: The Corporeal Turn in American Avant-Garde Film*, Manchester: University of Manchester Press, 2014.

19 Jonas Mekas et al., 'The First Statement of the New American Cinema Group,' in P. Adams Sitney (ed.), *Film Culture Reader*, New York: Praeger, 1970, pp. 79–83.

20 Juan Suárez, *Bike Boys, Drag Queens and Superstars: Avant-Garde, Mass Culture and Gay Identities in the 1960s Underground Culture*, Bloomington: Indiana University Press, 1996, pp. xvi–xvii.

21 Janet Staiger, 'Finding Community in the Early 1960s: Underground Cinema and Sexual Politics', in Hilary Radner and Moya Luckett (eds), *Swinging Single: Representing Sexuality in the 1960s*, Minneapolis and London: University of Minnesota Press, 1999, p. 52.

22 Suárez, op. cit., p. 95.

23 Ibid., p. xvii.

24 Jonas Mekas, 'Movie Journal', *Village Voice*, 30 January 1964, p. 17.

25 Callie Angell, *The Films of Andy Warhol Part II*, New York: The Whitney Museum of American Art, 1994, pp. 14–15.

26 Hebdige, op. cit., p. 121.

27 Anon, Advertisement for 'The Woman Show [Group Film Screening]', The Bridge, St Mark's Place, *Village Voice*, 12 August 1965, p. 15; Anon, Advertisement for 'Andy Warhol Shorties', Film-makers' Cinematheque, New York, *Village Voice*, 3 June 1965, p. 15.

28 Anon, Advertisement for P. U. F. F. [Pop Underground Film Festival], Cinema, Santa Monica, CA, *Los Angeles Free Press*, 5 August 1966, p. 6.

29 Tyler, op. cit., p. 13.

30 Ibid. Here, it is worth noting that Amos Vogel proposes an alternative conception; he categorises Pop with Dada as an 'anti-art' form: see Vogel, *Film as a Subversive Art*, New York: Random House, 1974, pp. 48–50.

31 Charles Boultenhouse, 'The Camera as a God', in P. Adams Sitney (ed.), *Film Culture Reader*, op. cit., p. 137.

32 Ibid., p. 138.

33 Ronald Tavel, 'The Banana Diary: The Story of Warhol's *Harlot*' (1966), in Michael O'Pray (ed.), *Andy Warhol: Film Factory*, London: British Film Institute, 1989, pp. 66–93.

34 Anon, 'Report from the Underground', *Life Magazine*, 29 January 1965, p. 23.

35 Pete Hamill, 'Explosion in the Movie Underground', *Saturday Evening Post*, 28 September 1963, p. 83.
36 Lawrence Alloway, 'Popular Culture and Pop Art', *Studio International*, 178:913, July/August 1969, p.17.
37 See, for instance, Sid Sachs and Kalliopi Minioudaki (eds), *Seductive Subversion: Women Pop Artists, 1958–1968*, Philadelphia: University of the Arts; New York and London: Abbeville Press Publishers, 2010; Darsie Alexander and Bartholomew Ryan (eds), *International Pop*, op. cit.; Jessica Morgan and Flavia Frigeri (eds), *The World Goes Pop*, New Haven: Yale University Press, 2015.

Part 1

Framing Pop Cinema

1

Notes on Pop Cinema, Revisited

William Kaizen

While the influence of cinema is acknowledged in histories of Pop Art, the production of cinema in relation to Pop Art has been largely ignored. In 2011, I curated *Pop Cinema*, the first screening series in the United States to show mid-century British and American films that operate at the intersection of popular culture, popular art and the cinematic avant-garde. The film programme and this essay, which was published in the accompanying catalogue, were my preliminary attempt to define Pop Cinema and celebrate the films included.[1] Many of these films remain practically unknown, and all are under-acknowledged in histories of both Pop Art and avant-garde film. I became interested in them because they are some of the most visually arresting avant-garde artworks of the twentieth century. Upon viewing several for the first time, I saw that their themes and formal operations clustered naturally together under the banner of Pop Art. Further viewing confirmed this. Although some of the makers of these films were directly involved with Pop Art, many of the films pre-date or parallel the invention of Pop Art as an art historical category. Given that the history of Pop Cinema starts in the early 1950s, when Pop Art was still nascent, it seemed to me that the history of Pop Art needed to be re-written to account for these films and filmmakers.

Pop Cinema is a category largely of my own invention.[2] There has never been a movement that officially went by this name. Few artists have declared themselves makers of Pop Art films. When they were released, the films of Andy Warhol – who was the most prolific filmmaker among the canonical Pop artists – were lumped under the broader terms 'underground' or 'avant-garde' cinema.[3] Pop Cinema is a useful term in so much as it more specifically identifies a variety of films whose subject-matter and formal operations were closely aligned with Pop Art. From the early 1950s through the early 1970s, a host of filmmakers working largely outside of the commercial film industry began to embrace the world of the mass media. Unlike their avant-garde filmmaking peers (Stan Brakhage, Jonas Mekas), they embraced film for its very connections to Hollywood movies and television as mass media. The works by these filmmakers share a focus on the increasing entanglement of the mass media with everyday life during a time when the daily presence not only of mass-produced goods but also of mass-produced popular entertainment was dramatically increasing. The representation of these goods in the context of entertainment (as in advertising) or as a form of entertainment in itself (as with pop music) is the subject-matter of many of these films. So is the consumption of movie stars, whose very humanity has been turned into a consumable product.

During the late 1950s, British art critic Lawrence Alloway began using the phrase 'the aesthetics of plenty' to describe the emerging world of postwar abundance represented in the mass media.[4] Riding a wave of prosperity, both the mass media and the goods it proffered were becoming widely available in both the US and even the UK, despite its continued postwar austerity. Alloway recognised that the mass media were not only the primary vehicle for selling images of affluent consumption, but that consuming mass media content was itself becoming the new basis for living an affluent life. This world of mass-mediated plenty had become increasingly seductive even to a particular segment of the hip avant-garde. Along with Alloway, like-minded critics and artists were beginning to admit their deep-seated appreciation for popular entertainment. Rather than dismiss the world of the mass media as a vampire sucking the blood of the avant-garde for profit, as earlier generations of critics had, they undertook a more open-minded examination of the mass media, recognizing that even mass-produced culture has an aesthetics of its own, which was ripe for appropriation.

Without denying the inherent tendency for the mass media to skew to the lowest common denominator, these early popular culture connoisseurs acknowledged that artistic greatness could be found in 'low' culture, and that the elitism of 'high' culture often masked fine-art productions as superficial as any so-called kitsch. They also recognised that the aesthetic codes of high and low art could be fertilely mixed. By the early 1960s, artists on both sides of the Atlantic had become connoisseurs of mass cultural aesthetics with the obsessive fan's nuanced ability to distinguish between good and bad examples, coupled with a critical ability to recognise the impositions made on its producers by profit motives.

Although unacknowledged in most art histories, what many art historians describe as the inaugural moment of Pop Art was a proto-cinematic event. In 1952, at the Institute of Contemporary Art in London, Eduardo

Paolozzi made an after-hours presentation to colleagues. The artists, architects and fellow travellers assembled there would soon adopt the name The Independent Group, becoming the progenitors of British Pop Art.[5] Paolozzi had been making collages of images cut from American magazines. Like Ken Burns panning across old photographs but without the nostalgia, he scanned across a selection of them using an opaque projector. One of the most famous brings together the cover of an issue of the pulp magazine *Intimate Confessions* featuring a half-dressed woman with a pasted-on revolver that points to her head. The word 'POP!' emerges in a puff of smoke out of the gun's barrel in a gesture that winkingly acknowledges the mass media's tendency to objectify women by turning them into a commodity fetish.

By projecting these images, Paolozzi was able to use a cinema-like experience as a means for remixing the aesthetics of plenty. The screen became a surrogate pinboard, that favourite tool of pop-cult fanatics, used for displaying their collections of mass-produced images. In his description of 1950s and 1960s art as a 'flatbed picture plane', Leo Steinberg likens the formal structure of such art to both 'bulletin boards' and 'a projection screen'.[6] This motif, which would permeate Pop Cinema, was used literally in Ken Russell's film *Pop Goes the Easel*, aired on BBC television in 1962. Russell depicted Pop artists Peter Blake, Peter Philips, Derek Boshier and Pauline Boty as obsessive fans whose consumption of pop culture sustains both their work and lives. The film opens with a pan across a wall plastered with hundreds of photographs. Most are of pop stars, many of them American (Figure 1.1). Images of Elizabeth Taylor, Marilyn Monroe and Elvis Presley fill the screen, echoing Paolozzi's earlier presentation. The camera pans down to the host, revealing that the images have been pinned behind his desk, fully covering the wall. While Russell's pinboard was constructed in the television studio, every one of the artists' studios that are visited over the course of the film contains a similar wall, depictions of which return continuously throughout the film. The host describes the world of Pop Art as consisting of things like 'film stars, the Twist, science fiction and pop singers', a world that these four artists take seriously, and not as 'tawdry' or 'second rate'. Like it or not, he acknowledges, we all live in this world today, and these artists are coming to grips with it, as their workspaces as much as their work demonstrates.

Paolozzi himself would eventually turn to film, as did numerous other artists, including Boshier. Film added another dimension to the pinboard's accumulative abilities by allowing images to change rapidly over time. As prefigured by Paolozzi, film could transform the pinboard from a static table into a moving tabular image whose data are constantly shifting, heightening the phantasmagorical effect of the mass media's already fast-paced flow.[7]

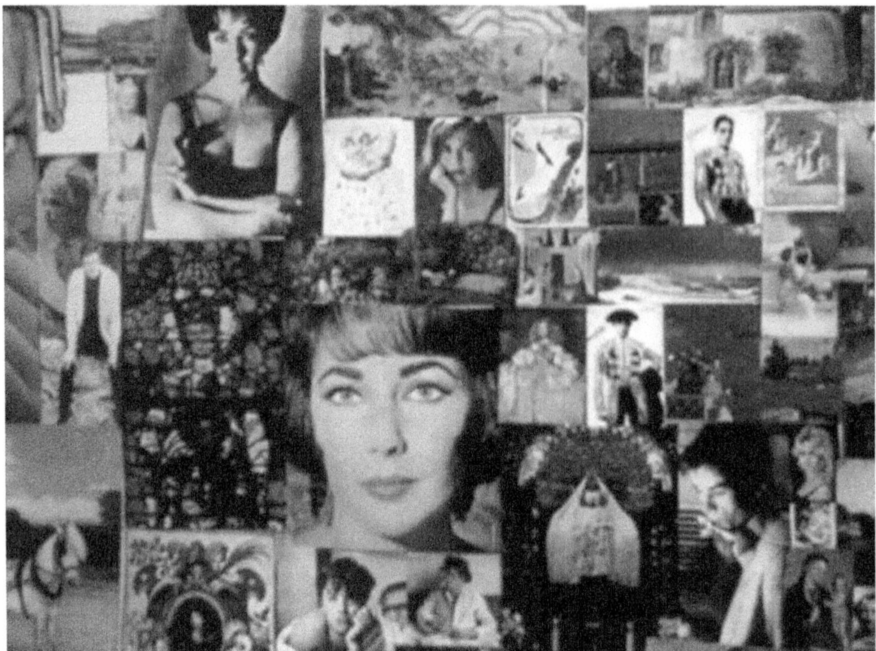

Figure 1.1 *Pop Goes the Easel* (Ken Russell, 1962).

Alloway said of Pop Art's use of appropriation: 'To achieve an effect of plenty in art, it is necessary to have an endless supply of imagery (supplied by mass culture) and an omnivorous all-overism'.[8] For many artists, film provided an essential tool for producing just such an omnivorous all-overism.

There are three main types of Pop Cinema, all of them aligned with the avant-garde. The first are documentary films about the consumption of popular culture and its effects on everyday life, shot using avant-garde techniques. These include films such as *Pop Goes the Easel,* made about Pop artists, who were typically portrayed as expert consumers of popular culture. The second are collage films made of readymade images ripped directly from the world of pop culture, including films made by Robert Breer, Stan VanDerBeek and Bruce Conner. The images used in these films were either things like magazine pages shot firsthand by the filmmaker or made from recycled film footage shot by others. The third are 'sub-z' movies, such as the Kuchar brothers' *I Was a Teenage Rumpot* (1960), whose makers recast the genres of commercial film in deviant forms using non-professional actors and quasi-narrative storytelling. All three types often feature pop music as a soundtrack in complement and counterpoint to the image.

The earliest examples of Pop Cinema were made in England in the context of the Free Cinema movement, which emerged during the mid-1950s alongside the Independent Group. Free Cinema films examined the lives of working-class Britons whose leisure time was increasingly occupied by mass amusement. The core group behind Free Cinema – Lindsay Anderson, Karel Reisz, Tony Richardson and Lorena Mazzetti – first showed their work together at a screening in 1956.[9] They chose 'Free Cinema' as an appellation because of the distance they sought to put between themselves and the British documentary film tradition. Rejecting John Grierson's voice-of-God narration, they used looser, less diegetic camerawork and the faster-paced editing of avant-garde cinema. They also turned away from the far-off communities of anthropological film, focusing instead on the sociology of working-class British life more sympathetically than had previously been captured.

Mass entertainment as a release from workday drudgery is an especially important theme in Free Cinema. Anderson's *O Dreamland* (1953) is at once a tribute and a rebuke to seaside carnivals as a popular spectacle. Filmed at the Dreamland amusement park in Margate using a hidden camera, Anderson captured the dazed fascination on the faces of the fairgoers. He depicts Dreamland as a cheap fantasia of mechanical technologies where the public is seen gawping at lowbrow distractions (Figure 1.2). Considerably

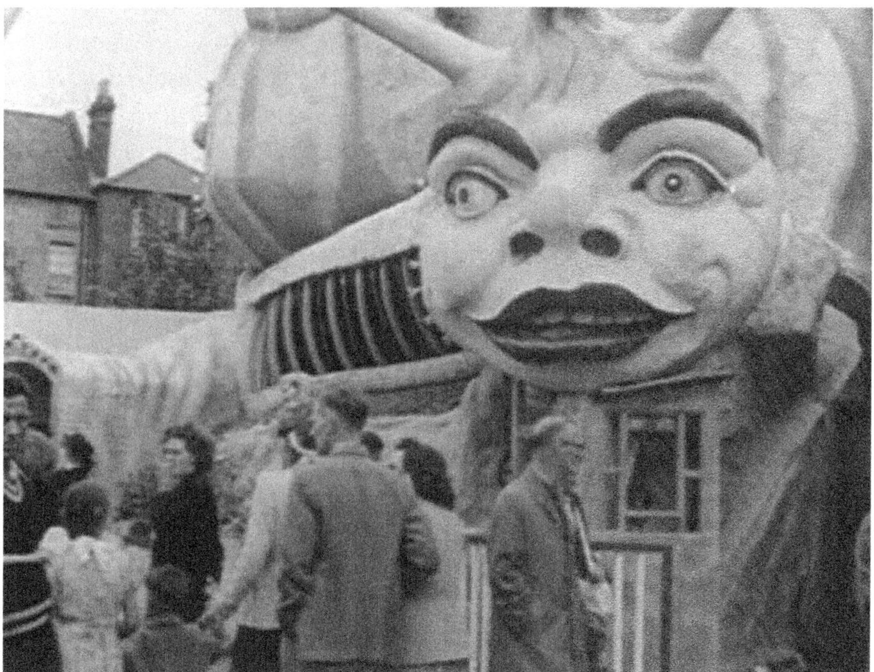

Figure 1.2 *O Dreamland* (Lindsay Anderson, 1953).

more upbeat, Reisz and Richardson's *Mama Don't Allow* (1956) celebrates the culture of working-class youth. It captures the emergence of postwar teen culture in the UK just before the onset of British rock 'n' roll. Fast-paced shots depict teddy boys and shop girls ecstatically Lindy Hopping at the Wood Green Jazz Club in North London. They reel and twirl to the Chris Barber Band, finding release after a long workday. The same year that Reisz and Richardson filmed *Mama Don't Allow,* Lonnie Donegan – a member of Barber's band who appears in the film – would have a huge hit with his rollicking cover of Lead Belly's 'Rock Island Line'. John Lennon, Jimmy Page and many other future rock stars got their start in skiffle bands influenced by Donegan. It is easy to imagine their older siblings as the teens in *Mama Don't Allow.* The film's excitement is infectious. Even after many viewings, my body still wants to jump up and dance along with its anonymous stars.

By moving away from strict narrative and increasing the pace of its editing, Pop documentary began to emulate the high-speed flow of imagery found on television and in the full-colour, advertisement-filled magazines crowding the newsstands.[10] American photographer William Klein began making films in 1957 with his city-symphony *Broadway by Light.*[11] Klein impressionistically shot the neon signs in New York City's Times Square, fragmenting them into bursts of artificial light illuminating the night sky. His camera cuts from sign to spectacular sign, moving from product logos and brand names to close-ups that reduce the signs to abstractions. The shifting rhythm from one brand to the next is subsumed by the whole in a dazzling ode to the hypnagogic powers of advertising. Documentaries that focus on the work of Pop artists, such as Juan Drago's *Superartist* (1967) on Andy Warhol and James Scott's *Richard Hamilton* (1969), make similar use of formal techniques that fragment film structure to capture a sense of pop culture as an image-saturated phantasmagoria.

By the middle of the 1950s, several American artists-turned-filmmakers began to leave traditional forms of documentary film behind entirely. Turning to collage, their films were aligned with the avant-garde even more closely than the Pop documentaries. A strong precedent for this practice existed in Joseph Cornell's 1936 film *Rose Hobart,* which abandoned all vestiges of classical Hollywood cinema to surreally evoke its star as an object of desire. Cornell obsessively focuses on Hobart as the epitome of a human being transformed by cinematic magic into a consumable commodity. Made wholly from recycled footage, he re-cut a print of George Melford's 1931 film *East of Borneo* down to individual scenes, even single shots, focused on Hobart. Cornell interleaved these images with other short bits of found film, projecting the finished film in slow motion through a blue-coloured piece of glass while playing longing-filled pop songs on a record player as a soundtrack.

Robert Breer made his first collage film, *Un Miracle*, in collaboration with Pontus Hulten in 1953. Just one minute long, it features a cut-up, animated photograph of the Pope juggling his own head. Breer would go on to make several other films in the 1950s using the same technique. These include *Jamestown Baloos* (1957) featuring similarly ridiculous depictions of soldiers along with rapidly scanned images of newspaper and magazine pages. Breer developed a host of other animation techniques, as did Stan VanDerBeek, who began making similar films during the mid-1950s using cut-up images culled from the mass media as his primary medium. VanDerBeek's films found wide acclaim, winning numerous film prizes and directly inspiring the animated sequences made by Terry Gilliam for *Monty Python's Flying Circus*.

Bruce Conner's *A MOVIE*, from 1958, is solely focused on the reuse of previously shot films. Highly regarded, it would set the tone for his own and many other filmmakers' subsequent collage-based work. Conner was spurred to make *A MOVIE* both by movie previews, with their condensed, often surreal use of narrative, as well as his own lack of money – it cost him less to buy old rolls of pre-shot film than to shoot his own. He recut found material, which ranged from bits of stag films over b-movies and industrial films to wartime documentaries, into new sequences focused on the darker sides of cinematic voyeurism. After an opening shot of a half-nude woman taking off her stockings, *A MOVIE* speeds through bomb explosions, car crashes and sports accidents. A tone of desublimated Cold War anxiety mixed with black humour runs throughout. Conner uncovers the repressed consciousness of mass consumption, as if behind all those teen adventure movies lurks a more terrible reality. The soundtrack (Ottorino Respighi's *The Pines of Rome*) swings from a lighter to a more serious tone while the images do the opposite. Contrasting the soundtrack with the image as yet another collage element would become a common practice in subsequent Pop films.

Most of Breer, VanDerBeek and Conner's collage films are composed of a ceaseless, high-speed montage driven by the rapid alternation of one image culled from the mass-media after another. With their focus on the radical juxtaposition of recycled imagery and little narrative development, these films amplified the flood of mass-mediated images that were becoming prevalent in everyday life. Even today, when viewers have become inured to such profusion, watching them can lead to an experience of psychic overload. The rapidity of their quotations emphasises the cut, and therefore the caesura, not as pause or closure but as an endless series of distracting interruptions. Nevertheless, mini narratives bubble up amid the chaos, generating recurring themes without recourse to a unified story or plot. In Conner's *REPORT* (1963–67), which focuses on the media coverage of the assassination of John F. Kennedy, the trappings of historical narrative remain but are transformed through speed, repetition and ellipsis.

Pop collage films extend the strategy of paradigmatic substitution developed in Surrealist film. Unlike Surrealist film, where one unlike thing is made to relate to the next by the sheer force of succession (as in the famous sequence of cuts between a hand filled with ants, a woman's hairy armpit and a sea urchin in Salvador Dalí and Luis Buñel's *Un Chien Andalou*, 1929), in films such as *A MOVIE*, one similar commodity follows the next, echoing the endless substitution of more of the same found in the mass media. These films tend to take a less favourable stance toward the mass media than some of the Pop documentaries or sub-z movies do. In these films, radical heterogeneity gives way to a radical homogeneity critical of the sameness of the mass marketplace.

In Pop collage films, one quoted image bumps up against the next, creating a portrait of the marketplace for mass-manufactured amusements as a whole. Astute viewers can recognise, in general and sometimes specifically, the sources of the quoted bits, and yet these bits are ripped from their original contexts and forced to obey new rules by being pressed into thematic purposes at odds with their original use. Pop collage films generate tension by harnessing this allegorical double valence as the reused images individually say one thing while, in their new succession, doing another. The soundtrack, which is similarly repurposed, adds yet another layer to the allegorical ironies.

As the 1960s progressed, pop music became an integral part of Pop Cinema. After *Mama Don't Allow*, Conner's *COSMIC RAY*, made in 1960, is one of the earliest examples of the music-based variant of Pop Cinema. At a dizzyingly fast pace set to the rhythm of Ray Charles performing 'What I Say', Conner collaged together original footage of a nude go-go dancer with readymade footage that includes film leader, war films and Mickey Mouse cartoons. He counterpoints collaged footage with the Charles song by cross-cutting military images with the nude dancer. As the music rises to a climax, an enormous cartoon cannon shoots its load then flamboyantly limpens, making absurdly literal the song's barely disguised sexual urgency. Conner would go on to make several more song-length music films in which collaged material is rhythmically counterposed against a pop song.

Conner's music films, and those made by other avant-garde filmmakers such as Peter Whitehead, are often cited as the precursors to the music videos of the 1980s. While Conner and Whitehead made some remarkable music films, record companies were producing a whole host of similar 'music promos' as advertisements for their songs. Music promos were shown on television and scopitones, jukeboxes that included small film projection screens. There was little difference between the majority of these films and the musical performances being done in television studios for live broadcast. Most were campy scenes of the performer lip-synching against a backdrop or location, accompanied by scantily clad back-up dancers. One of Whitehead's first jobs as a professional filmmaker was for the BBC's television music programme *Top of the Pops*. Hired to film bands that were unable to appear live, Whitehead made promos for numerous artists, including the Rolling Stones, Jimi Hendrix and Nico. Rather than shoot straight concert footage, his music films often mixed performance with strategies drawn from the avant-garde.

One of Whitehead's earliest films was 'When I Was Young'. Made in 1965 for Eric Burdon and the New Animals, it was an early reflection on the escalation of the war in Vietnam, disguised as a pointed look back at World War II and the sacrifices made by the previous generation. Fast-paced collage footage of military planes is intercut with the band performing in the studio. Whitehead reused documentary footage that heightens the song's already satirical lyrics by undermining the representation of war in popular media as a heroic enterprise in which the good guys always win. Given that the music promo is one of the crassest forms of advertising, Whitehead's anti-war message was remarkable.

Beyond his promos, Whitehead made numerous other films that focused on rock. *Charlie is My Darling* (1966) captures the Rolling Stones' 1965 tour of Ireland. *Tonite Let's All Make Love in London* (1967), subtitled a 'Pop Concerto for Film', features the work of Pink Floyd and others, along with footage of Pop artists such as David Hockney (Figure 1.3). He filmed several early concerts by Led Zeppelin. Not all of these are collage films, but all are deeply engaged with the intersection of popular culture as an art form and its passionate consumers. The same is true of several of Kenneth Anger's films from the same period, including *Scorpio Rising* (1963) and *Kustom Kar Kommandos* (1965). Anger's films depict young men aping the kind of macho poses found in Hollywood and the hipster subcultures of 1950s California. In both films, Anger uses rock songs as a Greek chorus to speak on behalf on the audience, as if the song's lyrics were calling out with longing from the sidelines for the men depicted.

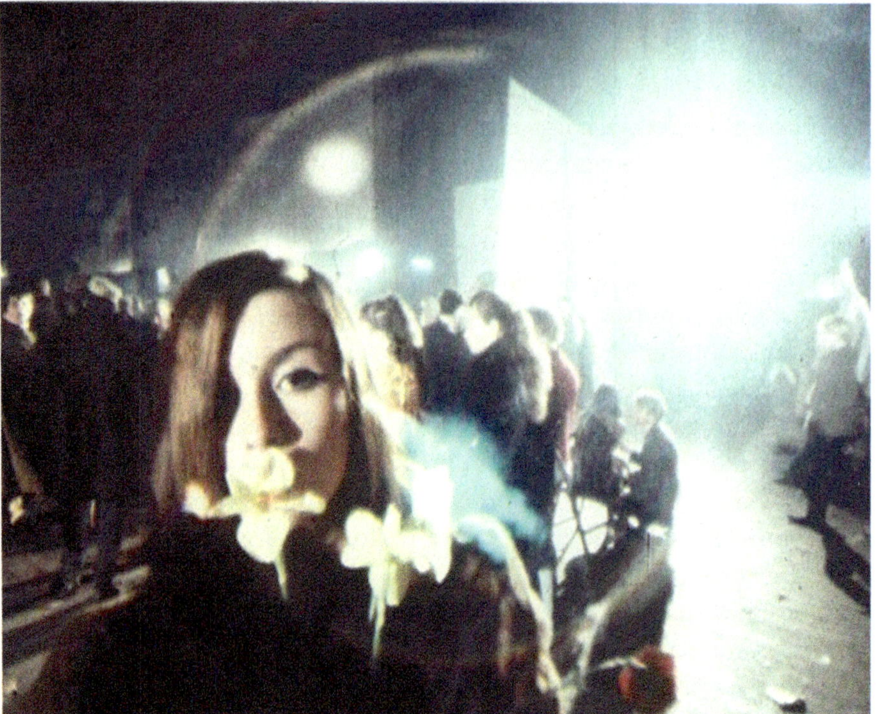

Figure 1.3 *Tonite Let's All Make Love in London* (Peter Whitehead, 1967).

In complement to the use of recycling in collage films, the makers of sub-z movies took the genres of mainstream cinema as readymades. The main practitioners of the sub-z movie were Anger, Jack Smith, Andy Warhol and the Kuchar brothers. Much has already been written on the subject.[12] Along with the above-mentioned Anger films, Smith's *Flaming Creatures* (1963), Warhol's *Tarzan and Jane Regained... Sort of* (1964), and George and Mike Kuchar's *I Was a Teenage Rumpot* (1960) are prime examples. Such films treat genre as a collage element, cutting up and shuffling the categories of Hollywood film as yet another recyclable medium. The primary genre that they all imitate is the b/z-movie, with their bad acting, thin plotting and hyperbolic tone. They secondarily imitate the subgenres of such movies: biker films, erotica, science fiction, melodrama. Some focus on a single genre, while others blur the lines between them. *I Was a Teenage Rumpot* turns the 'I was a teenage vampire, mummy, zombie, etc' comedy/horror genre on its head by focusing on the far more prosaic subject of alcoholism. Rather than kitchen-sink realism, the Kuchar brothers play this subject to high ridiculousness. Pop music figures as prominently in the soundtracks to sub-z movies as it does in other forms of Pop Cinema. The studied incompetence of sub-z movies distinguishes them from the unacknowledged, self-serious incompetence of truly camp films.[13] They histrionically pastiche Hollywood's tropes, allowing the seams to show in movies whose productions are continuously falling apart. Sub-z movies are hyper-camp, aping camp cinema with such impoverished means that they become something beyond – or beneath – even the z-movies produced by the likes of Ed Wood in the outer orbits of Hollywood. Forgoing collage, sub-z movies are purely ersatz imitations (of the z-movie) of imitations (of the b-movie) of classical Hollywood filmmaking. They rely on amateur acting and improvisation. Although they often nod at narrative, their plots continually get sidetracked.

Queer themes predominate in sub-z movies. Traditional masculinity is frequently turned on its head through impotence, drag and sexual ambiguity. Sub-z filmmakers embraced camp as a means of undermining stereotypes of masculinity. Smith, Warhol and the Kuchar brothers focused on the absurdities of machismo as a media phenomenon. In their femininity and failure to impose their will on the world around them, the stars of their films are like anti-Hollywood heroes. Anger's films move in the opposite direction. They show highly sexualised images of teen bikers and auto mechanics ('rough trade') straight out of then illicit gay magazines, turning an objectifying erotic male gaze on the male body.

Marie Menken was one of the few women filmmakers whose work is specifically associated with Pop.[14] Like Anger and the other sub-z filmmakers, in her film *Wrestling* (1964) she flipped Pop Cinema's typical presentation of gender on its head to explore the production of normative masculinity in the mass media. In a feminist gesture that undercuts the recycled images of femininity deployed by so many straight male Pop artists and filmmakers, she reuses an emblem of popular machismo to reclaim the male body for formal purposes. *Wrestling* consists of a series of highly sped-up shots of professional wrestlers that Menken filmed directly from a television set. Her signature hand-held camerawork distorts the figures on screen. Edited to hyper levels of animation, with no sound, the masculinity of the he-men she captures becomes a ridiculous caricature that ultimately gives way to a lyrical evocation of semi-abstract bodies in motion. The raster of the television's scan lines become an additional compositional element which she contrasts with the grain of her film stock.

Other women filmmakers challenged the normative images of femininity found in both the mainstream media and Pop Cinema itself. Eroticised women frequently appear in Pop films made by men, from Paolozzi's initial collage presentation, to Pauline Boty's glamorous sexuality in *Pop Goes the Easel* and elsewhere, to Conner's hippie nudes. Throughout Pop films, multitudes of recycled advertisements flash past, of female bodies being used to sell products starring models whose bodies themselves were a product. Because mass-mediated depictions of women, particularly during the 1950s and 1960s, were produced for either male arousal, female aspiration, or both, reusing them was tricky. There was (and remains) a thin line between reproducing gender stereotypes and critiquing them.

In several early films, Gunvor Nelson turned to the realities and sur-realities of women's bodies.[15] *Schmeerguntz*, made in 1965 with Dorothy Wiley, is a fast-paced collage film of images from women's magazines depicting the stereotypes of femininity with which such publications were filled and that so many male Pop filmmakers were also using. Set to surf rock and other pop songs, Nelson and Wiley intercut these images with footage that they shot themselves of the far more prosaic reality of women's lives. Repeated shots of a pregnant woman show her struggling to get dressed and vomiting in a toilet, presumably from morning sickness. There are close-ups of shit being wiped from a baby's bottom, a tampon being removed and other images that show taboo snippets of the behind-the-scenes reality of women's everyday lives. In the penultimate scene, the film stock is reversed and vomit flies back from the toilet into the woman's mouth.

In Nelson's *Take Off* (1972), which responds to Conner's work among others, an older female stripper disrobes in what ultimately becomes an act of total self-abnegation. The film begins as predictably as any stag film, with the performer tossing off a spangled bikini and cheekily twirling pastie tassels over raunchy grind-house jazz. Once she's fully naked, white flashes begin to disrupt the image, and the music turns dissonant. Using primitive special effects, she strips off her hair, legs, then her ears, nose, head and breasts until her arms wiggle away, leaving just her torso, which spins off into space. Both *Schmeerguntz* and *Take Off* use humour-tinged body horror to undermine not only mainstream depictions of women as paragons of beauty but also the work of Nelson's male filmmaking peers. They became iconic works of second-wave feminist film.

The Pop Cinema programme ended with two films that, while they fall somewhat outside of the purview of the others, responded as directly to representations of women as Nelson did. Activist film collective Newsreel's *Up Against the Wall Miss America!* (1968) is a documentary on the protest held against the 1968 Miss America beauty pageant in Atlantic City, New Jersey. The protest itself became a hot media item when the women performing street theatre outside the pageant hall were erroneously accused of setting fire to their bras, leading to endless quips about bra-burning feminists. Peter Whitehead and Niki de Saint Phalle's *Daddy* (1973) is a gothic fairytale in which Saint Phalle takes metaphorical revenge on the father who had molested her as a child. Whitehead and Saint Phalle turn the erotic film on its head by grappling candidly with the consequences of sexual abuse.

Pop Cinema proved influential on a wide range of film and video practices that followed, inside and outside the avant-garde. It is a short hop, thematically at least, from *Mama Don't Allow* to *American Bandstand*, *Top of the Pops*, *Ready Steady Go!*, even *Dancing with the Stars* and TikTok dance memes. MTV music videos were direct descendants of the music promos of Conner, Whitehead and others associated with Pop Cinema. (Conner even had videos he made for bands including Devo aired on MTV.) With their radical fragmentation and heterogeneity, 1980s music videos hewed even more closely to the form of the Pop collage film than many of the earlier music promos. In the 1980s and 1990s, Dan Graham, Pipilotti Rist and other contemporary artists turned to music video as a form. Around the same time, Scratch video emerged in the UK as an avant-garde variant on music videos. For pop stars today, such as Lady Gaga and Beyoncé, releasing an experimental moving-image project alongside their music projects is a given. Trash, punk and no-wave cinema, aka 'the cinema of transgression', continued the lineage of sub-z movies.[16] The work of John Waters, Nick Zedd, Richard Kern and Beth and Scott B. follows closely from that of Smith, Warhol and the Kuchars. Through video installation, contemporary artists such as Ryan Trecartin have more recently brought the sub-z movie into the art gallery.

In the digital media age, the aesthetics of plenty have become more bountiful than ever. We live in a world now dominated by the omnivorous all-overism of commercial images. Pop Cinema is an early instance of what the curator Nicholas Bourriaud calls 'postproduction', or the contemporary tendency of culture-makers to explicitly reuse existing cultural artifacts as the basis of their work, rather than starting from scratch.[17] Online video's proliferation of easily produced, appropriation-based mash-ups echoes many of the themes explored in Pop Cinema. So does the fast-paced recycling of material drawn from the mass media in meme culture.

The speed of much of Pop Cinema, its self-conscious awkwardness and its inward-looking obsession with popular culture have become a significant part of the language of gallery-based art as well as more popular forms of digital image making. Given that such techniques have long been adopted by the mass media, the films that I am ascribing to Pop Cinema deserve to be studied as closely as Pop Art is. The dissociative impact of their montage, the many clever ways in which they use pop music and other citations from commercial sources, even the violence of their critical impulses, make them rewarding to watch. I undertook this project in a self-conscious act of historical revision. Recognizing how great these films are caused me to re-evaluate my understanding of Pop Art. By mapping the field of Pop Cinema and creating a typology for it, my goal was to make these films more visible. That there remains interest in the project a decade later indicates that this is beginning to happen.

This is an updated version of an essay printed originally as 'Notes on Pop Cinema' in William Kaizen (ed.), Pop Cinema: Art and Film in the US and UK, 1950s–1970s, *Philadelphia, PA: International House Philadelphia, 2011, pp. 11–30.*

Notes

1 The series' full title was *Pop Cinema: Art and Film in the US and UK, 1950s–1970s.* It was held 28–30 April 2011 at the International House, Philadelphia. This is a revised version of the catalogue's introductory essay. The catalogue also contained a list of films screened with synopses of each that expanded upon this essay. These synopses focus on some of the lesser-known artists in the series. I gave Jeff Keen's work, for example, a synopsis in the catalogue rather than a discussion in the essay, although he is central to any history of Pop Cinema. Further discussion of Pop Cinema would necessarily address parallel developments in France in the films of the Lettristes and Situationist International, as well as the films of Yokoo Tadanori in Japan, and even the work of mainstream filmmakers such as Richard Lester and many others.

2 Tanya Leighton curated a film series that directly inspired mine. The programme, simply titled 'Pop' was one of six subsections (the others were 'Dreams', 'Expression', 'Play', 'Modernity' and 'Protest') compiled under the banner *Essentials: Secret Masterpieces of Cinema.* It ran in multiple venues across the UK from January 2008 to October 2009, including Tate Modern, the National Media Museum in Bradford and the Arnolfini Gallery in Bristol. David James addresses the relationship between Pop Art and cinema in his writings on avant-garde film in the 1960s. His work, as well as the work of William Wees on the use of found footage in film, has been influential on my account. See David E. James, *Allegories of Cinema: American Film in the Sixties,* Princeton: Princeton University Press, 1989; William C. Wees, *Recycled Images: The Art and Politics of Found Footage Films,* New York: Anthology Film Archives, 1993.

3 Other canonised Pop Artists who made films include Ed Ruscha in the US and the British Pop artists mentioned below.

4 Lawrence Alloway, 'The Long Front of Culture', reprinted in David Robbins (ed.), *The Independent Group: Postwar Britain and the Aesthetics of Plenty,* Cambridge, MA: MIT Press, 1990, p. 165.

5 For more on the British origins of Pop, see Robbins (ed.), *The Independent Group,* op. cit.

6 Leo Steinberg, *Other Criteria: Confrontations with Twentieth Century Art,* New York: Oxford University Press, 1972, pp. 82–91.

7 William Kaizen, 'Richard Hamilton's Tabular Image', *October*, 94 (Fall 2000), pp. 113–28.

8 Lawrence Alloway, 'The Independent Group: Postwar Britain and the Aesthetics of Plenty', in Robbins (ed.), *The Independent Group*, op. cit., p. 50.

9 Paolozzi was the star of Mazzetti's film *Together* (1956).

10 Warhol's silent films were shot at 24 frames per second (fps) but exhibited at the slow projection speed of 16 fps and are thus an obvious exception to the speed of other Pop films. Warhol used this technique specifically for its alienation effect, as a way of creating critical distance between the viewer and what they were viewing. Paradoxically, the slowness of his 'Screen Tests', a large collection of portraits of people projected at the slower frame rate, can cause the viewer to connect more empathically with the person on screen.

11 His later feature-length films *Who are You, Polly Maggoo?* (1966), *Mr. Freedom* (1969) and *The Model Couple* (1977) are also significant works of Pop Cinema.

12 For example, in James, *Allegories of Cinema*, op. cit.

13 As Susan Sontag describes them in 'Notes on Camp'. Sontag, *Against Interpretation: And Other Essays*, New York: Picador, 2001, p. 281.

14 Menken and her husband Willard Mass were friends with Warhol. Menken taught Warhol how to use a film camera and starred in several of his films. She also made the film *Andy Warhol*, starring Warhol, which constitutes yet another example of a Pop Cinema avant-garde documentary.

15 Her husband Robert Nelson also made significant contributions to Pop Cinema, including the films *Oh Dem Watermelons* (1965) and *Grateful Dead* (1967).

16 Jack Sargeant, *Deathtripping: The Extreme Underground*, New York: Soft Skull, 2008.

17 Nicolas Bourriaud, *Postproduction: Culture as Screenplay: How Art Reprograms the World*, ed. Caroline Schneider, trans. Jeanine Herman, New York: Lukas & Sternberg, 2002.

2

Pop and Cinema: Three Tendencies

Ed Halter

Film as a Pop Art

In contemplating the relationship of cinema to Pop art – and determining whether we can identify a strain of 'Pop cinema' that was part of, or paralleled, the international diffusion of a Pop aesthetic – the first thing to consider is the movies' foundational influence on the development of Pop and its visual vocabulary.

Artifacts fresh from contemporaneous film culture played a prominent role in the 1956 exhibition *This Is Tomorrow* at London's Whitechapel Gallery, notably in a section co-organised by Richard Hamilton, John McHale and John Voelcker. These three men comprised one segment of the Independent Group, a coterie of critics such as Lawrence Alloway and Reyner Banham and artists including Hamilton, McHale and Eduardo Paolozzi, who had been active at London's Institute of Contemporary Art in the early and mid-1950s and are today seen as the earliest practitioners of Pop art. *This Is Tomorrow* is remembered as one of the first Pop events, not least because Hamilton created his seminal piece *Just what is it that makes today's homes so different, so appealing?* (1956) to advertise the exhibition. Hamilton's collage includes a marquee billboard advertising Al Jolson's *The Jazz Singer* (1927), perhaps as a nod to the fact that the Hamilton-McHale-Voelcker section would be dominated by the ephemera of movie marketing. A sixteen-foot-tall model of Robby the Robot from the film *Forbidden Planet* (1956) loomed at the entrance to their space at *This Is Tomorrow*, along with an enormous display advertisement for the same science-fiction epic that had graced the façade of a London theatre (Figure 2.1). Elsewhere one could see a life-size cutout of Marilyn Monroe from *The Seven Year Itch* (1955); a poster for MGM's *Julius Caesar* (1953), featuring Marlon Brando

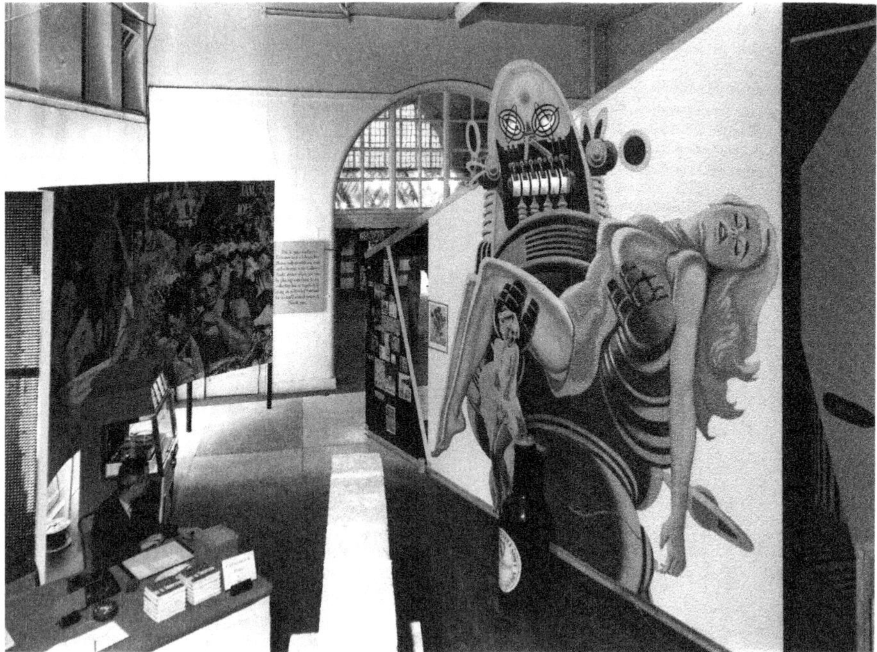

Figure 2.1 *This is Tomorrow* exhibition, Whitechapel Art Gallery, London: Group 2 exhibit, showing the advertisement for *Forbidden Planet* and an image of Marilyn Monroe from *The Seven Year Itch*. Source: Architectural Press Archive/RIBA collections.

as Mark Antony; and a wall-size photomontage celebrating CinemaScope, the wide-screen technology that had been used to spectacular effect in *Forbidden Planet.*[1]

Cinema shaped the visions of numerous Pop artists across the Atlantic, too. For example, Ed Ruscha approximated the aspect ratio of American widescreen motion pictures in the canvas dimensions of his paintings *Standard Station, Amarillo, Texas* (1963) and *Large Trademark with Eight Spotlights* (1962), which depicts the 20th Century Fox logo; Rosalyn Drexler employed the compositional logics of film frames and movie posters for *The Dream* (aka *King Kong*) (1963), *Home Movies* (1963) and other paintings; and James Rosenquist disassembled the face of a star for his *Marilyn Monroe, I* (1962). Undoubtedly, the American Pop artist most deeply invested in film was Andy Warhol, whose interest in the medium is evident in work from as early as 1963, when he began using Hollywood images as source material for his silkscreened paintings. For his Marilyn series, he employed a black-and-white photo made to promote the Monroe movie *Niagara* (1953); he based his Liz paintings on images of Elizabeth Taylor produced to publicise *Butterfield 8* (1960); and his Elvis series multiplies a publicity still for

Presley's western vehicle *Flaming Star* (1960). Warhol once mentioned that he took up silkscreening for the method's 'assembly-line effect', and that his first experiments involved photos of movie heartthrobs Warren Beatty and Troy Donohue.[2] By adopting such small-scale techniques of mechanical reproduction, Warhol's New York studio, the Factory, became an artists' atelier that reflected the culture industry at large. The same year Warhol began silkscreening, he entered film production proper with minimal 16mm films such as *Sleep* and *Kiss*, eventually bringing forth well over a hundred individual titles. The publicity Warhol's films generated, even more so than his paintings, cemented his mainstream celebrity.

The Pop activities of London's Independent Group, Warhol and other artists occurred during a time when such diverse mid-century intellectuals as Marshall McLuhan in Canada, Susan Sontag in the United States, Raymond Williams in England, Theodor W. Adorno in West Germany and Guy Debord in France were re-evaluating the function and value of mass culture. All these thinkers agreed that the spread of new communications technologies was displacing the traditional arts from their former status as the most privileged objects of critical scrutiny, although they differed in their individual analyses of the contours, causes and ramifications of this shift. The Independent Group also participated in this conversation, as the writers among them reported. 'Advertising, colour photography and colour reproduction, (big screen) films, (early English) TV, [and] automobile styling were regarded on equal terms with the fine arts', Alloway wrote. 'Not the same, but equally interesting'.[3] And John McHale summarised the larger cultural transition in a 1973 conversation with the futurist Alvin Toffler. 'The fine arts', he said, 'are now just one of many channels of communication within which images and metaphors of the society flow'.[4]

Linked to this alteration in attitude towards the mass media, cinema itself underwent an intense revaluation. As television became the dominant medium of mass entertainment, movies assumed a position of cultural legitimacy formerly held exclusively by the more traditional arts. The struggle for cinema to be understood as a true art form had been ongoing since the 1920s, when the European avant-garde embraced filmmaking. After World War II, however, a more broadly based cinephilia developed within a new generation whose members could see international imports and repertory classics through an increasingly large network of film societies, campus screening rooms, museum programmes and specialised movie houses. Before long, the 'art film' became a mass phenomenon. These changes accorded a new status to film critics, who began to take on a role once occupied by literary critics in the nineteenth and early twentieth centuries – using the form of the topical review to make larger observations on art and society. Journals such as *Cahiers du Cinéma* in France, *Movie* in Britain and *Film Culture* in the United States did more than merely review films: they produced critical and polemical writings that encouraged new ways to conceptualise and create cinema.

The fact that post-war filmmakers could now be considered artists made the encounter between Pop art and cinema different from that between Pop art and other mass media, and this led to some debate. Alloway was the International Group member most drawn to matters cinematic.[5] He weighed in on the evolving role of the film critic in his 1964 essay 'Critics in the Dark', written for the literary magazine *Encounter*.[6] Alloway assessed several then-recently published books devoted to the medium, including James Agee's two volumes of collected film criticism; the distributor Dan Talbot's compilation *Film: An Anthology*; and the sociologist Edgar Morin's early celebrity study *The Stars*. Alloway claimed that the main problem with intellectual film criticism as it had been practiced up to that point was it had not dealt with 'pop movies' (as opposed, the reader might assume, to 'art films') as the mass-produced, genre-driven experiences they were meant to be. He argued that critics focused too much on celebrating what they considered to be the best work, and thereby failed to explore more fully the contours of the field of cinema as a whole. This limitation was partly due to the toils of the weekly journalist, beholden to the output of distributors. After all, Alloway noted, the early nineteenth-century British essayist William Hazlitt had been free to write about only the best in literature, if he wished. By contrast, Agee, writing for *Time* magazine and the *Nation*, had to respond to whatever Hollywood released that week, good or bad.

Two major American critics took umbrage at Alloway's assertions and defended the evaluative role and intellectual heft of their métier. Pauline Kael concluded the introduction to her influential first collection of reviews and essays, *I Lost It at the Movies* (1965), on this note:

> In the West several of the academic people I know who have [the] least understanding of movies were suddenly interested by Lawrence Alloway's piece… By suggesting that movie criticism had never gotten into the right hands – i.e., theirs, and by indicating projects, and by publishing in the prestigious *Encounter*, Alloway indicated large vistas of respectability for future film critics. Perhaps also they were drawn to his condescending approach to movies as a pop art.[7]

Andrew Sarris paralleled Kael's sentiment in his own retort to Alloway, in the essay 'Pop Go the Movies!', first published in *Moviegoer* in 1964:

> In his eagerness to divest the cinema of personal responsibility and durable value, Alloway transforms what is too frequently a dismal fact into a visionary ideal. This is not the attitude of the true movie addict who is too experienced to like everything he sees, but more the rationale of condescending content awareness without any deep commitment to formal excellence.[8]

It seems odd that Kael and Sarris would chide Alloway for being 'condescending' toward the movies, given the British critic's clear love of genre films. In any case, Alloway fired back a bit later, in a 1968 article for *Vogue*. There he described *The American Action Film, 1946–1964* – a retrospective of Hollywood films he would co-curate in 1969 at the Museum of Modern Art in New York with the writer Toby Mussman and the artist Robert Smithson – as 'intended to reveal some of the characteristic patterns of cinema rather than the compulsive expertise of director recognition'. For Alloway, it was Kael and her circle who were condescending, particularly in their attitude toward the average moviegoer. 'Audiences understand these conventions', Alloway concluded. 'Now, perhaps, critics can begin to'.[9]

Pop Artists Onscreen

While Pop artists drew inspiration from the aesthetics of Hollywood, a new generation of international filmmakers was vehemently rejecting the notion of film as mere commercial entertainment and attempting to reshape it along more visionary and personal terms. The critic Parker Tyler noted in his landmark study *Underground Film: A Critical History* (1969) that Pop art 'came on the scene almost in step with the reawakening of the avant-garde film in the late Fifties'.[10] Indeed, the post-war period saw an explosion of cinematic styles and movements worldwide: neorealism in Italy, the Nouvelle Vague and Cinéma vérité in France, Free Cinema in Britain, Cinema Novo in Brazil, Parallel Cinema in India and numerous other 'new waves'. The underground film boom to which Tyler referred – focused more on shorter, non-narrative works than on documentaries or feature films, in contrast to the other new waves – staked out its own claim within this expanded scene. Such work was facilitated by the relatively low cost and accessibility of 16mm in that period. Filmmakers started collectively run distribution centres in London, Paris, Tokyo, Vienna, West Berlin and elsewhere, inspired by the New American Cinema's Film-Makers' Cooperative in New York, which was formed in 1962.[11] During this time, experimental cinema was 'typically American', the *Cahiers du Cinéma* critic Louis Marcorelles observed, by way of noting the influence of the New American Cinema on experimental film movements abroad: 'Deeply anarchical, it denies that the cinema is a mass medium'.[12]

Pop and cinema converged in this new generation of filmmakers. As Salvador Dalí and Marcel Duchamp had done decades earlier, many of those who entered this cinematic frontier arrived with experience in the fine arts, including several prominent figures associated with Pop. Warhol is the most obvious and prolific example of this phenomenon, and he served as an inspiration to later artists who turned to film. His feature *Chelsea Girls* (1966) was, for a time, the highest-grossing independent release in the United States, and its unprecedented success focused mainstream, international attention on underground cinema. Bruce Conner's found-footage films, such as *A MOVIE* (1958), *COSMIC RAY* (1961) and *REPORT* (1963–67), would become so celebrated for their sly wit and canny editing that their creator's renown as a filmmaker all but eclipsed his substantial reputation as a sculptor and painter. Red Grooms, Roy Lichtenstein, Claes Oldenburg and Ed Ruscha were among other American Pop figures who dabbled in film. Outside the United States, Sigmar Polke and Gerhard Richter in West Germany, Marcel Broodthaers in Belgium, Yves Klein in France and Nelson Leirner in Brazil all produced films in the 1960s and early 1970s, with varying degrees of commitment to the medium.

One of the most accomplished filmmakers on the international Pop scene was the second-generation British Pop artist Derek Boshier. Between 1970 and 1973, he made four short 16mm films that ingeniously translate the formal concerns of his painting and photography into moving images. His earliest, *Link* (1970), suggests a collage-like technique, presenting stills and brief motion-picture segments of otherwise unrelated images that are connected only by a set of primary shapes. One segment, for example, proceeds from an Islamic dome to a nude breast, to a bubble rising in a pool of yellow paint, to a flying saucer in a Superman comic book. Boshier juxtaposes Egyptian pyramids with the Paramount studios logo, the cube-shaped Kaaba in Mecca with a sleek cigarette lighter. The overall effect of *Link* is a levelling of all forms of status, equating high and low, fine art and mass art, ancient and modern, sacred and profane. The film's soundtrack, made up of mechanical chugs and electronic warbles, suggests that technological standardisations encourage the radical juxtaposition – or linking – of disparate elements. Boshier returned to this structure for his final film, *Change* (1973), this time using animation to make one image appear to melt into the next, a technique that, as the art historian Alex Kitnick has noted, predicts the digital-editing style of morphing.[13]

Eduardo Paolozzi also used collage techniques in his films of the early 1960s, but to vastly different ends. His black-and-white *History of Nothing* (1961–62) animates illustrations of industrial machinery, animals and architecture taken from damaged books found at a German school where Paolozzi taught. The disjunctive feel of *History of Nothing* seems clearly indebted to surrealism, particularly the work of Max Ernst, but in a way that connects Ernst's use of mass-produced images with Pop's interest in newer mass media. Paolozzi incorporated elements of this film in several other works, including the ink-on-paper print *History of Nothing* (1962) – a grid of hand-drawn filmstrips, complete with wobbly sprocket holes and fanciful cartoon images – and the screenprint *Four Stills from the History of Nothing* (1962), which adds colour to four of the originally monochrome illustrations. Pages of Paolozzi's artist's book *Metafisikal Translations* (1962) depict isolated collage elements from the animation as well as a stream-of-consciousness-style 'shooting script' for the film: 'LONG SHOT Clowns and dancers Robots aeroplanes ancient and modern Demolished ships Diamond transformations and German transformers dissolve MIDDLE SHOT Radial engine Floral gears Useful analogy military insignia transfer Lagoon seen through cars windscreen Aerial view of a city burning.'[14]

Paolozzi's animation seems elementary compared to the complex line-drawn movement and energetic photo-collage of Japan's Yokoo Tadanori, who produced three brief yet explosive films in the mid-1960s. In *KISS KISS KISS* (1964), images inspired by Western comic-strip romances transition from one to the next by means of holes in the centre of the pages. *Kachi Kachi Yama* (1965) inserts colourful cartoons of Brigitte Bardot, Alain Delon, Elizabeth Taylor and others in fantastical movie-scene tableaux. Beginning nearly a decade later, Tadanori's compatriot Tanaami Keiichi created many more films using similar techniques, but at times he also hinted at political commentary and a disturbing eroticism. Tanaami's *Good-by Elvis and USA* (1971) contains a gas-masked superhero in a costume emblazoned with 'USA', half-naked Statue of Liberty dancers and a grotesque caricature of Elvis Presley consuming golden penises, set to tape-manipulated snippets from his songs 'Love Me Tender' and 'Hound Dog'.

The West German artist Peter Roehr reportedly disliked being categorised as a Pop practitioner, despite the fact that his striking but limited body of work – cut short by his death in 1968 at age twenty-three – incorporates found, mass-produced materials and seems, therefore, to have affinities with the movement. This connection is particularly notable in a series of photomontages he began in 1964, in which shots of coffee, cars and other products, culled from magazine advertisements, are reproduced and assembled into austere grids. Roehr maintained, however, that he was more interested in the structure of repetition than in the content of the images. The coolness of his photographic work translates into something far more heightened and hypnotic in a series of 16mm films he made in 1965, collectively titled *Film-Montagen 1-3* (*Film Montages 1-3*). Here, Roehr reprints seconds-long segments, mostly from American TV commercials, so that each bit loops multiple times, in succession. His choice of images is highly enigmatic: a model flips her hair, nude athletes wrestle in the sun, an Esso gasoline sign rotates against the sky. Some sequences are stripped of soundtracks, while others retain their original music and dialogue – to exhilaratingly repetitive effect, not unlike the American composer Steve Reich's minimalist tape pieces of the same years. 'Phrases repeat seamlessly whether the words express a complete thought or not', the artist William E. Jones observed about Roehr. 'Describing banalities such as the action of a shampoo or the broadcast of a television programme, the fragments acquire an uncanny power in repetition; they become incantations'.[15]

During this same period, Pop artists were not just behind the camera; some became subjects themselves on the screen. Years before he began directing feature films, Ken Russell made *Pop Goes the Easel* (1962), a forty-four-minute documentary for the BBC meant to explain Pop art to the British public through profiles of the artists Peter Blake, Derek Boshier, Pauline Boty and Peter Phillips. Russell overlays examples of their work and footage of their daily lives with excerpts from audio interviews; the film ends with all four of them dancing the Twist at an apartment party. James Scott made four exemplary films on Pop artists for the Arts Council of Great Britain between 1967 and 1971, individually profiling Richard Hamilton, David Hockney, R. B. Kitaj and Claes Oldenburg. While the first three men are depicted at work (either in the studio or, in the case of Oldenburg, installing his art at the Tate Gallery in London), the Hamilton film shows only images of his works and their source materials, pairing these with a narration written by the artist analysing pieces of his such as *My Marilyn* (1965) and *Swingeing London* (1968–69). The Indian government's Films Division funded a psychedelic portrait of the painter and cartoonist Abid Surti by the experimental documentarian Pramod Pati. Simply titled *Abid* (1972), it animates Surti and his paintings through stop-motion techniques that are set to music by the composer Vijay Raghav Rao. The animation, Pati remarked, 'is agile, energetic and unpredictable just like the pop art movement'.[16]

In *Tonite Let's All Make Love in London* (1967), Peter Whitehead's lysergic chronicle and critique of 'swinging London', David Hockney receives the same celebrity treatment as actors Michael Caine and Julie

Christie, musicians Mick Jagger and Eric Burdon, and model Donyale Luna. Whitehead calls his documentary 'a pop concerto for film' in its opening titles, and he positions Pop art as one of several elements of hip youth culture, along with body painting, Pink Floyd light shows and mini-skirted Soho 'dolly girls'. Whitehead's later film, *Daddy* (1973), made with the French sculptor and painter Niki de Saint Phalle, began production as a documentary but ultimately became a fictionalised biographical narrative – shaped as much by Saint Phalle's ideas as Whitehead's – tracing a woman's struggle against the memory of her father.

This transfiguration of Pop *artists* into something more akin to Pop stars provides one indication that mass culture was transforming the previously rarified micro-culture of the art world. The practice of Pop did not merely entail the repurposing of mass-media images to revive traditional art forms; artists also appropriated the mass media's procedures, goals, methods and ideology. Not content simply to make works about the mass media, artists began taking over those media channels themselves. Warhol's embrace of the star system and his mastery of the press interview have international counterparts in Yves Klein's appearance in the Italian shockumentary *Mondo Cane* (1962): he is shown painting nude female models in his trademark blue. Other examples abound. There were, for instance, the prankish Fluxus actions of the artist Wim T. Schippers, who disrupted numerous Dutch television programmes in the 1960s and early 1970s and eventually became a mainstream TV personality himself;[17] Gerry Schum's *Fernsehgalerie*, a 'television gallery' that broadcast films on West German TV by Jan Dibbets, Walter de Maria, Robert Smithson and many others;[18] Korean-American artist Nam June Paik's first manipulation of television images in the mid-1960s; and the political actions of John Lennon and Yoko Ono, whose televised Bed-Ins for Peace (1969) protesting the Vietnam War could be considered artistic interventions on a mass scale. Although the Pop wave may have encouraged and enabled artists to use the mass media, many of these individuals would have considered themselves and their work distinct from Pop as such, despite certain obvious connections.

Ono's groundbreaking *Sky TV* (1966) is a case in point. One of the earliest examples of video art, it consisted of a television connected to a closed-circuit video camera, transmitting to its screen a live signal of the sky above the gallery. On one level, it presents a perfectly Pop object: a consumer TV set, appropriated by the artist and placed into a space associated with art. But Ono's gesture could also be seen as deeply anti-Pop. Rather than reuse media images, she removed them entirely, cleansing the channels of their frantic content so that they beamed a message of peacefulness and tranquillity, an invitation to contemplate the immediate and natural here-and-now, instead of corporate entertainments that originated elsewhere.[19]

The Pop Image and Its Politics

The relationship between Pop and cinema, then, can be considered in a more expanded fashion, if we look beyond the confines of Pop art proper – as it has typically been delimited by art history – and consider how works of advanced cinema from the heyday of Pop shared many of that movement's concerns. For example, through its embrace of mass media, Pop came to favour a certain kind of image, often powerfully simple in its form or colouration, designed to communicate quickly and directly. Thus, the frequent use of tropes and materials from newspapers and magazines, advertising, cartoons, product packaging and comic strips – or, indeed, images from popular movies, exaggerated and amplified. This is the species of image to which Alloway referred when he declared, in the catalogue accompanying *The American Action Film*, that 'the movies confer grandeur on the present by dealing with current events in maximal forms'.[20]

In the United States, underground filmmakers such as Kenneth Anger, Jack Smith and Ken Jacobs, George and Mike Kuchar, and of course, Conner and Warhol simultaneously parodied and celebrated mass culture's 'maximal forms' through a camp sensibility. And underground camp, like Pop, required its own menu of media artifacts: teeny-bopper songs and comic strips in Anger's *Scorpio Rising* (1963), syrupy easy-listening tracks in the Kuchars' mock-Hollywood mini-epics, or television commercial footage, interpolated whole into Warhol's *Soap Opera* (1964). Indeed, in the commentary of the day, Pop and camp may as well have been interchangeable terms.[21] While this strain of work was, as Louis Marcorelles noted, 'typically American', certain analogues existed in England, most notably in the over-stimulated 8mm films of Jeff Keen; inspired by b-movies and serials, comic books and children's toys, his work was notable for its superimpositions, ad hoc performances and rapid animation. Parallels can also be discerned in work by the eccentric artist and performer 'Professor' Bruce Lacey, whose cheeky *British Landing on the Moon* (1973) imagines the media spectacle of two Englishmen setting up a tea service on the lunar surface.[22]

Traces of Pop's DNA are evident in a spate of groovy, knowingly lowbrow films of the mid- and late 1960s. By now camp was something of an international style, drawing on pulpy science fiction and enlivened by artificial colours and winking sex appeal. Melding the sensibilities of the art house and the drive-in, such fare included Elio Petri's *The 10th Victim* (Italy, 1965), Fukasaku Kinji's *Black Lizard* (Japan, 1967) and *The Green Slime* (Japan/ United States, 1968), George Dunning's animated Beatles adventure *Yellow Submarine* (Great Britain, 1968) and Roger Vadim's *Barbarella* (France/ Italy, 1968), now regarded as a stylistic touchstone of its day. Indeed, distributors exploited *Barbarella*'s Pop reputation when the film was rereleased in West Germany in 1971, with poster copy touting it as 'the adventures of a POP-girl in outer space'.[23]

The marketing of *Barbarella* as a Pop movie illustrates how, as the 1960s progressed, the very term *Pop art* devolved into a hip but slippery buzzword. Alloway noted that it came to be used 'more like slang than the name of an art movement' and was eventually applied to 'fashion, films, interior decoration, toys, parties and town planning'.[24] He pointed to the evolution of Batman – from comic book, to Mel Ramos's paintings, to a knowingly campy American television series – as exemplifying this evolution.[25]

Certainly not all films that played with a Pop aesthetic were mere entertainments. The work of Jean-Luc Godard, for example, illustrates how the graphic sensibilities of Pop could be applied to more serious endeavours, particularly after the director adopted a politically radical approach in the mid-1960s. *Masculin-Féminin* (1966) alluded to this fusion of Pop and politics in its most memorable intertitle: 'This could be called *The Children of Marx and Coca-Cola*'. *Made in USA* (1966) hinted at the Pop-politics juxtaposition in three ways: in its red-white-and-blue design, in a scene set in an art-storage facility holding Lichtenstein-like paintings and in the oft-quoted line 'To live in society today is something like living inside an enormous comic strip'. In *La Chinoise* (1967), a primary-colour scheme, similar to that in *Made in USA*, frames the faces of beautiful young Communists discussing Marxist-Leninist theory; their dialogue is punctuated by close-ups on frames from superhero comics. Among the phrases written on the walls behind them is one that could serve as a Pop-revolutionary slogan: 'We must confront vague ideas with clear images' (Figure 2.2).

Films by the Cuban director Santiago Álvarez and the Polish artist Natalia LL point to how Pop tactics might function in works made in Communist societies. In *Now!* (1964), Álvarez's masterful work of agit-prop focused on racial discrimination in the United States, images lifted from American magazines and footage of police brutality at civil rights demonstrations are set to a fiery tune sung by Lena Horne, also titled 'Now!'; it was written for her by the Broadway lyricists Betty Comden and Adolph Green and the composer Jule Styne. Set to the melody of 'Hava Nagila', the song had been banned by several American radio stations due to its rousing activist lyrics.[26] In a

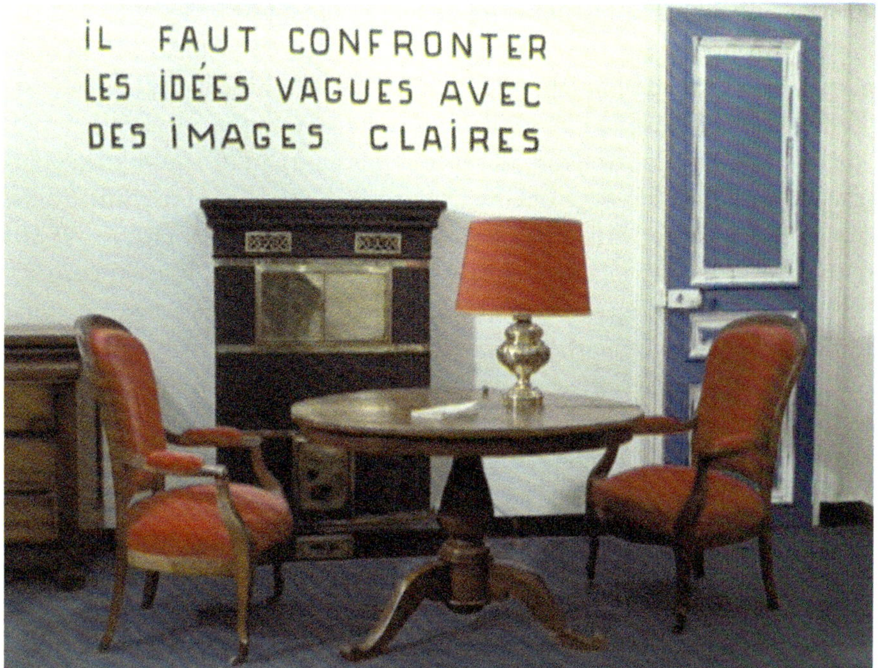

Figure 2.2 *La Chinoise* (Jean-Luc Godard, 1967).

lighter vein, Natalia LL literalises the modern consumer by eating bananas, ice cream and hot dogs on camera in her performance film *Consumption Art* (1975); to a Polish viewer of the day, such foodstuffs would have been considered expensive luxuries.

Perhaps the American expatriate photographer William Klein took Godard's graffito injunction to heart in making *Mr. Freedom* (1969), a French satire with crude American-English dialogue that imagines the struggle of world powers as a battle between oversized superheroes. The titular character, clad in star-spangled sports gear, attempts to stop a Commie insurgence in Europe after his ally Captain Formidable (representing France) is found dead. He then heads to Paris to battle the overstuffed Cossack Moujik Man and the inflatable dragon Red China Man. In Japan, Ōshima Nagisa likewise turned to comic-book images to tell a politicised tale in *Band of Ninja* (1967), an adaptation of Shirato Sanpei's multi-volume manga epic, set in feudal Japan, which had a cult following among young radicals due to its revolutionary themes. Rather than animating it in a conventional sense, Ōshima chose to film original pages of the work, giving motion to the drawings through camera movement, and adding character voices and sound effects. The narrative concerns the son of a disgraced warrior who joins a farmers' rebellion. In his notes for *Band of Ninja*, Ōshima wrote that the film's main premise is the conundrum of revolution: What compels ordinary people to shed blood in order to improve their lives?[27]

The tactics employed by Godard, Klein and Ōshima, in which comics and manga were deployed for radical ends, became part of a full-blown political philosophy in the work of Guy Debord. As a member of the Situationist International – a network of social revolutionaries active from the late 1950s to the early 1970s, that included artists, intellectuals and political theorists – he helped shape concepts such as détournement, the hijacking of popular forms such as the comic strip to propagate revolutionary rhetoric. His treatise *Society of the Spectacle* (1967), now regarded as one of the major intellectual legacies of the movement, also could be seen as a melding of Pop sensitivity to media images with the neo-Marxist philosophy of Frankfurt School *kulturkritik*. If Pop artists explored what it felt like to live inside a media-saturated culture, Debord asked how political agency might function within this system: he made clear in the book that 'the spectacle is not a collection of images, but a social relation among people, mediated by images', adding that what 'the spectacle makes visible is the world of the commodity dominating all that is lived'.[28]

His 1973 film version of *Society of the Spectacle* uses techniques familiar to Pop, such as splicing together found-footage sequences from Hollywood films with filmed images from fashion magazines and advertisements; he contended, however, that the true meaning of these images lies beyond their appearances. According to an injunction on one of the film's intertitles: 'What the spectacle has taken from reality must be taken back from it. The spectacular expropriators must be, in turn, expropriated. The world has already been filmed. The point now is to change it'. In this declaration, Debord proposes that thinking must move beyond Pop – investigating not merely the textures and forms of popular images, or even their symbolic potential, but also the specific structures of power that produce and circulate them.

First published in Phil Freshman, Kathleen McLean and Bartholomew Ryan (eds), International Pop, *Minneapolis: Walker Art Center, 2015, pp. 181–93, 366.*

Notes

1 On the Independent Group and *This Is Tomorrow*, see Anne Massey, *The Independent Group: Modernism and Mass Culture in Britain, 1945–1959*, Manchester: Manchester

University Press, 1995; and Erica F. Battle's essay 'A Nostalgia for Now: British Pop and the New Immediacy of Cultural Memory', in Phil Freshman, Kathleen McLean and Bartholomew Ryan (eds), *International Pop*, Minneapolis: Walker Art Center, 2015, pp. 101–18, 355.

2 Andy Warhol and Pat Hackett, *POPism: The Warhol Sixties*, New York: Harcourt Brace Jovanovich, 1980, p. 22.

3 Lawrence Alloway, 'Pop Art: The Words', in Alloway, *Topics in American Art since 1945*, New York: W. W. Norton, 1975, p. 119.

4 John McHale, 'The Future and the Functions of Art: A Conversation between Alvin Toffler and John McHale', in Alex Kitnick (ed.), *John McHale: The Expendable Reader*, New York: GSAPP BOOKS, 2011, p. 187.

5 The film historian Peter Stanfield has provided deeper accounts of Alloway's thinking on cinema that have been instrumental to my research on the International Group and its relation to film. See 'Maximum Movies: Lawrence Alloway's Pop Art Film Criticism', *Screen*, 49:2 (Summer 2008), pp. 179–93; and 'Regular Novelties: Lawrence Alloway's Film Criticism', *Tate Papers*, no. 16 (Autumn 2011), https://www.tate.org.uk/research/tate-papers/16/regular-novelties-lawrence-alloway-film-criticism.

6 Lawrence Alloway, 'Critics in the Dark', *Encounter*, 22:2 (February 1964), pp. 50–55.

7 Pauline Kael, *I Lost It at the Movies*, Boston: Atlantic Monthly Press, 1965, pp. 26–27.

8 Andrew Sarris, 'Pop Go the Movies!', in *The Primal Screen: Essays on Film and Related Subjects*, New York: Simon and Schuster, 1972, p. 69.

9 Lawrence Alloway, 'More Skin, More Everything in Movies', *Vogue*, 158:2 (February 1968), p. 213.

10 Parker Tyler, *Underground Film: A Critical History*, New York: Grove, 1969, p. 13. Other important histories of this moment – all of which privilege US work over that of other nations – include: J. Hoberman and Jonathan Rosenbaum, *Midnight Movies*, New York: Harper and Row, 1983; David James, *Allegories of Cinema: American Film in the Sixties*, Princeton: Princeton University Press, 1989; Sheldon Renan, *An Introduction to the American Underground Film*, New York: Dutton, 1967; P. Adams Sitney, *Visionary Film: The American Avant-Garde, 1943–2000*, New York: Oxford University Press, 2002; and Gene Youngblood, *Expanded Cinema*, New York: Dutton, 1970.

11 The global spread of the co-op movement during this time is best chronicled in the filmmaker Stephen Dwoskin's account *Film Is: The International Free Cinema*, Woodstock: Overlook Press, 1975. The British filmmaker Malcolm Le Grice proposed theories of experimental cinema grounded in both American and European developments of the period in his *Abstract Film and Beyond*, Cambridge, MA: MIT Press, 1977. In his influential essay 'The Two Avant-Gardes', first published in the November-December 1975 issue of *Studio International*, Peter Wollen argued that there were important differences between new waves in the United States and Great Britain and those in Europe. Curator Mark Webber reconsidered the early history of the London Co-op in *Shoot Shoot Shoot*, a major international touring exhibition that debuted at Tate Modern in London in 2002; for a dossier of related materials, see http://www.luxonline.org.uk/tours/shoot_shoot_shoot(1).html.

12 Louis Marcorelles, *Living Cinema: New Directions in Contemporary Filmmaking*, London: Allen and Unwin, 1973, p. 139.

13 Alex Kitnick, programme notes, 'Films by Derek Boshier', 19 October 2013, Light Industry, Brooklyn, New York, http://www.lightindustry.org/boshier (accessed 3 July 2014).

14 A reproduction of this page can be seen on the website of London's Tate Modern, http://www.tate.org.uk/art/artworks/paolozzi-no-title-p09059.

15 William E. Jones, 'William E. Jones on Peter Roehr', http://www.williamejones.com/collections/about/31 (accessed 14 May 2014).

16 Programme notes, 'Cinema of Prayog', Experimenta 2005, http://experimenta.in/?page_id=200 (accessed 7 July 2014).

17 Schipper's work is detailed in Sven Lüttiken, *History in Motion: Time in the Age of the Moving Image*, Berlin: Sternberg, 2013, pp. 130–34.

18 See Ulrike Gross (ed.), *Ready to Shoot: Fernsehgalerie Gerry Schum: Videogalerie Schum*, Cologne: Snoeck, 2004.

19 The blue sky has since become a major motif in Ono's work. She links it to early childhood memories of being sent to the countryside in Japan after the atomic bombings of Hiroshima and Nagasaki; there she spent hours with her brother looking up at the clouds. See the notes provided by the Museum of Contemporary Art, Australia, for the 2013 retrospective *War Is Over! (if you want it): Yoko Ono*, at http://www.mca.com.au/news/2013/11/15/mca-insight-war-over-if-you-want-it-yoko-ono/.

20 Lawrence Alloway, *Violent America: The Movies, 1946–64*, exh. cat., New York: Museum of Modern Art, 1971, p. 53. On pages 11 and 12, Alloway cites the German literary scholar Ernst Robert Curtius' analyses of ancient Greek oratory as inspiring this use of 'maximal', variants of which appear throughout Alloway's arguments. For example: 'In the movies we are faced with figures that embody in terms of contemporary references maximum states of age, beauty, strength, revenge, or whatever' (p. 12).

21 Noting this development in his review of Alain Resnais's *Muriel* (1963), Andrew Sarris facetiously proposed that the two words be merged: 'The least I can do is coin a new term, and not plagiarize Lawrence Alloway (pop) and Susan Sontag (camp). How about PAMP, or pop and camp in perspective[?]' Andrew Sarris, 'Films', *Village Voice*, 3 June 1965, p. 15.

22 George Melly considered a certain strand of Surrealist-inspired comedy central to the development of a pop style in Britain, particularly the BBC television series *The Goon Show* (1951–60) and the films directed by Richard Lester, including one he made with Lacey, *The Running, Jumping, and Standing Still Film* (1960). See *Revolt into Style: The Pop Arts*, New York: Anchor, 1971, pp. 175–87.

23 International Group member Reyner Banham was an early defender of Vadim's film as a Pop masterpiece. In 'Triumph of Software', an essay written for *New Society* in 1968, Banham argues that *Barbarella*'s 'responsive environments' and soft architectures were more in tune with the Now than Stanley Kubrick's hardware-driven *2001: A Space Odyssey* (1968). The essay is included in Banham's collection *Design by Choice*, London: Academy Editions, 1981, pp. 133–36.

24 Alloway, 'Pop Art: The Words', op. cit., p. 121.

25 Alloway does not cite specific works by Ramos, but the artist began painting 'portraits' of comic-book superheroes as early as the 1950s. By the mid-1960s, these figures were seen as quintessentially Pop.

26 The artist and theorist Hito Steyerl discusses the histories of both the song 'Now!' and Alvarez's film in her essay 'Archive in Motion', first published in *frieze d/e*, 3 (Winter 2011–12), http://frieze-magazin.de/archiv/features/ein-archiv-in-bewe gung/ (accessed 20 November 2014).

27 Ōshima's *Band of Ninja* has been given relatively little critical consideration in English-language studies of the director, but the film's relationship to the history of anime and manga has generated some recent scholarship. See Yuriko Furuhata, 'Audiovisual Redundancy and Remediation in *Ninja bugeicho*', *Mechademia*, 7 (2012), pp. 249–62; and Miryam Sas, 'Moving the Horizon: Violence and Cinematic Revolution in Ōshima Nagisa's *Ninja bugeicho*', idem, pp. 264–80.

28 Guy Debord, *Society of the Spectacle*, Detroit: Black and Red, 1983. This edition is not paginated, but the text is divided into numbered theses; the two quotations here are from theses 4 and 37, respectively.

Part 2

Pop Cinema's Parameters

3

Times Square as Pop Readymade: William Klein's *Broadway by Light* (1958)

Tom Day

In early 1957, the American-born artist William Klein was in the offices of his Parisian publisher Éditions du Seuil. The house had recently printed Klein's first book of street photography, an experimental, Pop-inflected vision of the artist's home city, titled *Life is Good and Good for You in New York: Trance, Witness, Revels* (1956) (hereafter *New York*). The work was published at the behest of Klein's friend Chris Marker, who worked at the publisher from the early 1950s until the late 1960s. While at Seuil, Marker had spearheaded *Petite Planète* (1954–64), a popular series of travel books which contained evocative photography and featured idiosyncratic approaches to book layout and design. Klein had turned to his friend following *New York*'s rejection from every American publisher he had approached. Because of the popularity of his travel books, Marker held a significant amount of clout at Seuil and upon seeing Klein's photographs promised: 'We'll do a book… We'll do a book, or I'll quit!'[1] Standing in Marker's office after the publication of the book in 1957, Klein was joined by another famous post-war French filmmaker and Marker collaborator, Alain Resnais. Resnais had been shown Klein's book by Marker and was deeply enamoured with its gritty realism. During the meeting he turned to Klein and opined: 'Now you've done the book you must do the film!'[2]

Later that year, Klein returned to New York and rented a 35mm film camera. Over a handful of night-time shoots, he composed *Broadway by Light* (1958), a short, non-narrative documentary study of the light signs of Midtown Manhattan's Times Square. The photobook had been widely dismissed by prospective publishers as being, in Klein's words, 'too ugly, too seedy and too one-sided'.[3] The artistic director of American *Vogue*, Alexander Liberman, who in part helped to fund Klein's travels to and from New York and Paris during the 1950s, said that the photographs possessed a 'violence

I'd never experienced in anyone's work.'[4] Klein himself saw *Broadway by Light* as an attempt to present another side of New York. He later summarised his feelings in an interview with *Aperture* magazine:

> [T]he New York photographs were criticised initially because they presented a vision of New York and America that was very harsh, black and white, and grungy. So I thought the next step would be to do a movie; I could do the same thing, but with something as beautiful as Times Square and the incessant ballet of advertising. The first thing people photograph or digest in New York is Broadway and Times Square – it's the most beautiful thing in New York, and in America.[5]

Reflecting on *Broadway by Light* in 1995, Klein referred to it as 'the first Pop film' ever made.[6] Given the timing of the piece's production and the positive gloss Klein puts on the work in relationship to its subject-matter, it could be instructive to place *Broadway by Light* in the lineage of early Pop art, mostly emanating from the UK, which celebrates and affirms the emblems and artifice of popular and mass culture. But later in the *Aperture* interview Klein contradicts his initial assessment, noting that, despite his conception of the film as an antidote to 'New York', it was at best ambivalent about this commercial space:

> But what is it? What are people actually seeing? They are seeing the spectacle of advertising; it's buy this, buy that, it's beautiful but it's made up of sales pitches, and people are fascinated and seduced by advertising […] *Broadway by Light* was a celebration of this whole process of selling – Of taking people by the lapels of their suits and saying, 'Buy this! Buy that!' and being immersed in the graphic world of advertising.[7]

Taken together, Klein's book and film represent significant interventions in the history of Pop art. They not only stand as two of the first iterations of Pop in their respective mediums of photobook and non-narrative cinema, but together the works cut to the heart of the potential of Pop as a site of ambivalence. The history of Pop art's reception can be traced as a journey towards a nuanced understanding expressed by writers such as Hal Foster and Bradford Collins, who see the movement on a continuum defined neither wholly by critique or complicity but by vacillation.[8] Adopting such a perspective, this essay unpacks *Broadway by Light*'s form, aesthetics and content to identify what is at stake in such ambivalence.

Klein's photographic and book work has revived scant attention in academic writings on Pop art (the work is mentioned, albeit not excerpted for examination, in Mark Francis' *Pop* survey from 2005).[9] Several photography historians and critics have alluded to the possibility of reading Klein's work as proto- or even full-blown works of Pop. In a 1981 *Aperture* book of Klein's pictures, John Heilpern summarises the ambiguous placement of Klein's work in relation to the movement:

> It is sometimes said that Klein belongs to the surface vitality and flash of the 1960s, or that he really belongs to Pop art. If so, his pictures (which were taken in the mid and late 1950s) anticipated the next generation. Only his films and fashion photography grew out of the mood of the 1960s.[10]

Here, Heilpern brackets Klein's photography into two distinct periods: a first, comprising the street photography books of the 1950s, which he argues could be read as prefiguring or pre-empting Pop; and his later work in cinema and fashion photography, which Heilpern aligns ambiguously with what is dubbed the 'surface vitality and flash of the 1960s'. Heilpern offers no further analysis of specific photographs by Klein that could be isolated and read directly as Pop; it is ultimately a vague allusion. This stands in contrast to considerations of Klein and Pop by Martin Harrison, who is more prescriptive in his interpretation, arguing that 'Klein's appropriation of symbols of ad/mass consumerism in the introductory booklet to *New York* was already proto-Pop, his captions interspersed with newspaper and magazine advertisements for chewing gum, Mercury cars, body-building, *Mad* magazine and toothpaste'.[11] The inclusion of advertisements and other elements of the popular press are inflected with 'sarcasm' by Klein, according to Harrison, resulting in a comment on the 'mass brainwashing' of consumer culture.[12] Curiously, Harrison does not go beyond the *New York* book's introduction to the photographs within, which contain both spontaneous and rigorously composed scenes where people are juxtaposed against and amongst advertisement hoardings and signs, and where walls of posters assume the position of subjects in urban photographic still lives. In his catalogue, Francis' own interpretation of Klein collates the positions of Heilpern and Harrison; Klein's street photography is fused with typography in an unprecedented way, he argues, 'creating one of the first examples of a sustained "Pop" approach to word and image'.[13]

Critical readings, then, of Klein's photographic output in relation to Pop place emphasis on his photo editing and book layout, seemingly leaving his actual photography to one side. This disservice to the image is not found in the critical reception of *Broadway by Light*. Perhaps because of Klein's own assessment of the film, as an *urtext* of Pop cinema, *Broadway by Light* has been featured on nearly every museum and gallery programme of Pop cinema since 'Pop Cinema' was held at International House Philadelphia in 2011. The film is a foundational and influential example of Pop art aesthetics applied to the moving image. Combined, the book and film were labelled substantive 'alphabets' and 'manifestos' of Pop art by *The Guardian* at the turn of the new millennium, terms that could be equally applied to Klein's later feature films, the fashion satire *Who Are You, Polly Magoo?* (1966) and the acerbic, cartoonish Vietnam War critique *Mister Freedom* (1968).[14] In this essay, I argue that the film represents the culmination of Klein's early New York period. For four years (from the conception of *New York* in 1954 to the release of *Broadway by Light* in 1958), Klein created a Pop vision of his home city. It is a vision defined by a shift from stillness to movement. This shift is not only represented by Klein's graduation from still photography to moving pictures but is also present in a constant *shifting*: a restless attitude which refuses to uphold photography and photobook display as emblematic of stillness, or completely give his early filmmaking practice over to a conventional style. Klein's experimentations with both photo and book forms are attempts to infuse their inherent stillness with a latent movement, staging mobility within the confines of the still image through blur and shudder and weaving a cinematic montage into the page layout of the *New York* book. These cine-interventions into his photography and design work anticipate *Broadway by Light*.

Klein's work from this New York period has a Pop subject-matter, observing life amongst the advertisement signage of a bustling metropolis. The through-line which guides and underpins this Pop vision of the city is, however, a deep commitment to the aesthetics of cinema. This is played out finally in *Broadway by Light*, a text indebted as much to the street photography which preceded it as to the cinematic language of rapid editing, superimposition and speed which define it as the example par excellence of the City Symphony. It is here, I argue, that one can situate Klein's very particular brand of Pop: between the actuality of documentary and the non-representative strategies of abstraction, aesthetic postulations that define the City Symphony form. *Broadway by Light* will be understood in this essay in relation to ideas of documentary formalism and to modes of City Symphony filmmaking. Klein's manipulation of the image becomes defined by simulation and abstraction, resulting in blur, noise and radical layout in his photography; and temporal dissonance (jump cuts, superimpositions and speed) in *Broadway by Light*. This is made palpable by his engaging with and representing areas of New York City wherein the senses are dizzied by competing visual discourses – with spaces at once fully comprehensible and deeply abstruse. It is within Klein's aesthetic collision of abstraction and figuration, mobility and immobility, that his work can be aligned with a very particular strain of Pop's criticality: an ambivalence that insists on being read two ways at once, and one that harks back to the original function and design of Times Square as a paradoxically seductive urban space.

In a statement opening his guest-edited 2004 issue of *Artforum* on Pop, Jack Bankowsky summarised what remained, for many, Pop's almost odious character: 'Pop art is a nasty bit of work. It toadies to the powers that be *and* plays to the peanut gallery; broadcasts our dirty secrets but never lets us in on its own. Pop art is pushy, unapologetic, expedient – and amnesiac. It glories in the way things are and doesn't worry much about the way they should be.'[15] In contrast, in her 2005 book *Pop Art and the Contest over American Culture* Sara Doris comes down emphatically on the side of Pop as critical of consumer culture by arguing that the movement amounted to an expression of 'resistant cultural practice'.[16] Hal Foster's comments on Pop in his book *The First Pop Age* seem to accept that such disparities exist, but he argues that this does not and should not preclude us from seeing a productive critical worth, or moments of 'criticality' in Pop: 'Here the very ambivalence of Pop toward high and low cultures becomes double: often, rather than having it both ways, Pop values the two cultures even as it injects a modicum of doubt into our relations to each'; 'at times', he surmises, 'I want to insist, Pop highlights cultural contradictions in ways that do produce critical consciousness'.[17] Foster's comments offer a combination of previous outlooks on the critical validity or lack thereof of Pop; but ultimately, in his view, its critical potential wins out. Pop, it could be said, has throughout the history of its reception existed between these two poles: as a set of potent subversions, or as a crass and hollow pandering to the status quo of mass culture. Published in the same year as Foster's book, Bradford Collins' study also wishes to re-orientate the field, the author stating that his own history of Pop will be an attempt to lay to rest the debate of whether Pop was 'for' or 'against' popular and mass culture. 'To be sure', he writes, 'the focus of much Pop art was popular culture. Some of this was critical, some complicit, some ambiguous. But Pop artists also dealt with an extraordinary range of other individual, artistic and historical issues – from sex, love, and death to aesthetics, from the Civil Rights Movement and the Vietnam War to feminism'.[18] It is this muddy thicket of ambivalence that I see *Broadway by Light* wading in, acting ultimately as a prophetic text for Pop cinema.

Between Stillness and Movement

Following a successful showcase of early paintings (completed under the tutelage of Fernand Léger in Paris after World War II) in Milan at the Galleria del Milione in 1952, Klein was invited by architect Angelo Mangiarotti to create a mural of sliding panels to decorate and divide a local apartment he had just finished. The panels consisted of mismatched black stripes on a white background. They could be interchangeably rotated and manipulated, creating an array of possible combinations. While Klein was documenting the installations, his wife Jeanne spun the panels, and they blurred in the camera's long exposure time. This was a major turning point for Klein, forming the basis for his first proper engagement with the medium of photography. David Campany describes the possibilities that were opened up: 'Klein grasped straight away how the camera records and expresses, how it inevitably depicts and abstracts at the same time. Hard-edged painting could turn into soft edged photography'.[19] From this time onward, Klein devoted himself almost entirely to experimenting with his new medium of choice.

The culmination of these early, exploratory sessions with abstract photography were collected in a photo maquette, which was completed in 1952 but not formally published until 2015. To accompany the publishing of these early works, a touring exhibition was held, starting at London's HackelBury gallery in the spring of 2015. The show displayed many of the abstract maquette prints for the first time, alongside a looped screening of (and still, large-format prints excerpted from) *Broadway by Light*. This is one of the first instances when Klein's moving-image work was placed in direct dialogue with his photography. The standard practice in many Klein retrospectives up to this point was to have his feature fiction and non-fiction film-making presented as a side programme. This juxtaposition permitted a way of looking at Klein's abstracted works and early film experiments as being in conversation with each other. Just as Klein had taken the sliding panels of the apartment divider as a 'ready-made', which the camera could aestheticise and stylistically shape, in *Broadway by Light*, New York's Times Square was taken on similar terms as a 'ready-made' space available for manipulation. Through Klein's lens the space is opened out, mediated, abstracted and commented upon. For Klein this process was simple, and thematic comparisons with the *New York* book are completely legitimate: 'New York electric lights and neons were ready-mades – just film the cycles of the ads and I would be saying the same thing I said in the book', he recalled.[20] As will be demonstrated below, while there are thematic similarities, *Broadway by Light* is not that easily deducible. Its complex manipulation of film language and ambivalent approach to its subject matter cast it as a cumulative expression of Klein's work up to this point and most significantly as a key meditation on advertising and public space, through the prism of Pop.

The film opens with a short exegesis penned by Marker that sets the scene, claiming that Americans have invented the lights of Times Square as a means of 'consoling its citizens against the night'. It continues:

> Every evening an artificial dawn breaks in New York City. It aims to advertise shows and promote products. But these advertisers would be truly amazed to learn that the most fascinating show of all, the most valuable product, is the street transformed by their neon signs. The artificial day has people, shadows, illusions and rites of its own. It also has its own sun.

The film then immediately cuts to a wide-angle shot of a yet-to-be-illuminated Pepsi Cola sign at dusk. Slowly zooming into the centre of the symbol, the film abruptly cuts to the dancing sparks of its illumination. With the lights now on, the film begins its cacophonic ten-minute exploration of the sights and lights of Times Square. The film moves from one half in which images remain broadly figurative and identifiable to a frenzied and geometrically abstract second section; throughout, it is soundtracked by a nervous, disjointed and restless modernist score composed by Maurice Le Roux that seems to marry with the frenzied, impatient tempo of Klein's editing.

The first half of the film, while not devoted entirely to stillness, embraces a certain stasis and legibility in the composition of its shots. Cutting from the Pepsi Cola sign to a sharp whip pan across a set of advertising facades, Klein then offers a dense shot of many of Times Square's light signs superimposed alongside one another, as if to offer a legible preview of each of the images that will be explored, abstracted and fragmented (Figure 3.1). This first part of the film contains dozens of shots; but unlike the second half, which employs a frenzied, overdetermined pace, here Klein seems to linger over discreet, individual light spectacles, seemingly in thrall to their pleasures, their animation and their chromatic intensity (Figure 3.2). The pacing in this sequence is more sedate and grounded than what comes later and because of this relative stillness, this passage of the film echoes quite directly Klein's photobook work.

The fusion of film and photography in Klein's still image work has been pointedly commented upon by Raymond Bellour. One of the first things he examines about Klein is his self-conscious occupation of a position which is wholly devoted neither to stillness nor to movement. Klein's work, so Bellour claims, contains both concurrently: Klein is seen as coming 'from

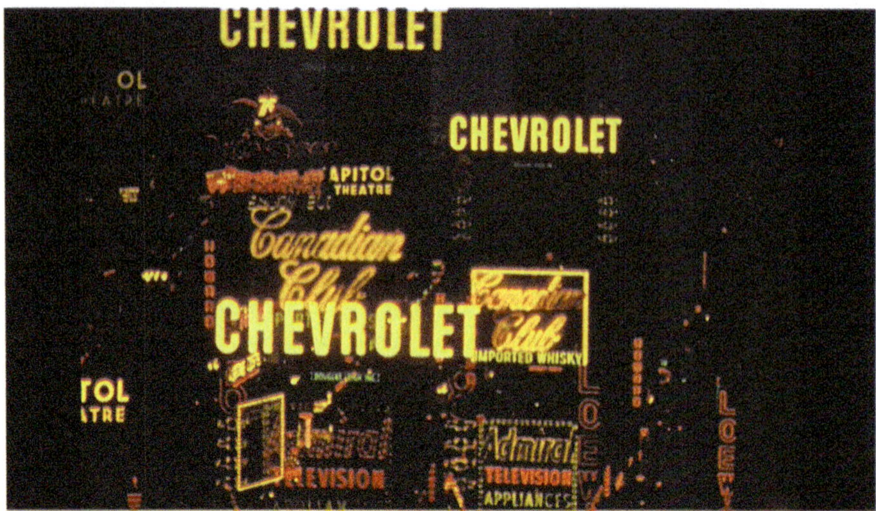

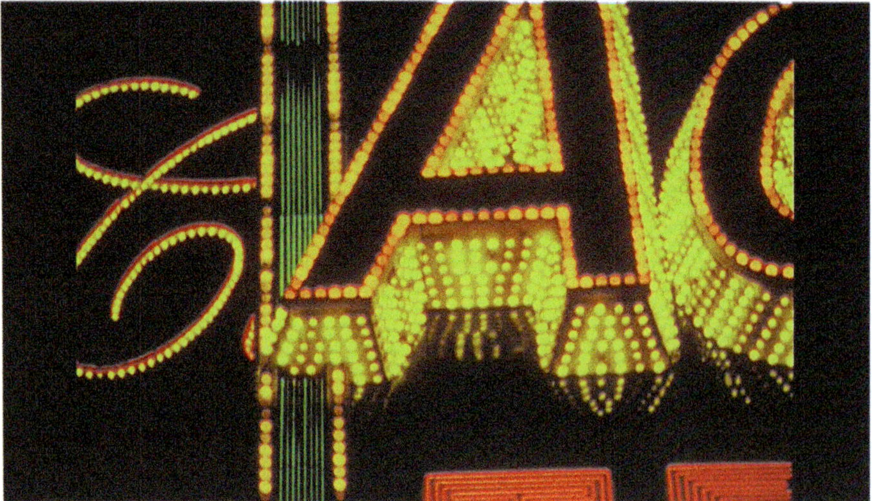

Figures 3.1 and 3.2 *Broadway by Light* (William Klein, 1958). 35mm, colour, sound, 12 minutes. Source: Courtesy of Argos Films.

between photography and cinema'.[21] Bellour's comments could be combined with those of Roland Barthes about Pop painting as it relates to photography: just as Pop painting's use of photography gave rise to an indistinct admixture, Klein's Pop photography could be said to be a 'nameless mixture' that conflates the stillness of photography books with the movement of cinema.[22] This combination is commented upon by Klein:

> For me, the design, the graphic scenario, the layout was almost as important as the photographs. So I did everything to make it a new

visual object. Double pages with twenty images jammed together in comic strip style, colliding facing pages, bleed doubles, catalogue parodies, a dada blast… there is no layout, it's even anti-layout. Just full pages and double pages, only the sequencing counts, like a movie. Like the movie I thought this book should be.[23]

Seeing the film as an adaptation and a furthering of concerns from the book seems logical. Taken on its own terms, *Broadway by Light* is essentially a non-narrative documentary in much the same way as the book is. While the book is more haphazardly fragmented in terms of narrative, the film has a clear trajectory: the duration of an evening, with the film beginning at dusk and ending at sunrise (an end it shares with the *New York* book's final image). This sense of an unmediated temporal trajectory is, however, undermined by the fact that the film was shot over several evenings. Furthermore, it is plain to see that Klein is not concerned with forms of documentary practice which privilege modes of realism and actuality (like the then flourishing Direct Cinema movement); his use of speed, abstraction and reflection lend the film an expressive function. For Michael Renov, the manipulation of images for poetic or aesthetic effect is no afterthought – not simply 'aesthetics as the icing on the cake'.[24] They are more broadly evidence of an expressive function; one of the four cornerstones which constitute a poetics of non-fiction cinema.[25] Renov defines expressivity as one of the many poles of enunciation through which a filmmaker speaks: 'It is important to note that expressivity is always the support of other discursive goals. The greater the expressive power of the piece, that is, the more vividly the film communicates [and] the more likely an audience is to feel persuasion, educative value or revelation'.[26] *Broadway by Light* is constant in its twisting of the expectations of documentary, never allowing our perspective to stabilise. Its formalism places the film between the poles of representation and abstraction, often achieving this effect through temporal dissonance. 'The formal regime', Renov argues, 'is the very portal of sense-making: it determines the viewer's access to the expression of ideas, its power to move and transform an audience'.[27] Consequently, such moments within this formal regime, 'while never entirely departing from the realm of ethnography', actually allow us to see the world of the film in 'unexpected ways, ways that cause us to reflect upon our preconceptions and move us towards new imaginings'.[28] While Renov is commenting more generally on a selection of films contemporaneous to his writing, I think that some of his ideas can be transplanted onto Klein's work and the realm of Pop's concerns regarding representation and abstraction. It is true that *Broadway by Light* does offer a representation of Times Square's illuminations as they were in 1958, but it is the 'formal regime' employed by Klein that guides our perception of the space. Such a regime can indeed move us towards 'new imaginings', of the effect of such spaces, where the senses are overwhelmed by a cacophony of light-based and neon signage which demands our attention and participation.

Klein's collision of abstraction and documentary examination of the commercial sign culture finds corollaries in other artists' approaches to Times Square and its immediate environs. These include sculptors, painters and sound artists such as Chryssa, Jane Dickson and Max Neuhaus. A veritable subgenre of experimental film and video art which takes the space as a subject also exists: *Weegee's New York* (Arthur 'Weegee' Fellig, 1948); *Jazz of Lights* (Ian Hugo, 1954); *Night Crawlers* (Peter E. Goodman, 1964); *Square Times* (Rudy Burckhardt, 1967); *Sodom and Gomorrah* (Rudy Burckhardt, 1976); *Times Squared* (Brenda Miller, 1988); *Doin' Time in Times Square* (Charlie Ahearn, 1992); and *Jane in Peepland* (Charlie Ahearn, 1993). Unlike these moving image works, perhaps the most notable and signal element of Klein's film is its affinities with the thematics and aesthetics of the City Symphony. It is this particular body of films to which this essay will now turn its attention.

Broadway by Light: Pop Symphony

The City Symphony film is a product of the 1920s, transnational in scope and varied in its ambitions. Experimental film chronicler Scott MacDonald offers a succinct, broad definition of the genre: 'a film that provides a general sense of life in a specific metropolis, by revealing characteristic dimensions of city life from the morning into the evening of a composite day'.[29] Alexander Graf has identified that the genre reached its full maturity in the late 1920s with Walter Ruttmann's *Berlin, Symphonie einer Großstadt* (*Berlin, Symphony of a Great City*, Germany, 1927) and Dziga Vertov's *Man with a Movie Camera* (USSR, 1929).[30] These films continue to be considered touchstones, despite the fact that the tradition has expanded itself since the 1920s to, in the words of Erica Stein, 'encompass the mid-century New York cycle as well as contemporary global entries more closely aligned with an observational documentary tradition'.[31] It is this later lineage, particularly the New York City cycle, with which I would like to put *Broadway by Light* in conversation.

Broadway by Light can be aligned with the 1920s mode, but a certain inversion must take place. Take Graf's account of the formal style of the City

Symphony in its 1920s expression: 'an almost total suppression of intertitles, narrative and plot elements, and a rejection of the documentary form in the traditional sense, in favour of asserting rhythmic and associative montage as formal devices, and a dawn to dusk strategy in the search for a pure film form'.[32] This could serve as an accurate description of the strategies at play in Klein's film, with a couple of caveats. Klein gives us the temporal frame of an evening, not a whole day, in *Broadway by Light*. Furthermore, the film is, it seems, less about locating an ideal film form in and of itself (in this way the film is very much a disavowal of modernist tendencies regarding medium specificity which early City Symphonies are seen as exploring) and more preoccupied with articulating a certain way of seeing its subject. However, this is not to say that Klein abandons questions of form and medium specificity entirely.

Moreover, New York City Symphony films have been seen as allowing viewers to focus on 'carefully articulated geographic spaces' as opposed to sweeping panoramas which attempt to grasp the feeling of a city in its entirety, as seen in efforts from Europe.[33] This perspective echoes the words of sociologist Robert Park, who in 1925 noted that the city is a 'mosaic of little worlds which touch but do not interpenetrate'.[34] For curator and critic Jon Gartenberg, in cinematic terms, New York City Symphony films 'represent the articulation of a defined time frame' within specific spaces, be these 'atop skyscrapers, under bridges, through parks, down Broadway [or] in Coney Island'.[35] In other words, one does not need to comprehend the vastness of New York City as a whole to be given select perspectives on it, an invitation to see the spaces of the city anew. *Broadway by Light*'s focus on one specific area of the city serves as a contrast to Klein's previous project, the *New York* book, which takes in all manner of geographical locales across the metropolis. In making *Broadway by Light*, Klein has commented that he had hoped to capture something different from the book, but he ended up with similar conclusions: 'In the book I showed a New York which was not the big apple. A New York which was tragic. [I was] filming the electric lights to show the most beautiful thing in New York. A direct contrast to the book. But it said the same thing. The obsession of commercial brainwashing'.[36]

Do any previous efforts to understand or conceptualise Times Square approximate Klein's play with stillness, movement and abstraction? Such a question can be linked back to both formative examples of the City Symphony genre and to the theoretical debates around modernism that relate to cinema, spectacle and city life in the 1920s. In his monograph on Times Square, part memoir of his own interactions with and relationship to the space, and part cultural history of its representation, Marshall Berman reflects on the cacophonous nature of the light-filled crossroads, importantly linking it to both a modernist art movement and a classic text of both the City Symphony and avant-garde cinema:

> The signs come at us from many directions; they colour the people next to us in complex blends, and we become coloured, all of us overlaid with the moving lights and shadows. The development of Cubism in the early twentieth century was made for spaces like this, where we occupy many different points of view while standing nearly still. Times Square is a place where Cubism is realism. Being there is like being inside a 1920s Cubist experimental film: *Man with a Movie Camera* as a home movie. Signs are the essential landmark, yet generally what grips our hearts is less any one sign than the complex, the totality, the superabundance of signs, *too many signs*, a perfect complement for the Square's too many people.[37]

Berman's interpretation of Times Square points towards aspects of the space as it is represented in Klein's film. First is the definition of the space as one of surface experience: a fleeting, ethereal and almost ritualistic 'bath of light', as Berman terms it, recalling his mother's naming of the family strolls they would take there when he was a boy.[38] Second is the abstraction of lights and signs that, for Berman, is already present in the immediate reality of the space, in which a multiplicity of visual discourses vie for attention. Berman connects this abstract visual texture to the disparate fragmentation of Georges Braque and Pablo Picasso's Cubism. This is enhanced by the film's further breaking-up of the square's architecture of lights through editing. Third is the analogy that Berman sees between Times Square and cinema, with specific reference to Vertov's *Man with a Movie Camera*, a classic of the City Symphony form that shares filmmaking stylistics with Klein's project, especially the use of superimposition, fast cutting and a consistent interplay between a fixed and a roving camera. There is an important element present within the Soviet documentary but largely absent in *Broadway by Light* which Berman also touches upon: the presence of people, which in Klein's film are seen only fleetingly; the '*too many signs*' which Berman speaks of have taken over completely.

This excerpt from Berman can also point us towards a deeper analysis of the surface and spectacle which appear to be so intrinsic to both the space of Times Square itself and its representation in *Broadway by Light*. Often appearing in writing about the City Symphony, the German cultural critic Siegfried Kracauer's famous essay 'The Mass Ornament' (1927) describes modernity in terms of its surface, as a world in which the crowd has transformed into a spectacle (in Kracauer's conception this included chorus lines, stadium crowds, the throngs of people passing through commercialised spaces like that of Times Square and the audiences in attendance at packed movie palaces). Kracauer understands the individual subject being subsumed into the mass ornament of spectacle and spectatorship as a paragon for modernity itself, and the capitalist system which underpins its rise to prominence by the 1920s: 'the mass ornament is the aesthetic reflex of the rationality aspired to by the prevailing economic system'.[39] The rise of the society of the mass ornament had been made possible by the explosion in urban populations and the commercialisation of public space within cities and towns; for Kracauer 'the electric texture of the urban surface' becomes the definition of the 'modern urban condition'.[40]

Unlike canonical examples of the City Symphony film such as Paul Strand and Charles Sheeler's *Manhatta* (1921), which has been discussed in relation to Kracauer's essay and which places significant emphasis on the spectacle of crowds throughout the island of Manhattan, *Broadway by Light* is almost completely devoid of human presence.[41] The people who make up Kracauer's mass ornament have been usurped by the surface of signs and lights. This is commensurate with Kracauer's thought; 1950s New York had borne witness to an unprecedented economic boom following World War II, and the Eisenhower years saw an explosion in the material wealth of the nation and a vast expansion of the country's middle class.[42] This unbridled rise in spending, production and consumption meant that advertising had graduated from a specialist and narrow interest to become a profession of significant cultural cachet, garnering comment from sociologists, novelists and filmmakers and appearing everywhere.[43] The mass ornament shifts and mutates as capitalism itself transforms, as Kracauer writes: 'The structure of the mass ornament reflects that of the general contemporary situation'.[44] No area in the United States or the rest of the world could claim to be more laden with advertising than Times Squares, a space by then built into both the American and global consciousness as the 'crossroads of the world'. Such status had been attained by the space some thirty years before Klein filmed there, as William Leach writes in his study of the rise of American consumerism: 'Nowhere else in the world, by the end of the 1920s, was so much commercial colour and light to be found concentrated in one place'.[45] The forms, structures and shapes that emanated from the Broadway streets could be easily thought of in relation to Kracauer's words: 'The ornament [...] consists of degrees and circles like those found in textbooks of euclidean [sic] geometry. Waves and spirals, the elementary structures of physics'.[46] Kracauer's description of the amassed subjects of modernity transformed into spectacle seem to anticipate the neon tubes, truncated and twisted into varying shapes, which came to dominate Broadway and Times Square. This space is, in Kracauer's words, an 'aesthetic reflex' to the increasingly centralised position of consumerism and advertising in American life, which had begun to define the mass ornament for the post-war age, where advertisements were appearing on all manner of surfaces, from newspapers and billboards to television screens and building facades.

Speeding through Times Square

In contrast to the first part of the film, which gives us often unimpeded views of such sights, the closing half of *Broadway by Light* is dominated by speed, in the guise of time-lapse photography and a sporadic use of fast editing patterns. The combination of these approaches gives the second half a visual tone distinct from the film's previous sequences, which persists until the climactic sunrise. Directly following a moment of dense, formally rigorous abstraction, an effect generated by Klein zooming in on and rapidly cutting across an illuminated news ticker, which provides separation from the more stasis-orientated first half, Klein shifts to a series of shots which privilege the horizontal flow of light and motion.

Immediately after the news tracker abstraction disappears, with a subtly conceived in-camera frame wipe left, we are in close-up, with six letters of a neon shop window sign at the centre of the image, cropped enough at all edges to resist legibility. As soon as the viewer can begin to orient themselves within the frame, it begins to shift. The spectator becomes aware that they are, in fact, viewing this sign through the window of a bus which is on the move. The opening of this passage of the film is shot at a frame rate comparable to the rest of the sequences up until this point. The same tempo continues over into the next two shots, both reflections of signs and marquees in bus windows, as the vehicles travel from left to right, out of the frame. Then, the application of time-lapse moves the film into a temporal register which stands in stark contrast to the rest of the film. Cars and buses now jolt past, zipping through the frame in a flash of bright movement as Broadway's lights reflect on their windows and mirror-like bodies. There are six shots like this, amounting to just over ten seconds of screen time. The movement of automobiles is then usurped by the movement of lights, as we observe stationary cars, their reflective surfaces inscribed by the movement of light shows above at the same high-tempo velocity with which the previous machines had moved through the street. Nine shots comprise this car-as-canvas moment, before Klein cuts to another equally temporally

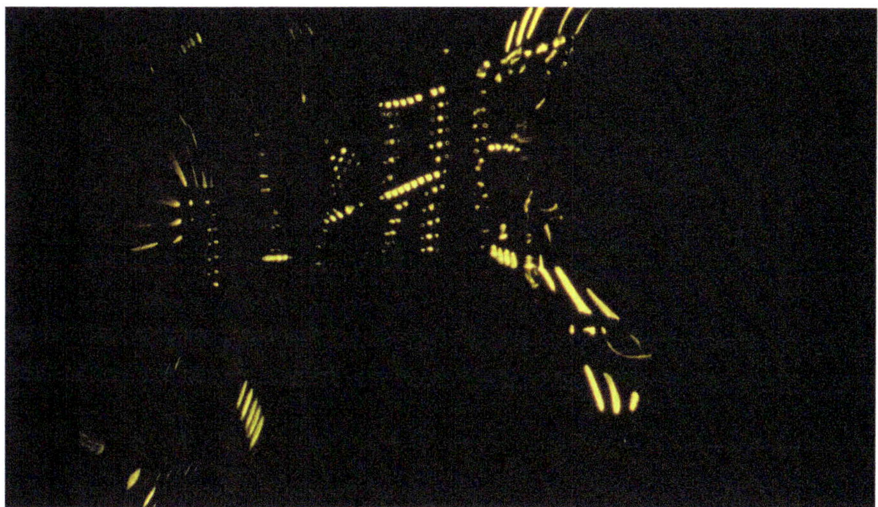

Figure 3.3 *Broadway by Light* (William Klein, 1958). 35mm, colour, sound, 12 minutes. Source: Courtesy of Argos Films.

charged series of reflections of neon lights in puddles (Figure 3.3). What one loses sense of in these sequences is the very subject of the film itself, the signs of Times Square. When filtered through the paradigm of temporal velocity, they become unreadable and unattainable as advertisements and turn into objects of aesthetic pleasure. Through what Paul Virilio terms the 'primitive dimension of speed' the signs are lost in the bustling hubbub of the city in motion. They cease, to put it bluntly, their *modus operandi*: to be an intelligible place of advertisement. While this sequence can be seen as revelling in a kind of spatial and temporal anarchy, there is a much subtler register of pleasure and commentary in operation. *Broadway by Light* articulates less the 'emptiness of the quick' than a style of speed which exists on a playful double edge, holding both aestheticism and criticism in balance.[47]

The use of speed in this sequence can highlight once again a significant link between Klein's film and some of the theoretical concerns which have become inherently linked with the City Symphony as it relates to modernity. This link allows us to see the film as an articulation of early planners' and entrepreneurs' visions of the space of Times Square itself. For Kracauer, '[c]apitalist thinking can be defined by its abstractness'.[48] If one takes the signs of Times Square to be an articulation of the wants and desires of consumer capitalism, an updated version of the mass ornament, this abstract quality makes sense. It does not wish to appeal to the subject in any rational way; its appeal is precisely through the senses.

Or, as Kracauer has it: 'The abstract and general dimensions of meaning [...] do not render unto reason that which belongs to reason. In this scheme empiricism is neglected; any kind of utilitarian application can be drawn from abstractions devoid of meaning'.[49] Under the sway of advanced consumer capitalism, the abstract can be grounded in a function other than description: 'Despite the substantiality which is to be demanded from them, abstractions are only concrete in one sense. They are not concrete in the vulgar sense which uses the term to designate those ideas which are rooted in natural life – The abstractness of contemporary thinking is therefore ambivalent'.[50] In Kracauer's thinking, capitalism modifies form, removing abstraction from its roots as a descriptor of geometric forms or natural beauty; it is repackaged as a spectacle which performs a function in capitalist modernity. If abstraction has become ambivalent through capitalism, then 'the *Mass Ornament*', defined as it is by a willingness to abstract, 'is just as ambivalent'.[51] This is what Klein seems to be tapping into with *Broadway by Light*: his film accentuates the ambivalence at the heart of the spectacle of the mass ornament. Moreover, it seems appropriate that the subject for the film should be a space which has the ambivalence between sensation and seduction at its very core.

Our checklist of interpretive schema for *Broadway by Light* has moved us through a variety of fields, from questions of documentary formalism and the City Symphony's relationship to the mass ornament; over notions surrounding the delicate balance between representation and abstraction articulated by the film; and finally, to ideas of speed and surface. If the film does capture a significant ambivalence – a snapshot of simultaneous fascination with and disdain for the marketisation of Manhattan – perhaps this is not only owed to the lineage of Pop in which the film has been placed. It can also be considered as fulfilling the promise of Times Square that was articulated during the process of its invention as the home of lights and spectacle in Manhattan at the turn of the twentieth century.

Times Square has had a rich history of mutability. Its contemporary incarnation is the result of over a century of legal battles and merchant squabbles, arguments amongst city planners and moral guardians about both the ownership of advertising space and the licentious vice of many of the area's (now former) business operations.[52] 'The Great White Way' was intended as a term of both affection and advertisement for the space. It was coined by the entrepreneur O. J. Gude, himself responsible for the invention and proliferation of a great many of the sign types first found in Times Square and captured in Klein's film, such as 'electric signs studded with lamps, illuminated signboards, and the floodlighting and outlining of exteriors'.[53]

Gude's own commentaries on the world of the signs that he made so much a part of urban life, and how people on the street relate to them, are intriguing. They offer an extremely rich complement to Klein's suspicions about and admiration for the space.

Many of Gude's pronouncements were originally published in the trade paper *Signs of the Times* (1874–). Within its pages, he outlined a theory that argued for the aesthetic validity of his business while also, at the same time, attempting to account for its success. He believed that his signs offered people more aesthetic pleasure than any other medium. In an article from 1912, titled 'Art and Advertising Joined by Electricity', he writes that '[o]utdoor advertising has […] felt and shown the effects of the artistic spirit of the people in this country'.[54] Its spectacle should be considered 'beautiful' as opposed to 'brutally' dominant.[55] Such a statement is contrary to comments made by Gude five months earlier in another article for *Signs of the Times*. Instead of the 'beauty' of the signs, here he offers explicit commentary on Klein's assessment of the space as a location for brainwashing:

> [Electric sign advertising] literally forces its announcement on the vision of the uninterested as well as the interested passer-by […] Signboards are so placed that everybody must read them, and absorb them, and absorb the advertiser's lesson willingly or unwillingly […] The constant reading of 'Buy Blank's Biscuits' […] makes the name part of one's sub-conscious knowledge.[56]

Gude's comments here are at a far remove from any aesthetic considerations: he gives us the hard sell. This is the language of coercion, with signs organised and mapped onto the space of Times Square, announcing their presence and selling their wares through the unavoidable and literal 'force' of perceptual engagement. Indifference or ambivalence on the part of the spectator is not an option: 'willingly or unwillingly' the job of public engagement will be done. In *Broadway by Light*, this sense of being overwhelmed is furthered and intensified by Klein's manipulation of film language. The space is not left to its own devices. Klein uses 'chance techniques' and '"found" rather than invented images' as his means; these techniques, used within Abstract and Pop art-making, are deployed, in the words of Suzi Gablik, to 'achieve a tougher art, to avoid tasteful choices, and to set the stakes higher'.[57] The film's interrogation of Times Square's spectacle links back not only to Gude's formative commentary on the space but also taps into a fundamental ambivalence at the heart of the culture of mass ornamentation which Kracauer sees as a defining feature of capitalist modernity in the twentieth century. Directing the gaze away from the teeming mass of the crowd, one finds the mass ornament located at the heart of the urban city centre. Here it is not people but advertising which assumes an integral role in capitalist modernity; it is a language directed at people. However, interpretations do not seem to be clear-cut. Are we being cynically goaded by such spaces, brainwashed into obeying their demands, or are we willingly experiencing a radiant and heightened experience, a sensuous 'bath' in the light?[58] Klein's film seems to suggest, through the aesthetic of Pop, that the paradox is unresolvable.

Klein's attitude possesses many affinities to Pop. It is a complex negotiation of Pop aesthetics; one which gives aesthetic fascination and critical engagement equal footing. Much like Gude's pronouncements, Klein's work appears to have its feet in two camps consistently. From attempts to collapse distinctions between stillness and movement, to his insistence on the malleability of representations which flit between the figurative and the abstract, Klein's work operates through a succinct dialectical understanding of everyday existence within a society predicated on mass consumer culture and mass spectacle. New York is the subject par excellence in which to observe the duality of mass culture and modernity playing out. Klein's work frames New York and specifically Times Square within the Pop idiom. I have argued throughout this essay that Klein's casting of the city through a Pop lens is a journey which is best viewed as a shift or shifting between the stillness of representation and the abstraction of heightened movement. Importantly, this taps into debates which impinge on the very epicentre of Pop art and its meanings; its conflation of representational and abstracted visuality and its critically potent ability to exude ambivalence. Klein's translation of this attitude is multi-layered and complicated, stretching as it does from photography and photobook design to filmmaking. There is a consistency throughout these works, a strain of irreverence which playfully ignores and attempts to collapse distinctions between media, which results in Klein's Pop vision of New York City being tinged with a pulsating drive towards the cinematic as an organising aesthetic principle. Times Square may at its most basic function be a space in which 'Art and advertising [is] joined by electricity', but here a third ingredient is added: the intervention of an artist who uses the still camera, the book page, the gallery wall and the film camera to produce a series of images and experiences that are not hollow, not all pure surface, but which act as, in Foster's summation of Pop images, a 'probe into a given matrix of cultural languages, both high and low – a probe that, far from facile, is complex in its making and viewing alike'.[59]

Notes

1 Brian Dillon, 'The Interview: William Klein', *Sight & Sound*, 23:1 (January 2013), p. 62.

2 Ibid.

3 John Heilpern, 'Profile', in *William Klein: Photographs*, London: Aperture Books, 1981, p. 7.

4 Ibid., p. 15.

5 Aaron Schuman, 'William Klein', *Aperture*, 220 (Fall 2015), p. 28.

6 William Klein, *New York, 1954–1955*, Manchester: Dewi Lewis, 1995, p. 11.

7 Schuman, op. cit., p. 28.

8 Hal Foster, *The First Pop Age: Painting and Subjectivity in the Art of Hamilton, Lichtenstein, Warhol, Richter and Ruscha*, Princeton: Princeton University Press, 2012; Bradford Collins, *Pop Art: The Independent Group to Neo Pop, 1952–90*, London: Phaidon, 2012.

9 Mark Francis, *Pop*, London: Phaidon, 2005.

10 Heilpern, op. cit., pp. 13–15.

11 Martin Harrison, 'Afterward', in *William Klein: In and Out of Fashion*, London: Jonathan Cape, 1994, p. 253.

12 Ibid.

13 Francis, op. cit., p. 46.

14 Alix Sharkey, 'Angry Icon', *The Guardian* (22 April 2000): https://www.theguardian.com/theguardian/2000/apr/22/weekend7.weekend1.

15 Jack Bankowsky, 'Performing the Future', *Artforum*, 43:2 (October 2004), p. 39.

16 Sara Doris, *Pop Art and the Contest over American Culture*, Cambridge: Cambridge University Press, 2007, p. 62.

17 Foster, op. cit., p. 250.

18 Collins, op. cit., p. 12.

19 David Campany, 'Into the Light', in *William Klein: Black and Light*, London: Imprint/HackelBury, 2015, unpaginated.

20 William Klein, 'William Klein: Regis Dialogue with Paulian Del Paso', 26 June 2009, Minneapolis: Walker Art Center: http://www.walkerart.org/channel/2009/william-klein-regis-dialogue-with-paulina-del.

21 Raymond Bellour, *Between-the-Images* (1990), ed. Lionel Bovier, Zurich: JRP Ringier, 2012, p. 106.

22 Roland Barthes, 'That Old Thing Art…' (1980), trans. Richard Howedard, in Stephen Henry Madoff (ed.), *Pop Art: A Critical History*, Berkeley, Los Angeles and London: University of California Press, 1997, p. 283.

23 Klein, *New York*, op. cit., p. 5.

24 Michael Renov, 'Expressivity: The Art of Documentary Practice', in Charles Merewether and John Potts (eds.), *After the Event: New Perspectives on Art History*, Manchester: Manchester University Press, 2010, p. 159.

25 Michael Renov, 'Towards a Poetics of Documentary', in Renov (ed.), *Theorising Documentary*, New York and London: Routledge, 1993, pp. 12–36.

26 Renov, 'Expressivity', op. cit., p. 158.

27 Ibid., p. 159.

28 Ibid., p. 161.

29 Scott MacDonald, *The Garden in the Machine: A Field Guide to Independent Films About Place*, Berkeley and Los Angeles, CA: University of California Press, 2001, p. 151.

30 Alexander Graf, 'Paris – Berlin – Moscow: On the Montage Aesthetic in the City Symphony Films of the 1920s', in Alexander Graf and Dietrich Scheunemann (eds), *Avant-Garde Film*, Amsterdam and New York: Rodopi, 2007, pp. 77–93.

31 Erica Stein, 'Abstract Space, Microcosmic Narrative, and the Disavowal of Modernity in *Berlin: Symphony of a Great City*', *Journal of Film and Video*, 65:4 (Winter 2013), p. 3.

32 Graf, op. cit., p. 79.

33 Jon Gartenberg, 'NY, NY: A Century of City Symphony Films', *Framework* 55:2 (Fall 2014), p. 248.

34 Robert E. Park, 'The City: Suggestions for the Investigation of Human Behaviour in the Urban Environment' (1925), in Robert E. Park, Ernest W. Burgess and Roderick D. McKenzie (eds), *The City*, Chicago and London: University of Chicago Press, 1967, p. 40.

35 Gartenberg, op. cit., p. 248.

36 Klein, 'William Klein: Regis Dialogue', op. cit.

37 Marshall Berman, *On the Town: One Hundred Years of Spectacle in Times Square*, London and New York: Verso, 2009, p. 6.

38 Ibid, p. xxvi.

39 Siegfried Kracauer, 'The Mass Ornament' (1927), trans. Barbara Correll and Jack Zipes, *New German Critique*, 5 (Spring 1975), p. 70.

40 Giuliana Bruno, 'Fabrics of Light: On the Structure of Film and Architecture', in Synne Bull and Marit Paasche (eds), *Urban Images: Unruly Desires in Architecture and Film*, Berlin: Sternberg Press, 2011, pp. 47–61.

41 Juan A. Suárez, 'City Space, Technology, Popular Culture: The Modernism of Paul Strand and Charles Sheeler's *Manhatta*', *Journal of American Studies*, 36 (2003), pp. 85–106.

42 For a general history of this period which places significant emphasis on consumerism and social mobility, see Gary Donaldson, *Abundance and Anxiety: America, 1945–1960*, Westport: Praeger, 1997. For an overview of notable Pop artists, including Andy Warhol, Roy Lichtenstein, Thomas Wesselmann and Claes Oldenburg in relation to consumer culture, see Christin Mamiya, *Pop Art and Consumer Culture: American Super Market*, Austin: University of Texas Press, 1992.

43 Concerns about advertising's possible uses of coercion and underhanded tactics are reflected by the popularity of Vance Packard's best-selling exposé of the ad industry and media manipulation, *The Hidden Persuaders* (New York: David McKay, 1957). Notable novels such as Sloan Wilson's *The Man in the Grey Flannel Suit* (1955) and the writings of Richard Yates and John Cheever concern themselves with the despondency and fallout from the pressures associated with this world of new-found prosperity, material consumption and middle-class conformity. Films like *Will Success Spoil Rock Hunter?* (Frank Tashlin, 1957) comically skewered the advertising industry for benefiting from the rise of television at the expense of cinema and revelling in vacuity.

44 Kracauer, op. cit., p. 69.

45 William Leach, *Land of Desire: Merchants, Power and the Rise of a New American Culture*, New York: Vintage, p. 343. For broader histories of Times Square, see William R. Taylor (ed.), *Inventing Times Square: Commerce and Culture at the Crossroads of the*

World, Baltimore: Johns Hopkins University Press, revised ed., 1996; James Traub, *The Devil's Playground: A Century of Pleasure and Profit in Times Square*, New York: Random House, 2004; and Lynn B. Sagalyn, *Times Square Remade: The Dynamics of Urban Change*, Cambridge, MA and London: MIT Press, 2023.

46 Kracauer, op. cit., p. 69.

47 Paul Virillo, *The Lost Dimension*, trans. David Moshenberg, Cambridge, MA: MIT Press, 2012, p. 78.

48 Kracauer, op. cit., p. 72.

49 Ibid.

50 Ibid., pp. 72–73.

51 Ibid., p. 73.

52 Writing on the history of Times Square as a contested urban space is plentiful. Perceived as a playground of vice in the 1970s, 42nd Street and its immediate environs have commonly been home to sex workers and erotic entertainment. See, for instance, Peter Braunstein, '"Adults Only": The Construction of an Erotic City in New York during the 1970s', in Beth Bailey and David Farber (eds), *America in the Seventies*, Lawrence: University of Kansas Press, 2004, pp. 129–56, and Terry Williams, *The Soft City: Sex for Business and Pleasure in New York City*, New York: Columbia University Press, 2022. The neoliberal sanitisation of the space especially under the mayoralty of Rudy Giuliani has been covered extensively. See especially Lynn B. Sagalyn, *Times Square Roulette: Remaking the City Icon*, Cambridge, MA and London: MIT Press, 2001, and Benjamin Chesluk, *Money Jungle: Imagining the New Times Square*, New Brunswick: Rutgers University Press, 2007.

53 Leach, op. cit., p. 235.

54 O. J. Gude, 'Art and Advertising Joined by Electricity', *Signs of the Times*, November 1912, p. 3.

55 Ibid.

56 O. J. Gude, '10 Minute Talk on Outdoor Advertising', *Sign of the Times*, June 1912, p. 77.

57 Suzi Gablik, 'Introduction', in Suzi Gablik and John Russel (eds), *Pop Art Redefined*, London: Thames and Hudson, 1969, p. 18.

58 Berman, op. cit., p. xxvi.

59 Foster, op. cit., p. 251.

4

Arocha's Black and White Pop: History, Desire and Politics in 1960s Colombia in *Las ventanas de Salcedo* (1966)

Juan Carlos Guerrero-Hernández

Luis Ernesto Arocha's *Las ventanas de Salcedo* (1966, black-and-white 16mm, sound, 6 minutes), the first experimental film with animation produced in Colombia, has received scant attention. Arocha (1932–2016), an architect born in Barranquilla, Colombia, who graduated from Tulane University in Louisiana in 1953, never attended film school but grew up close to cinema. During his childhood, he played with a 35mm projector and cans of silent films his family had at home; he also frequented the Teatro Apolo[1] that was built by his grandfather in 1930 and used as a cinema and theatre for about fifteen years.

Inspired by experimental films he first watched in New York in 1964, Arocha produced his first films in the USA and Colombia – among them *Pasión y Muerte de Margarita Gautier* (*The Passion and Death of Margarita Gautier*, 1965). Later, when teaching at Universidad Nacional in Bogotá, the architect, who would go on to become a pivotal figure in experimental and expanded cinema in Colombia,[2] met architect and artist Bernardo Salcedo (1939–2007), a slightly younger man who was to play a leading role in the renovation of the fine arts.[3] The pair soon began working on *Las ventanas*, a film produced in a few days, with no script, in Salcedo's studio. It is not a documentary about Salcedo's oeuvre, as James Scott's *Richard Hamilton* (1968) is about its eponymous artist, but a production where Arocha enters into a dialogue with Salcedo's emerging work to develop a Pop commentary on society and politics.

Arocha is one of the few filmmakers who intentionally considered his work a Pop film and used it to develop a humorous and ironic approach to Colombian society and what has become canonical Pop. As *Las ventanas* and his later film *La ópera del mondongo* (1975) – the latter formulated as a pseudo-documentary of the Barranquilla Carnival's popular side, including the poor and working classes participating in it – attest, he distanced himself from those discourses that assumed that Pop Art was, as Sontag put it, 'only possible in an affluent society, where one can be free to enjoy ironic consumption'.[4] Significantly, he created the single-film film company 'Pop Film' to produce *Las ventanas* during a deep economic recession in Colombia.

Arocha was interested in pointing to a context that diverged from that of the rise of the middle class and the modernisation of society in the so-called First World, which was the 'background' of the art and film produced in cities such as New York and Paris, and even in Buenos Aires where Pierre Restany identified the 'physical and psychological conditions for cosmopolitanism'.[5] By contrast, the signs of economic deterioration in Colombia were clear following a long period of violence that lasted until around the mid-1960s and had as its landmark event of collective trauma the assassination of Liberal and populist presidential candidate Jorge Eliécer Gaitán in 1948. In 1966, the country's unemployment rate was 11 percent, the devaluation of the national currency exacerbated inflation and shrank the level of the living wage, the production and importing of commodities were at their lowest since 1958, and the central bank's international reserves were negative, drastically reducing Colombia's capacity to import goods and services.[6]

In this context, this chapter discusses Arocha's *Las ventanas* as part of the understanding of Pop art in a global sense. Yet, 'global' here does not mean the expansion of the notion of Pop art and cinema, as suggested by *The World Goes Pop* exhibition at Tate Modern (2015–16) – a show that left unquestioned the anglophone canon referenced in what the curators of the show described as a 'pop style or a pop spirit'.[7] If the word 'Pop' is meant to be used in global terms, we need to challenge, as Arocha did, what in 1966 was already considered to be the anglophone canon that art critics such as Restany, Barbara Rose, Lawrence Alloway and Jasia Reichardt linked to capitalist mass culture and consumption, a colourful style and anti-experimentalism.[8] This challenge made by Arocha, which is arguably also present in Mário Pedrosa's notion of the 'Pop artist of the underdevelopment',[9] invited audiences and critics to consider Pop in a more open and complex manner by assuming different, sometimes contradictory approaches to and uses of experimentation with media, visual materials and forms of popular culture.

***

Las ventanas has a one-minute-long introduction, a central section and a one-minute-long ending. The introduction opens with the syncopated rhythm of the 'Ragtime' movement taken from the Indo-Dutch experimental composer Henk Badings' *Evolutionen – Ballet Music* (1958), which evokes a circus act. With a fast-paced editing rhythm and in medium close-up, the film shows – with a shallow depth of field – a chain painted white moving like a pendulum, attached to a round and adjustable white rotary piano or art stool. The following sequence reveals the chain as part of an assemblage placed in front of a black background. This includes a mutilated, white, life-size mannequin's legs (just the complete left leg, with the right leg cut off just below the buttock resting on the stool seat) and Salcedo dressed in black. As an acrobat in an uncomfortable and unstable position, he sits on top of the mannequin's legs while holding and using a black pyramidal-like viewer (Figure 4.1). The latter recalls the para-cinematic experience of viewing portrait-like and shallow-depth-of-field pictures in small-scale peepshow viewers – an activity that was popular in the early 1960s in Colombia.

Arocha begins to animate the assemblage. It appears to spin towards its right. The animation continues while the camera moves out, up and in, until reaching a close-up of Salcedo's face and the viewer's larger end, on which one can read the production company's name. The assemblage spins again,

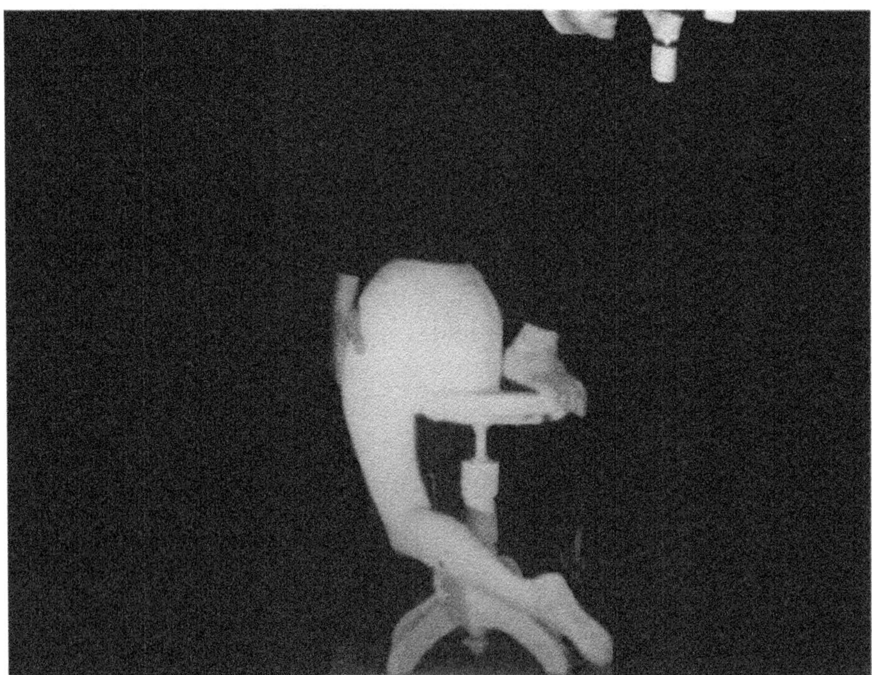

Figure 4.1 *Las ventanas de Salcedo* (Luis Fernando Arocha, 1966). Source: Courtesy of Fundación Patrimonio Fílmico Colombiano.

and the film's title now appears on the viewer's end. Salcedo's head and hand are then replaced by a mannequin's head and hand, which rotate to the right. The close-up suggests that the head may well be of an artist's jointed model, a dress form, or an articulated doll used as religious sculpture. The upper back of the mannequin head has been removed, allowing the viewer to see a couple of loose power cables inside it. The mannequin's hand holds the viewer, which now has the film production credits naming Arocha on it. The assemblage spins again, three more times, during which the mannequin's head and hand are replaced by Salcedo's. We are shown a full shot of the initial assemblage spinning at a faster pace, followed by a shot of the assemblage at rest without Salcedo, while the chain moves again like a pendulum.

Las ventanas partially nods toward a broader history of cinema that underpins the animated image, rather than merely presenting the illusion of movement. The film's introduction recalls Vertov's 'frame shot' and his Taylorist take on film – and especially animated films – as an art linked to 'advanced industrial labour'[10] and as the art of 'inventing movement of objects in space'.[11] Nonetheless, Arocha's aims are different. Significantly, instead of Vertov's constructivist approach, he manually took the filmed register of movement and got rid of film frames; he then assembled sets of a few frames in order to create an intentionally 'clumsy-appearing' and artisanal animation of a deranged assemblage.

Instead of conceiving of cinema as an analytic machine of movement and commodity production, Arocha's choreographed movements highlight the artificiality of assemblage itself. They underline a dialectics at the heart of animation between movement and stillness, illusion and disillusion, grace and awkwardness, where, as Alan Cholodenko argues, the 'nonhuman (including all other organic forms, as well as the inorganic) and the object' are privileged.[12] Arocha also emphasises what Karen Beckman identifies as cinema's capacity to 'anthropomorphize inanimate objects, including humanoid dolls', and to 'turn actors' as well as the artist and the director into 'lifeless dolls or signs'.[13] He offers a humble commingling of human and mannequin, resisting the spectacle of Fordist production and consumption.

Arocha's position as a filmmaker who had also worked as an architect for large industries in Bogotá, Barranquilla and New Orleans during the 1950s and 1960s allowed him to recognise that the assembly line – adopted in Colombia in the 1950s – displaced predominantly craft-based production, increased mechanisation and fragmented the 'traditional work relationships, friendship and solidarity among workers in factories', thus creating general discontent.[14] Contrary to the mass consumerism and emergence of the middle class referenced and celebrated by Pop art in New York, he was aware that poverty was increasingly becoming a clear 'contradictory corollary of Fordism's prosperity'[15] in cities such as New Orleans, Bogotá and Barranquilla, with their significant populations of poor labourers of colour. In this sense, Arocha's reference to ragtime reminds us that, in ragtime's energetic rhythm, Black communities breathed into 'the rhythm and the sound of machines', as Le Corbusier recognised.[16] Ragtime also placed folk music in a mechanised context and embodied a subversive way of 'ragging time' (that is, tearing time apart), mocking the industrial clock and Fordist machinery and imperatives.[17] Arocha's artisanal and subtractive montage and his adoption of ragtime subversion, hence, should be understood in the context of post-World War II Colombia.[18]

The introduction is followed by a collage of short sequences, mostly of around three to five frames in length. The montage creates flickers and a staccato or disconnected visual rhythm reinforced by the audio. For instance, the film passes from three blank frames to two frames in black; to ten frames of a close-up of a car's 1965 license plate, and then to a frame of a grid; to seven frames of vertical white and black bars; to five frames of the number two in black possibly taken from a countdown; and to an abstract advertising symbol found on a façade on a Bogotá street.

The frames appear to have been part of film leaders sourced from found footage and other movies made by Arocha, who was aware that, in commercial cinema, leaders were neglected as 'blank' because they supposedly carried no information for the general public. Like in Bruce Conner's assemblage film *A MOVIE* (1958), which also included leaders, Arocha was interested in paying attention to 'what everybody took for granted'.[19] Unlike Conner's inclusion of the complete countdown leaders following the traditional countdown order, Arocha included only some numbers and did not follow any order whatsoever. He knew that the leaders were used for synchronisation of sound and image, and that they served as – in Matt Soar's words – 'identification, statements of ownership, and instruction' for film distribution.[20] Yet, he was apparently most interested in making leaders the place of operations that defy interpretation. In this regard, since commercial cinema leaders were usually produced by the studios' 'art departments – the same folks who were likely responsible for props featuring type and lettering, intertitles, and publicity posters'[21] that influenced Pop artists in the 1960s – it is possible that Arocha made his own leaders, intending to create signs divorced from clear meaning and purposefully separated from Pop art's interest in mass media images that offered direct communication.

This brief section of *Las ventanas* combines syncopated rhythmic sounds and the fast change of short sequences in a manner that echoes the flickering of some structural film and its transformation of traditional cinemagoers' steady perception into an acrobatic exercise. Towards the end of it, the leaders yield their prominent role – without disappearing altogether – to short shots of façades, windows and balconies in Bogotá, including the window of the retail store LEY, where women and men in line look at the camera, and close-ups of Salcedo moving the viewer as if it were a camera. Contrary to what many would perhaps expect from a Pop film, Arocha's film avoids as much as possible recording goods, public spaces and outdoor advertisements, such as billboards, banners and window and neon signs in the modern city, which were important in Spanish filmmaker José María Arzuaga's *Rapsodia en Bogotá* (1963) – a piece much influenced by William Klein's *Broadway by Light* (1958).

Despite his training as an architect, in *Las ventanas* Arocha departs from both the traditional ways in which architecture is depicted in films about modern cities and from representations of windows as portals of surveillance (a topic explored in, to give just one example, Hitchcock's *Rear Window*, 1954). The film captures people standing by windows or on the balconies of neoclassical and modern buildings, at times watching voyeuristically with binoculars, chatting frantically, sometimes apparently interested and expectant, sometimes reserved. The short and fast tilts and pans, however, neither allow time for identifying persons and goods, acts, events or images, nor do they offer a clear idea of public space and the buildings' three-dimensionality. Arocha's montage treats the shots of windows and balconies as shallow stages of a Pop theatre where the viewers by the windows (and the audience in the cinema) see no commodities at all.

***

The central part of the film gives the protagonist role to 'windows' (*ventanas*), namely, Salcedo's humorous furniture-box-like assemblages that – as presented by Arocha – are less like windows in the traditional sense, but instead nod to popular peep show viewers, chambers of toy cameras (such as the famous Diana camera), puppet theatre and architecture. The film reveals Arocha and Salcedo's interest in establishing a critical distance from the modern legacy of the Albertian window, appealing instead to Le Corbusier's 'horizontal window' – a concept associated with furniture,[22] the 'space of photography'[23] and, equally important, the architectural threshold. Le Corbusier's photographs produced in the 1920s, particularly a picture taken at the Maison Cook in Boulogne-sur-Seine, where a wooden drawing mannequin sits on the sill, attest to how his horizontal windows displaced the verticality of the modern human figure,[24] interrupted the voyeuristic gaze, foregrounded frontality, collapsed space (as Arocha also did in the above-mentioned shots of windows and balconies) and created situations where light and objects live together.

This theatre of light, puppets and toys is the dominant mise-en-scène of the central part of *Las ventanas*, reminding us that Salcedo's 'windows' may be considered as para-cinematic stages of a drama of light and shadow, where objects are animated by the movement of the light source and the public in front of the piece. With a playful, childlike and surreal tone, the central part shows, for instance, short shots of a child playing with a toy truck, shots of two mannequin heads wearing diving masks, as if they were swimming in deep waters within one of Salcedo's 'windows', and a clumsy animation of a ball emerging from a tap as well as white and black bottles appearing and disappearing in a vertically-oriented bottle-basket (Figure 4.2). The animation attains a more ironic, political and sexual tone when Swan Lake's well-known waltz leitmotif is accompanied by short shots of 'windows' inside of which a white swan toy moves across as if in a shooting gallery, and Salcedo's hand appears aiming a white toy revolver as if ambiguously shooting the swan or

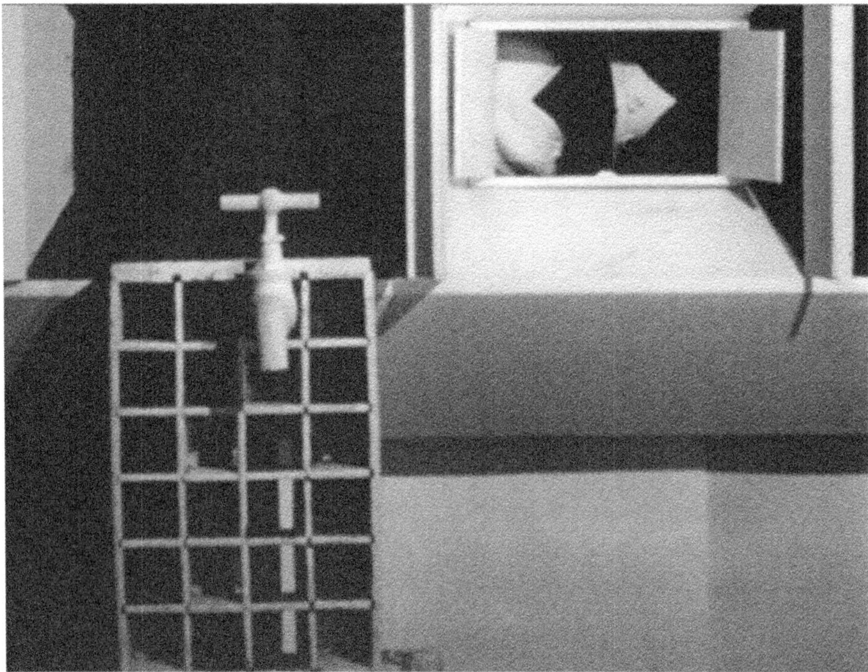

Figure 4.2 *Las ventanas de Salcedo* (Luis Fernando Arocha, 1966). Source: Courtesy of Fundación Patrimonio Filmico Colombiano.

the audience. The sound of gunshots subsequently accompanies alternated flickering frames of leader numbers and a broken window glass panel, and a repetition of the shot of the toy swan and the hand with a revolver, as well as a set of frames of a close-up of the promotional poster of Joseph Mawra's film *Olga's Girls* (1964) and an extreme close-up of a 'chastity lock' depicted in the centre of that poster.

Arocha's selection and assemblage of frames are highly suggestive, especially regarding the rapid use and close-up of the poster of a sexploitation film largely ignored by Cinema Studies – a film which, in the context of the USA, exudes Cold War paranoia and a social and political repression that is symbolised by the poster's lock.[25] In the context of Colombia, the close-up recalls a striking picture that was part of a criminal trial against a husband for systematic sexual abuse of his wife. Printed out of context on a full page in the cultural magazine *Mito* in 1957 and still present in the collective memory in 1966, it was the close-up of a padlock and barbed wire sewing up the vaginal lips of an eighteen-year-old impoverished peasant. Arocha's smart montage recalibrated the poster as an allegorical marker connecting the 'local' and the 'foreign'.

On the local side, the film pointed to what Octavio Paz described as an 'atrocious testimony' of sexual repression in Hispanic America,[26] and what Jaime Jaramillo Vélez would have regarded as a symptom of the conservatism and deferred secularisation in Colombia.[27] On the foreign side, the film subtly pointed to the USA's National Security Act of 1947 and Kennedy's Alliance for Progress (1961–70) that not only grounded an interventionist agenda and support for the Frente Nacional (1958–74) in Colombia (a pact among the political elites that agreed to rotate the presidency to secure power and exclude left-wing political options) and the repression and state terror around the world (including the 1964 military dictatorship in Brazil), but also restricted the other countries' room for experimentation with their own models of development. In relation to these models, an important case for architects such as Arocha was the World Bank's imposition of modernisation and urban processes in Latin America, and the Bank's apparent interest in supporting Le Corbusier's 1950 Pilot Plan for the transformation of Bogotá after the Bogotazo (that is, the massive riot in 1948 that followed the assassination of Gaitán and which destroyed hundreds of historical buildings downtown). This was a plan that initially recognised the value of the downtown core but was later altered and left unexecuted due to instructions and pressure from both Washington and local interests.

Las ventanas plays with and also suggests a rearticulation of and response to the local and foreign repressions of the 1960s. The film's central and final parts include short shots registering a bored, nonchalant eight-year-old girl chewing gum and lying on a window sill, two mannequin legs coming out from two 'windows', opening and moving in a happy rhythm, a flickering frontal frame of the half-open tights of a woman lying down (probably taken from a contemporary erotic film), Salcedo rapidly putting eggs into his mouth with the help of a mannequin hand and shots of soldiers and presidential elections, to which I will return later. To add another layer to the allegorical sexual turns, subversions and ironies, Arocha also inserted in the central part of the film the highly recognizable voice of the popular icon Libertad Lamarque singing the Spanish version of the waltz 'Frou-Frou'. Lamarque was known as the Sweetheart of the American Continent; her iconicity as an actress and singer was well established by the 1930s. Her voice singing a song that makes fun of late-nineteenth-century female décor was extracted from the popular Argentinian melodrama film *Puerta cerrada* (*Closed Door*, John Alton/Luis Saslavsky, 1939), a celebrated production in which the lighting design by co-director Alton preceded and served as a model for Hollywood's film noir.[28]

As an architect and filmmaker, and in line with figures such as the Brazilian artist Antonio Dias, whose sculptural work *Nota sobre a morte imprevista* (1965) was inspired by local comic books from the *sertão* (hinterlands) and the tradition of woodcut illustrations in *cordel* literature, Arocha apparently understood Pop as an assemblage of layers and images that broke from the stable and coherent condition that modern functionalist architecture intended to achieve. Also like Dias, he understood Pop as neither the USA's 'new naturalism' of the industrial commodity in the bastions of privilege transferred to other places of the world,[29] nor as having, as a 'primary precondition', what Hal Foster has referred to as 'the new configuration of cultural space entailed by consumer capitalism'.[30]

Arocha's use of black and white film in *Las ventanas* (rather exceptional in his broader colourful output) invites us to recognise that Pop means a renovated historical and increasingly global consciousness – within the realm of art and cinema in the post-World War II era – of the complex, vital and incoherent character of cities and popular cultures around the world, including former European colonies and the *Gran caribe* (the extended Caribbean) that includes New Orleans and Barranquilla. The primary precondition of Pop should be seen as the consciousness and practice of transculturalism already present in ethnomusicologist and scholar of Afro-Cuban culture Fernando Ortiz's notion of the transcultural,[31] as well as in ragtime's blending of African polyrhythms, the military march and even the European waltz. Instead of uncritically assuming the cultural hegemony of capitalism and the USA as if they were central references for the changing world of decolonisation, transnationalism and the emergence of the Non-Aligned Movement in the 1960s, the historical consciousness of popular culture is positioned by Arocha as a critical approach to modernism's aesthetic of technique and functionalism that tended to be abstract, elitist, (neo)colonialist and amnesiac.

Contrary to Restany's understanding of Pop as a rehabilitation of the explicit imagery of art and publicity for which interpretation was not necessary,[32] at the centre of Pop Arocha's *Las ventanas* finds a historical consciousness that recruits, and at times commingles, elements from the past and present in the flickering of different time-images. This is why the use of black-and-white film is significant: compared to colour stock, it can more easily register, level and assemble disparate materials from different times into a homogeneous whole (something Santiago Álvarez also did in his masterpiece *Now* [1965]). In addition, the use of black-and-white finds a fit with Salcedo's drama of light, and it allows the director to avoid what Lawrence Alloway identifies as the reigning colourful Pop 'aesthetics of plenty'[33] – an aesthetic that dominates in most of the Pop films that William Kaizen and Ed Halter list and discuss in their approaches to Pop cinema.[34]

Like many architects after World War II, including the Independent Group's Alison and Peter Smithson – who also criticised Le Corbusier's functionalism while valuing some aspects of his understanding of the contemporary city – Arocha and Salcedo were aware of the crisis of modernist art and architecture and of its associated instrumental rationality. Nonetheless, within the context of Bogotá, which still bore the wounds of the Bogotazo, they were not interested in ideas such as those which Robert Venturi later formulated for a new architecture and city where he identified the civic with 'the commercial strip'.[35] Viewed retrospectively, the position of Arocha and Salcedo falls closer to that of Vittorio Gregott, Aldo Rossi and the Neoliberty movement's post-World War II dialogue with and criticism of modernism.

There is a clear connection between Arocha and Salcedo's interests and the Neoliberty movement's invitation to consider the role of history and time in architecture, to think of the city as (in Aldo Rossi's words) 'retaining the traces of time' and past and present dreams, desires and struggles.[36] Like the Neoliberty movement, Arocha and Salcedo understood the architect as someone who inventories forms such as the window, which are 'handed down from history and established in the collective memory', in order to formulate the problems presented by the city and identify eventual solutions.[37] Indeed, Arocha's film and Salcedo's 'windows' nod to

Fernando Martínez Sanabria's rearticulation of Le Corbusier's horizontal window in his design of loose, dilated and detached-from-the-facade balconies made in concrete for the modernist Giraldo Building (1958) in Bogotá. These balconies reformulated the colonial Spanish closed wooden balconies that protrude from façades in the old downtown and are central to the city's collective memory – no matter if some were falling into ruin during the social and economic crisis. In *Las ventanas*, Arocha and Salcedo recalibrated Sanabria's design, as well as the architectural relic used by eighteenth-century female nobles for privacy and surveillance, transforming it into a threshold of public visibility in the 1960s. A threshold, that is, between traditional morality, social and political repression, the emergent sexual liberation and the countercultural revolution that would no longer defer secularisation and modernisation in Colombia.

***

The final part of *Las ventanas* opens with a medium close-up of a woman turning the crank of a popcorn machine (Figure 4.3) and is accompanied by an electronic and circus-like sound evoking penny arcade machines.

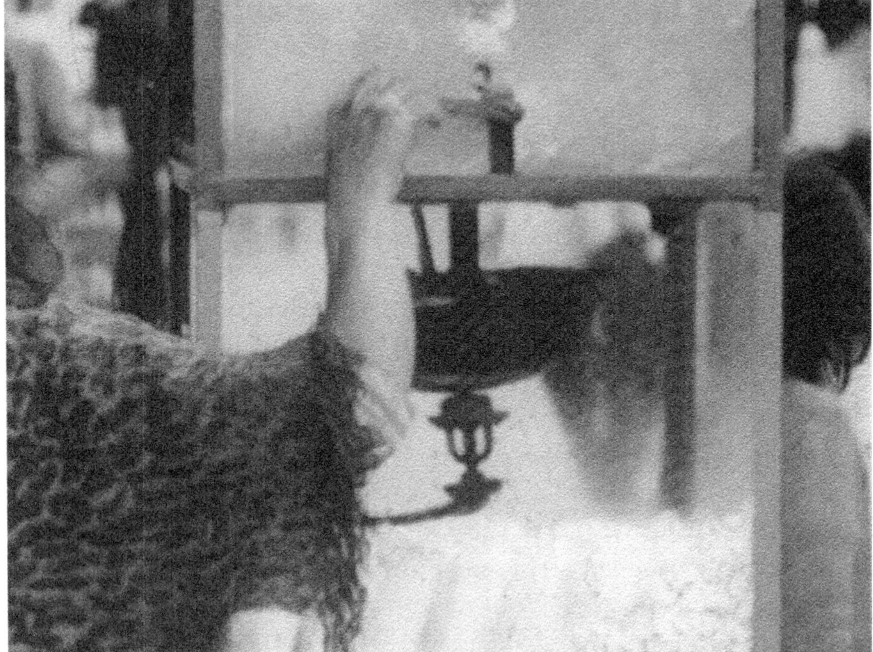

Figure 4.3 *Las ventanas de Salcedo* (Luis Fernando Arocha, 1966). Source: Courtesy of Fundación Patrimonio Filmico Colombiano.

With the ironic use of a pop(corn) machine, *Las ventanas* distances itself from celebrating industrial mass production as a fundamental or necessary reference for Pop art. From the popcorn machine, the film rapidly cuts to a sequence of a medium shot of a nun passing between the camera lens and a food display, the animated movement of an umbrella opening and closing, and a fast-paced and repeated animation of a frontal close-up of Salcedo spitting out the eggs he ingested earlier. Later, and accompanied by the sounds of gunshots and fireworks, the section includes a mid-shot of two armed soldiers watching over a square, a full shot of a poster of the presidential candidate José Jaramillo (who represented the opposition to the Frente Nacional) holding a Colombian flag, over which the text 'Atras las oligarquias! 1966–1970' ('Down with the oligarchies!') has been printed, Salcedo's hand aiming the toy revolver, another poster of Jaramillo depicted within a target-like composition with the text 'Educacion y Trabajo' ('Education and Jobs'), and a demonstration in support of Jaramillo in Bogotá's main square with the Senate building's façade as the background. The section goes on to include a shot of the rose window of a church, another of soldiers and women passing by the church's main doors, shots of white mannequin heads within a 'window' with targets pasted on their eyes or back, and a mannequin's hand aiming the revolver.

The shots and the pace of the montage do not allow the public to register the magnitude of the demonstration for Jaramillo and the public spaces. The film here suggests a gaze and a society caught – like the bodies of Salcedo on the stool and of those standing by the windows in the film's introduction – in a truncated threshold space, restricted to a to-and-fro movement between a tradition still to be overcome and possibly related to the interior space, and an incipient and differently-charged modernity arguably related to a public space as the still-to-be locus of public freedom. The stunted growth of industry, inequity, the stagnation of agricultural production, repression, the USA's interventionism, the emerging communist guerrilla faction and social discontent were all prominent factors in the presidential elections where Jaramillo gathered support from diverse forces and offered a populism that addressed the lack of inclusiveness and awkwardly assembled contradictory and ideologically incoherent proposals combining leftist, nationalist and liberal ideas of revolution, as the sequence suggests. This was a combination that in turn – even if it received scant support in the ballot and Arocha might have regarded it with suspicion – suggested heterogeneous directions of potential development for democracy and a type of modernity in Latin America that would follow neither the North American nor the Soviet models.[38] In other words, and playing with the title of Vertov's famous animated film *Soviet Toys* (1924), *Las ventanas* was not interested in displaying communist or capitalist advertising, animations, or toys.

The film ends with a ten-second-long sequence that, after a short animation of the shooting gallery swan exploding into feathers, shows a shot of three contiguous 'windows' where the legs that were happily moving now fall, as if the mannequin's desire has imploded, as the accompanying sound suggests. Short shots of long balloons then follow, emerging from the 'windows' and frenetically released with clear sexual and war-like innuendo, emphasised by the sounds of gunshots and small explosions. This is followed by a sequence overlaid with the sounds of a fire alarm. It includes a fast-paced countdown, ten different flickering close-ups (in about three seconds) of pictures of nuclear mushroom clouds, a short close-up of a boy pulling a truck and a close-up of a mannequin's hand halting the animated movement of a pendulum, thus signalling the end of the animation just before the credits.

Besides the continuation of themes of sex, play and violence, the film ends with (what seems to me to be) a tribute to Colombian poet Gonzalo Arango, the founder of the countercultural and anti-establishment poetic movement known as Nadaísmo:

> History is in liquidation [… It] no longer evolves. It jumps like a crazy crab against the rhythm of the waves of time. Its frenzy does not indicate that it is progressing in its somersaults. But contemporary history launches itself from war to war, in search of progress, uselessly.[39]

Instead of using found footage of nuclear explosions, as Conner did in *A MOVIE*, Arocha used pictures probably taken from local newspapers or international magazines. He used flickering to animate the explosion in such a way that, contrary to the animation opening the film, it created a short, frenzied vibration of the picture, much like Arango's crazy crab. He also registered the pictures within a black 'window', as if transforming the frame into a TV monitor, creating another assemblage.

This choice of the TV-like 'window' for the closing of Arocha's film is significant. It not only precedes Arocha's future production of newsreels for the TV news programme *Noticiero del Caribe* between 1968 and 1970 (coincidently, the director Santiago Álvarez also worked in newsreels), but the use of the TV-like window serves as a valuable device for exploring the ways in which the end of *Las ventanas* mobilises different forms of feedback. First, it suggests a close relationship, closer than desired by some cinephiles, between film and television and how one nurtures and has been nurtured by the other. The flickers, the fast jumps (of the film, of the crab) from one image/theme to another, the movement of the camera and the flattened space were all rarely found in commercial cinema and were easily identified in experimental film and television's operation and news. Arguably, television also influenced the flat, frontal shooting of Salcedo's 'windows'.

Second, feedback refers to the more critical idea and praxis of registering elements of social reality and history, processing them through animation, montage and editing, and sending them back to the public and society in the cinema. It even suggests that the public should re-assemble reality and that such an active role in front of a flickering screen was far more complicated and limited than what Marshall McLuhan liked to assign to TV viewers. *Las ventanas*, unlike advertising, was not meant to have a direct meaning but only slant and oblique ones, requiring from the public a crab's movements against the flux and temporalities of commercial cinema.

Third, *Las ventanas* is a film that takes Salcedo's work from the artist's studio, and through teamwork production processes – as in theatre, film, or television – and post-production in the editing room, sends it 'back' to the art and cinema world. *Las ventanas* intended to open up a literal stage and present possibilities for cinema in Colombia in the 1960s. In other words, *Las ventanas* not only brought art out of the traditional gallery spaces where Salcedo's works were exhibited, but it also nodded towards the broad and popular scope of cinema that is still marginalised by some art and film criticism, including animation – whose side-lining Tom Gunning described as 'one of the great scandals of film theory'[40] – and sexploitation films.

Las ventanas invites us to consider not only that Pop cinema – which is still a notion under construction – may help us to nurture and complicate our understanding of Pop art, but it also argues that we must complicate our general understanding of Pop. If we want to think and study Pop – cinema and art – in an open and pluralistic sense, we need to do more than expand the canon or make it inclusive. We need to do more than question the Euro-American citizenship of Pop.[41] Works such as Dias' *Nota sobre a morte imprevista* and Arocha's *Las ventanas* did more than follow or react to the canon of Euro-American Pop; they were the consequence of a historical consciousness that, in the 1960s, rediscovered the force, complexity, heterodoxy and relevance of popular cultures – not just mass culture – for contemporaneity and a world in the process of globalisation. They rediscovered popular cultures' pertinence for understanding and questioning political, social, sexual and transnational realities and for intuiting emergent challenges for the modernist aesthetics of technique, Washington's imposed model of development, and Pop's aesthetics of mass consumption and plenty.

Notes

1 Christopher Tibble, 'El cine experimental de Luis Ernesto Arocha', *Semana* (Bogotá), 10 December 2015, https://www.semana.com/impresa/cine/articulo/cine-experimental-de-barranquilla-luis-ernesto-arocha/45465/.

2 Marta Lucía Vélez, 'The Barranquilla Group, La Cueva, and Experimental Film', in Jesse Lerner and Luciano Piazza (eds), *Ism, Ism, Ism / Ismo, Ismo, Ismo: Experimental Cinema in Latin America*, Oakland: University of California Press, 2017, p. 338.

3 María Iovino, *Bernardo Salcedo: El universo en caja*, Bogotá: Biblioteca Luis Ángel Arango, 2001, p. 13.

4 Susan Sontag, *As Consciousness is Harnessed to Flesh: Journals and Notebooks, 1964–1980*, New York: Farrar, Straus and Giroux, 2012, p. 21.

5 Pierre Restany, 'Buenos Aires y el nuevo humanism', *Planeta*, 5 (1965), p. 122.

6 Carlos Caballero Argáez, 'La impronta de Carlos Lleras Restrepo en la economía colombiana de los años sesenta del siglo XX', *Revista de Estudios Sociales*, 33 (2009), pp. 91–103.

7 Jessica Morgan, 'Political Pop: An Introduction', Tate Research Publication, 2015, https://www.tate.org.uk/whats-on/tate-modern/exhibition/ey-exhibition-world-goes-pop/jessica-morgan-political-pop-an-introduction.

8 Restany, op. cit.; Barbara Rose, 'Dada Then and Now', *Art International*, 7:1 (January 1963), p. 25; Lawrence Alloway, 'Pop Art: The Words', in Richard Kalina (ed.), *Imagining the Present: Context, Content, and the Role of the Critic: Essays by Lawrence Alloway*, Oxon: Routledge, 2006, pp. 147–50; Jasia Reichardt, 'Some Notes about Definitions of New Trends', in Wim Beeren (ed.), *Nieuwe Reaslisten June 24 – August 30*, The Hague: Gemeente Museum, 1964, pp. 4–5.

9 Mário Pedrosa, 'Do Pop americano ao sertanejo Dias', *Correio da Man* (Rio de Janeiro), 29 October 1967.

10 Mihaela Mihailova and John MacKay, 'Frame Shot: Vertov's Ideologies of Animation', in Karen Beckman (ed.), *Animating Film Theory*, Durham, NC: Duke University Press, 2014, p. 148.

11 Dziga Vertov, 'WE: Variant of a Manifesto', in Annette Michelson (ed.), Kevin O'Brien (trans.), *Kino-Eye: The Writings of Dziga Vertov*, Berkeley: University of California Press, 1984, p. 8.

12 Alan Cholodenko, '"First Principles" of Animation', in Beckman (ed.), *Animating Film Theory*, op. cit., p. 102.

13 Karen Beckman, 'Animating Film Theory: An Introduction', in Beckman (ed.), *Animating Film Theory*, op. cit., p. 5.

14 All translations from Spanish are mine. Alberto Mayor Mora, 'Institucionalizado!! Perspectivas del Taylorismo', *Boletín Socioeconómico*, 24/25 (1992), p. 215.

15 David Gartman, *From Autos to Architecture: Fordism and Architectural Aesthetics in the Twentieth Century*, New York: Princeton Architectural Press, 2009, p. 253.

16 Le Corbusier, *When the Cathedrals Were White*, New York: McGraw-Hill, 1964, p. 154.

17 Terry Waldo, *This is Ragtime*, New York: Hawthorn Books, 1976, p. 36.

18 On subtractive editing in Bruce Conner's film works, see Kevin Hatch, *Looking for Bruce Conner*, Cambridge, MA: MIT Press, 2012, pp. 124–26.

19 William C. Wees, *Recycled Images: The Art and Politics of Found Footage Films*, New York: Anthology Film Archives, 1993, p. 79.

20 Matt Soar, 'Standardized Film Leaders', in Mark J. P. Wolf (ed.), *The Routledge Companion to Media Technology and Obsolescence*, New York: Routledge, 2019, p. 183.

21 Ibid., p. 187.

22 Claudio Vásquez, 'Light in the Work of Le Corbusier', *ARQ*, 76 (2010), p. 23.

23 Beatriz Colomina, 'Le Corbusier and Photography', *Assemblage*, 4 (1987), p. 20.

24 Thomas Keenan, 'Windows: Of Vulnerability', in Bruce Robbins (ed.), *The Phantom Public Sphere*, Minneapolis: University of Minnesota Press, 1993, p. 126.

25 Elena Gorfinkel, *Lewd Looks: American Sexploitation Cinema in the 1960s*, Minneapolis: University of Minnesota Press, 2017, p. 161.

26 Octavio Paz, *Puertas al campo*, Barcelona: Seix Barral, 1981, p. 107.

27 Rubén Jaramillo Vélez, *Colombia: La Modernidad Postergada*, Bogotá: Editorial Temis, 1994, p. 48.

28 Iván Morales, 'Las Sombras Llaman a Mi Puerta: John Alton y El Melodrama en *Puerta Cerrada* (1939)', *Studies in Spanish & Latin American Cinemas*, 16:3 (2019), p. 296.

29 Waldemar Cordeiro, 'Arte Concreta Semântica', in Waldemar Cordeiro, São Paulo: Galeria Atrium, 1964.

30 Hal Foster, 'Image Building', *Artforum*, October 2004, https://www.artforum.com/print/200408/image-building-7661.

31 Fernando Ortiz, *Cuban Counterpoint: Tobacco and Sugar* (1947), Durham, NC and London: Duke University Press, 1995.

32 Pierre Restany, quoted in María José Herrera, *POP! La consagración de la primavera*, Buenos Aires: Fundación OSDE, 2010, p. 9.

33 Lawrence Alloway, 'The Long Front of Culture', in Kalina (ed.), op. cit., p. 61.

34 See the essays by Ed Halter and William Kaizen in this volume.

35 Robert Venturi, *Learning from Las Vegas: The Forgotten Symbolism of Architectural Form*, Cambridge, MA: MIT Press, 1972, p. 6.

36 Aldo Rossi, *The Architecture of the City*, Cambridge, MA: MIT Press, 1982, p. 128.

37 Gartman, op. cit., p. 253.

38 Michael Conniff, 'Introduction', in Conniff (ed.), *Populism in Latin America*, Tuscaloosa: University of Alabama Press, 2012, pp. 1–22.

39 Gonzalo Arango, '13 poetas nadaístas: El infierno de la Belleza', *El Tiempo – Lecturas Dominicales* (Bogotá), 25 August 1963, p. 6.

40 Tom Gunning, 'Moving Away from the Index: Cinema and the Impression of Reality', *differences: A Journal of Feminist Cultural Studies*, 18:1 (2007), p. 38.

41 Sônia Salzstein, 'Cultura pop: Astúcia e inocência', *Novos Estudos CEBRAP*, 3:76 (2006), p. 261.

5

Psychedelic Agit-Pop: The Animated Films of Tadanori Yokoo

Clint Enns

In the 1960s, the social and political conditions of postwar Japan generated a frenzy of artistic innovation within a wide range of practices including theatre, cinema, literature, music, illustration, graphic design, dance and performance art. As art historian Alexandra Munroe states, it was 'undoubtedly the most creative outburst of anarchistic, subversive and riotous tendencies in the history of modern Japanese culture'.[1] It was in this artistic climate that the renowned Japanese artist Tadanori Yokoo first began to experiment with graphic design. Through blending Pop art, psychedelia and traditional Japanese aesthetics, in particular *ukiyo-e* (a genre of Japanese art which has been considered proto-Pop), Yokoo created works that are playful, humorous, personal and idiosyncratic.[2] In 1968, Yokoo's friend, author Yukio Mishima, provocatively declared that Yokoo's graphic works connected 'a straight line through the sorrow of Japanese local customs (*dozoku*), and the idiotic and daylight nihilism of American Pop art'.[3] It was this particular aesthetic cocktail that landed him the reductive and Western-centric nickname of the 'Japanese Warhol'. At the time, Yokoo was at the centre of the Japanese counterculture, collaborating with pivotal figures in the scene, including filmmaker Nagisa Ōshima, playwright-poet-filmmaker Shūji Terayama, playwright-director-actor Jūrō Kara, choreographer Hijikata Tatsumi and musician Toshi Ichiyanagi. Although predominantly known as a graphic designer and painter, Yokoo also produced three short animations.

This chapter will situate Yokoo's animated films in relation to his overall artistic practice, as well as the social and political context in which they were made. A brief analysis will be performed on all three of Yokoo's animations: *Anthology No. 1* (アンソロジーNO. 1, 1964), *KISS KISS KISS* (1964) and *Kachi Kachi Yama Meoto no Sujimichi* (堅々獄夫婦庭訓, 1965).[4] Expanding on this analysis, a close reading will be provided of Yokoo's most complex animation, *Kachi Kachi Yama*, a work that alludes to the revolutionary potential of popular culture. While working on his animations, Yokoo abandoned commercial graphic design. At this time, he began to pursue his own idiosyncratic artistic expressions, blending psychedelia and Pop art aesthetics, producing artworks that advocate for political change through expanding consciousness and through everyday actions rather than explicit political action.

Climax at the Age of Twenty-Nine

In 1965, Yokoo created a graphic poster titled *Made in Japan, Tadanori Yokoo, Having Reached a Climax at the Age of 29, I Was Dead* (Figure 5.1). The poster embraces a Pop style with its simplified flattened imagery, bright artificial colours and combination of text and image, while also incorporating elements which were distinctly Japanese, both modern and traditional. At the centre of the composition is a man hanging from a noose, holding a drooping flower in front of the Rising Sun, an image inspired by the *Kyokujitus-ki* military flag, a controversial symbol of Japan's imperialism banned during the US occupation from 1945 to 1952. It also contains many of the aesthetic and visual motifs that Yokoo would continue to employ, including atomic explosions, an erupting Mount Fuji and the speeding Shinkansen bullet train. The poster was shown at Tokyo's Matsuya department store in a group exhibition titled 'Persona' and established Yokoo's reputation as a graphic artist. The piece is intended to be allegorical; however, according to art critic Christopher Mount, 'some believed at the time that [Yokoo] had really died'.[5]

The graphic announcement of Yokoo's symbolic death marked his departure from traditional commercial design to a more self-conscious and radical form of practice. As art historian Hiroko Ikegami has argued, at the time Yokoo had 'uneasy feelings about being known as a mere "designer" as opposed to an "artist", and was skeptical of the art-world term "Pop"'.[6] These sentiments were expressed in a 1966 graphic poster titled *Ballad for the Chopped-off Little Finger*, an homage to the thespian achievements of Ken Takakura, an actor best known for playing ultra-hip tough guys with dignity and honour in gangster (*yakuza*) films. The text on the image, which lies somewhere between a loyalty oath of a *yakuza* member and the strict samurai code of the *bushido* (the way of the warrior), reads: 'Although still inexperienced in the world, I, with the spirit of a false Pop man, pursue the proper road of graphic design in Japan'.[7] Scholar Steven Ridgley argues that,

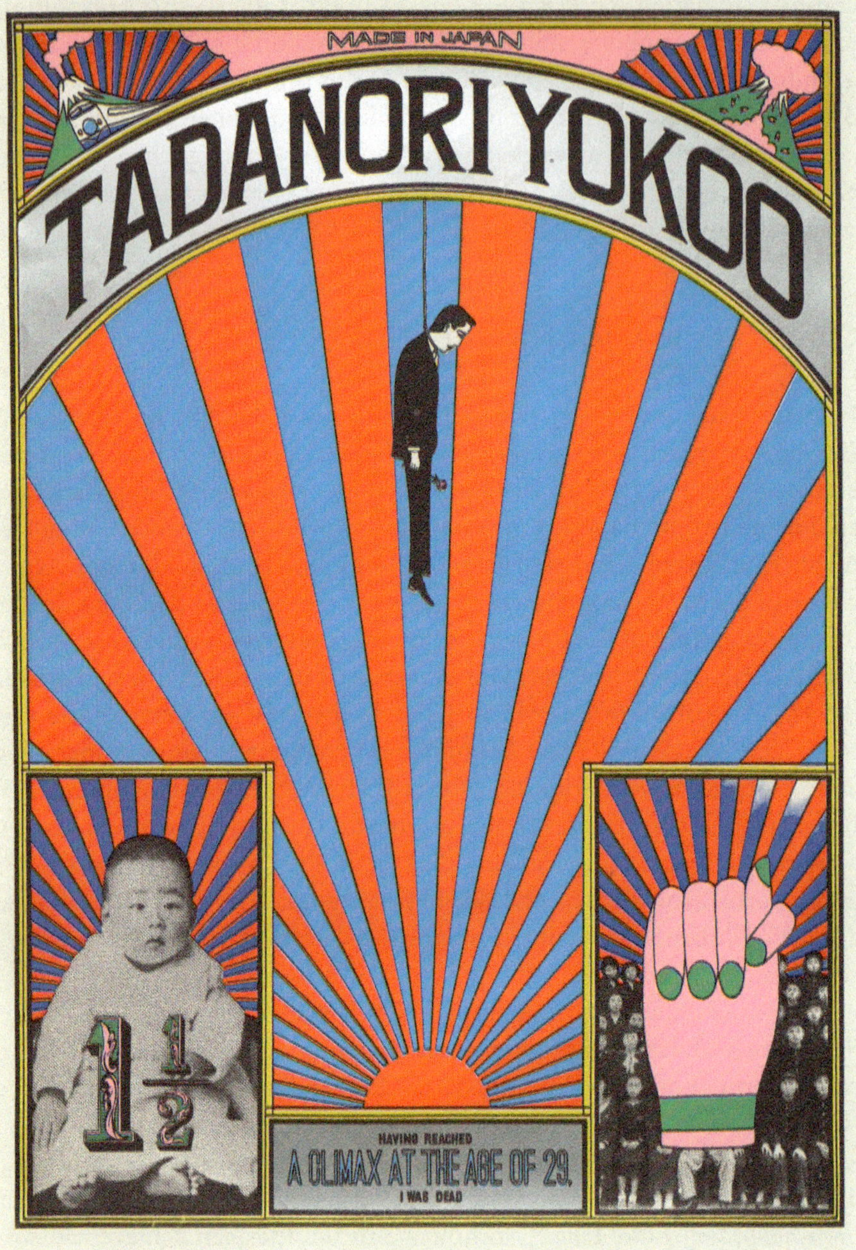

Figure 5.1 Tadanori Yokoo, *Made in Japan, Tadanori Yokoo, Having Reached a Climax at the Age of 29, I Was Dead*, silkscreen, 43 × 31⅛".

by January 1969, Yokoo had completely overcome all of his reservations about being a 'commercial designer' and had begun to practice 'without remorse'.[8] By this time, Yokoo had developed an awareness of the potential dangers of commercialism and a consciousness regarding contemporary sociopolitical conditions. As Ridgely reasons, 'what we find in Yokoo's position on commodified art is a perfect example of counterculture's adjustment from full-spectrum market boycott toward a more precise consideration of who is exchanging what with whom, where that exchange is occurring, and on whose terms'.[9] As such, Yokoo continued to produce commercial design that was both idiosyncratic and personal. As art critic Yasushi Kurabayashi observes, 'Yokoo's posters are not designed around conventional poster-like ideas. Rather his posters have been executed from his own desire for creative expression, with little regard for cognitive clarity or message'.[10]

Yokoo's animation *Anthology No. 1* was made at the end of his four-year stint at the Nippon Design Centre (1960–64) and prior to *Made in Japan*. Like all of Yokoo's animations, the work was produced through the Sōgetsu Art Centre, a Toyko-based experimental hub for postwar avant-garde art. At the time, experimental animation was relatively new to Japan, and *Anthology No. 1* and *KISS KISS KISS* premiered at the inaugural Sōgetsu Animation Festival in September 1964. The source materials for *Anthology No. 1* are Yokoo's commercial graphic design work (publicity posters, magazine and book covers) produced between 1961 and 1964. The film is literally an anthology; however, the film is not simply a documentation of his commercial graphic designs given that none of the works are shown in their entirety. The animation consists of details from his graphic designs and, in a few cases, elements from these works are re-configured into new designs and given animated motion.[11] As scholar Yuriko Furuhata suggests, Yokoo's animation 'foregrounds the static, graphic quality of unanimated images'.[12] In the film, the camera minimally animates the source material producing a form of discontinuous animation that is not necessarily intended to produce the illusion of movement. As Furuhata notes, many Japanese graphic designers of the era were exploring 'graphic animation', a term coined by animation critic Takuya Mori to 'describe the intermedial form of graphic design and animation'.[13]

It has been argued that *Anthology No. 1* functions as an archive of Yokoo's early graphic design while also revitalising the work through remediation. For example, Furuhata suggests that 'animation allows Yokoo to both preserve otherwise ephemeral works of graphic design and to breathe new life into them, all the while highlighting his investment in repetition as a central component to his artistic process'.[14] While *Anthology No. 1* successfully reinvigorates his older work, it is, at best, a rather poor attempt at *preserving* his graphic design work. A film that fully documents his works in their entirety would have made for a better archive. Nevertheless, to expand on Furuhata's line of reasoning, the film not only attempts to 'breathe new life into' his previous work, but also attempts to *artistically* reclaim his commercial work in a desire to move beyond it.

One of the last images in the film, the one immediately before the end title (with '終' ['End'] emerging from a mouth) is a detail from a 1964 graphic poster, *The Performance of Gekidan Mingei: Under the Magnolia Tree*.[15] The image depicts a cross marking a grave beneath a tree, which is consistent with the play which Yokoo's poster was advertising; however, given that this was the last image of the animation and that it is shown without any reference to the play, it can be seen as signifying the end of life. Although not as striking or as explicit as *Made in Japan*, this gesture can also be seen as further indicating Yokoo's departure from traditional graphic design and subsequent rebirth as a graphic artist in pursuit of his own personal, psychedelic, Pop art aesthetic.[16]

Lichtenstein, Warhol and Yokoo Sitting in a Tree, K-I-S-S-I-N-G

KISS KISS KISS is a 1964 animation that borrows the aesthetics of American romance comics and features hand-coloured illustrations of couples kissing. The soundtrack, composed by Akiyama Kuniharu (who also made the electronic soundtrack for *Anthology No. 1*), begins with crooner Dean Martin singing his 1953 pop hit 'Kiss', which abruptly changes after the title cards disappear, to electronic bloops that mimic the 'muah' sounds of people kissing.[17] In addition, the word 'kiss' appears in speech bubbles around the figures embracing (see Figure 5.2). The animation itself is minimal, with little movement, and makes use of lo-fi transitions – one repeated form of which is a ripping of paper, beginning as a small hole at the place of two lips kissing, swiftly becoming larger until the next kiss is revealed. The film ends with a title card ('The End') and the sound of Martin repeating the phrase 'kiss me, kiss me again', as if the record were skipping, until it slowly fades out.

The images in *KISS KISS KISS* are reminiscent of Roy Lichtenstein's *Kiss* series (1962–64), which was a source of inspiration for Yokoo.[18] Following Lichtenstein, Yokoo sourced the material for his film from American romance comics produced after World War II. Both artists are playing with

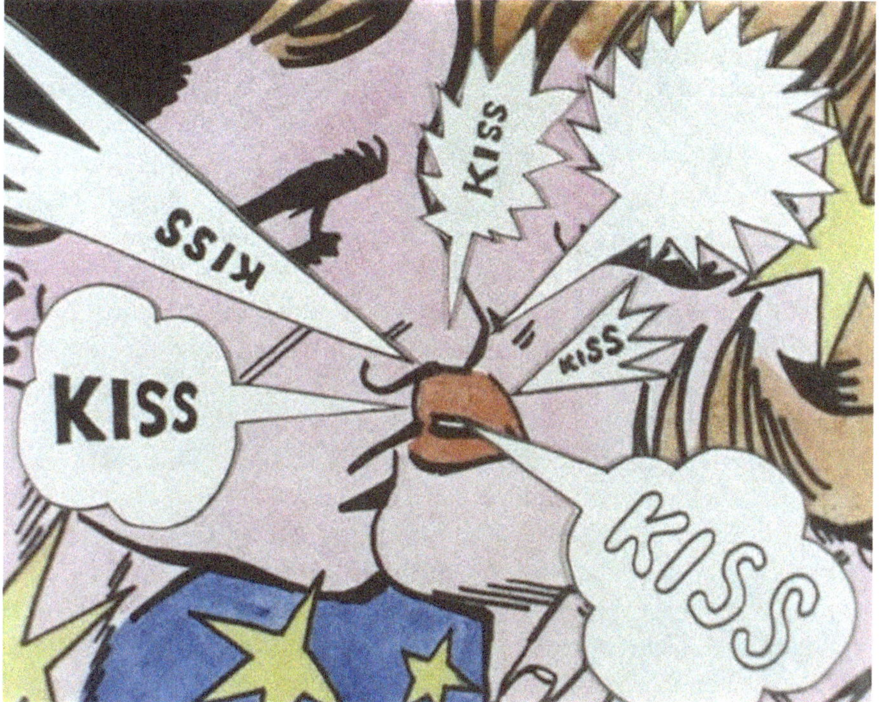

Figure 5.2 *KISS KISS KISS* (Tadanori Yokoo, 1964).

the tension between the artwork and the newsstand source from which they were appropriated. One difference between the two artists' works is that Yokoo's images lack Lichtenstein's signature Ben-Day dots since he created new illustrations for his film; that is, he did not photograph them directly from comic books. Beyond removing the Ben-Day dots, Yokoo also includes an image of the moon which Ikegami suggests is taken from the Japanese card game *hanafuda*.[19] In this way, Yokoo is subtly mixing Japanese and Western images, juxtaposing indigenous Japanese popular culture with Western popular culture, a gesture which can be interpreted as a response to the Westernisation of postwar Japan.

Both Yokoo and Lichtenstein extract the objects that they are appropriating from their original context, a strategy that both celebrates them and opens them to scrutiny. In addition, both artists employ a number of different techniques to manipulate, remediate and transform the objects that they appropriate from mass culture. Beyond an actual transformation, Lichtenstein argued that his work effected a slightly more abstract form of *critical* transformation: 'the closer my work is to the original', he stated, 'the more threatening and critical the content. However, my work is entirely transformed in that my purpose and perception are entirely different. I think my paintings are critically transformed, but it would be difficult to prove it by any rational line of argument'.[20] While the degree to which Lichtenstein simply copied his source materials has been the subject of much debate, it is certain that he transformed what some critics perceived as 'low brow' material into 'high art'.[21] Yokoo describes his use of appropriated images in a slightly different way, arguing that 'each of these mass-produced works that appear on screen [in *KISS KISS KISS* and *Anthology No. 1*] are ruins of the former works, robbed of their short life after being exhausted on the commercial front. [...] I am playing the role of a spiritual medium who conjures their spirits from the ghostly past and confers on them a new light of life'.[22] In other words, Yokoo sees both *KISS KISS KISS* and *Anthology No. 1* as providing a second life to mass-produced, popular images that had 'exhausted' their intended commercial function.

By the mid-1960s, Lichtenstein's aesthetic was already being appropriated by commercial advertising agencies. In June 1964, Brazil Coffee released a one-page advertisement in the *New York Times Magazine* in a style similar to Lichtenstein's romance paintings, only one month after the magazine had published a substantial article on Pop art by John Canaday.[23] As Thomas Crow has demonstrated, Pop art aesthetics were quickly re-absorbed into the commercial sphere, with commercial designers appropriating the self-conscious nature of the artworks. By 1965, Lichtenstein had stopped using comic book panels as source material, and by the end of the 1960s, Pop art was largely abandoned by the art world (although it was to re-appear in different forms).[24] However, the influence of both Lichtenstein and Yokoo's works have outlasted the ephemeral, mass-produced images from which they borrowed.

While *KISS KISS KISS* engages with a Pop aesthetic similar to that employed by Lichtenstein, the film also employs formalist strategies that date back to the Edison film depicting the first on-screen kiss. *The May Irwin Kiss* (1896), directed by William Heise, is a filmic adaptation of the final scene of the musical stage comedy *The Widow Jones*, a kiss between actors May Irwin and John C. Rice. Approximately fifteen seconds in length, the film was originally projected on loop using a Vitascope. In other words, the shot of Irwin and Rice kissing was repeated multiple times. The film was 'the most popular Edison film of the year', notes film historian Charles Musser.[25] Many of the critics of the era saw the film as humorous. For instance, one described the 'evident delight of the actor' and 'the undisguised pleasure of the actress' as '"too funny" for anything'.[26] Exactly what was the anything? Others were scandalised:

Film theorist Linda Williams describes this *vulgarity* as cinema's 'first sex act'.[28]

In the mid-1960s, the decontextualised kiss would return to the screen in Andy Warhol's serial *Kiss* (1963–64). Warhol's *Kiss* consists of different couples kissing and was originally shown as a 'serial', with 'a new segment shown every week at the [Film-Makers'] Cinematheque, like *Merrie Melodies*'.[29] The final film is made from twelve black-and-white, 100-foot 16mm reels, spliced together, complete with burns and perforated end tags. There are no titles or credits; like most of Warhol's silent films, it was shot at 24 frames per second but projected at 16 fps, producing a dream-like effect, stripping away the sexual impact to reveal the banality of the action and providing space for quiet contemplation of the on-screen performances.[30]

Warhol's *Kiss* and Yokoo's *KISS KISS KISS* share particular formal affinities with Edison's *The May Irwin Kiss*, including fragmentation, repetition and magnification. For Yokoo, each kiss is just one panel from a comic book, a single drawing representing a frozen moment. In the case of *The May Irwin Kiss*, the kiss is removed from its original context within a play. Warhol rejected any semblance of traditional narrative, allowing new sets of questions to arise. As filmmaker and theorist J. J. Murphy observes,

All three films consciously remove the kiss from any narrative constraints, emancipating it from previously established cultural conventions.

The looping of *The May Irwin Kiss* was a by-product of the technology.[32] In contrast, the repetition with variation found in both Warhol and Yokoo's work was intentional. The repetition of *The May Irwin Kiss* potentially contributed to the laughs, whereas for Yokoo it enhances the banality of the act. When asked about the use of erotic or sexual imagery in his work, Yokoo stated: 'I think that I wanted to show the banality of sex in the best possible way. For the generations that came before in Japan, sex was not something that needed to be made pornographic, it was natural. If everyone's working out in the field and mom and pop want to have a break and take five or ten to do a sweet one – that was normal.'[33] The repetition in Warhol's films contributes to their monotony; however, they also force the viewer to consider slight variation. As Warhol famously declared, '[e]verything repeats itself. It's amazing that everyone thinks that everything is new, but it's all a repeat.'[34]

Finally, all three films use a form of magnification. In *The May Irwin Kiss*, the couple is framed in chest-up shot, a marked close-up compared to the theatre production. Warhol uses a two-person close-up for every couple, except for the third reel where there is a slight narrative set-up. In the third reel, the camera zooms back to reveal experimental filmmakers John Palmer and Andrew Meyer topless and kissing. This may have been shocking to some since, in close-up, some viewers might have assumed that the couple kissing was heterosexual, given Palmer's androgynous features. In Yokoo's work, the illustrated kissing couples are framed both chest-up and as two-person close-ups. Yokoo also uses another technique to isolate the kiss, a simple matting device: a black frame which blocks out much of the image and draws focus to the kissing lips.

KISS KISS KISS blends two aspects of Yokoo's political philosophy – namely, the revolutionary potential of everyday gestures and sexual liberation. In an interview with curator Takayo Iida, Yokoo explains that 'the real revolution was perhaps in those simple everyday gestures. I think the most important inner activity is not to deliver political messages, but rather to transform consciousness and our daily activities.'[35] To Yokoo, sexual liberation is directly linked to political revolution. As Ridgely elegantly states, Yokoo 'was on the psychosexual side of 60s politics, interested in a transformative heightening of consciousness that could direct the libidinal trauma of war and the repressed Thanatos of the Cold War into a broad cultural response rather than a limited political action.'[36] Viewing *KISS KISS KISS* through this lens, the kiss serves as a *simple everyday gesture*, an act of intimacy shared between two people that contains the potential to heighten consciousness and transform the dominant culture.

The psychosexual aspect of Yokoo's political philosophy becomes particularly apparent in Nagisa Ōshima's *Diary of a Shinjuku Thief* (*Shinjuku*

Dorobō Nikki, 1969), a film for which Yokoo not only designed the poster, but that also features him as one of the main actors.[37] The film explicitly links sexual liberation with political revolution. As Ōshima explained in an interview with Joan Mellen, the sexual inadequacies of the two lead characters Birdey Hilltop (Yokoo) and Umeko (Rie Yokoyama) are political inadequacies; sex and politics cannot be separated.[38] Given that Birdy Hilltop was based on Yokoo's real persona, the film further demonstrates Yokoo's belief that there is a connection between revolution and consciousness expansion – in this case, as a form of sexual liberation.[39] A similar line of reasoning can be identified in a flip book animation that Yokoo produced for Shūji Terayama's experimental novel *Throw Away Your Books, Rally in the Streets* (*Sho o Suteyo Machi e Deyō*, 1967). The kineograph begins with a countdown from sixty-nine to zero, prompting the pushing of a button which is revealed to be a woman's breast. This sets off three explosions, blowing the world into tiny pieces. END. Reading the work literally, a sexual act sets off a transformation of the world. This anarchic animation uses humour to demonstrate the power of the sexual impulse.

While *KISS KISS KISS* is not as explicit as these two works, it puts into action Yokoo's political philosophy. In the film, Yokoo extracts the kiss from its original context within a romantic narrative, sexualising the act; it becomes, literally, a gesture of sexual liberation. Its revolutionary potential is not linked to an overtly political act, but rather to an everyday gesture, a passionate demonstration of affection. The animation eschews an overt political message, but instead magnifies an act of intimacy.

Illustrated Stories of Cannibalism for Children

Yokoo's animation *Kachi Kachi Yama Meoto no Sujimichi* is arguably the most complex of his animated works. Like *KISS KISS KISS* and *Anthology No. 1*, the film is an example of remediation; however, it is also an adaptation or, more precisely, a re-adaptation of an adaptation. The animation is based on a graphic story by Yokoo and poet Mutsuo Takahashi, which originally appeared in a 1964 anthology titled *Nihon Minwa Gurafikku* (*Japanese Folktale Graphics*, 日本民話グラフィック*), which paired graphic artists with writers to re-imagine Japanese folktales.[40] Yokoo and Takahashi collaborated on an adaptation of *Kachi Kachi Yama* (*Crackling Mountain* or *Click-Click Mountain*, かちかち山), one of the best-known Japanese folktales.[41] Both the graphic story and the animation make use of a Pop graphic aesthetic and blend Japanese and Western iconography.[42]

Kachi Kachi Yama is a violent tale of torture and revenge that involves an old farmer and his wife, a mischievous shape-shifting *tanuki* (a Japanese raccoon dog that is often mistakenly translated as a badger or raccoon) and a rabbit. A succinct summary of the story appears in the *Nippon Bungaku Daijiten* (*Standard Dictionary of Japanese Literature*, 日本古典文学大辞典):

> An old man traps a bad badger [the raccoon dog or *tanuki*] in the mountain, brings it home and hangs it from the ceiling, tying its legs together. After he has gone to work again, the captive badger persuades the wife to untie the rope. When freed, the badger kills her and makes soup of her. He disguises himself as the wife, and when the old man comes home, serves him the soup calling it badger soup. The badger taunts the old man that he has eaten his own wife, then flees.
>
> A rabbit comes along while the old man is crying and promises to seek revenge for him. The rabbit by deception makes the badger carry firewood on his back, and from behind strikes a flint, 'click-click', to set fire to the firewood. The badger questions the sound, and the rabbit says that there is such a noise here because the place is the Click-Click Mountain. A similar explanation is given to the sound of burning wood on his back, before he realises that he is afire.
>
> Red-pepper plaster is applied as an ointment to the burns by the rabbit. When the burns have finally healed, the rabbit invites the badger for boating. Riding a wooden boat himself, the rabbit provides the badger with a boat of mud, which dissolves in the water and drowns the badger.[43]

Granted, this is only one version of the tale, and many variations exist; however, this version contains all of the core elements of the story and provides an explanation of the title.

Notably, the folktale is educationally ambiguous and does not contain an obvious moral, but instead uses violence and torture for entertainment value. Scholar Lucrezia Morellato observes that '*Kachi Kachi Yama*, on the surface, presents a violation-punishment structure featuring a violent retaliation to justify a vendetta, which seems the ideological end of the story'. Although the violence in the story seems directed towards a moralistic end, she continues, the 'violence stops being an accessory to the narration and becomes its protagonist in an excessive, festive way for a gruesomely comic effect'.[44] While many Japanese folktales make use of violent retaliation, they usually incorporate an educational component. As Morellato suggests, 'the bulk of the most popular Japanese folktales conforms to this description by overtly celebrating values such as obedience, perseverance and loyalty with no shortage of violent retaliation, punishment and reward plots and prohibition-violation-punishment schemes'.[45]

To read Yokoo's adaptations of *Kachi Kachi Yama* requires an intertextual approach that references the original folktale and several pop culture sources. In the graphic story and animation, Alain Delon plays the *tanuki* and is lovers with Brigitte Bardot, both sex symbols of 1960s French cinema. Delon attained international success for his role in René Clément's *Plein soleil* (*Purple Noon*, 1960), a film in which Delon plays Tom Ripley, a character who assumes another person's identity, similar to the shape-shifting abilities of the *tanuki* in the folktale. At the time, it was also commonly assumed that Alain Delon and Brigitte Bardot were real-life lovers after the two had met and become close friends on the set of Michel Boisrond's anthology film *Les Amours célèbres* (*Famous Love Affairs*, 1961). To further confirm that Delon is the *tanuki*, in the graphic story he is shown with his back on fire after returning home to Bardot, an image that is missing from the animation.

The old couple in the graphic story and animation is played by Richard Burton and Elizabeth Taylor. In 1961, during the production of Joseph L. Mankiewicz's *Cleopatra* (1963), Burton and Taylor had begun a scandalous affair, both being married to other people at the time. The affair was well publicised and transformed from rumour into fact when a paparazzi shot of the couple embracing emerged. It is the Beatles and Bardot that perform the role of the rabbit in Yokoo's adaptations. They team up with the grief-stricken Burton in order to exact revenge upon Delon for the murder of Taylor. In the animation, Marilyn Monroe is also listed in the credits along with these other previously mentioned pop culture icons; however, she only appears for a few seconds on a billboard advertising Coca-Cola and does not appear in the graphic story at all. As such, her 'cameo' is an example of 'false advertising'.

The folktale, the graphic story and the animation follow similar structures but also have a few key differences. To begin with, all are stories of revenge. Following the folktale, Delon murders Taylor in an attempt to steal her money, which is consistent with some versions of the folktale where the *tanuki* is caught stealing from the farmer. In the animated version, after Taylor is murdered, Burton *needs somebody* and screams *"Help!"* Of course, *not just anybody* shows up – it is the Beatles to the rescue. In both the animated version and the graphic story, the Beatles, with tears in their eyes and dressed as priests, sing a poem at Taylor's funeral (Figure 5.3). In the animation, after the funeral and a brief commercial break advertising beer, we witness Burton sucking on Taylor's toes: the cannibalism of the folktale is replaced by podophilia.

In a slightly perplexing scene, Delon, shown with the body of a skeleton, appears to Bardot. In the text of the graphic story, it is hinted that Bardot

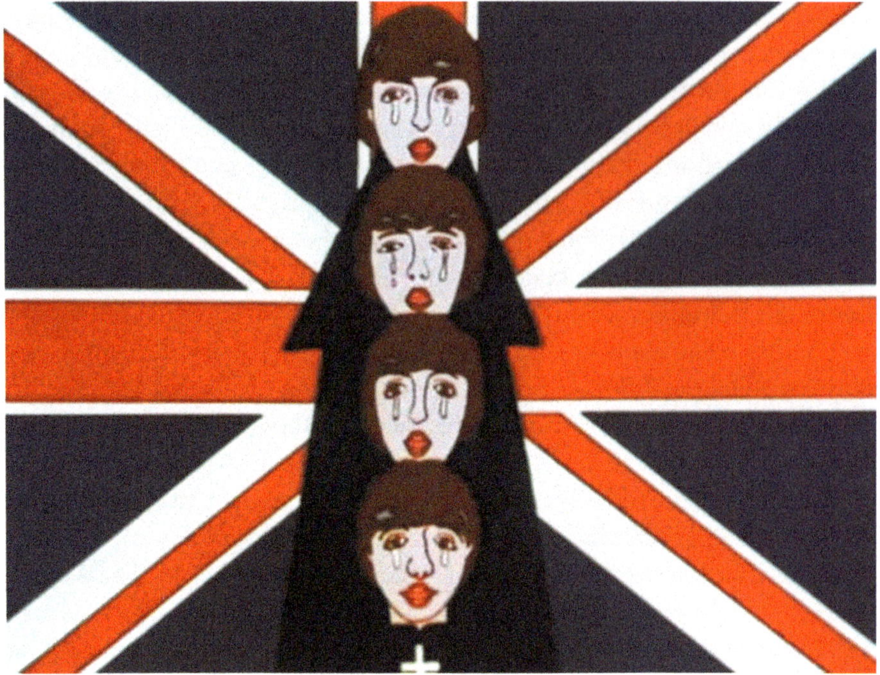

Figure 5.3 *Kachi Kachi Yama Meoto no Sujimichi* (Tadanori Yokoo, 1965).

will help Burton avenge the death of Taylor, re-affirming that she, along with the Beatles, performs the role of the rabbit. As in the folktale, she will betray Delon, participating in Burton's revenge. In the animated version, Burton and the Beatles, each in their own fighter jet flying in military formation, engage in a dogfight with Delon and Bardot's plane, which is shot down with the couple narrowly escaping in parachutes. Later, the Beatles and Burton, now in a submarine, track down Delon and Bardot who are shown necking on an inflatable pool mattress in the middle of the ocean. The couple are blown up by three torpedoes, but again somehow manage to escape. In both the graphic story and the animation, Delon and Bardot escape from Burton and the Beatles by riding on a Shinkansen bullet train ascending Mount Fuji. The animation ends with Delon crying, in distress, and unable to embrace Bardot, with the sound of a woman laughing as a funeral note, with '家' ('Home') written on it, blows in front of the Rising Sun. From the graphic story, we can assume it is Bardot who has the last laugh as money rains on her from Mount Fuji.[46]

In his autobiography, Yokoo claims that in his adaptation of *Kachi Kachi Yama* he was imitating the work of Ingmar Bergman and John Ford.[47] Bergman's influence can be seen in the dialogue, which is filled with bleak, poetic expressions of existential angst, philosophical profundities and fearsome visions of spiritual unrest, with Buddhism replacing Christianity. In addition, the graphic story and animation both begin with Bergmanesque symbolism – namely, Taylor holding an hourglass and Burton holding a scythe. Ford's influence can be seen where Delon and Bardot are shown riding on horseback between two mesas (which have the text 'かちかち山' ['Kachi Kachi Mountain'] and 'ぼうぼう山' ['Bōbō Mountain'] rising out of them).[48] In the animation, they are being chased by a posse consisting of Burton and the Beatles riding horses; everyone is wearing a cowboy hat.

Both adaptations also contain a playful beer advertisement. The beer's label reads 'USAGI' ('Rabbit') and depicts Bardot wearing only bunny ears and stockings (Figure 5.4). The bottle cap blends the Asahi trademark with the Playboy motif: a Rising Sun with a bunny head in the middle. In the graphic story the bunny declares:

> Many sins in this world
> are horrifying
> What can be more horrible than
> to eat an aging woman?
> It is sinful to devour
> the one you shared a bed with
> Know that a heart filled with hate
> ends in hell like so[49]

In other words, the bunny explicitly makes a connection between the graphic story and the folktale and expresses Burton's emotional state. In his autobiography, Yokoo explains that while working at Nippon Design Centre he saw Asahi's 'Nami ni asahi' ('Rising Sun and Waves') trademark almost every day and that this was the inspiration for the Rising Sun in his work.[50] It was also in 1964 that the Asahi Steiny mini bottle with the Rising Sun on its bottle cap was launched. Before the advertisement appears in the animation, a Buddhist sutra appears on the screen: '色即是空　空是即色' ('Form is empty, emptiness is form').[51] Zen in an era of consumer capitalism.

The graphic story, in many ways, can be seen as the birth of some of Yokoo's visual motifs. In an interview, Yokoo stated that 'it wasn't until I was 28 or 29 [1964–65], after I became freelance, that I really developed my own voice',[52] and *Kachi Kachi Yama* visually marked a transition point in Yokoo's work. Both of Yokoo's adaptations contain the Rising Sun, Mount Fuji and a speeding Shinkasen train. Christopher Mount explains the significance of these images while discussing *Made in Japan*:

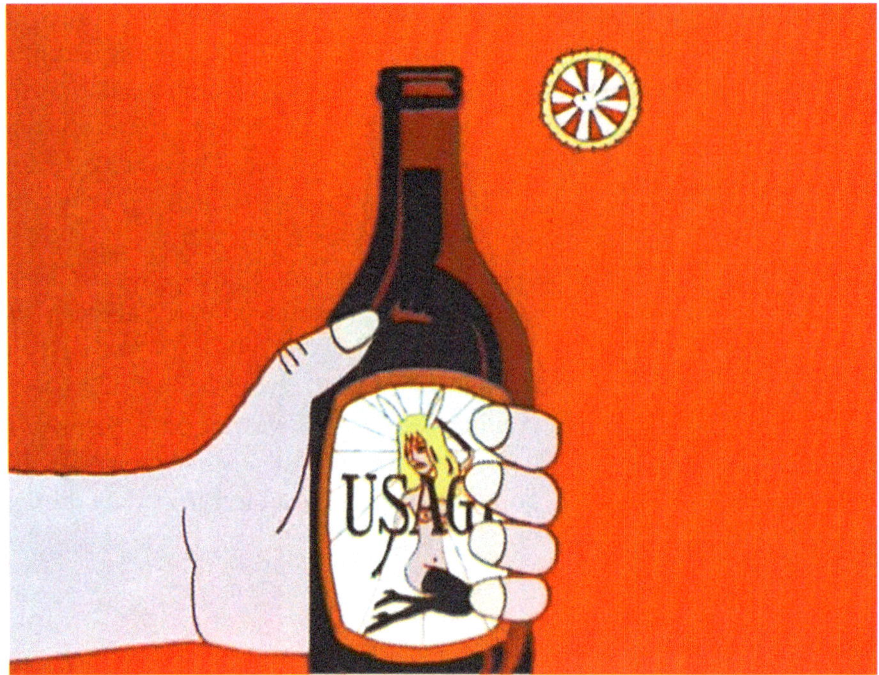

Figure 5.4 *Kachi Kachi Yama Meoto no Sujimichi* (Tadanori Yokoo, 1965).

> The train represented postwar Japan's rapid and ultimately problematic development, which some felt had destroyed the country's nobler traditional culture. Mount Fuji stood for that old world, and the rising sun symbolized the militaristic folly that led to Japan's modern condition.[53]

The complexity of Yokoo's work stems from the way in which it juxtaposes traditional and contemporary Japanese culture, as well as the way in which it blends Western and Japanese iconography. Yokoo's use of nationalistic imagery is just as complicated. He explains:

> I was specifically bringing in fascist or wartime imagery wrapped in the ambivalence and criticism and support of what it meant to me in my lifetime. [Yukio] Mishima, on the other hand, specifically would not allow those symbols in his work. He liked my work and appreciated that I could bring in ambivalence [...] He told me, 'I criticize these things by not including them, but you criticize them by ambivalently including them'.[54]

Yokoo and Mishima were both responding to the anxieties experienced under the conditions of post-war Japan. Despite explicitly engaging with these symbols, Yokoo is less politically extreme than Mishima. Yokoo claims to treat this imagery with ambivalence in order to undercut its power; however, it is precisely due to this ambivalence that these images can also be read as a form of nationalistic pride, adding an additional layer of complexity to his work.

The ability to *criticise culture ambivalently* is precisely one of the strategies employed by Pop artists. However, this has also been one of the critiques leveraged against Pop art – namely, that this ambivalence leads to an ambiguity as to whether the work is complicit with or criticising consumer culture. The ambivalent juxtaposition of American and Japanese iconography was also a strategy employed by other Tokyo Pop artists of the era, seen for instance in the work of Tiger (Kōichi) Tateishi, Keiichi Tanaami and Hiroshi Nakamura. The effect was two-fold: it was both a way of countering post-war American cultural imperialism through asserting Japanese culture and a way of demonstrating the impact that American culture had on the Japanese cultural landscape. As Ikegami has argued, 'the products of Tokyo Pop can be seen, collectively, as a commentary not only on the colonizing effect of U.S. art and culture, but also on the "internal America" embraced by the Japanese'.[55] In 1969, Yokoo literally expressed this sentiment in a cover of *Shūkan Anpo* (*Anpo Weekly*), which featured a Pop-style illustration of Prime Minister Eisaku Satō, with his name printed over the image with the letters 'U', 'S' and 'A' highlighted in red.

The soundtrack for *Kachi Kachi Yama* was composed by Toshi Ichiyanagi and comprises sound effects, musique concrète, classical music, traditional Japanese folk music and Buddhist chanting.[56] Like the film itself, the sound design is idiosyncratic while still directly responding to the action on screen. For example, there is the sound of a crowd cheering when Delon steals the money from Taylor, and the film ends with a woman laughing feverishly. The Buddhist chanting was done by Takahashi and is repeated throughout the animation. The lyrics come directly from the opening of the graphic story, where Elizabeth Taylor, holding an hourglass, states:

> This is not of this world
> An old story from the past
> Delusional but horrifying, the story of infinite hell
> may frighten the young mind
> but best to tell it with good intentions
> As the old saying goes
> spare the rod and spoil the child[57]

This self-reflexive statement seemingly addresses the horrific nature of the violence and torture in the original folktale while also suggesting that the tale can lead to personal development. While the graphic story alludes throughout to the teachings of Buddha, the animation is more in line with the original folktale in its use of violence for entertainment value.

Radical Approaches to Conflict Resolution

Kachi Kachi Yama was made before the Beatles' animated television show (1965–67), before the Beatles would record *Yellow Submarine* at Abbey Road Studios, and three years before George Dunning would direct the animated film *Yellow Submarine* (1968). Stylistically, *Yellow Submarine* and *Kachi Kachi Yama* share similarities; in particular, both make use of limited animation, explore a style of psychedelic Pop art, and involve the Beatles manning a submarine. The Beatles are the 'heroes' in *Kachi Kachi Yama*, but a type of hero very different from the one portrayed in *Yellow Submarine*, where they defeat the Blue Meanies by performing some 'transformation magic' and by singing 'All You Need is Love'. In *Kachi Kachi Yama*, the Beatles are heroes for hire who fire nuclear missiles from a submarine, a representation very different from the likeable, silly lads of *A Hard Day's Night* (Richard Lester, 1964) or the peace-loving hippies of *Yellow Submarine*.

Kachi Kachi Yama asserts the revolutionary potential of popular culture through the use of the Beatles by representing them as heroes willing to hunt down villains who commit murder for personal profit. In a 1969 essay, Yokoo argued 'that if revolution were going to come in the 60s, it would be via a pop group like the Beatles'.[58] The radical potential of the Beatles was unleashed with John Lennon and Yoko Ono's peace campaign (1969–70). This consisted of two bed-ins for peace, one in Amsterdam and one in Montréal, and an ad campaign that consisted of billboards reading 'WAR IS OVER! If You Want It – Happy Christmas from John and Yoko', which was intended to appear in Amsterdam, Athens, London, Los Angeles, Montréal, New York, Paris, Rome, Toronto, West Berlin and Tokyo. However, the 'WAR IS OVER!' billboard that was slated for Tokyo did not make it; rather, Yokoo was hired to make a variation of the poster in order to advertise a 'Christmas Party for Love and Peace' in the city.[59]

The peace campaign employed a commercial marketing strategy, with Lennon leveraging his celebrity status as a member of the Beatles to claim the attention of the press. As Ono explained in an interview with *Penthouse* magazine, 'many other people who are rich are using their money for something they want. They promote soap, use advertising propaganda, what have you. [...] We're using our money to advertise our ideas so that peace has equal power with the meanies who spend their money to promote war'.[60] Lennon and Ono were using the commercial marketing system to promote counter-cultural ideology. As Ono explained to a reporter, 'instead of becoming violent about it and saying "Stop the War" or something, with violence, it's better to say: it's spring, stay in bed'.[61] Similar to Yokoo, Ono argued not for delivering political messages through abrasive tactics, but in favour of a transformation of consciousness, revolution through the everyday gesture. Of course, many in the press expected scandalous photo ops and salacious copy, assuming that the couple would be doing more than just lying in bed, given that the first bed-in was on their honeymoon. However, the celebrity couple was serious about talking peace. Moreover, there was a gesture of inaction, as opposed to action, designed to lead to peace. As Lennon infamously declared, if everyone stayed in bed for a week, all wars would end.

Although the cartoon violence in Yokoo's *Kachi Kachi Yama* may go against the non-violent stance of the peace campaign, the film portrayed the Beatles as more than just pop stars. Even though the revolution did not materialise, the Beatles and Yokoo left an undeniable impact. Since reaching his climax at the age of twenty-nine, Yokoo has been pursuing his own personal visions inspired by psychedelic and Pop art. He designed records such as Santana's *Amigos* (1976) and Haruomi Hosono's *Cochin Moon* (1978), books such as Eikoh Hosoe's *Barakei* (*Ordeal of Roses*, 1971) and David LaChapelle's *LaChapelle Land* (1996), as well as thousands of posters. In the early 1980s, Yokoo moved further away from commercial graphic design and began to pursue painting.[62] By examining his early animations, it is possible to trace the origins of the visual motifs and political beliefs that ultimately made him one of Japan's most renowned and influential artists.

Notes

1 Quoted in Donald Richie, 'Japan Shattered Stereotypes in the 60s', *The Japan Times*, 9 October 2000, https://www.japantimes.co.jp/culture/2000/10/09/books/japan-shattered-stereotypes-in-the-60s/.

2 For a discussion of proto-Pop in the context of Japanese art, see Reiko Tomii, 'Oiran Goes Pop: Contemporary Japanese Artists Reinventing Icons', in Jessica Morgan and Flavia Frigeri (eds), *The World Goes Pop*, New Haven: Yale University Press, 2015, pp. 95–103.

3 Mishima, quoted in ibid., p. 103.

4 *Anthology No. 1* is also known as *Tokuten eizō* which has been translated as *Privileged Images. Kachi Kachi Yama Meoto no Sujimichi* has been translated as *Creaking Mountain, The Couples' Precepts* and *Hermetic Prison – A Couple's Home Education*. See Maria Roberta Novielli, *Floating Worlds: A Short History of Japanese Animation*, Boca Raton:

CRC Press, Taylor & Francis Group, 2018, p. 51; Doryun Chong (ed.), *Tokyo, 1955–1970: A New Avant-Garde*, New York: The Museum of Modern Art, 2012, p. 212.

5 Christopher Mount, 'Japan's Greatest Avant-Garde Artist', in Masahiro Yasugi (ed.), *The Complete Posters: Tadanori Yokoo*, Japan: Kokushokankokai, 2010, p. 448.

6 Hiroko Ikegami, '"Drink More?" "No Thanks!": The Spirit of Tokyo Pop', in Darsie Alexander and Bartholomew Ryan (eds), *International Pop*, Minneapolis: Walker Art Center, 2015, p. 174.

7 Ibid. Original text in Japanese.

8 Steven C. Ridgely, 'Total Immersion: Steven Ridgely on the Design of Tadanori Yokoo', *ArtForum*, 51:6 (February 2013), p. 207.

9 Ibid., pp. 207–8.

10 Quoted in Mount, 'Japan's Greatest Avant-Garde Artist', op. cit., p. 448.

11 For example, some of the elements from Yokoo's 1963 poster *Kyoto Ro-on Concerts, Series B, No. 33* (J. Fujio & T. Watanabe and Habana Cuban Boys) are re-configured and put into motion. Details from the actual poster are also shown in the film.

12 Yuriko Furuhata, 'Animating Copies: Japanese Graphic Design, the Xerox Machine, and Walter Benjamin', in Karen Redrobe Beckman (ed.), *Animating Film Theory*, Durham: Duke University Press, 2014, p. 184.

13 Ibid., p. 185.

14 Ibid.

15 Gekidan Mingei (The People's Art Theatre) was formed in 1950 by Jūkichi Uno. *Under the Magnolia Tree* is a play by Yushi Koyama.

16 'As with *Tadanori Yokoo* [*Made in Japan*], these works [in his 1968 book *Isakushu* (*Posthumous Works*)] represented a form of rebirth for me'. Yokoo quoted in Ashley Rawlings, 'Dark was the Night', *Art and AsiaPacific*, 74 (2011), p. 104.

17 The kiss sound is a segment of the Dean Martin song recorded in reverse. Ikegami, '"Drink More?" "No Thanks!"', op. cit., p. 362.

18 Tadanori Yokoo, *Haran E!! Yokoo Tadanori Jiden*, Tokyo: Bunshun Bunko, 1998, p. 85.

19 Ikegami, '"Drink More?" "No Thanks!"', op. cit., p. 174.

20 John Coplans, *Roy Lichtenstein*, New York: Praeger, 1972, p. 52.

21 For instance, see Dorthy Seiberling, 'Is He the Worst Artist in the U.S.?', *Life*, 56:5 (31 January 1965), pp. 79–83; Doug McClellan, 'Roy Lichtenstein, Ferus Gallery', *Artforum*, 2:1 (July 1963), pp. 44–47; Michael Lobel, *Image Duplicator: Roy Lichtenstein and the Emergence of Pop Art*, New Haven: Yale University Press, 2003. The critics Brian O'Doherty and Erle Loran found it absurd that others were defending Lichtenstein by stating that he 'transformed' rather than copied his sources since this went against the Pop spirit and artistic appropriation which already had a long-standing history within the arts. See David Deitcher, 'Unsentimental Education: The Professionalization of the Artist', in Graham Bader (ed.), *Roy Lichtenstein (October Files #7)*, Cambridge, MA: MIT Press, 2008, pp. 73–102.

22 Yokoo, quoted in Furuhata, 'Animating Copies', op. cit., pp. 184–85. Translation by Furuhata.

23 John Canaday, 'Pop Art Sells On and On – Why?' *New York Times Magazine* (31 May 1964), pp. 7, 48, 52–53. For more on the re-commodification of Lichtenstein's appropriation style, see Cécile Whiting, 'Borrowed Spots: The Gendering of Comic Books, Lichtenstein's Paintings, and Dishwasher Detergent', *American Art*, 6:2 (1992), pp. 9–35.

24 For more on how Pop art migrated through different spheres, see Thomas Crow, 'The Absconded Subject of Pop', *RES: Anthropology and Aesthetics*, 55/56 (Spring-Autumn 2009), pp. 5–16.

25 Charles Musser, *The Emergence of Cinema: The American Screen to 1907*, New York: Scribner, 1990, p. 118.

26 'The Vitascope at Keith's', *Boston Herald* (19 May 1896), p. 9. Quoted in Charles Musser, 'The May Irwin Kiss: Performance and the Beginnings of Cinema', in Vanessa Toulmin and Simon Popple (eds), *Visual Delights Two: Exhibition and Reception*, London: John Libbey, 2005, p. 103.

27 John Sloan, 'Notes', *The Chap-book*, 5:5 (15 July 1896), p. 240. Emphasis in the original. The remarks are unsigned and have often been attributed to the editor Herbert Stone; however, they were actually written by the painter John Sloan. See Linda Williams, *Screening Sex*, Durham: Duke University Press, 2008, p. 331.

28 Williams, *Screening Sex*, op. cit., p. 26.

29 Stephen Koch, *Stargazer: Andy Warhol's World and His Films*, New York: Praeger, 1973, p. 36.

30 For more information about *Kiss* including cast, crew and a reel-by-reel breakdown, see Bruce Jenkins, 'Kiss', in John G. Hanhardt (ed.), *The Films of Andy Warhol Catalogue Raisonné, 1963–1965*, New Haven: Yale University Press, 2021, pp. 67–77.

31 J. J. Murphy, *The Black Hole of the Camera: The Films of Andy Warhol*, Berkeley: University of California Press, 2012, pp. 23–24.

32 'Their smiles and glances and expressive gestures and the final joyous, over-powering, luscious osculation was repeated again and again, while the audience fairly shrieked and howled approval'. *Los Angeles Times* (7 July 1896), p. 6. Quoted in Musser, 'The May Irwin Kiss', op. cit., p. 104.

33 Norman Hathaway and Dan Nadel, *Electrical Banana: Masters of Psychedelic Art*, Bologna: Damiani, 2011, p. 176.

34 Andy Warhol, 'Andy Warhol Interviewed by K. H.', in Mark Francis and Margery King (eds), *The Warhol Look: Glamour Style Fashion*, Pittsburgh: Bullfinch Press and the Andy Warhol Museum, 1997, p. 273.

35 Takayo Iida, 'An Interview with Tadanori Yokoo', in Sophie Perceval (ed.), *Tadanori Yokoo*, Paris: Fondation Cartier pour l'art contemporain, 2006, p. 120.

36 Ridgely, 'Total Immersion', op. cit., p. 206.

37 On a side note, in 1967 Ōshima directed *Band of Ninja* (*Ninja Bugei-chō*), a film that took the remediation style of *KISS KISS KISS* to its logical conclusion. The film brought Sanpei Shirato's popular manga to life by shooting the original illustrations (complete with speech bubbles and onomatopoeia) and adding a soundtrack with music, sound effects and voice.

38 Joan Mellen, *Voices from the Japanese Cinema*, New York: Liveright, 1975, p. 271.

39 Iida, 'An Interview with Tadanori Yokoo', op. cit., p. 121. Yokoo explains: '[Ōshima] was the king of improvisation [...] it was through those untimely improvisations that the actors' real personalities emerged and took on more depth'.

40 Tadahito Nadamoto et al., *Nihon Minwa Gurafikku*, Japan: Bijutsu Shuppansha, 1964. The title of the graphic story is 'Kachikachiyama'. Pairings included: Tadahito Nadamoto / Toshiyuki Takirai, Kazumasa Nagai / Yusuke Kaji, Akira Uno / Yusuke Kaji, Ikko Tanaka / Hiroshi Sakagami and Tadanori Yokoo / Mutsuo Takahashi.

41 Kachi Kachi is onomatopoeia for the sound made when using flint to light a fire.

42 For a discussion of *manga* (Japanese comics or graphic novels) as proto-Pop and its relationship to Pop art, see Ryan Holmberg, 'When Manga was Pop', *Art in America* (January 2016), pp. 56–63.

43 Hiroko Ikeda, '"Kachi-Kachi Mountain" – An Animal Tale Cycle', in Wayland D. Hand, Archer Taylor and Gustave O. Arlt (eds), *Humaniora: Essays in Literature, Folklore, Bibliography Honoring Archer Taylor on His Seventieth Birthday*, Locust Valley: J. J. Augustin, 1960, p. 230. Lighting the badger on fire is a version of *kugatachi*, a trial in which the innocence of a person is judged by the divine will. In other words, if the badger were innocent, it would not burn.

44 Lucrezia Morellato, 'Symbolic Violence in Contemporary Japanese Children's Literature: Case Study of a Japanese Folktale in Its Twenty-First Century Picture Books Renditions', unpubl. Master's thesis, Lund University, 2016, p. 23.

45 Ibid., p. 24.

46 The funeral note also appears in the graphic story behind Delon who is sitting with Bardot on the bullet train, which features the rising sun in its window. Funeral notes usually have the name of the deceased in the middle; however, these ones do not, making them ominous and foreboding.

47 Yokoo, *Haran E!!*, op. cit., p. 87.

48 Bōbō is onomatopoeia for the sound made when something is vigorously burning.

49 Translation by Aya Aikawa.

50 Yokoo, *Haran E!!*, op. cit., p. 88.

51 This is a well-known Buddhist sutra.

52 Hathaway and Nadel, *Electrical Banana*, op. cit., p. 177.

53 Mount, 'Japan's Greatest Avant-Garde Artist', op. cit., p. 448.

54 Hathaway and Nadel, *Electrical Banana*, op. cit., p. 177.

55 Ikegami, '"Drink More?" "No Thanks!"', op. cit., pp. 176, 180.

56 In 1969, Toshi Ichiyanagi would again collaborate with Yokoo on *Opera 'From the Works of Tadanori Yokoo'*, a two-LP picture disc set, which sonically blended musique con-crète, Brechtian folk songs, field recordings and heavy psych rock. The set was designed by Yokoo and came with a four-page booklet containing twenty-four of his posters.

57 Translation by Aya Aikawa. Translation note: It is written 'infinite hell', but this can be seen as wordplay on 'Avici hell' since they are pronounced the same.

58 Ridgely, 'Total Immersion', op. cit., p. 204. Ridgely adds that 'they already had a global following, so the sleeper-cell structure was already in place'.

59 For a well-researched account of the organising of the Tokyo component of the peace campaign, see Kevin Concannon, 'War Is Over! John and Yoko's Christmas Eve Happening, Tokyo, 1969', *Review of Japanese Culture and Society*, 17 (December 2005), pp. 72–85.

60 Charles Childs, 'Penthouse Interview: John and Yoko Lennon', *Penthouse*, 1:4 (October 1969), pp. 29, 34.

61 John Lennon and Yoko Ono being interviewed by Niek Heizenberg for NCRV televi-sion ('Hier en Nu' programme), filmed on 25 March 1969.

62 Rawlings, 'Dark was the Night', op. cit., p. 104.

6

Some Like It Pop: Replication and Repetition in Bruce Conner's *MARILYN TIMES FIVE* (1968–73)

Justin Remes

'I need say nothing. Only show'. – Walter Benjamin[1]

Ceci n'est pas Marilyn

Kevin Hatch: '[Bruce Conner's *MARILYN TIMES FIVE*, 1968–73] grew from fragments of a one-reel silent nudie loop [called *The Apple-Knockers and the Coke*, 1948] starring Arline Hunter, a Marilyn Monroe look-alike. (Hunter was often erroneously reputed to be Monroe, an assumption Conner appears to have made as well at the time he was working on the film). In the original stag film, "Marilyn" strips and performs topless, with an apple and Coke bottle as props; in Conner's version, segments of her seductive movements are interleaved with varying lengths of black leader' (Figures 6.1 and 6.2).[2]

'Arline Hunter [was not] Marilyn [...] [She was] "Marilyn"'.[3]

Louis Pelletier: 'The source material for *MARILYN TIMES FIVE* is a nudie film [...] featuring the very same model seen lounging in the U-boat captain's sight in [Bruce Conner's] *A MOVIE* [1958], Arline Hunter (b. 1931). Variously titled *Intrigue* or *The Apple-Knockers and the Coke*, the film was long alleged to feature a pre-fame Marilyn Monroe. Indeed, Conner himself appears to have been convinced that the film featured the actual Marilyn Monroe during the five years he spent (intermittently, one hopes) working on the film, as well as at the time of the first public screenings of the film in 1973'.[4]

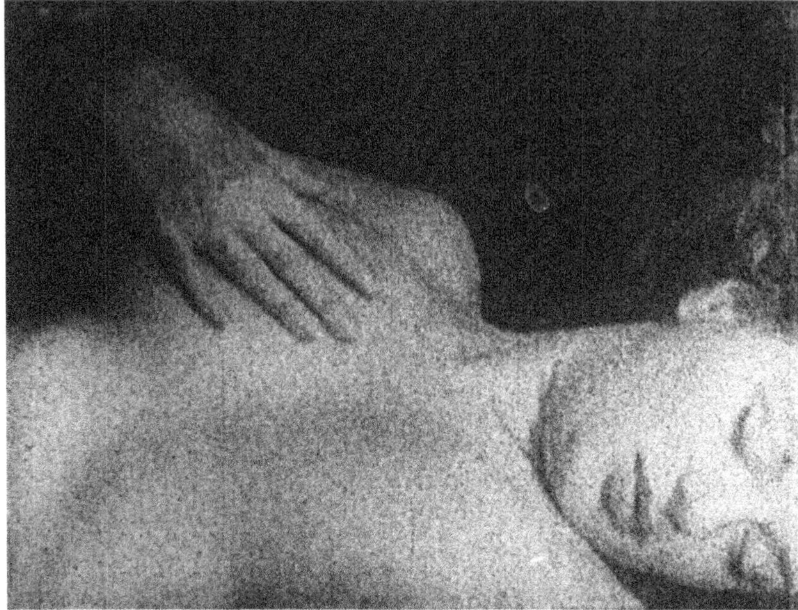

Figure 6.1 Marilyn look-alike Arline Hunter caresses her right breast in Bruce Conner's *MARILYN TIMES FIVE* (1968–73). Source: © Conner Family Trust, Courtesy of the Conner Family Trust.

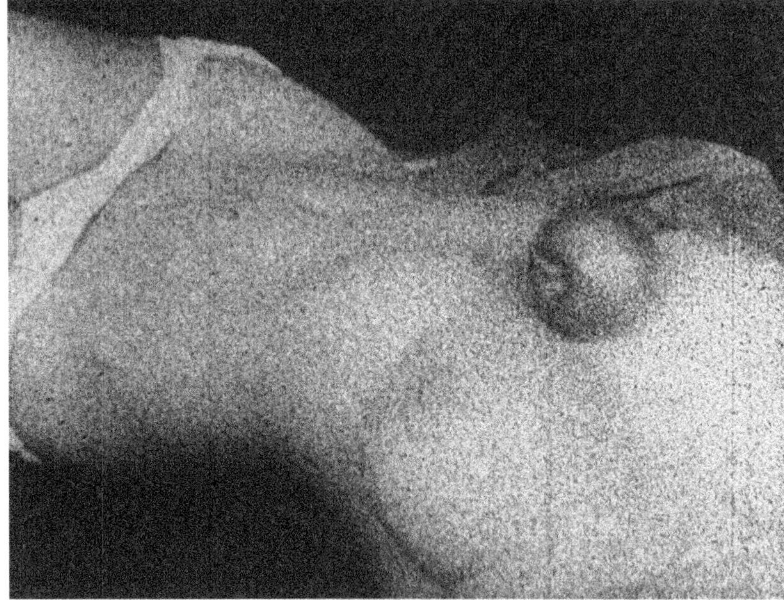

Figure 6.2 Arline Hunter rolls an apple down her body in *MARILYN TIMES FIVE* (1968–73). Source: © Conner Family Trust, Courtesy of the Conner Family Trust.

William C. Wees: '[*The Apple-Knockers and the Coke*] was distributed with an opening title, "High Quality Films Presents Marilyn Monroe"'.[5]

Bruce Conner: '[Norman] Mailer has speculated that this may not be Marilyn because the breasts are so large, but I have written him a long letter arguing that she is real'.[6]

Correction: '[T]his [is] not [...] Marilyn'.[7]

Harry M. Geduld and Ronald Gottesman: 'Marilyn Monroe's *Apple Knockers and the Coke* [...] was a skin flick in which she appeared in the nude playing suggestively with apples and a Coke bottle'.[8]

Correction: '[*The*] *Apple*[-]*Knockers and the Coke* [...] was a skin flick in which [Arline Hunter] appeared in the nude playing suggestively with apples and a Coke bottle'.[9]

Michael O'Pray: 'Marilyn Monroe appears briefly in Conner's first film, *A MOVIE*, as the target, espied through a submarine periscope, of a phallic torpedo attack. Posing cheese-cake style in a two-piece swim-suit, her resulting sexual encounter with the torpedo is expressed by the image of an atomic-bomb explosion. When she reappears in *MARILYN TIMES FIVE*, she has been dead for ten years and the mood is very different'.[10]

Correction: '[*Arline Hunter*] appears briefly in [...] *A MOVIE* [and] reappears in *MARILYN TIMES FIVE*'.[11]

Michael Shedlin: 'Nicholas Ray declared at a showing of the film in Berkeley that the image was indeed *not* Marilyn. Conner, however, seems certain. Perhaps new experts with inside information will step forward'.[12]

'Nicholas Ray [was correct:] the image was indeed *not* Marilyn'.[13]

Scarlett Higgins: 'Arline Hunter appeared as "Playmate of the Month" in the August 1954 issue of *Playboy* magazine, posing in a fashion that was clearly meant to recall Monroe's pose from 1949'.[14]

'Arline Hunter [...] was [a] pose[r]'.[15]

Holly Willis: 'That the woman may not be Monroe haunts the film in fascinating ways. Does it matter who the woman is? What value is gained in the film, and in our viewing, if it is Monroe? And what is lost if it isn't?'[16]

Scarlett Higgins: 'Does it matter whether or not this is the "real" Monroe in the images? From an economic standpoint, the original film, as a commodity, would have been worth a great deal more money if it had been Marilyn Monroe and not Arline Hunter in the images, or even if its intended audience simply believed that it was. The images of Hunter in the film constantly invoke her status as a shoddy "copy" of Monroe.'[17]

'[F]ilm[s,] [...] commodit[ies,] [...] money [...] and [...] images [require] belie[f].'[18]

Scott MacDonald: 'By the way, is that really Marilyn Monroe in *MARILYN TIMES FIVE*?'
Bruce Conner: 'Well, I understand that it may not be. I tell people that while it may or may not have been Marilyn Monroe in the original footage, it's her now. Part of what the film is about is the roles people play, and I think it fits either way. It's her image and persona.'[19]

Bruce Conner: 'I couldn't tell if it was Marilyn Monroe or not, but I realized that sooner or later [*The Apple-Knockers and the Coke*] would be exploited as a Marilyn Monroe film.'[20]

Ed Halter: '[O]ne of the earliest star-attributed films to circulate widely was a nameless one-reel nudie loop purporting to depict a young Marilyn Monroe, who would have shot it around 1948, prior to her posing nude for the inaugural issue of *Playboy*. In the film, a lone young woman does a striptease, rolls an apple across her chest, and then sips a soda. Later dubbed *The Apple*[-]*Knockers and the Coke*, it was distributed to colleges and cinemas in the early 70s by Grove Films, packaged in a collection of vintage erotic shorts and experimental works like Carolee Schneemann's *Fuses* [1967]. Today, it's recognized that *Apple*[-]*Knockers* and several other so-called Monroe porn films depict another early *Playboy* model named Arline Hunter.'[21]

'[*MARILYN TIMES FIVE*] [f]uses [...] Monroe [and] Hunter.'[22]

Bruce Conner: 'I try to make separate things become one.'[23]

Joan Rothfuss: 'I AM BRUCE CONNER button[s] [were] conceived and produced by Conner in 1964 for [a] proposed Bruce Conner Convention [which would have been attended by other individuals named Bruce Conner]. […] I AM NOT BRUCE CONNER button[s] [were also] conceived and produced by Conner in 1964 for [the] proposed Bruce Conner Convention.'[24]

'I AM BRUCE CONNER. […] I AM NOT BRUCE CONNER.'[25]

'I AM [MARILYN]. […] I AM NOT [MARILYN].'[26]

Jonas Mekas: 'Is MM playing herself or creating a part?'[27]

Andy Warhol: 'I […] see Monroe as just another person.'[28]

'Monroe [*is*] another person.'[29]

Akira Mizuta Lippit: 'Found-footage works […] undermine the originality of the original.'[30]

Joan Rothfuss: 'According to Conner, one of his (unsigned) collages had once been "positively" identified by a "prominent art historian" as a work by Max Ernst. Did calling Conner's collage "an Ernst" momentarily increase its value or significance?'[31]

'Did calling [Arline Hunter] [Marilyn] momentarily increase [her] value or significance?'[32]

Joan Rothfuss: 'In 1964 […] Conner […] asked [his friend Henry Moss] to substitute for him […] at a lecture and film screening in Worcester, Massachusetts. […] Moss […] said that although he drew suspicious scrutiny at first because of his jeans and sneakers, no one in the audience questioned his identity. In fact, Conner relates that as soon as Moss identified himself as Bruce Conner, "a glorious transformation took place. They listened seriously to everything he had to say". Conner had engineered a fine demonstration of the power of his name, and its detachment from any real aspect of his ego.'[33]

'[A]s soon as [Conner] identified [Arline] as [Marilyn], "a glorious transformation took place".'[34]

'Conner had engineered a fine demonstration of the power of [Marilyn's] name.'[35]

Michel Foucault: 'A little like the anonymous hand that designated the pipe by the statement, "This is not a pipe", Magritte names his paintings in order to focus attention upon the very act of naming.'[36]

'[Conner] names his [film *MARILYN TIMES FIVE*] in order to focus attention upon the very act of naming.'[37]

Scarlett Higgins: '[T]his "fake" copy of Monroe is a copy made *before* she was "Monroe". Hunter in *MARILYN TIMES FIVE* becomes a copy of a copy of what is imagined, popularly, as an "original", Norma Jean Baker, whose nude photos graced the first issue of *Playboy* magazine.'[38]

'[…a] copy of […] a copy [of] a copy of a copy […]'[39]

Kevin Hatch: 'For [*MARILYN TIMES FIVE's*] soundtrack, Conner used "I'm Thru with Love", the signature song from Monroe's movie *Some Like It Hot* [Billy Wilder, 1959], played in its entirety five times over.'[40]

Scarlett Higgins: 'Jack Lemon [*sic*] and Tony Curtis's characters impersonate women badly […] in [*Some Like It Hot*], but Monroe's performance is just as much of an impersonation, a fantasy of female availability taken to laughable extremes. The film seems to propose on the one hand that gender is malleable and a type of performance and on the other hand that the romance between Curtis's and Monroe's characters can only be possible when they shed their respective drags (for Curtis's character, both of his drags – as a woman and as a millionaire) and show their "true" selves.'[41]

Louis Pelletier: 'By bringing the materiality of his chosen medium to the foreground, Conner somehow succeeds in separating the media image from the pre-existing reality, which is to say that in dissolving "Marilyn Monroe" the icon, he manages to expose "Marilyn Monroe", the human being. His use of leader and repetition puncture the illusion and create brief moments of intimacy with the performer. All of this while the fantasized Marilyn still hovers on the soundtrack, and with a performer who is not Marilyn Monroe at all.'[42]

'[*MARILYN TIMES FIVE* is about] image[s,] […] icon[s,] […] illusion[s] and […] fantasi[es].'[43]

William C. Wees: 'Recycled images call attention to themselves as images'.[44]

Laura Mulvey: 'As Marilyn became an ultimate signifier of sexuality – from her pinups, to her early ultrasexualized cameos, to her superstardom in the mid 1950s – she was always more image than character; she personified a "to-be-looked-at-ness" in which interiority would be, by and large, irrelevant. This was, of course, due to her highly evolved masquerade, stylized gestures, and performance. In semiotic terms her signification floated, referring not to any Hollywood impersonation of reality but to a series of signifiers that could themselves shift, as flexibly as sexual fantasy itself'.[45]

'Marilyn […] was […] more image than […] reality'.[46]

'Marilyn […] was […] a […] fantasy'.[47]

Marilyn Monroe: 'That's the trouble, a sex symbol becomes a thing. I just hate to be a thing'.[48]

Feminism and Misogyny

Bruce Conner: 'I am […] a feminist [and] a profound misogynist'.[49]

Marc Selwyn: 'Do you consider yourself a feminist?'
Bruce Conner: 'I don't think that's a term I could reasonably put to myself. First of all, if those women who have talked to me about [*MARILYN TIMES FIVE*] call themselves feminist, how could I possibly define myself as a feminist? If I have a feminist stance, it's that I find it unbelievable how difficult it was for women who have quality in their work to be of any importance in the art world'.[50]

Sean Buffington: 'Women artists associated with Pop Art [have been] banished from its mythology and even written out of its formal history'.[51]

Bruce Conner: 'People have reacted to [*MARILYN TIMES FIVE*] with the greatest range of responses. I've had people who identified themselves as feminists say that this was a funny film. I've had several women tell me how tragic it is. I've had women attack me for my sexism and say that I have murdered Marilyn Monroe'.[52]

Sally Banes: 'The bevies of pinup girls in Bruce Conner's films and collages […] are typical emblems of feminine helplessness, wiliness, and sexiness, only made more gigantic. Reproducing the iconography of mainstream culture, these transferences of female images leave gender codes intact'.[53]

Amy Taubin: 'In my brief period of scorched-earth feminism (around 1978) […] I had no patience […] with *MARILYN TIMES FIVE*, which now seems to me not only one of Conner's greatest films but also among the most witty and poignant of so-called structural films'.[54]

Kevin Hatch: '[Jonas] Mekas and others in the experimental film world praised [*MARILYN TIMES FIVE*], and Freude Bartlett, the Bay Area pioneer in feminist film criticism, was a particularly strong supporter. But for others – particularly many critics who self-identified as feminist – the film's lack of a clear political statement was troubling'.[55]

'[Must a] film [make] a clear political statement[?]'[56]

Kevin Hatch: 'In 1985, Conner noted he had not been able to show *MARILYN* for years because the screening would devolve into a political forum while the film itself would not be discussed, nor even really watched'.[57]

Kevin Hatch: '[*MARILYN TIMES FIVE*] earnestly endeavors to deconstruct the popular culture objectification of woman'.[58]

Holly Willis: 'Throughout the five segments, Conner by turns eroticises the woman's body with a caressing eye, twists it into uncomfortable poses with zesty humour, and ultimately suggests that the body's objectification is deeply troubling, all through the careful cutting and rearranging of shots'.[59]

'Conner […] objectifi[es]'.[60]

'Conner […] suggests that […] objectification is deeply troubling'.[61]

William C. Wees: 'Looped again and again, Monroe's inept gestures are almost graceful, yet their mechanical repetition undercuts their playfulness and naïve simulation of erotic pleasure. They become increasingly artificial and anti-erotic. Despite its stag movie and pin-up girl clichés, the film reneges on its initial invitation to the voyeur. Instead of a closer, more intimate view of a woman's body, the repetition of shots and the extreme graininess of the film increasingly draw attention to the body of the film itself, to the film's own image-ness'.[62]

'[*MARILYN TIMES FIVE* is] erotic [...] and anti-erotic'.[63]

Kevin Hatch: 'The film is erotically charged [...] Yet it undercuts its eroticism'.[64]

Rebecca Solnit: 'Conner saw the footage as conveying tremendous loneliness – a solitary female meant to be watched by lonely males, the antithesis of genuine lovemaking'.[65]

Scarlett Higgins: 'Conner is unable (or unwilling) to erase fully the eroticism of the original film, or unwilling to strip it of aesthetic beauty'.[66]

'[Should] Conner [...] erase [...] eroticism[?]'[67]

Joan Rothfuss: '[T]he history of postwar America might be read as the gradual proliferation of images, especially, it seems, images of the human visage. We all like looking at each other'.[68]

'We all like looking'.[69]

Take Five

1. Scarlett Higgins: '[*MARILYN TIMES FIVE*] begins in silence, with three repeated shots of Hunter moving her hand up to her hair while on her back, and bending sideways at the waist. The music begins on the fourth such shot. There is a fifth repetition, then break to black leader'.[70]

'[*MARILYN TIMES FIVE*] begins [...] with [*five*] repetition[s]'.[71]

2. Malcolm Turvey: 'Monroe's recording of "I'm Thru with Love", featured in the film *Some Like It Hot* (1959) in which she starred, is repeated *five* times back-to-back on the soundtrack'.[72]

3. Holly Willis: '[*MARILYN TIMES FIVE* has] *five* sections'.[73]

4. Kevin Hatch: 'The editing of *MARILYN TIMES FIVE* consumed *five* working years'.[74]

5. Marcel Duchamp: '[W]hen you do a thing, you don't do it in five minutes or in five hours, but in five years. I think there's an element in the slowness of the execution that adds to the possibility of producing something that will be durable in its expression, that will be considered important five centuries later'.[75]

Givers of Gifts: Conner and Duchamp

Arturo Schwarz: 'There is no doubt that Duchamp formulated the most radical aesthetic conception of our time. With him, something changed forever. Just as human history is ordered in B.C. and A.D., art history has to be reckoned with in terms of "Before Duchamp" and "After Duchamp"'.[76]

'Before Duchamp [objects are made]. After Duchamp [objects are found]'.[77]

'Before Duchamp [footage is shot]. After Duchamp [footage is found]'.[78]

Tom Gunning: 'Many found footage films have been at least partly inspired by Duchamp's ready-mades'.[79]

Joan Rothfuss: 'Conner had long admired [Marcel Duchamp]'.[80]

Elizabeth Armstrong: 'What questions come to mind when you think of Duchamp?'
Bruce Conner: 'The very idea of questioning'.
[...]
Elizabeth Armstrong: 'Do you think that one needs to have great knowledge to understand Duchamp?'
Bruce Conner: 'No. The question is whether you *can* understand Duchamp'.[81]

Bruce Conner: 'I would save sequences of images that I didn't know what reason I wanted to save them for, or what they might represent, except they were fascinating to me. Many times when making [...] films, I have not been able to consciously understand what they are communicating'.[82]

'[The question is whether you *can*] understand [Conner]'.[83]

Warren Bass: 'Bruce Conner told me a story about the first piece of film he had ever owned. As a teenager, he was at a friend's house and discovered his friend had a collection of "girlie" movies in a chest-of-drawers. Each film was only one shot, maybe ten feet long. Conner's friend gave him one of the films. It consisted of a side view of an almost totally naked lady removing stockings. Years later, Conner and Larry Jordan were running a film society called Camera Obscura in San Francisco. Conner fixated on the idea of splicing his single shot stag film unannounced into the film society's showing of [Leni Riefenstahl's] *Triumph of the Will* [1935].

Before Conner was able to do it, Jordan found out and was appalled. This would have been Conner's debut into filmmaking, an impish, dadaist prank of Duchampian stature, an ultimate contextual disjuncture that would have hardly been appreciated by its unsuspecting 1950s audience! Within a year [...] Conner did make his first film, *A MOVIE* (1958), and this same single-shot stag film is the first human image to appear in it after a build-up created by a purposely pompous title sequence (reminiscent of *Triumph of the Will?*) and some false endings'.[84]

'Bruce Conner [...] was [...] Duchampian'.[85]

Joan Rothfuss: 'By 1961, when the twenty-eight-year-old Conner was included with Duchamp in the Museum of Modern Art's landmark exhibition, *The Art of Assemblage*, he might have discovered a number of correspondences between their practices (an interest in humour and wordplay, the employment of alter egos, the exploration of many media)'.[86]

Bruce Conner: 'But before I went [to Duchamp's 1963 lecture at Brandeis University], I took a case, like a glass case that I had gotten in Mexico [...] there were just like a few pearls stuck in it [...] and [...] I had a rubber stamp made from [my] signature [...]. Then I put it in this little case [...]. And so I put a candle on top of it and it burned for a while and it sort of dribbled around. Then I had it sitting on top of a radiator and that winter the radiator got real hot and the candle went over the edge of it, sort of like a limp six-inch prick [...]. And it was like right over the opening of the box so you really couldn't open it without breaking the candle [...]. And then [...] I picked up a ball of string [and wrapped it around the box]. I remember once [Duchamp] had organized a surrealist exhibit where he had run string all over the place'.[87]

'[Duchamp] really couldn't open [Conner's gift]'.[88]

Bruce Conner: 'Then they had question-and-answer, and at one time one person said to Marcel Duchamp, "Mr. Duchamp, don't you think it's time that you *confessed*?" And he said, "Confessed *what*?" "Well, confessed what you've been *doing* all this time with all of these *things* that you make, and what you've been doing putting 'em in art museums and calling 'em ART". And Marcel Duchamp explained *exactly* what he was doing, which I've never heard anybody quote [...]. [H]e said, **"I never called this 'art'. I never put it in art museums". And, "They were all gifts. I never realized any money from them; they were gifts of love to my friends".** [...] Nobody talks about these things being gifts'.[89]

'[Bruce Conner and] Marcel Duchamp [are givers of] gifts'.[90]

'[Bruce Conner and] Marcel Duchamp [are] gift[ed]'.[91]

Bruce Conner: 'I wondered what it was that I was doing there with that box, and I realized that I had wanted to give the box to Marcel Duchamp. But, I also understood that I could not give this to him because it was too much of an imposition to give it to him directly as a gift, which would have a burdensome character to it [...]. [After the lecture] I carried the box with me and held it in front of me and I asked, "Would you take this box and give it to [art collector] Mr. Charles Alan?" [...]. He said, "*I WILL!*"'[92]

Joan Rothfuss: 'The box was eventually donated to the Guggenheim Museum under the title THE MARCEL DUCHAMP TRAVELLING BOX'.[93]

V. Vale: '[F]or the twentieth century, the three most *original* artists were Marcel Duchamp, Andy Warhol, and Bruce Conner'.[94]

'[In] the twentieth century, the three [artists who questioned the very idea of] original[ity] [...] were Marcel Duchamp, Andy Warhol, and Bruce Conner'.[95]

A Coke is a Coke: Conner, Warhol and Repetition

James Peterson: 'Besides Warhol there is, of course, another avant-garde filmmaker who is consistently associated with Pop Art and images appropriated from popular culture: Bruce Conner'.[96]

Bruce Conner: 'Warhol was very up on advertising imagery and how to confront people to get the kind of response that he wanted. He would study a particular aspect of what already existed in the art world and do a distillation of it'.[97]

'Warhol [and Conner] confront[ed] people [with] what already existed'.[98]

Bruce Conner: '[A]nything which was taken for granted as not serious, not art, just things that are thrown away, were exactly what I paid attention to. By the 60s this attitude was codified into a structure called Pop Art – as if it was a big new discovery. But all that Pop Art did was to follow philosophical premises that have been around for a long time: if you want to know what's going on in a culture, look at what everybody takes for granted'.[99]

'Pop Art [...] look[s] at what everybody takes for granted'.[100]

'[*MARILYN TIMES FIVE*] look[s] at what everybody takes for granted'.[101]

Malcolm Turvey: '[Conner's films] take images of familiar, even iconic events and people, banalized by frequent repetition in the mass media, and endeavor to make us see their subjects anew [...] [They] aspire to reawaken in us an appreciation of the extraordinary, even bizarre quality of commonplace images'.[102]

Joan Rothfuss: 'Conner was interested in multiplicity rather than wholeness'.[103]

Camille Paglia: 'This multiplicity of meanings is caught by Warhol's chance variations in inking and printing: none of the fifty faces [in Warhol's *Marilyn Diptych*, 1962] are exactly alike'.[104]

Vilis R. Inde: 'Warhol began to paint images as if they were rolling off a printing press: *200 Campbell's Soup Cans* [1962], *210 Coca-Cola Bottles* [1962], *Marilyn x 100* [1962]'.[105]

William C. Wees: 'In Conner's film [...] Monroe (or her look-alike) [...] coyly drinks from a bottle of Coke until some of its contents spill out on her face and breasts' (Figure 6.3).[106]

Scarlett Higgins: 'The hourglass shape of the Coke bottle mirrors Hunter's (and Monroe's) physical form'.[107]

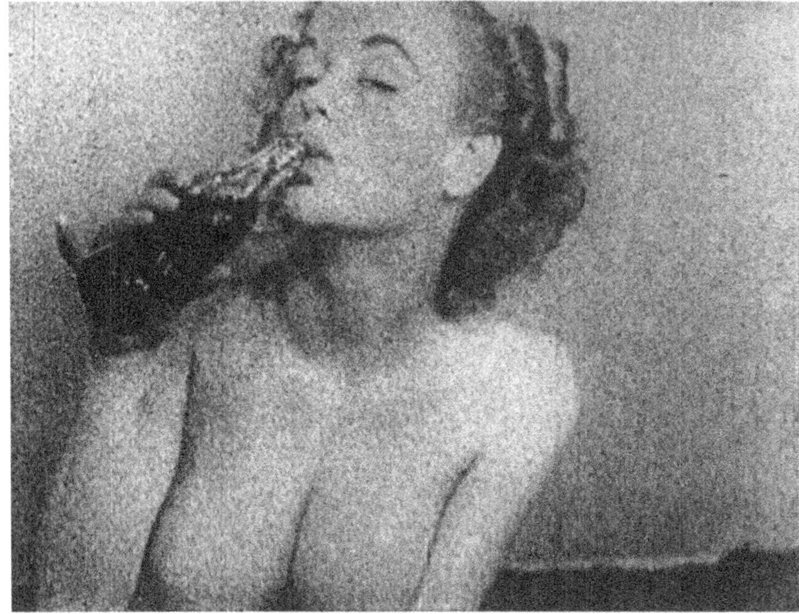

Figure 6.3 Arline Hunter drinks Coke in *MARILYN TIMES FIVE* (1968–73). Source: © Conner Family Trust, Courtesy of the Conner Family Trust.

Ted Ryan: 'The Coke bottle has been called [...] the "Mae West" bottle after the actress's famous curvaceous figure'.[108]

Gertrude Stein: 'Rub her coke'.[109]

Excerpt from a 1953 Advertisement for Coca-Cola:
Man's Voice: 'Coke time!'
Voices of Women Singing: 'There's nothing like a Coca-Cola, nothing like a Coke!'
Jack Paar: 'What do you say we have dinner together?'
Marilyn Monroe (in a bikini and holding a bottle of Coke): 'Wonderful! Where?'
Jack Paar: 'Oh, someplace where we don't have to dress, like [*pause*] your apartment'.
Man's Voice: 'Coke time is anytime, anywhere. It's always time for ice-cold Coca-Cola!' (Figure 6.4).[110]

Interviewer: 'What does Coca-Cola mean to you?'
Andy Warhol: 'Pop'.[111]

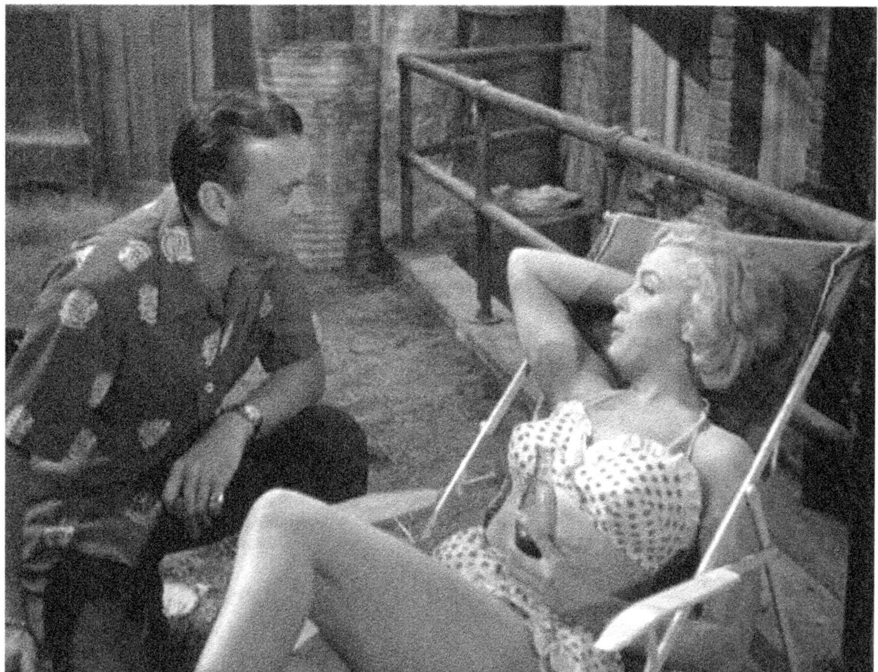

Figure 6.4 Marilyn Monroe drinks a Coke in *Love Nest* (Joseph Newman, 1951), footage that was later used in a 1953 advertisement for Coca-Cola.

Andy Warhol: 'What's great about this country is that America started the tradition where the richest consumers buy essentially the same things as the poorest. You can be watching TV and see Coca-Cola, and you can know that the President drinks Coke, Liz Taylor drinks Coke, and just think, you can drink Coke, too. A Coke is a Coke and no amount of money can get you a better Coke than the one the bum on the corner is drinking. All the Cokes are the same and all the Cokes are good. Liz Taylor knows it, the President knows it, the bum knows it, and you know it'.[112]

> 'You can be watching TV and see Coca-Cola, and you can know that [Marilyn Monroe] drinks Coke, [Arline Hunter] drinks Coke, and just think, you can drink Coke, too'.[113]

> '[A] Coke [is a] Coke [is a] Coke is a Coke'.[114]

2019 Super Bowl Ad for Coke: 'A Coke is a Coke is a Coke'.[115]

Marcel Duchamp: '[W]ords are taken and repeated, and after a certain number of repetitions the word takes on an aura of mysticism, of magic [...].

[L]ike the idea of repeating, "Coca-Cola, Cola-Cola [*sic*]". After a while magic appears around Coca-Cola'.[116]

> '[Images] are taken and repeated, and after a certain number of repetitions the [image] takes on an aura of mysticism, of magic'.[117]

Jaimie Baron: 'Techniques of repetition [...] defamiliarize bodily actions and speech acts that might otherwise appear natural'.[118]

> '[R]epetition [is] [un]natural'.[119]

Andy Warhol: 'I started repeating the same image because I liked the way the repetition changed the same image'.[120]

Joseph D. Ketner II: 'Warhol [...] creat[ed] literally thousands of paintings and prints of Marilyn'.[121]

Andy Warhol: 'The more you look at the same exact thing, the more the meaning goes away, and the better and emptier you feel'.[122]

Bruce Jenkins: 'By the end of [*MARILYN TIMES FIVE*], ["Marilyn"] is emptied of meaning'.[123]

Michel Foucault: 'A day will come when [...] the image itself, along with the name it bears, will lose its identity. Campbell, Campbell, Campbell, Campbell'.[124]

> 'A day will come when [...] the image itself, along with the name it bears, will lose its identity. [Marilyn], [Marilyn], [Marilyn], [Marilyn]'.[125]

Malcolm Turvey: '[T]he rhythmical repetition of a human facial expression or movement can rob it of psychological depth and turn the human body into a plastic object, much as the repetition of a word drains it of meaning and transforms it into pure sound'.[126]

> 'Repetition [...] drains [...] meaning'.[127]
> 'Repetition [...] drains [...] meaning'.[128]
> 'Repetition [...] drains [...] meaning'.[129]
> 'Repetition [...] drains [...] meaning'.[130]
> 'Repetition [...] drains [...] meaning'.[131]

Stan Brakhage: 'Repetition [...] is among the characteristic marks of Conner's films. Yet, he proves that there is no such thing as repetition, in the sense that Gertrude Stein made clear in her book *Making of Americans*. She demonstrates that when you "repeat" a thing, you charge it with another level of energy; so that if you vary it, however slightly, it is dynamic. It is much more dramatic if you repeat an image and make slight variations'.[132]

Gertrude Stein: 'I am inclined to believe there is no such thing as repetition'.[133]

Michael O'Pray: 'Conner's device of repeating a body movement, and with each repetition lengthening the shot so that finally we are given the full movement, not only emphasises the voyeuristic "moment", the freezing of the erotic in a sadistic captivity, but also attempts the impossible – that is, giving us so much that the eroticism finally leaks from the image, leaving it drained'.[134]

Laura Mulvey: '[T]he closeup "Marilyns" that Andy Warhol silk-screened as a tribute to her after her death in August 1962, are easily projected backwards on to Marilyn's own closeup, fossilizing the emblematic Marilyn with connotations of death'.[135]

'[T]he [...] "Marilyns" [of] Warhol [...] connot[e] [...] death'.[136]

Michael Shedlin: 'The last image of [*MARILYN TIMES FIVE*] is a quick clip of Marilyn [*sic*] sprawled face down on the floor, motionless. It seems calculated to convey a feeling of death' (Figure 6.5).[137]

Marilyn Monroe: 'There was something special about me, and I knew what it was. I was the kind of girl they found dead in a hall bedroom with an empty bottle of sleeping pills in her hand'.[138]

Bruce Conner: '[Marilyn Monroe] was an icon. I was aware of it while she was alive, not after she was dead. She had created an image she couldn't control and it didn't belong to her. Ultimately, it destroyed her'.[139]

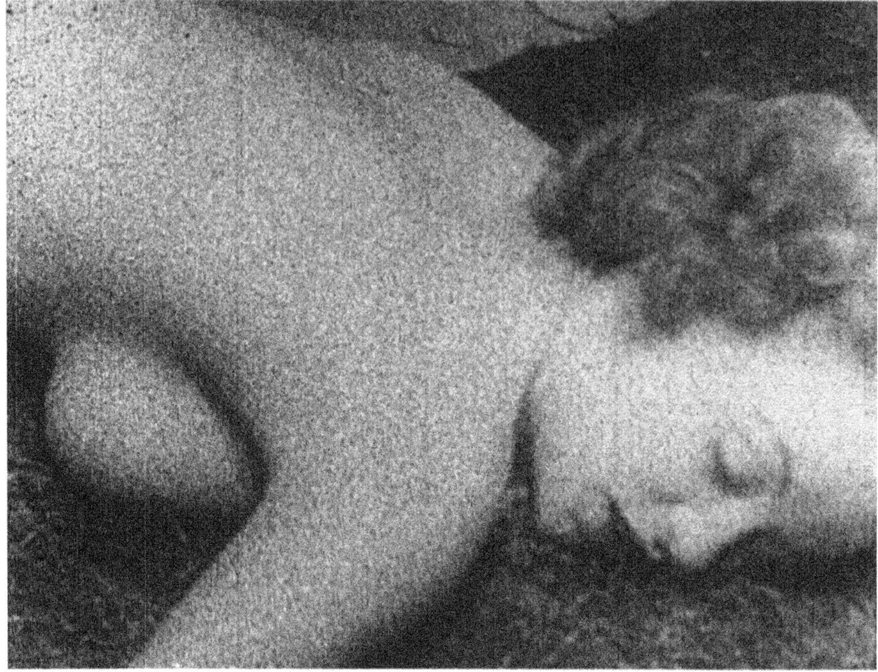

Figure 6.5 Arline Hunter's pose evokes Marilyn Monroe's death in *MARILYN TIMES FIVE* (1968–73). Source: © Conner Family Trust, Courtesy of the Conner Family Trust.

Notes

1 Walter Benjamin, 'Theoretics of Knowledge; Theory of Progress', *The Philosophical Forum*, 15:1–2 (Fall/Winter 1983–84), p. 5.
2 Kevin Hatch, *Looking for Bruce Conner*, Cambridge, MA: MIT Press, 2012, pp. 176–77.
3 Ibid.
4 Louis Pelletier, 'Hidden in Plain Sight: Castle Compilations and Nudie Films as Lost Intertexts for Bruce Conner's *A MOVIE* and *MARILYN TIMES FIVE*', *Found Footage Magazine*, 5 (March 2019), p. 59.
5 William C. Wees, 'The Ambiguous Aura of Hollywood Stars in Avant-Garde Found-Footage Films', *Cinema Journal*, 41:2 (2002), p. 12.
6 Quoted in Michael Shedlin, 'Marilyn', *Film Quarterly*, 27:3 (Spring 1974), p. 47.
7 Ibid.
8 Harry M. Geduld and Ronald Gottesman, *An Illustrated Glossary of Film Terms*, New York: Holt, Rinehart, and Winston, 1973, p. 82.
9 Ibid.
10 Michael O'Pray, '*Marilyn Times Five*', *Film Bulletin*, October 1987, p. 317.
11 Ibid.
12 Shedlin, op. cit., p. 47. Italics in original.
13 Ibid.

14 Scarlett Higgins, *Collage and Literature: The Persistence of Vision*, New York: Routledge, 2019, p. 164.

15 Ibid.

16 Holly Willis, 'Marilyn Times Five', *Senses of Cinema*, 50 (March 2009), http://sensesof cinema.com/2009/cteq/marilyn-times-five/.

17 Higgins, op. cit., pp. 153–54.

18 Ibid.

19 Scott MacDonald, 'Bruce Conner', in *A Critical Cinema: Interviews with Independent Filmmakers*, Berkeley: University of California Press, 1988, p. 253.

20 Marc Selwyn, 'Bruce Conner: Marilyn and the Spaghetti Theory', *Flash Art*, 156:1 (January/February 1991), p. 96.

21 Ed Halter, 'Secrets and Thighs', *The Village Voice*, 3–9 December 2003, p. 44.

22 Ibid. Italics removed.

23 MacDonald, op. cit., p. 249.

24 Joan Rothfuss, 'Escape Artist', in Peter Bosell, Bruce Jenkins and Joan Rothfuss (eds), *2000 BC: The Bruce Conner Story Part II*, exh. cat., Minneapolis: Walker Art Center, 2000, pp. 161, 167. Capitalisation in original.

25 Ibid.

26 Ibid.

27 Jonas Mekas, 'Marilyn Monroe and the Loveless World', in Gregory Smulewicz-Zucker (ed.), *Movie Journal: The Rise of the New American Cinema, 1959–71*, New York: Columbia University Press, 2016, 2nd ed., p. 32.

28 Gretchen Berg, 'Andy Warhol: My True Story', in Kenneth Goldsmith (ed.), *I'll Be Your Mirror: The Selected Andy Warhol Interviews*, New York: Carroll and Graf, 2004, p. 88.

29 Ibid.

30 Akira Mizuta Lippit, *Ex-Cinema: From a Theory of Experimental Film and Video*, Berkeley: University of California Press, 2012, p. 158.

31 Rothfuss, op. cit., p. 163.

32 Ibid.

33 Ibid, p. 170.

34 Ibid.

35 Ibid.

36 Michel Foucault, *This Is Not a Pipe*, trans. and ed. James Harkness, Berkeley: University of California Press, 1983, p. 36.

37 Ibid.

38 Higgins, op. cit., p. 154. Italics in original.

39 Ibid.

40 Hatch, op. cit., pp. 176–77.

41 Higgins, op. cit., p. 154.

42 Pelletier, op. cit., p. 61.

43 Ibid.

44 William C. Wees, *Recycled Images: The Art and Politics of Found Footage Films*, New York: Anthology Film Archives, 1993, p. 32.

45 Laura Mulvey, 'Thoughts on Marilyn Monroe: Emblem and Allegory', *Screen*, 58:2 (Summer 2017), p. 207.

46 Ibid.

47 Ibid.

48 Richard Meryman, 'Marilyn Lets Her Hair Down About Being Famous', *Life*, 3 August 1962, p. 37.

49 Quoted in Rudolf Frieling and Gary Garrels (eds), *Bruce Conner: It's All True*, exh. cat., San Francisco: San Francisco Museum of Modern Art, 2016, p. 1.

50 Selwyn, op. cit., p. 97.

51 Sean Buffington, 'Foreword', in Sid Sachs and Kalliopi Minioudaki (eds), *Seductive Subversion: Women Pop Artists, 1958–1968*, New York: Abbeville Press Publishers, 2010, p. 11.

52 Selwyn, op. cit., p. 96.

53 Sally Banes, *Greenwich Village 1963: Avant-Garde Performance and the Effervescent Body*, Durham, NC: Duke University Press, 1993, p. 228.

54 Amy Taubin, 'Leaders of Men: Amy Taubin on Bruce Conner', *Artforum*, 10 November 2020, https://www.artforum.com/film/amy-taubin-on-bruce-conner-26797.

55 Hatch, op. cit., p. 179.

56 Ibid.

57 Ibid, p. 181.

58 Ibid, p. 177.

59 Willis, op. cit.

60 Ibid.

61 Ibid.

62 Wees, *Recycled Images*, op. cit., p. 11.

63 Ibid.

64 Hatch, op. cit., p. 177.

65 Rebecca Solnit, *Secret Exhibition: Six California Artists of the Cold War Era*, San Francisco: City Lights, 1990, pp. 121–22.

66 Higgins, op. cit., p. 158.

67 Ibid.

68 Rothfuss, op. cit., p. 164.

69 Ibid.

70 Higgins, op. cit., p. 149.

71 Ibid.

72 Malcolm Turvey, 'Bruce Conner and the Power of Repetition', in Ursula Blickle, Gerald Matt and Barbara Steffen (eds), *Bruce Conner: The 70s*, exh. cat., Vienna: Kunsthalle Wien, 2011, p. 70. Italics added.

73 Willis, op. cit. Italics added.

74 Hatch, op. cit., p. 176. Italics added.

75 Calvin Tomkins, *Marcel Duchamp: The Afternoon Interviews*, New York: Badlands, 2013, pp. 44–45.

76 Arturo Schwarz, *The Complete Works of Marcel Duchamp*, vol. 1, New York: Delano Greenidge Editions, 1997, p. 46.

77 Ibid.

78 Ibid.

79 Tom Gunning, 'Finding the Way: Films Found on a Scrap Heap', in Marente Bloemheuvel, Giovanna Fossati and Jaap Guldemond (eds), *Found Footage Exposed*, Amsterdam: Amsterdam University Press, 2012, p. 50.

80 Rothfuss, op. cit., p. 173.

81 Elizabeth Armstrong, 'Interview with Bruce Conner', *October*, 70 (Autumn 1994), p. 57. Italics in original.

82 Quoted in Wees, *Recycled Images*, op. cit., p. 83.

83 Ibid.

84 Warren Bass, 'The Past Restructured: Bruce Conner and Others', *Journal of the University Film Association*, 2 (Spring 1981), p. 15.

85 Ibid.

86 Rothfuss, op. cit., p. 174.

87 V. Vale, *Bruce Conner: The Afternoon Interviews*, San Francisco: Re/Search, 2016, pp. 60–61. According to Sarah Keller, 'Duchamp's piece, sometimes titled "Sixteen Miles of String" [1942], stretched string across the walls of [the *First Papers of Surrealism* exhibition at the Whitelaw Reid Mansion in Manhattan], attenuating the view of several works of Duchamp's contemporaries, and obstructing movement throughout the exhibition on the part of those who attended it'. See Sarah Keller, *Maya Deren: Incomplete Control*, New York: Columbia University Press, 2015, p. 64.

88 Vale, op. cit., p. 61.

89 Ibid, pp. 62–63. Italics, bold and capitalisation in original.

90 Ibid. Bold removed.

91 Ibid.

92 Quoted in Rothfuss, op. cit., p. 173. Italics and capitalisation in original.

93 Rothfuss, op. cit., p. 174.

94 Vale, op. cit., p. 125. Italics in original.

95 Ibid. Italics removed.

96 James Peterson, *Dreams of Chaos, Visions of Order: Understanding the American Avant-Garde Cinema*, Detroit: Wayne State University Press, 1994, p. 141.

97 Selwyn, op. cit., p. 95.

98 Ibid.

99 Quoted in Wees, *Recycled Images*, op. cit., p. 79.

100 Ibid.

101 Ibid.

102 Turvey, op. cit., p. 64.

103 Rothfuss, op. cit., p. 168.

104 Camille Paglia, *Glittering Images: A Journey Through Art from Egypt to* Star Wars, New York: Pantheon, 2012, p. 152.

105 Vilis R. Inde, *Art in the Courtroom*, Westport, CT: Praeger, 1998, p. 151.

106 Wees, 'The Ambiguous Aura of Hollywood Stars', op. cit., pp. 12–13.

107 Higgins, op. cit., p. 155.

108 Ted Ryan, 'The Story of the Coca-Cola Bottle', *Coca Cola Journey*, 26 February 2015, https://www.coca-colacompany.com/stories/the-story-of-the-coca-cola-bottle.

109 Gertrude Stein, 'Tender Buttons: Objects, Food', in Joan Retallack (ed.), *Gertrude Stein: Selections*, Berkeley: University of California Press, 2008, p. 142.

110 See 'Marilyn Monroe Coke Commercial 1953 Coca-Cola', *YouTube*, https://www.youtube.com/watch?v=d1HMGytwFCA. The exchange between Jack Paar and Marilyn Monroe originally appears in Joseph Newman's *Love Nest* (1951).

111 'Pop Art? Is It Art? A Revealing Interview with Andy Warhol', in Kenneth Goldsmith (ed.), op. cit., p. 5.

112 Andy Warhol, *The Philosophy of Andy Warhol (From A to B and Back Again)*, Orlando: Harvest, 1975, pp. 100–1.

113 Ibid.

114 Ibid. Cf. Gertrude Stein: 'A rose is a rose is a rose is a rose'. Gertrude Stein, 'An Elucidation', in Joan Retallack (ed.), op. cit., p. 186.

115 'A Coke is a Coke', *YouTube*, https://www.youtube.com/watch?v=6Hcrz4Jq9WE.

116 Tomkins, op. cit., pp. 61–62.

117 Ibid.

118 Jaimie Baron, '(In)appropriation: Productions of Laughter in Contemporary Found Footage Films', in David Laderman and Laurel Westrup (eds), *Sampling Media*, Oxford: Oxford University Press, 2014, p. 180.

119 Ibid.

120 Gerard Malanga, 'A Conversation with Andy Warhol', in Kenneth Goldsmith (ed.), op. cit., p. 193.

121 Joseph D. Ketner II, *Andy Warhol*, New York: Phaidon, 2013, p. 66.

122 Andy Warhol and Pat Hackett, *POPism: The Warhol Sixties*, San Diego: Harvest/HBJ, 1990, p. 64.

123 Bruce Jenkins, 'Explosion in a Film Factory: The Cinema of Bruce Conner', in Peter Bosell, Bruce Jenkins and Joan Rothfuss (eds), op. cit., p. 203.

124 Foucault, op. cit., p. 54.

125 Ibid.

126 Turvey, op. cit., p. 70.

127 Ibid.

128 Ibid.

129 Ibid.

130 Ibid.

131 Ibid.

132 Stan Brakhage, *Film at Wit's End: Eight Avant-Garde Filmmakers*, Kingston: Documentext, 1989, p. 135.

133 Gertrude Stein, 'Portraits and Repetition', in Gertrude Stein, *Writings: 1932–1946*, New York: Library of America, 1998, p. 288.

134 O'Pray, op. cit., p. 317.

135 Mulvey, op. cit., pp. 207–8.

136 Ibid.

137 Shedlin, op. cit., p. 47.

138 Marilyn Monroe with Ben Hecht, *My Story*, Lanham: Taylor Trade, 2007, p. 79.

139 Selwyn, op. cit., p. 96.

7

A Lost White Girl of Pop: Writing the Drive to Fantasise in *Daddy* (1973)

Kimberly Lamm

Writing Fantasies

Niki de Saint Phalle was a French American assemblage artist who moved easily across materials, genres, schools and influences. In 1973, with the British filmmaker Peter Whitehead, Saint Phalle made the underground film *Daddy*. 'Making films', she declared, 'enabled me to give free rein to my fantasies'.[1] Staging the symbolic murder of a white patriarchal father, *Daddy* reveals the incest and sexual abuse that ruptured Saint Phalle's childhood and reverberated disastrously into her adult life.[2] In a global media culture saturated with sex crimes and therapeutic discourse, revelations about rape, incest and sexual trauma are ubiquitous now, but *Daddy* shows just how shocking such revelations can be, whether in the present moment or in the 1970s.[3] Alissa Clarke describes the film as a 'sexually explicit surrealist pop-art Freudian rape revenge fantasy', which is not an exaggeration.[4] *Daddy* is a disturbing feminist horror flick that explores the symbolic burdens specific to the white woman's body in western culture and challenges the repression of her capacity to fantasise.

Daddy was originally intended to be a 'semi-documentary' about Saint Phalle's work as a sculptor, but became, as Whitehead put it, a 'crazy pseudo-fictional biopic' that delved into the psychic connections among the artist, her childhood and her artwork.[5] As Whitehead explains, *Daddy* 'continues [Saint Phalle's] work into the broader spectrum of the film medium'.[6] Well known for rock documentaries that foresee the music video – *Charlie is My Darling* (1966), *Tonite Let's All Make Love in London* (1967) and *Led Zeppelin: Live at the Royal Albert Hall* (1970), to name just a few – Whitehead was well-suited for this project. He was an emergent contributor to Pop cinema, and his immersive, fast-paced films, which blur and spin with his kaleidoscopic camera work, capture the sensuous release of the sexual revolution. By contrast, *Daddy* turns back in time to represent a dark and stubborn history of gender hierarchies and sexual dominance that haunted the period's ecstatic claims to sexual freedom. A feminist engagement with Pop cinema is part of this exposure.

By making the artwork of Saint Phalle one of *Daddy's* primary subjects, the film engages with a key feature of Pop cinema. *Daddy* creates what Tom Day calls a 'conversation' between film and art that highlights their inter-relations, without, I would argue, fully becoming its own form of Pop art.[7] An extension of the collaboration between Saint Phalle and Whitehead, the film's conversation with her artwork attests to her determination to create something from the sexual abuse to which she was subjected and to materi-alise her fantasies in an extended visual form. But by maintaining the distinc-tion between the artwork and the film, the directors attest to the difficulties that a woman artist faced in claiming film as a space for materialising her fan-tasies. In other words, *Daddy* does not absorb, but instead resists dominant understandings of gender upon which film so often relies.

The connections among film, art, sexuality and fantasy in *Daddy* aligns with the understanding of fantasy offered by psychoanalysts Jean Laplanche and Jean-Bertrand Pontalis. In their 1964 essay 'Fantasy and the Origins of Sexuality', they declare that '[f]antasy is not the object of desire, but its setting. In fantasy the subject does not pursue the object or its sign: he appears caught up himself in the sequence of images'.[8] It is hard to miss the connection between fantasy and cinema (a 'sequence of images'), but Laplanche and Pontalis also suggest passivity in the idea that our sexuali-ties are 'caught' by and constituted through images. This passivity is often displaced onto images of women as the premier objects of desire, and in *Daddy* Saint Phalle refuses that displacement and expresses an artist's drive to compose the mise-en-scène of fantasy.

Utilising images of women frozen in the visual grammar of gender sub-ordination, Pop art and cinema have contributed to the displacement of passivity on to women. Exemplified by Andy Warhol's silk screen portraits of Marilyn Monroe, Pop's images of white women are readymades from consumer culture that signal the artist's ability to master commodifica-tion. Look at the women in Richard Hamilton's mixed-media portrayals of domestic interiors: collaged into spaces crowded with consumer imagery, they are almost indistinguishable from the objects that surround them. And remember the women from comic strips and advertisements that Roy Lichtenstein makes the focus of his romance paintings: rehearsing clichéd scripts, drowning in melodramatic feelings, these figures occupy moments in visual culture's assembly-line production of gender. Lost in the superficialities of consumption, these images of women not only critique late capitalism's visual cultures, but they also buttress the notion that white women are capitalism's most permeable objects. Pop's work reinforcing this assumption creates significant challenges for women artists. Linda Nochlin insightfully identifies the dilemma: 'Comic-strip heroine, mass-produced portrait, flattened faceless nude – how could the woman artist find a position that didn't either objectify her or run roughshod over her own subjecthood?'[9]

Martha Rosler underscores Nochlin's point when she argues that the image of woman in Pop is a 'conquered' sign.[10] To explain what this vanquishing served, Rosler writes that '[Pop's] main tasks required a silencing of women that related to its ambiguous theatre of mastery through the transcoding and rearranging of magical images, many of them images of women.'[11] Full of Saint Phalle's own 'magical' imagery, *Daddy* makes the patriarchy's domestic theatre of silenced women its subject. It explores the sexual power and sadistic pleasure of objectifying women, 'run[ning] roughshod over' them (to borrow Nochlin's phrasing),[12] flattening their subjectivities, halting their drives, and, as Saint Phalle shows, capturing and negating their capacities to rearrange images – that is, to fantasise.

Like many women artists who entered Pop, Saint Phalle has an uncertain place within it. Her choice to draw so explicitly from her life story makes her connection to Pop unstable, as does the feminism of her oeuvre, which pulsates through every expressive detail. According to art historian Kalliopi Minioudaki, Pop 'became synonymous with women's exploitation in visual culture, rendering the female Pop artist into an oxymoron.'[13] And yet, Pop has feminist potential. Rosler often notes that, by focusing on everyday consumer imagery, it opened the possibility that feminist artists could make the domestic sphere their subject.[14] In a similar vein, Jennifer Doyle argues that the queer sexuality of Warhol's films allows women to 'be something other than the straight sex object' and thereby enables them to express the 'ambivalence, abjection, and rage' that accompanies 'empowered female desire.'[15] In *Daddy*, Saint Phalle takes up these darker dimensions of empowerment to challenge the idea that women are not Pop's primary makers and that images of their bodies should carry and transmit the meaning of consumption.

Given this challenge, it does not come as a surprise that William Kaizen claims that *Daddy*, which he describes as a 'gothic fairytale', 'fall[s] somewhat outside the purview of Pop Cinema.'[16] Although Pop cinema is an elastic term that can be understood through its attachment to other cinematic genres,[17] in Kaizen's characterisation, it most often eschews narrative structure for a fast-paced montage that creates a dizzying flow of consumer imagery. Bruce Conner's *A MOVIE* (1958) exemplifies this feature and shows how images of women figure into it. A meditation on visuality and violence, in *A MOVIE* clips of women's sexual display are central to the film's reflection on the seductions of mass media. Conner's clips are citations of Hollywood glamour, anonymous and sexualised surfaces, floating between the 'mass-produced portrait' and the 'flattened faceless nude' that Nochlin identifies.[18] Conner presents these images to critique them, but they also might express the artist's desire to portray the feminised visibility, interchangeability and emptiness inherent to images of women in capitalism. Kaizen argues that in *A MOVIE* Conner 'uncovered the deeper drives that underlie consumption, which the marketplace represses' – but did Conner rely on the idea that woman, a 'commodified figure of desire', stands for the repression of those deeper drives in order to reveal them?[19]

We can see Whitehead relying on an idea of woman as a 'commodified figure of desire' in *Tonite Let's All Make Love in London*, subtitled a 'Pop Concerto for Film'. Evoking the 'hedonistic rush' of 1960s London, *Tonite* documents, in the words of Mark Jones, a 'mélange of pop, pomp, stardom, clubbing, fashion, art, sex, and psychedelia'.[20] Devoted to the performances of Pink Floyd as well as other musicians, Whitehead creates sexualised images of women that embody the ecstatic splendour and dazed superficiality of this world. *Tonite* is rife with images of women modelling the shiny and risqué fashions of the period – the mini-skirt is a point of focus – all of which evoke sexual freedom as well as moral danger, which Whitehead alludes to by filming panicked newspaper headlines that express the fear that sexuality is for sale and out of control. By interviewing a young woman on an amusement ride explaining what 'dolly girls' are, Whitehead highlights the sexual freedom newly available to women. The dolly girl is a feminine type associated with a youthful, doll-like, mini-skirt style, but this young woman has a more far-reaching definition: 'she dresses how she feels, does what she likes, she is free'. Footage of the artist Alan Aldridge painting flowers on the torso of a woman complicates this freedom, as the woman's body is the 'canvas' for the marks and meanings of others.

Compared to *A MOVIE* and *Tonite*, *Daddy* is laboriously slow. Images are not spliced together to create a swift and intoxicating visual surface. There is nothing of the unscripted happenstance or detachment of a Warhol film, or their banal self-evidence. Many of the scenes are staged to look like plays, and every detail has been sculpted by the artist's intentions. Working with the cinematic unfolding of narrative time, Saint Phalle and Whitehead slow Pop cinema down to reveal the stories of sexuality that images so often hide and the possibility that they can be rewritten. By doing so, they create a painstaking exposure of the sexual abuse that Saint Phalle's father inflicted on her as a young girl, the foundation for her depiction of the artist sadistically staging her revenge against the white Euro-American aristocratic family and its lineage of violence. This attack extends to modes of perception that insist on making girls and women 'commodified figures of desire', a figuration that makes them containers for fantasies, but restricts their abilities to realise their own.[21]

Daddy refutes the association between femininity and passivity and the entrenched idea that girls and women should relinquish their drives. Sigmund Freud's work suggested that the drives are lines of libidinal force that prop themselves on biology's instinctual pathways. They appear in the virtual space of the psyche, between the mental and the physical, where sexuality extends beyond biology and the idea of the natural that accompanies it. This is the space of fantasy that art and cinema occupy. Elsewhere I have argued that the drives *write* the instincts, distance them from biological needs and reveal the unpredictable correspondences between the body and sexuality.[22] Linked to movement, aggression and agency, the drive can be understood as the impulse to see one's fantasies materialise in the world. Usually, this impulse is not evenly distributed across gender divisions. As Freud demonstrates in *Three Essays on the Theory of Sexuality*, girls and women are often expected to keep the drives in check and create a pretty picture of 'normal' sexuality, ostensibly free from disgust and shame, and made to contain the sexual perversities that provoke those responses.[23] *Daddy* represents Saint Phalle refuting these assignments and writing her drives, which gives the film a depth that counters Pop cinema's swift ride on late capitalism's visual surfaces.

Presenting *Daddy* at its London premiere in 1973, Laura Mulvey observed that the film is 'about the unconscious: repression and desire and the phantasies they produce'.[24] My aim in this essay is to draw on the psychoanalytic understanding of the unconscious to uncover how *Daddy* writes a feminist fantasy of revealing and dismantling the deeply repressive power wielded through the white patriarchal family. By exposing the arrangements in which the girl child is made to internalise the idea of her sexual passivity, *Daddy* restages the traumatic events of father-daughter incest as a form of psychoanalytic 'working-through' to reclaim her drive to fantasise. That is, Saint Phalle and Whitehead rewrite the denigrated place of the girl in the dominant Euro-American family system and connect that denigration to Pop's reliance on iconic images of the white woman as a passive object of desire. Pursuing this parallel, I show that *Daddy* is a feminist take on Pop cinema and tells a story of how images of white girls serve as embodiments of western culture's commodified surfaces that cover over the disgust and shame which they are made to contain.

Drawing and Writing a Girl

The beginning of *Daddy* features a sequence of tender drawings from Saint Phalle's story book *The Devouring Mother* (1972), which narrates her family origins. First and foremost, *The Devouring Mother* places Saint Phalle's writing of her life story, and its connection to her artwork, at the centre of the film. It also introduces the book-like structure, complete with parts and chapters, through which the film is organised, albeit loosely. Although she composed them as an adult, the drawings in *The Devouring Mother* are like those of a child. They demonstrate that Saint Phalle used writing and drawing to follow the associative logic of her fantasies instead of displaying the maturity of her artistic skill. Colourful, two-dimensional and cartoony, the images create a dynamic interaction between the illustrations and words so that they resemble the children's books that make learning to read playful and imaginative. Whitehead's static camera lingers over the images, as if to encourage the intertwined process of looking and reading. One can see the drawings as tender frames for holding the image of the child, which Saint Phalle linked to the image of herself as the artist. As she explains, 'I feel that the part of me that stayed a child is the artist in me'.[25]

In the opening image, the title of the film has been placed below a drawing of a father wearing a double-breasted suit with a tie. The letters of the word 'Daddy' are composed from wide and rounded shapes that Saint Phalle has partially filled in with black blots. Rendering the suit with razor thin black lines, Saint Phalle announces that the attention to the visual shapes and surfaces of clothing will be a consistent theme of the film. He stands in front of a red cross, which is part of a three-tiered altar composed of undulating lines of uneven widths. Daddy's arms are stretched out in a cross-like pose, and there is a small gravestone to his right. This portrayal reveals the girl's loving identification with her father. A victim, a martyr, a figure of pity, this image will be transgressed over the course of *Daddy*.

The point of this transgression is to open a space for the artist to reclaim her drive for fantasy that sexual abuse muted. As psychoanalyst Sandor Ferenczi argues in his 1932 essay 'Confusion of the Tongues Between the Adults and the Child', in sexual abuse, the 'overpowering force and authority of the adult' can 'rob [children] of their senses', which can lead them to 'subordinate themselves like automata to the will of the aggressor'.[26] That is, sexual abuse mutes the child's voice and the sensations it can register, carry and express. *Daddy*'s score, which forcefully makes itself heard in the opening sequence, suggests how challenging it can be for victims of abuse to speak of their sensory experiences in their own tongues. Loud and out of tune, the piano music of the score expands with ponderous, gothic clangs.

Saint Phalle's handwriting – bubbly, curvy, girly – makes the letters of the story into visual objects that pulsate with sensations. Her word-images make drawing and writing extensions of each other and suggest that her hand slips easily between them. The lines they share open paths to psychic relief: 'Drawing, drawing', Saint Phalle writes, 'as soon as I have a pen in hand, the anxiety goes'.[27] The mark-making of drawing and writing allow her to connect images of her childhood to dimensions of her psyche that are not shut down and determined by abuse. In this way, Saint Phalle's work aligns with Freud's understanding of writing as a metaphor for memory and a practice intimately associated with the psychoanalytic project of accessing the unconscious.[28]

After announcing the title of the film with the image of the father on the cross, the next image tells viewers what *Daddy* is: 'A Bedtime Story'. Saint Phalle depicts the bed as a rectangle that stands up straight in the picture plane. A little girl with yellow hair lies underneath the bed cover, which has been drawn with dark undulating lines that offer narrow glimpses of the white paper. Sitting on a chair near the bed is a man – the 'Daddy' from the previous image – who reads to the girl from a book. This drawing of a father reading to a daughter evokes care, sleep, dreams, vulnerability, sexuality and the unconscious. As the film will show, the father betrays the care normally associated with the scene of the bedtime story and indoctrinates the girl into sexual subservience.

The girlish aesthetic on display in *Daddy* is a defence against this subservience and an assertion of the girl's independent value. Viewers see this value in Saint Phalle's self-portrait as a girl that follows the drawing of the 'Bedtime Story'. Titled 'ME', the drawing is a claim to the self as an object in language and images. Saint Phalle appears in a dress outlined in pink (Figure 7.1). There are pink squiggly lines to suggest ruffled trim and the skirt of the dress is decorated with a jagged pattern of small pink squares. She wears black saddle shoes and ankle socks with scalloped edges. The girl's hair is yellow gold, and she is jumping rope. Suspended in the air and creating a half circle over her head, the line of black rope is a sign of play that connects Saint Phalle's writings and drawings to the oscillations of fantasy.

Saint Phalle writes and draws to disinter the drive to fantasise and gives it back to the figure of the girl. In this way, the film not only represents her

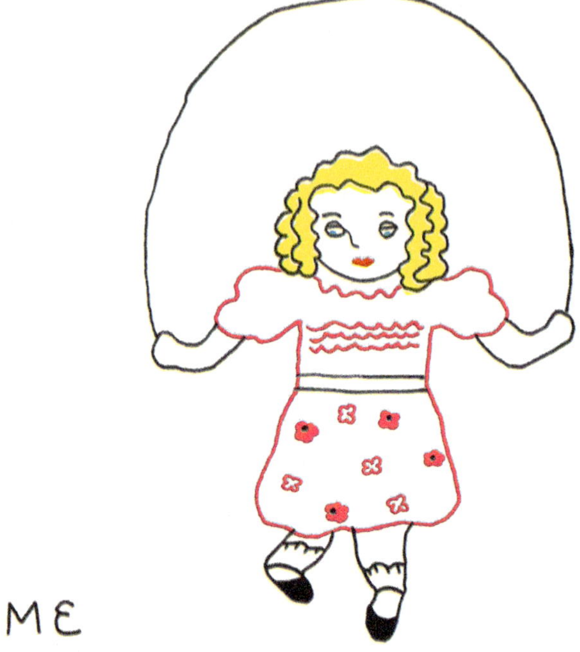

Figure 7.1 Niki de Saint Phalle, 'ME', from *The Devouring Mother* (1972). Source: © Niki Charitable Art Foundation/ARS, NY/ADAGP, Paris.

erotic attachments but also undercuts the defensive delusion articulated by psychiatrists that she seduced her father. Writing about her hospitalisation after suffering a nervous breakdown and attempting suicide, Saint Phalle describes reading a letter to her doctor in which her father confesses to 'trying to make [her] his mistress'.[29] Saint Phalle explains that this Jungian psychiatrist 'declared that a man such as my father, who was raised in a pious Catholic home with strict moral principles, could never have committed any of [these] transgressions'.[30] Familiar to so many people subjected to sexual abuse, the confrontation with psychiatry's patriarchal bias tells us why Saint Phalle turned to the imaginary spaces of art and cinema to testify to her losses. *Daddy* will not reinforce the link between girlhood and an uncomplicated idea of purity – it is angry, sexual and vengeful, teeming with aggression and tabooed desires – but the images in *The Devouring Mother* underscore the erotic tenderness of her childhood attachments and reject the presumption, which heavily relies on the idea that the bodies of girls and women are repositories of shame, that she instigated the incest.

Throughout *Daddy*, the mother is implicated in the father's abuse. In this opening sequence, she is a large, menacing figure with an unruly appetite, a devouring mother who 'eats daddy'. She raises questions about identification: if the daughter identifies with the mother, and the mother consumes the father, has the daughter also internalised the subordination of femininity that his authoritarian force requires? Mulvey writes that *Daddy* 'shows how women are thrown into an ambiguous relationship with their femininity when femininity is equated with passivity and lack of power'.[31] By depicting the mother's positive relationship to femininity and linking it to her own creativity, Saint Phalle creates the conditions for delinking images of women from subordination and the burial of their drives in the graveyard of white masculinity.

In the drawing 'Mummy Makes Up', Saint Phalle depicts her mother at the vanity table. Viewers see the mother's back and a few tools of beauty – scissors, comb, brush – that have been placed on a rectangular table before her, along with smudges of yellow and pink to suggest makeup. Linked to Pop's attention to fashion, masks and performance, the image of her face appears in the mirror, encircled with spiky black triangles. Her face has dots of red rouge, and her golden yellow hair, which rhymes with the girl's, suggests that Saint Phalle is seeing herself through her mother's self-reflection. While makeup is normally thought to be a superficial practice that reinforces the vanity associated with femininity, Saint Phalle turns those denunciations around. This drawing connects the feminine practice of putting on makeup to Saint Phalle's work as an artist. 'I did not reject Mother', Saint Phalle declares, 'I retained things from her that have given me a lot of pleasure – my love of clothes, fashion, hats, dressing up, and mirrors. These things I took from her, and they helped me to stay in touch with my femininity'.[32] This statement helps us understand why costume and fashion are part of *Daddy*'s feminist claim to the drive. Set against the film's grim history, the costumes have a flashy, colourful boldness that evoke the aggression which Saint Phalle had to claim in order to 'stay in touch' with a concept of femininity that is not conflated with shame and subordination. The costumes are one part of the film's attempt to imagine, create and possess images of femininity that are not robbed of the drive to fantasise.

Shooting Revenge

Beginning *Daddy* with the drawing and writing of *The Devouring Mother* underscores the fact that Saint Phalle and Whitehead worked in a psychoanalytic register and made the depth of the unconscious central to the film, a stark contrast to Pop's flat detachment. For many, this claim that the unconscious is *Daddy*'s subject makes it '[h]opelessly caught within a Freudian compulsion to repeat', as Clarke puts it.[33] But this assessment relies on an idea of psychoanalysis without a concept of 'working-through' and skips over the drawing, writing, staging, shooting, performing and filmmaking that are expressions of Saint Phalle's desire to free herself from the patriarchal concept of the girl and give free rein to her fantasies.

Disidentifying with the patriarchal concept of the girl requires aggression. While the tender drawings of *The Devouring Mother* discover a way to repair femininity, the next scene is devoted to revenge. Shifting to black-and-white film tinted with a light bluish green, Whitehead's handheld camera moves jaggedly across objects arranged on the surface of an altar. The altar echoes the drawing of the father on the cross that opens the film. Replacing a crucified Daddy are broken dolls, portrait busts, taxidermy animals, sculptures of saints and Madonnas, and crosses that extend from the altar's triangular gables. Some of the animals are entangled in predatory clutches. Below a crucifix on the uppermost point of the central panel is a bat with enormous wings that presides ominously over the scene. This staging of fantasy resembles the proto-Surrealist horror of Hieronymus Bosch's *Garden of Earthly Delights* (1490–1500), but there is no reverence for masterpieces in *Daddy*. Saint Phalle and Whitehead expose the altar as a perverse arrangement of images that commands viewers to submit themselves to the moral authority of patriarchal dominance. Without warning, these objects start exploding with blue, red and black paint. A gun is firing outside the camera's frame, and the film stock shifts to colour. Paint bleeds down and spatters across the objects. The altar has become an archive of injuries, a messy testimony to a symbolic assassination.

Whitehead's camera then takes a wide view of the altar. The back of Saint Phalle's head is now in the frame, along with her black pistol. The angle of the camera aligns with both the artist's perspective and the barrel of her gun. This wide shot allows viewers to see that the altar is in front of a chapel, and its three gables rhyme with the chapel windows. Mossy grey and worn with age, the chapel seems to extend from the ground like a gravestone. Wearing a black suit with long white ruffled sleeves, Saint Phalle stands at the centre of the image with her gun and creates a slim black line that runs straight through it. She is clearly in charge. In the words of Johanna Fatemen, Saint Phalle 'take[s] up arms against the church, the Father, and the picture plane'.[34] After she fires another round of shots, a white mist envelops the altar in loose clouds of powder. Its diffuse white silt heightens the bright, deep green of the grass and foliage that surrounds Saint Phalle (Figure 7.2). It is a striking image that materialises her ambitions to transform the conditions of visibility and aggressively reclaim her capacity to fantasise.

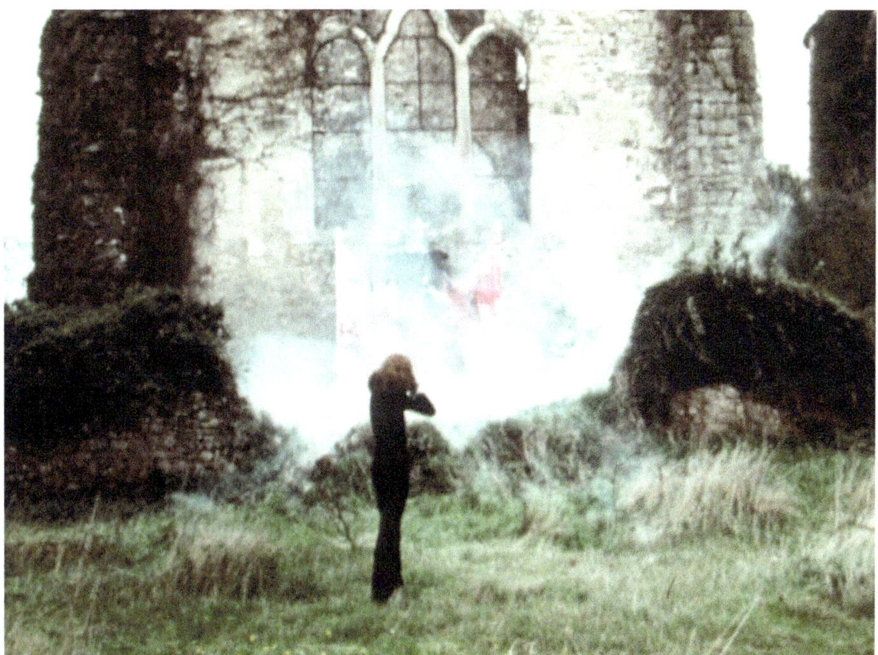

Figure 7.2 *Daddy* (Niki de Saint Phalle and Peter Whitehead, 1973). Source: © Niki Charitable Art Foundation/ARS, NY/ADAGP, Paris.

This is a cinematic depiction of Saint Phalle's *Tirs*. Known as 'Shooting Paintings', Saint Phalle began the *Tirs* in 1961. Often performed before an audience, these events catapulted her career into visibility. For each *Tir*, Saint Phalle would shoot at a white plaster relief with a real rifle. She embedded bags and cans of coloured paint into the relief so that each shot created a spontaneous explosion that spilled down the plaster surface. Playing with the figurative relay between firing guns and directing films that the word 'shooting' captures, in *Daddy* the camera becomes weaponised against the history of film, which has helped to make aggression a property of masculinity.

The *Tirs* gave Saint Phalle an ecstatic release and psychic relief. As she explains: 'In 1961, I shot at my art because it was fun and it made me feel great. I shot because I was fascinated watching the painting bleed and die. I shot for that moment of magic. Ecstasy'.[35] The drips of paint running down the surface are traces of long-stifled aggression allowed to spill out, but 'aggression' is not the word that Saint Phalle uses. Her word is violence. 'I was shooting at my own violence', she once stated.[36] Linking her desire for 'imaginative revenge' against her father to American culture at large, Saint Phalle writes: 'Extremism is part of America's vitality and part of its problem. Also mine. Violence. My own violence is linked to my personal history, energy and temperament, and the city I grew up in. Later I would use violence to shoot at paintings. Murder with no victim.'[37] Making herself part of the violence she diagnoses, stressing that the *Tirs* stage a symbolic rather than an actual murder, Phalle reveals *Daddy*'s complicated stakes.

By staging a '[m]urder with no victim', Saint Phalle signals her interest in art as a form of 'working-through'. In the psychoanalytic clinic, 'working-through' is the process of bringing the unconscious into consciousness through free association and dream interpretation. It is distinct from unconsciously 'acting out' a forgotten past. With its metaphorical affinities with performance, 'acting out' is often on the blurred line between pathology and cure. It can provide material for working-through, but it can also be a symptomatic, unconscious repetition. *Daddy* is an effort to move away from the danger of unconsciously acting out and toward the possibility of creating a future less captured by a damaging past.[38]

Seeking to escape his capture, the rest of *Daddy* stages the father's symbolic death. Playing multiple iterations of 'Agnes', an angry feminist daughter, Saint Phalle's performance is vengeful and bitter, full of loathing and hard to watch, but revenge is not the only point. It is about creating a fantasy space in which a woman can watch herself move among multiple psychic positions within a sequence of images, aggressive as well as passive, sadistic as well as masochistic, thereby unsettling their fixed connections to gender hierarchies. In *Daddy*, this oscillation is part of expressing the desire to challenge the historical silencing of women, break the chains that lock masculinity and aggression together and extend masochism beyond the pathologised passivity attributed to women and make it about the drive to fantasise.

Entering the Castle

If the subordination of femininity is often justified through the assumption that it is free from drive, aggression and will, *Daddy* refutes that assumption. In the next scene, Saint Phalle's claim to the psychic drives manifest in a small black car that speeds up a gravel, tree-lined road. Hurtling toward the camera, it cuts through the middle of the image. Agnes gets out of the car wearing a black dress with ruby-pink stripes, designed by Dior. Placed across the black bodice in diagonals, the bold stripes are composed of glittering sequins. The skirt of the dress is made of black tulle, and the hem is asymmetrical. Saint Phalle is a living sculpture that moves through the film and, like her artwork, becomes part of its visual patterns. Holding her black suitcase, she says goodbye to the driver – who is not visible – and begins to survey the scene she is about to enter. She carries her body with the poise of a model, and the scene resembles a fashion shoot. Whitehead's camera follows the line of her gaze and pauses on the exterior of a chateau, with its dilapidated grandeur, and lingers for a moment on a stone cross to highlight the moral hypocrisy of its authority.

As Saint Phalle walks through the grounds, a small white sculpture can be glimpsed in the top left corner of the frame. It is one of Saint Phalle's *Nanas*. Next to the *Tirs*, the *Nanas* are her most famous artworks. They are large bulbous female figures, descendants of Paleolithic Venuses who joyously leap through space defying gravity. Each one is made with wool and plaster strips layered over a wire trellis; they have a handmade, vernacular feel. According to Minioudaki, the *Nanas* 'validate women's work, feminine materials, and decorativeness.'[39] Indeed, the *Nanas* encapsulate many of Saint Phalle's stylistic signatures – her undulating lines, bright colours and embellished surfaces. They share a cartoony accessibility with Claes Oldenburg's soft Pop sculptures from the 1960s and embody Saint Phalle's fairytale aesthetic, what Amelia Jones describes as her 'magical view of the world.'[40] In this view, things associated with girls, women and femininity are valued, not made to serve as the subordinated ground over which patriarchal culture establishes its dominance. If the *Tirs* represent the psychic struggle with destruction, the *Nanas*, like the tender drawings of *The Devouring Mother*, evoke the desire to repair. Noting the conversation that *Daddy* creates with Saint Phalle's artwork, Mulvey remarks that the sculptures 'appear in the reality of the location like traces or stains in the unconscious', which means that they point to places beyond what a film can reveal.[41]

Agnes' father has died, and she has returned home, not for a funeral gathering, but for a solitary exploration of the crime scene in her psyche. The chateau and its grounds become the stage for materialising the world of her psychic interior. While walls suggest that space is heavily defended, the artworks represent the possibility of those defences eroding. Indeed, Saint Phalle encounters one of her large sculptures that loosely resembles a bird, painted white with blue and red shapes, and gently caresses it (Figure 7.3). Then, after walking through the labyrinthian maze of the large topiary garden – the ruby pink stripes of her dress standing out against the dark green density of the manicured bushes – Agnes happens upon a black coffin and pauses before it. She circles the coffin and opens it to reveal a white plaster phallus as big as a body. Hyperbolically overdetermined, this revelation has been shot from a high upper-storey window inside the castle, which makes the penis appear small, but Whitehead's camera zooms into a closeup to reveal Agnes' response. Her detached stare suggests that the

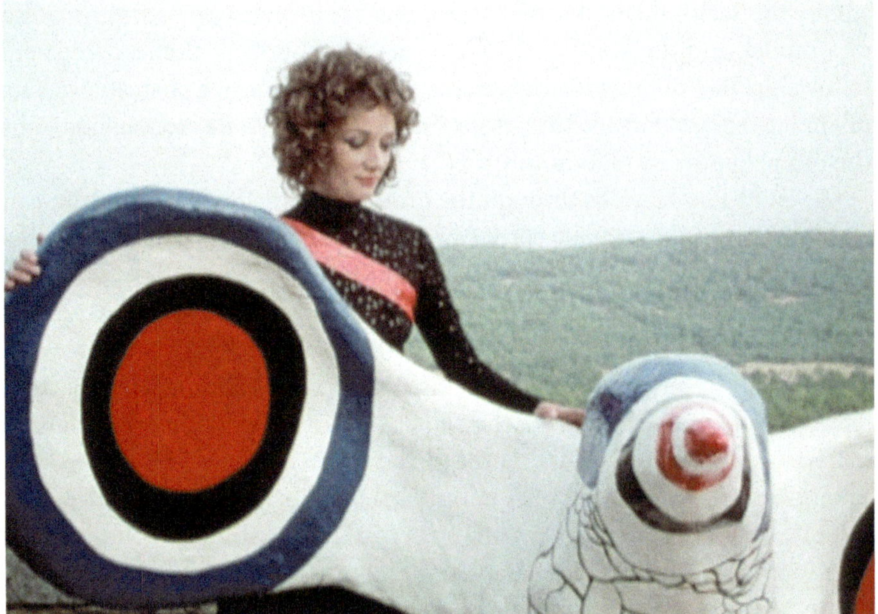

Figure 7.3 *Daddy* (Niki de Saint Phalle and Peter Whitehead, 1973). Source: © Niki Charitable Art Foundation/ARS, NY/ADAGP, Paris.

exaggerated size of the penis is not just a feminist joke – though it is funny – but materialises its psychic significance. Tenderly, she strokes its roughly composed testicles. Creating this large phallic sculpture, placing it in a coffin and exhibiting Agnes' attachment to this sexual fetish, *Daddy* begins a process of exposing and murdering the pompous grandiosity attributed to white masculinity.

Agnes enters the interior of the castle. She walks toward a table and turns the pages of a book placed on it. Quickly shifting back to black-and-white film tinged with grey-green, Saint Phalle and Whitehead portray a five-year-old Agnes (Gwynne Rivers) sitting under a tree flipping through the pages of another book. Viewers see the images, and they are drawn in the same style as those in *The Devouring Mother*. Announcing that this is 'Part 1', the first drawing portrays a girl with wings instead of arms and the title 'Daddy's Little Girl' written across them. Accompanying this drawing is the voice of Saint Phalle addressing 'Daddy': 'Once upon a time there was a little girl who dreamt she lived in a castle. Do you remember, Daddy, how much I loved you? You made my life into a fairytale'.

All of this sounds sweet enough, but there is a darkness to this fairytale that quickly finds its way into Saint Phalle's address. She asks 'Do you remember Blind Man?' Her voice, tinged with seduction and sarcasm, lingers on the title of the game. Whitehead shifts to a wide shot of the topiary garden and the father (Rainer von Dietz) chasing the daughter through its intricate maze. This is the restaging of Blind Man, a game in which Saint Phalle led her father, blindfolded, by the hand. Connected to the blindness of Oedipus and the value western culture places upon men's losses and desires, Blind Man was a ruse for sexual abuse. Dietz plays up the father's faux vulnerability and fear and Whitehead's camera reveals what the father wants to block from view. It focuses on the father's increasingly aggressive pursuit of the little girl and her efforts to escape his rough, sexualised clutch. Without actually portraying rape, the images certainly suggest it. The little girl's blue striped socks, which the father tries to pull down, become a point of focus and signifiers of sexual assault. With their thick and bold lines of bright blue, the socks echo the bold cartoony style of Saint Phalle's artwork.

There is another flashback that reveals the familial mise-en-scène out of which this abuse emerged and the fantasies it provoked. Through a keyhole that gives her a glimpse of a stately dining room, Agnes spies on her parents sitting down for dinner and witnesses what her mother has to consume and internalise. Seated at the head of the dining table wearing a tuxedo and a monocle, the father blames the loss of his oil shares on the 'bloody Arabs and boring Jews'. Wearing a platinum blonde wig, 'Mummy' (Clarice Rivers) describes these declarations as 'rubbish'. Reacting to her rejection of his racism, the father throws a tantrum and starts breaking dishes. Each time he throws a dish to the ground, he shouts the word 'rubbish', which gives his words a harsh gravity. Daddy is a tyrant who controls the determinations of value and is free to act out his aggressions at the slightest provocation. His wife and children are expected to swallow his declarations without question.

Physical and sexual violence are extensions of this verbal domination. After throwing his wife down the stairs, yelling and whipping her along the way, the father pushes her into a parlour room with painted portraits on the wall. Donning a military uniform that links him to fascism, Daddy identifies the painted images of white European faces and enumerates their aristocratic titles. With open arms he declares that the portrait gallery is a 'holy assembly of witnesses that looks down on our shame'. Alibis for his fictions of racial purity and masculine superiority, the portraits command his acts of denigration. After throwing her over the back of a sofa, he rapes the mother with the handle of his whip. Her body becomes the source of shame, and his relentless and maniacal shouting shows that rape is a 'speech act of aggression' that denies the victim's relationship to language.[42] This explicit display of the sexism and racism animating white patriarchal power illustrates the precarious role that white women play within it. If their allegiance to the 'holy assembly of witnesses' is not complete, if they speak words of dissent, their status as disposable objects will be exposed, and they will be treated as rubbish.

Daddy has a personal investment in maintaining the fictional homogeneity of Euro-American whiteness, what Gillian Harkins identifies as the 'ruse of racial purity'.[43] Neither explicit nor sustained, the film's attention to white supremacy nevertheless reveals something about the position of white women in patriarchal cultures and how the dominant images through which they appear might be challenged for the project of expanding gender and racial justice. Although allowed to claim a space in the public spotlight by aligning with the demands of the white male gaze, that space is heavily circumscribed. In this way, *Daddy* illustrates Camilla Griggers' argument that, while white women are 'icon[s] of social privilege', they are also 'its sacrificial victim[s]'.[44] Furthermore, while white women are positioned 'inside' Euro-American families and their sanctimonious "values", they are also 'the battered, the raped, the incested, and the murdered'.[45]

An image of the girl at the threshold of the parlour door reminds viewers that we are seeing a scene of sacrifice through her eyes, and it may be her fantasised recollection of events, but are her fantasies limited to this violent domestic scene? The girl puts on her mother's platinum blonde wig and looks into the mirror, an image that echoes the drawing 'Mother Makes Up' in *The Devouring Mother* and the mirroring, resemblance, identification and femininity that it stages. Dressing up as her mother and looking at her reflection in the mirror, perhaps the young Agnes is trying to see herself within the frame of a maternal gaze in which her femininity can be valued. However, in Daddy's world, the girl's act of staging her desire for and identification with her mother's femininity – which opens the possibility of a cinematic gaze that does not reinforce patriarchal values – is a criminal offense. Her father punishes the girl by dragging her into a kitchen closet, which connects to Pop's use of the domestic sphere, and locking her in it. She screams: 'Let me out!' Her demands reverberate beyond this dark kitchen closet. They give voice to the desires animating the film and reveal *Daddy* to be an extended sculpture that imagines beyond the dark ugliness of his punitive enclosures where her drives fold back on herself.

Working-Through a Girl

The horror of *Daddy* has only just begun. Becoming more surreal, lurid and confusing, getting closer to underground Pop cinema and its taboo-breaking explorations of gender identity and sexuality, the rest of the film gives free rein to Saint Phalle's fantasy of humiliating the father.[46] Confronting Daddy with repetitive illustrations of his abuse and its effects, the adult Agnes aims to show him the 'whole truth' and 'open his eyes to all those things [he] refused to see'. A meta-commentary on the film that Saint Phalle and Whitehead are making, Agnes commands him to 'watch the screen' and turns to the dark shadow which her body casts on the wall. He is caught in the sequence of images that she creates. Bound to a silver wheelchair, his hands locked in silver chains, he is disabled and debilitated, a feminised father who now embodies the paralysing past she was made to carry.

Agnes forces him to listen to a harrowing 'bedtime story'. Amidst a performance in which she dances seductively with a cape made of sheer red fabric, she addresses fantasy as a psychic space that is beyond his control: 'Oh how you longed to know what a woman's fantasies were, didn't you Daddy, so that you could have the same power over a woman's mind as you had over her body'. The father's voice, punitively describing her as a 'dirty little girl' and ordering her to 'stop touching herself', overlays this dance. A small *Nana* has been placed in the frame, signalling that her artwork defies this denial of her subjectivity and expresses her desire to compose the setting of desire (Figure 7.4). With a red bodice that rhymes with Saint Phalle's cape and legs painted with blue and white stripes, the *Nana* sculpture stands out; it is placed within the scene, but its stylistic features – bright, bulbous and cartoony – does not seamlessly fit within the gothic darkness of the film. This *Nana* gestures beyond this sequence of images.

Prompted by the voice over, Agnes starts describing her fantasies. They make it clear that proving that sexual abuse happened is not the point of *Daddy*. Rather, the film shows how it shaped her fantasy life, even as it was premised on the denial of her subjectivity. Agnes confesses to dreaming of what is was like to be him; in turn, she dreamt of what it was like to be one of his women. The commodification of sex is part of this fantasy picture: she imagines buying sex at a brothel with 'men for sale'. With her voice expanding with aggression and force, she describes buying a man with '*my* money', choosing one 'just like you of course', and then 'return[ing] him for the next woman to enjoy'. In this fantasy of consuming the sexuality of men, Saint Phalle reverses the gendered logic of woman as an interchangeable and disposable object and man as the subject of capitalist agency who wields the power of sexual possession.

Agnes is giving free rein to her fantasies, letting herself oscillate between sadistic and masochistic positions and unsettling the gender hierarchies that divide and isolate these positions in the most recognizable fantasies of

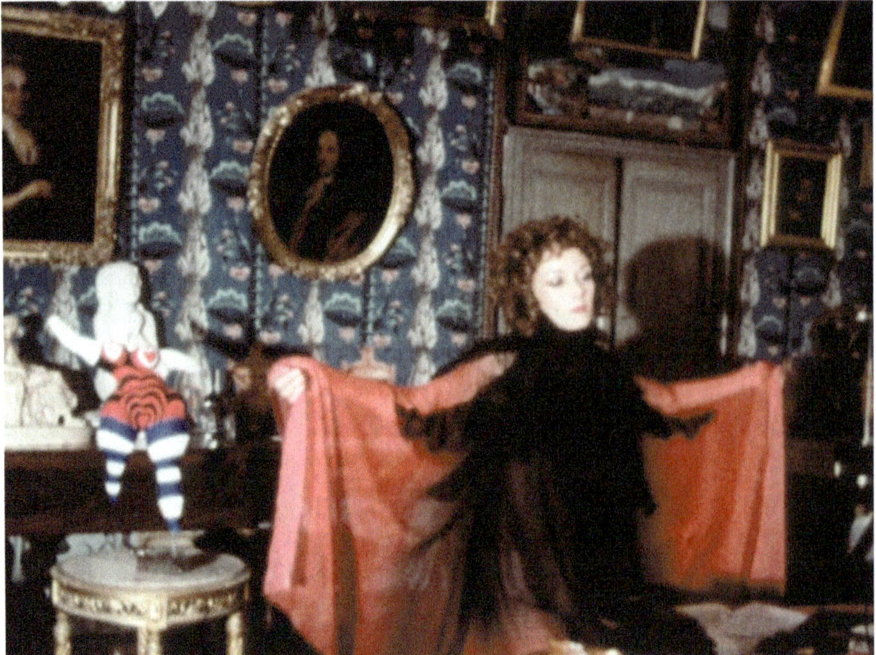

Figure 7.4 *Daddy* (Niki de Saint Phalle and Peter Whitehead, 1973). Source: © Niki Charitable Art Foundation/ARS, NY/ADAGP, Paris.

western culture. She also brings the reparative to this familiar set of oppositions and expresses the desire to free her mother from the snare of her marriage: 'How I would dream of taking mummy away from you Daddy so she could live the life she was really made for'. This desire for repair is not separate from the scenography of power and punishment but manifests through it. Mummy and daughter become lovers and dominatrix-like collaborators in scenes of shaming the father, making his body vulnerable, forcing him to eat, drink and serve. It is payback time for the master: now he is forced to internalise their power.

Working-through can be ugly. When Agnes recruits an adolescent girl (Mia Martin) to be part of her revenge fantasy, the film comes close to the nightmarish and all-too-real consequences of sexual abuse: the victim identifying with and then becoming the perpetrator by inflicting damage on more vulnerable people. Staging this reversal, Agnes offers up the younger girl as a birthday present for Daddy. She has long blonde hair and is dressed in a sexy schoolgirl costume. This Lolita figure is a younger version of Agnes. Relishing in the pleasure of expressing her aggression, Agnes teaches the girl how to seduce the father and, in doing so, re-stages the perverse seduction of a young girl that was construed to be the source of the abuse.

After bathing the girl and dressing her in undergarments and the stockings with blue stripes that link back to the portrayal of the Blind Man game, Agnes presents her as an object for the father's pleasure. Agnes is a madame in a brothel, and the girl is a prostitute. Following this presentation is a training session that instructs the girl to be a 'proper lady', which includes making her lick and eat a cake baked into the shape of a white phallus. These lessons culminate in a scene in which the girl performs a striptease during a church ceremony set to organ music. Saint Phalle has painted her skin in the bright colours and undulating forms associated with the *Nanas*. The girl is a living sculpture who acts out the meaning of sexual abuse and its link to the commodification of women's sexual display, but also the desire to create a fantasy that can retaliate against that history. This symbolic work raises questions about the challenges of working-through and its proximity to acting out. Even if Mia Martin was a skilled actor who could appear much younger than she actually was, and her performance took place on the terrain of the cinematic image, these scenes provoke ethical questions: How was the actress affected by participating in this scene? Have Whitehead and Saint Phalle reinscribed the idea that the image of a white girl is empty and interchangeable?

Within the frame of *Daddy*, the feminised subordination inflicted on the image of the white girl ultimately gets projected back onto the father's body. In another chapter, 'Daddy's Just a Girl in Disguise', Agnes appears in a number of close-ups against a black background. She speaks to the camera and interrogates her father, identifies his misogyny and names his delusional need to control women. She speculates that he was jealous of their access to the imaginative dimensions of femininity: 'how you envied us our world, our clothes, the roles we could play'. While Agnes makes these declarations, hands are putting makeup on his face: gold glitter on his eyelids, pink lipstick on his lips and cheeks. He becomes a garish image of the girlish femininity he used and denied.

This feminisation continues after his death. At a celebratory feast, Daddy appears in a coffin wearing a blonde wig, striped stockings, a large bonnet with flowers and a red boa. Mother and daughter, dressed in elaborate costumes and heavily made up, sing together and toast each other in a garish spectacle of ecstatic relief. Their abilities to realise fantasies of transformation have prevailed. While it is easy to see *Daddy*'s vengeful restaging as an ethically suspect identification with the aggressor, it might be more accurate to read the film as an effort to work through the most pernicious aspects of white patriarchal culture that suppress, in Minioudaki's words, 'a woman's right to desire' and thereby impede her fantasy life – with all its aggressions, pleasures and oscillations – from materialising in visual form.[47]

Conclusion: Traces of Daddy

While Daddy is dead, he has not disappeared. He is written into the erotic and psychic life of Agnes. The epilogue for the film, titled 'Resurrection', portrays Agnes as a young woman arriving at the castle with her lover, a young man with long blonde hair, played by Rainer von Dietz, the actor who also played Daddy. Shot in that black-and-white film tinged with bluish-green that appeared earlier, these scenes revisit Agnes' initial arrival at the castle. The young hippies run around and explore. They play dress up and erotic games. It is a little horrifying to see the young man donning the father's military costume and then gently spanking Agnes, who wears striped underwear. They even play their own version of 'Blind Man'. These repetitions are meant to shock. Agnes put so much effort and energy into staging the father's symbolic death, and now he is back as her lover.

'Resurrection' could substantiate Clarke's argument that, when read through psychoanalysis, *Daddy* is 'hopelessly caught within a Freudian compulsion to repeat'.[48] To my mind, however, this conclusion attests to the real challenges of 'working-through' and the fact that one is never completely cured. When it comes to sexual abuse, the scene of desire might always hold its unconscious traces. For Saint Phalle, 'working-through' was a lifetime process and intimately connected to her work as an artist. By creating a conversation between art and film, *Daddy* accesses a woman's capacity to fantasise and writes its depth into a cinematic narrative. Saint Phalle's drawings, sculptures and performances declare that her imagination is not restricted to the sexual power that the father wielded with such impunity and that the film provides a frame for that assertion. At the same time, the artwork points away from the mise-en-scène of film and suggests there might be more to see. By creating this fraught conversation layered with complication, Saint Phalle and Whitehead refuted the assumption that woman is a passive visual surface that emblematises capitalism's efficient work saturating everyday life. In so doing, they gave Pop cinema an unconscious that challenges the deep-seated assumption that girls and women should contain the delusion that masculinity can be secured by subordinating and flattening their drive to fantasise.

Notes

1 Quoted in 'From the Artist to the Icon, and the Icon to the Artist: Key Biographical Dates', in *Niki de Saint Phalle: Shadow and Light*, exh. cat., Côte d'Azur, Cannes: Fine Editions Art, 2019, p. 140.

2 I trace these reverberations in my catalogue essay '"I Felt I Had Been Assassinated": Niki de Saint Phalle's Imaginary and the Feminist Claim to Aggression', in Caroline Ugelstad (ed.), *Niki de Saint Phalle*, exh. cat., Oslo, Norway: Heine Onstad Kunstsenter, 2022, pp. 20–26.

3 On the proliferation of incest narratives, see Janice Doane and Devon Hodges, *Telling Incest: Narratives of Dangerous Remembering from Stein to Sapphire*, Ann Arbor: University of Michigan, 2001, and Gillian Harkins, *Everybody's Family Romance: Reading Incest in Neoliberal America*, Minneapolis and London: University of Minnesota Press, 2009.

4 Alissa Clarke, '"Am I Providing a Good Show for You?" Female Performance, Labour, and Collaborative Agency in Niki de Saint Phalle and Peter Whitehead's *Daddy* (1973)', *Feminist Media Histories*, 5:2 (2019), p. 148.

5 Virginie Sélavy, '*Daddy*: Interview with Peter Whitehead,' 2015: https://feminaridens. com/2015/01/30/daddy-interview-with-peter-whitehead/; Peter Whitehead, 'Dear Diana- *Daddy* Film Treatment, 1972,' *Framework*, 52:2 (Fall 2011), p. 599.

6 Whitehead, op. cit., p. 600.

7 Tom Day, 'Pop Cinema: Aesthetic Conversations between Art and the Moving Image', unpubl. PhD thesis, University of Edinburgh, 2019, p. 27. Day argues for the importance of seeing iterations of Pop cinema as 'themselves works of Pop art'.

8 Jean Laplanche and Jean-Bertrand Pontalis, 'Fantasy and the Origins of Sexuality' (1964), in Dana Birksted-Breen, Sara Flanders and Alain Gibeault (eds), *Reading French Psychoanalysis*, London and New York: Routledge, 2010, p. 335.

9 Linda Nochlin, 'Running on Empty: Women, Pop and the Society of Consumption', in Sid Sachs and Kalliopi Minioudaki (eds), *Seductive Subversion: Women Pop Artists, 1958–1968*, Philadelphia: University of the Arts; New York and London: Abbeville Press Publishers, 2010, p. 15.

10 Martha Rosler, 'The Figure of the Artist, the Figure of the Woman', in Sachs and Minioudaki (eds), op. cit., p. 182.

11 Ibid.

12 Nochlin, op. cit., p. 15.

13 Kalliopi Minioudaki, 'Pop Proto-Feminisms: Beyond the Paradox of the Woman Pop Artist', in Sachs and Minioudaki (eds), op. cit., p. 94.

14 Martha Rosler, 'Feminism and the State: Art, Politics, and Resistance', keynote lecture, MOCA, Los Angeles, 24 February 2018, https://www.youtube.com/ watch?v=FXPUTgbKdXA.

15 Jennifer Doyle, '"I Must Be Boring Someone": Women in Warhol's Films', in Jennifer Doyle, *Sex Objects: Art and the Dialectics of Desire*, Minneapolis: Minnesota University Press, 2006, p. 72.

16 William Kaizen, 'Notes on Pop Cinema', in Kaizen (ed.), *Pop Cinema: Art and Film in the US and UK, 1950s–1970s*, Philadelphia, PA: International House Philadelphia, 2011, pp. 28, 27. See also the re-worked version of this essay in this volume.

17 Providing an overview of significant accounts of Pop cinema, Day links it to discourses of 'popular, mainstream and narrative film and experimental/underground cinema', but ultimately argues for seeing the genre 'broadly'. Day, op. cit., pp. 54–86.

18 Nochlin, op. cit., p. 15.

19 Kaizen, op. cit., pp. 19, 27.

20 'Raffish filmmaker of the Sixties counterculture', *Independent*, 29 June 2019, p. 40; Mark Jones, 'Sex Spy: Sexuality and the Revolution in Peter Whitehead's Post-Sixties Works', *Framework*, 52:2 (Fall 2011), p. 819.

21 Kaizen, op. cit., p. 27.

22 Kimberly Lamm, 'Writing the Drives in Nancy Spero's *Codex Artaud*', in Lamm, *Addressing the Other Woman: Textual Correspondences in Feminist Art and Writing*, Manchester: Manchester University Press, 2018, pp. 107–45.

23 Sigmund Freud, *Three Essays on the Theory of Sexuality* (1905), in James Strachey (ed. and trans.), *The Standard Edition of the Complete Psychological Works of Sigmund Freud*, vol. 7, London: Hogarth Press, 1958, pp. 123–246.

24 Laura Mulvey, '*Daddy:* The Subversive Potential of an Aesthetic of Masochism (with Original 1974 Notes for Screening)', *Framework*, 52:2 (Fall 2011), p. 606.

25 Niki de Saint Phalle, *Traces: An Autobiography Remembering 1930–1949*, Lausanne: Acatos Publishers, 1999, p. 69.

26 Sandor Ferenczi, 'Confusion of the Tongues Between the Adults and the Child (The Language of Tenderness and Passion)', *The International Journal of Psychoanalysis*, 30 (1949), p. 227.

27 Nicole Rudick, *What is Now Known Was Once Only Imagined: An (Auto)biography of Niki de Saint Phalle*, New York: Siglio, 2022, p. 14.

28 Sigmund Freud, 'A Note Upon the "Mystic Writing Pad"' (1925), in James Strachey (ed. and trans.), *The Standard Edition*, op. cit., vol. 19, pp. 225–32.

29 Rudick, op. cit., p. 38.

30 Ibid.

31 Mulvey, op. cit., p. 607.

32 Rudick, op. cit., p. 103.

33 Clarke, op. cit., p. 153.

34 Johanna Fatemen, 'Self Made', *Artforum*, May 2021, https://www.artforum.com/print/202105/johanna-fateman-on-the-art-of-niki-de-saint-phalle-85478.

35 Saint Phalle, *Traces*, op. cit., p. 24.

36 Quoted in Ruba Katrib, 'Niki de Saint Phalle: Building for the Future,' in exh. cat., *Niki de Saint Phalle: Structures for Life*, New York: MoMA, PSI, 2021, p. 13.

37 Saint Phalle, *Traces*, op. cit., p. 75.

38 Sigmund Freud, 'Remembering, Repeating and Working-Through (Further Recommendations on the Technique of Psycho-Analysis II)' (1914), in James Strachey (ed. and trans.), *The Standard Edition*, op. cit., vol. 12, pp. 145–56.

39 Minioudaki, op. cit., p. 103.

40 Amelia Jones, 'Wild Maid, Wild Soul, a Wild Wild Weed: Niki de Saint Phalle's Fierce Femininities, ca. 1960–1966', in *Niki de Saint Phalle, 1930–2002*, Bilbao: Guggenheim Museum; Paris: Réunion des Musées Nationaux-Grand Palais, 2015, p. 157.

41 Mulvey, op. cit., p. 608.

42 Mieke Bal, *Reading Rembrandt: Beyond the Word-Image Opposition*, Amsterdam: Amsterdam University Press, 2006, p. 61.
43 Harkins, op. cit., p. 20.
44 Camilla Griggers, *Becoming-Woman*, Minneapolis: University of Minnesota Press, 1997, p. x.
45 Ibid, p. xii.
46 Day, op. cit., p. 73.
47 Minioudaki, op. cit., p. 119.
48 Clarke, op. cit., p. 153.

Part 3

Pop Cinema, Mass Production and the Politics of Consumption

8

Always Crashing in the Same Car

Glyn Davis

Around nine minutes into Eduardo Paolozzi's short black-and-white film *The History of Nothing* (1962), a static collaged image of a disconcerting collision appears: through the windscreen of a car, the ancient Hellenistic sculpture *Laocoön and His Sons* (otherwise known as 'the Laocoön Group') rears up, seemingly about to be hit by the speeding motor vehicle. An array of lines emanates from the car's dashboard: this section of the collage is clearly taken from a vehicle manual, with the lines indicating the placement and function of various dials, buttons and levers around the steering wheel. Although the collaged image is motionless, these lines provide an intimation of velocity. The naked bodies of Laocoön and his two sons, Antiphantes and Thymbraeus, stretch and contort, apparently anticipating an imminent demise from impact with a car. (In fact, the contortion of the figures in the sculpture is due to an attack from sea serpents, which wind their slippery ways around the limbs of the trio of figures.) The Laocoön-car collision image recalls a similar shot from six minutes earlier in the film: another view through a car windscreen, this time of an arid desert vista, mesa rising in the middle distance. The disjointed nature of Paolozzi's film – its images and soundtrack assembled from disjunctive fragments, pressed into proximity – invites viewers to find rhymes and connections between individual isolated moments, distributed across its running time. Is this the same car, the same driver? Is there a further shot to come later in the film which details the aftermath of the collision?

The car-Laocoön moment in *The History of Nothing* is merely one instance in the thirteen-minute film in which landscapes and their inhabitants (whether visible or implied) are threatened by large machines, or vehicular modes of transport are brought into uncomfortable relations to specific spaces. As Diane Kirkpatrick writes of these moments, 'whimsical machine beings are installed in 1920s/1930s interiors, placed in outdoor urban scenes, or transformed into architectural monuments in photographic landscapes'.[1] A gigantic vehicle, assembled from a rudimentary cart-like chassis and a blocky mechanical body, towers and glowers over a built-up seaside town. A biplane is jammed into a rather cramped (but empty) public space, with very little room for manoeuvre; a sign above a door in the space reads 'Entrance for Baggage' in English and German and names a sinister-sounding location ('Schlachthofstrasse' – 'Slaughterhouse Street'). A flat mechanical butterfly-like form, redolent of a carnival mask (or, from a present-day perspective, a drone) hovers over a landscape of skyscrapers. However, it is in the car-Laocoön image that the juxtaposition articulated in these other moments, as well as other similar scenes, threatens to become a disaster: the spectacle of a car crash looms on the horizon, yet fails to materialise.

The History of Nothing was made in 1962, at a point when Paolozzi (who was born in Scotland) had just returned to the United Kingdom after two years of teaching in Hamburg. As Robin Spencer identifies, the film 'consists of collage material gathered in Hamburg and landscapes and domestic interiors haunted by uncanny mechanical sphinxes'.[2] *The History of Nothing* was produced with the assistance of Denis Postle at the Royal College of Art in London. The visuals mainly take the form of John Heartfield / Hannah Hoch-style collages, or of found and appropriated materials presented without manipulation; there is occasional camera movement, panning across an individual collage or image. Some images recur (including a simplified illustration of a striped feline, the focus partially blurred); some collage fragments reappear across images (including *Laocoön and his Sons*, who are variously visible through a window, in the three sections of a winged vanity mirror and, as already identified, through a car windscreen). No one image is held for very long, and the editing pace is often rapid. The soundtrack similarly edits together disparate materials, in the style of musique concrète: an aeroplane taking off, a dog barking, thudding drums, an angular tune played on a mouth harp. Clumsy audio tape edits are left in place, accentuating the disjointedness of the whole assembly. And yet some sequences approach thematic coherence: in the fifteen seconds after the first shot through a car windscreen, for instance, to a consistent audio track of a chiming instrument being played at a hectic pace (and which is possibly speeded-up), a quick montage includes an illustration of a figure on a motorbike, a collage that includes an upside-down car, a diagram of a tank, a photograph of a boy in an outsized life-vest and a drawing of a woman in an aeroplane seat adopting the brace position. Images of various forms of transport, that is, give way to signs of danger, to the behaviours and practices needed to escape from (and potentially survive) vehicular disaster.

The trope of vehicular catastrophe can be traced through Paolozzi's output, predominantly in the form of plane and car crashes. This essay will focus in particular on the place of the automobile accident in Paolozzi's oeuvre and engage with a number of works from across his career – collages, sculptures, films – in which car cataclysms play a significant role. These works will be situated in relation to paintings and films by other artists associated with Pop, including Andy Warhol and Bruce Conner, that also engage with automotive disaster. I will argue that the pervasive fascination with car crashes in Pop art and, especially, Pop cinema, articulates and anchors Pop's interest in speed, repetition and danger. Where Pop art's car crashes – whether sculptures, screenprints, or paintings – freeze-frame disaster, dwelling on moments of imminent impact or aftermath, the time-based motion of Pop cinema's headlong unfurling brings the noise and brutality of the car crash to ugly, threatening life, articulating a trauma to be revisited through repeated viewings.

Paolozzi and Pop

The History of Nothing was described by Robin Spencer as 'a surrealist homage to the ghosts of Germany's past'.[3] Diane Kirkpatrick also linked the film to Surrealism, writing that it 'creates a flowing evanescent dream imagery in which surrealist reveries merge with urban, industrial, and technological fantasies'.[4] While it is possible to trace threads of surrealism, Dada, art brut and Pop (and other artistic movements) running throughout the wide-ranging tapestry of Paolozzi's output – and, indeed, in operation within this one film work – I here want to place emphasis on *The History of Nothing*'s Pop credentials and thematics, and to ground it as a key work of Pop cinema. Its fascination with the blurred relationships between humans and machines, sustained use of lightly-manipulated mass-reproduced popular culture materials and equivocal political register all clearly align the film with Pop and its concerns.

Scottish-Italian Paolozzi (1924–2005) only made four films in his career: *The History of Nothing*; *Kakafon Kakkoon* (1965); *Mr Machine* (1971); and *1984 – Music for Modern Americans* (1983).[5] Rather than film, he is predominantly known for working with sculpture, collage and screen printing. He is often recognised by art and cultural historians as a major figure in the pantheon of British Pop art; specific collage series, screen prints, sculptures and installations from the 1950s, 1960s and 1970s are regularly identified as canonical works of the art movement. A key contributor to this framing of Paolozzi was the cultural critic Lawrence Alloway, whose 1962 essay '"Pop Art" since 1949', published in *The Listener*, sketched out three phases in the brief history of British Pop art. The use of the term 'Pop art', he wrote, in a refreshingly simple definition, 'refers to the use of popular art sources by fine artists: movie stills, science fiction, advertisements, games boards, heroes of the mass media'.[6] The first phase, he claimed, ran from 1951 to 1958; the Pop artists working during this period had a special interest in technology, science and visions of the future. 'Typical of this first phase of Pop art in England is the work of Eduardo Paolozzi', he wrote.[7] 'Science fiction', Alloway observed, 'because it was pro-technology, but highly fantastic, was popular at this time'.[8] This comment prompts a question: should *The History of Nothing*, made in the same year that Alloway's essay was published, be read as an abstract science fiction film, Pop SF? If so, do its conflicting collage elements and often dissonant soundtrack offer up a utopian or dystopian take on things to come?

Paolozzi's childhood, the artist recalled, was 'drenched in cinema' – specifically, in popular and generic cinema. He spent his early years in Leith, Edinburgh, and remembered the city in the 1930s as 'a maze of little cheap cinemas. […] From a very early age, from possibly even the age of four, I was going to the cinema. And there was a particular fleapit […] called The Laurie that used to show nice films about slime and submarines and all these things that little boys liked'.[9] In Alloway's account of the history of British Pop, he highlights the importance of these forms of cinema to the artist:

> As a boy Paolozzi had seen Karloff monster movies, and retained the massive, lumbering contours in his memory until it returned in his sculptures of the human image. Paolozzi and I used to go to the London Pavilion, which was the first-run house for monster movies in the fifties. And our feeling was never that we were slumming, or getting away from it all, or not being serious. It was our assumption that what we felt at, say, *Tarantula* [Arnold, 1955], was as serious and interesting and worthwhile as our other aesthetic feelings. What happened was that these emotionally charged images from the mass media dramatically reduced aesthetic distance.[10]

Here, Alloway is identifying at work the common Pop tactic of inverting or disrupting cultural hierarchies, the (re-)valuation of 'low' culture as just as worthwhile of attention, affection and analysis as any more 'middlebrow' or 'highbrow' cultural material. In addition, he pinpoints the powerful affective charge of popular culture and a crucial question it poses of the art establishment: should not all forms of art have the same immediacy, force, resonance?

A few years later, in a revisitation of the history of British Pop for Lucy Lippard's 1966 book on Pop art, Alloway reiterated Paolozzi's association with the movement: 'we find in Paolozzi a full statement of the ideas that were necessary for the development of Pop art: a serious taste for popular culture, a belief in multi-evocative imagery, and a sense of the interplay of technology and man'.[11] However, he expressed a minor reservation about unreservedly aligning Paolozzi with Pop, claiming that '[h]is own work is not straight Pop art'.[12] In most subsequent accounts of Paolozzi's career or of Pop art's history, the two are connected – not always unproblematically. Daniel Herrmann, for example, identifies Paolozzi as a 'prime exponent of UK Pop art and one of its most prominent representatives in international exhibitions', while recognizing that by the early 1970s the artist was reject-ing the label.[13]

Paolozzi's association with Pop is rooted in his activities with the Independent Group, a loose cluster of young artists who met at the Institute of Contemporary Arts (ICA) in London in the 1950s. The Group included Alloway, the painter Richard Hamilton, architects Alison and Peter Smithson, photographer Nigel Henderson and the architectural historian Reyner Banham, among others. In the spring of 1952, the Independent Group organised a series of talks at the ICA; Paolozzi was the first speaker. For his contribution, the artist used an epidiascope, a sort of slide projector, to project collages and pages from his scrapbooks onto a screen. Herrmann recounts:

> There was not much talking involved. Instead, the audience was witness to an event that the few actual records mainly describe in terms of its physicality […] Automobile advertisements were followed by sequences of pin-up girls; arrangements of magazine cut-outs led to the covers of pulp science-fiction journals. Aliens, Coca-Cola, strippers, cars, robots: gaudy colours and images popped up in rapid succession […] Paolozzi had launched an onslaught of images at his audience, and the reaction was one of bafflement.[14]

This event has subsequently and retrospectively become known as 'the *Bunk! lecture*', in reference to one of Paolozzi's collage works, *Bunk! Evadne in Green Dimension* (1950), which is emblematic of the sorts of materials that Paolozzi projected at the ICA in 1952. As Anne Massey notes, '[t]hese images have subsequently acquired a mythical aura, often cited as the first examples of British Pop art or even Pop art'.[15] However, what exactly was projected remains unclear. Complicating the narrative, in the early 1970s, working with collage and scrapbook materials that he had been assembling in the late 1940s and early 1950s, Paolozzi put together a portfolio of forty-five screen prints with the title *Bunk!*; which of these materials were projected in 1952 at the ICA is impossible to establish.[16]

The Independent Group was short-lived, only lasting from 1952 to 1955. The following year, a dozen of the group's members – along with another twenty-four participants – took part in the landmark exhibition *This is Tomorrow* at the Whitechapel Art Gallery, which was open to the public from 9 August to 9 September 1956. The intention behind the show was to bring together individuals working in distinct fields of practice: architecture, painting, sculpture. As Ed Halter notes, the exhibition 'is remembered as one of the first Pop events'; in significant part, this is due to artist Richard Hamilton creating his canonical Pop collage work *Just what is it that makes today's homes so different, so appealing?* in order to advertise the show.[17] Eduardo Paolozzi worked with Nigel Henderson and Peter and Alison Smithson on one of the contributions to the exhibition; their collaborative installation did not evidence any distinctly Pop traits. As Graham Witham writes, '[t]he Patio and Pavilion, as the exhibit was called, was a habitat symbolic of human needs – space, shelter, and privacy – and the objects it contained represented the range of human activity'.[18] In contrast, the room that Hamilton worked on with fellow artist John McHale and architect John Voelcker was littered with popular culture materials: film posters, a jukebox, a giant bottle of Guinness.

Over the decades of his career, Paolozzi's personal relationship to Pop was always unsettled: at times he courted the art movement, at others he dismissed it. In a 1971 screen print that he created, titled *Pop Art Redefined (Lots of Pictures – Lots of Fun)*, for instance, a cheery cartoon elephant dressed in a bright red jumper, blue trousers and sporting a polka-dot neckerchief sits at an easel. The anthropomorphic animal is painting the American flag; it holds a tin of Spam in its trunk; its paintbrush pot is an empty tin of Campbell's vegetable soup. Key artists associated with Pop art are being bluntly referenced: Jasper Johns, Ed Ruscha, Andy Warhol. The screen print is not a celebration of Pop, but a critique: as Daniel Herrmann writes, …

> All its ingredients are exaggerated to the point of utter saturation. The colours are too bright, the forms too simplified, the references too obvious. This is no coy criticism of an art movement; it is a delightful sarcastic broadside, revelling in calling out Pop as a parody of itself – an easily imitated style, dominated by American artists.[19]

With this screen print, published in an edition of 1,000 (and thus, ironically, adopting a mass production technique used by a number of Pop practitioners), Paolozzi publicly denounced a prominent art movement, 'position[ing] himself belligerently in opposition to his own reputation and to other artists'.[20] In the same year that he produced *Pop Art Redefined*, Paolozzi gave an interview in which he aligned himself with an alternative tradition: 'It's easier for me to identify with [Surrealism]', he stated, 'than to allow myself to be described by some term, invented by others, called "Pop", which immediately means that you dive into a barrel of Coca-Cola bottles. What I like to think I'm doing is an extension of radical Surrealism'.[21] And yet, 1971 was also the year of a major Paolozzi retrospective at the Tate gallery in London – an exhibition at which the full set of *Bunk!* screen prints received their first public showing. One of the *Bunk!* collages, *I was a rich man's plaything* (1947), features (among other components) a doctored cover of an issue of *Intimate Confessions* magazine; a gun is pointed at the head of an oblivious cheesecake model, the word 'Pop!' emitting from its barrel. In the catalogue for the Tate exhibition, Paolozzi annotated the image with the words 'The first use of Pop?' – seemingly identifying himself as a key progenitor (if not the primary origin point) of the art movement.[22] Paolozzi's relationship to Pop was fraught, then, embattled; however, it remains a crucial and valid frame for approaching and unpacking his work.

Crash!

In 1964, two years after making *The History of Nothing*, Paolozzi created the large metal sculpture *Crash*, a key work in the 'machine-style' phase of his sculptural output (Figure 8.1). In shape and size, the sculpture resembles a car that has been in a smash, the force of the collision tipping the chassis up on to its side. Admittedly, this is a clean up-ended vehicle, a spotless and monochromatic accident made only of metal; there is no torn or burnt fabric, no smashed mirrors, lights or windows, no charred or blistered paintwork. At the centre of the sculpture is a wheel-like shape, a strip of metal jutting from its rim suggesting a tyre burst, rendered, irreparable. At one edge, a drooping and somewhat phallic thick metal tube with a corrugated rim near the spout resembles an exhaust pipe. Rigid axes imply a largely intact vehicular frame. Various other pipes and bars, however, jut and weave dramatically outwards, seemingly ripped from their original, 'correct' rectilinear position. The cleanliness of *Crash*'s form aligns it with the wider Pop art movement and its depictions of gleaming consumer goods – albeit with

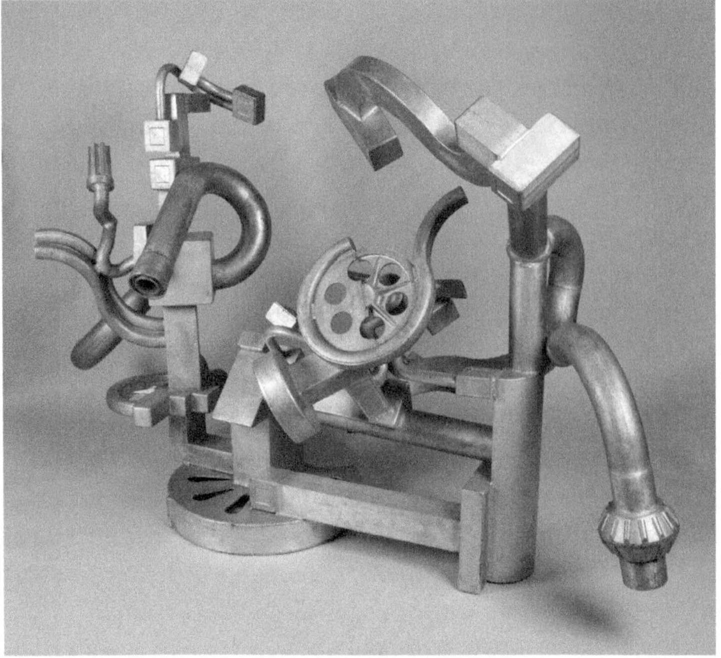

Figure 8.1 Eduardo Paolozzi, *Crash* (1964), Ulster Museum Collection: BELUM.U951. Source: © The Paolozzi Foundation, Licensed by DACS 2023.

evocative echoes of Léger's tubular compositions and Boccioni's dynamic rendering of human bodies in machinic motion.

Indeed, the implication of motion is central to *Crash*'s power. Diane Kirkpatrick describes *Crash* as 'a machine-style metaphor for an action-packed event'.[23] Despite the sculpture's motionless form, she argues that its shape and method of assembly suggest dynamism:

> With *Crash*, there is […] the feeling of being an eyewitness to the moment of the crash itself. Gravity seems suspended. Welding makes possible such an apparent freedom from the laws of nature, and the artist has happily exploited the technical possibilities to express the moment before complete disintegration.[24]

The work is caught in 'suspension', then, but is fragmenting, splitting apart; the horror of being the eyewitness to a car crash, watching calamity unfold in slow motion, is evoked. A similar point about stasis and movement is made by Elly Thomas: in the work, they claim,

> We see a fascination with the explosive and the unresolved. The parts connect and interrelate in such a way that they are not subsumed

within the totality. The result, in a piece such as **Crash**, is that although the elements are welded together, the sculpture seems caught in a continuing, unfolding process.[25]

For both Kirkpatrick and Thomas, *Crash* seems to be in motion, rent through or underscored by a narrative force: the testimony of the witness, the documentary or cinematic power of the 'action-packed event'. While it would be overstating the case to call this sculpture by Paolozzi a work of Pop cinema, the propulsive force of the car crash as a spectacular and horrific event rendered in time animates *Crash*.

Paolozzi would go on to make other car crash-related works across the decade. In 1967, the novelist J. G. Ballard became the prose editor of *Ambit*, a small but influential experimental literary journal founded in London in 1959 by Martin Bax, a paediatrician and novelist. Ballard and Bax approached Paolozzi about providing collages and visual essays for the publication; between 1967 and 1995, the artist made thirteen contributions. As David Brittain notes, 'Ballard had been an admirer of Paolozzi's work since the early fifties and they had long shared many of the same interests, obsessions and themes. […] Each was attracted to the apocalyptic: Ballard's early "catastrophe" novels foretold the end of civilisation by unstoppable natural or man-made forces, while the hulking half-man, half-machine sculptures of Paolozzi reminded Ballard of "survivors of a nuclear war"'.[26] For issue 50 of *Ambit*, Paolozzi provided several pages of 'unfilmed scripts'. The title page for this contribution features two images collaged together on a plain white background: a rear view of a VW Beetle car, its boot hatch open to reveal the workings of its engine, the gaping orifice resembling a mechanical mouth; and below this, the prone figure of a sniper holding a gun sight to his right eye. Despite a lack of movement, the car looks as though it is about to attack, drive into, or drop on top of the gunman. The following, largely nonsensical pages of film script – assembled from fragments of cut-up text – apparently take place in a dystopian location: 'some tremendous posters in rubber seem to be in the destruction of the city and do not stand side by side as in a picture'.[27]

At the end of the decade, Paolozzi made the bronze work *Crash Head* (1970, Figure 8.2), modelled on the head of a crash test dummy. Paolozzi collected images of crash test dummies – or 'road research simulators' – and his archive contains examples of these materials as well as letters to and from organisations responsible for manufacturing the mannequins.[28] In *Crash Head*, bolts on either side of the neck of the figure echo those of depictions of Frankenstein's monster; a chain attached to the top of the head makes it

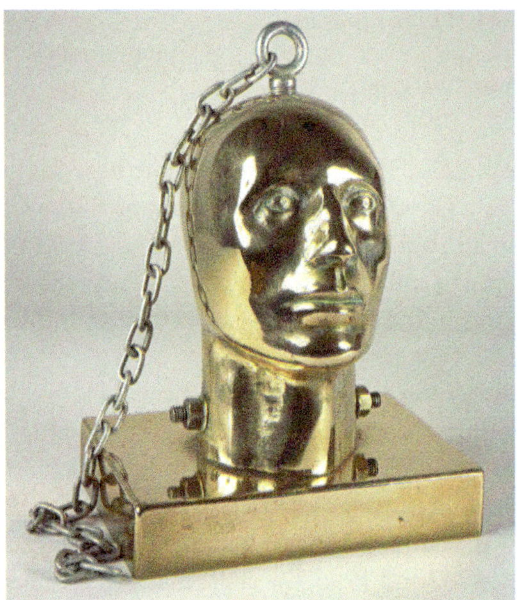

Figure 8.2 Eduardo Paolozzi, *Crash Head* (1970), National Galleries of Scotland. Bequeathed by Gabrielle Keiller, 1995. Source: © The Paolozzi Foundation, Licensed by DACS 2023.

simultaneously deployable as a mace-like weapon, and as a decorative (if far too large) key-ring. The slick rectangular plinth on which the head is secured and displayed raises a mass-produced industrial device to the level of precious object, while also suggesting a severed head on a platter (served up, perhaps, by Salome or Judith). As with the earlier sculpture *Crash*, the neatness and buffed metallic sheen of *Crash Head* disavow catastrophe, but the content and form of the piece evoke violence: how did the head come to be sliced so cleanly from its shoulders? Once again, motion is insinuated: not only of the decapitation, but also of the violence committed as a matter of course against road research simulators – a violence regularly captured on film or video and subsequently included, often in slow motion, in driving safety advertisements. The 'Crash' named in the sculpture's title, then, has already transpired, leaving the artist/scientist with a severed head to experiment with, bolt onto a fresh assembly, provide with new life.

In 1970, the same year that Paolozzi made *Crash Head*, J. G. Ballard published his experimental story collection, *The Atrocity Exhibition*. The book contained a short story, 'Crash!', written in 1968, which engages with the attractions and perverse erotics of auto-crash fatalities; the piece began to address some of the concerns that would be explored at greater length in Ballard's novel *Crash* (1973).[29] The short story (and, indeed, the whole of *The Atrocity Exhibition*) uses a cut-up format similar to that adopted by Paolozzi in his text-based experiments and artworks. The dry tone of social science reports is adopted, presenting violent and sexual content in an objective manner:

> Numerous studies have been conducted to assess the latent sexual appeal of public figures who have achieved subsequent notoriety as auto-crash fatalities, e. g. James Dean, Jayne Mansfield, Albert Camus. Simulated newsreels of politicians, film stars and TV celebrities were shown to panels of (a) suburban housewives, (b) terminal paretics, (c) filling station personnel. Sequences showing auto-crash victims brought about a marked acceleration of pulse and respiratory rates. Many volunteers became convinced that the fatalities were still living, and later used one or other of the crash victims as a private focus of arousal during intercourse with the domestic partner.[30]

Soon after authoring the story, in 1969, Ballard put on an exhibition of crashed cars at the New Arts Lab in London. Three cars were exhibited: a Mini, an Austin A40 and a Pontiac. As Ballard recounted in an interview conducted two years later, the staging of the exhibition seemed to coax barely-sublimated aggressive and sexual impulses out of attendees:

> The show went on for a month. In that time [the vehicles] came up against massive hostility of every kind. The cars were attacked, windows ripped off. Those windows that weren't broken already were smashed. One of the cars was upended, another splashed with white paint. Now the whole thing was a speculative illustration of a scene in *The Atrocity Exhibition*. […] It was not so much an exhibition of sculpture as almost of experimental psychology, using the medium of the fine-art show.[31]

Distinctions blur, causing ruptures in propriety. In Ballard's short story, scientific subjects fail to distinguish between real celebrity deaths and 'simulated newsreels', and they indulge in sexual fantasies about crash victims; at an art exhibition of damaged vehicles, audiences fail to act appropriately, interacting physically with the objects on display as if taking part in an experiment, exacerbating the automobile mutilation.

The 1971 interview with Ballard, in which he discussed the exhibition of crashed cars, also involved Paolozzi. At one point in the conversation, Frank Whitford, the interviewer, posed a question: 'Both of you often choose images which have to do with crashes, violence of all kinds, but particularly with car crashes. For which particular ideas or feelings does the car crash act as a metaphor?' Ballard provided an answer: 'The car crash is probably the only act of violence most of us in Western Europe are ever going to be involved with, is probably the most dramatic event in our lives apart from our own deaths, and in many cases the two are going to coincide.'[32] In a brief afterword on 'Crash!', published in a 1990 edition of *The Atrocity Exhibition*, Ballard expanded on this point, reflecting on the cultural significance of the car crash:

> Aside from the fact that we generally own or are at the controls of the crashing vehicle, the car crash differs from other disasters in that it involves the most powerfully advertised commercial product of this century, an iconic entity that combines the elements of speed, power, dream and freedom within a highly stylised format that defuses any fears we may have of the inherent dangers of these violent and unstable machines.[33]

Car crashes, that is, achieve their particular power in the social and cultural imaginary through the damage they enact upon the extraordinary power of advertising imagery. Pop art repeatedly features images of polished, glistening cars, cropped or copied from advertising: Paolozzi's *Bunk!* screen prints, for instance, feature a number of examples. Occasionally, however, Pop also contemplated the darker flipside of these commercial images, dwelling on the smashed and dismantled consumer product, on car carnage.

Pop Smash

A key artist in this regard is Andy Warhol. In June of 1962, Warhol met the curator Henry Geldzahler for lunch, who advised the artist to move away from focusing on emblems of 'life' in his art (Campbell's soup cans, Coca-Cola bottles) and to turn his attention to 'death'. The following day, Warhol created *129 Die in Jet*, based on the cover of an issue of the *New York Mirror*, and one of his final hand-painted pieces of work. This painting can be seen to inaugurate a large body of works that the artist produced between 1962 and 1967, collectively known as the 'Death and Disaster' series. These include images of a gangster funeral; of an atomic bomb explosion; dozens of paintings of car crashes and suicides; screen prints of an electric chair; images of a race riot in Birmingham, Alabama; and screen prints of a newspaper story about two women poisoned by eating tainted cans of tuna fish. Also related to the series are Warhol's screen prints of Marilyn Monroe, which he began making within weeks of her suicide in 1962; of Liz Taylor, whose ill health almost capsized the making of *Cleopatra* (Mankiewicz, 1963); and of Jackie Kennedy, whose widowing in 1963 pushed Warhol towards what Thomas Crow calls 'a sustained act of remembrance'.[34]

Some of the images that Warhol used for his 'Death and Disaster' series were taken from widely distributed newspapers and magazines. Others were more carefully and selectively sourced: as Crow notes, '[f]ar from limiting himself to newspaper photographs that might have come his way by chance, he searched out prints from the press agencies themselves, which only journalistic professionals could normally have seen'.[35] Some of these 'were apparently deemed too bizarre or horrific ever to be published'.[36] Certainly, the lurid detail of some of the car crash and suicide screen prints – even though they may be somewhat hidden by poor image registration or paint smearing – is marked, retaining the capacity to surprise and revolt. In many of the 'Death and Disaster' images, a selected photograph will be screen-printed multiple times onto the same canvas, creating a pattern across the work's surface. Crow offers insight into the car crash works, and the place of repetition in them. Echoing Ballard's comments on the cultural significance of the car crash, Crow writes that Warhol's images of automobile disasters 'commemorate events in which the supreme symbol of consumer afflu-ence, the American car of the 1950s, lost its aura of pleasure and freedom to become a concrete instrument of sudden and irreparable injury'.[37] He asks whether the repetition of the imagery in the screen prints 'cancel[s]' our 'attention to the visible anguish in the faces of the living or the horror of the limp bodies of the unconscious and dead' and notes that 'it might just as well be taken to register the grim predictability, day after day, of more events with an identical outcome, the levelling sameness with which real, not symbolic, death erupts into daily life'.[38] Other authors have been more critical about Warhol's use of repetition in these works: Bradford Collins, for instance, argues that the device both 'numbs the senses' and prompts us to search for differences between largely identical images.[39] 'What we see in these paintings', he argues, 'is a determined campaign to prevent the viewer from fully experiencing the shocking horror of the original events'.[40]

An alternative take on Warhol's car crash screenprints would approach them as cinematic – perhaps even as prime instances of Pop cinema. The repeated images on the canvases resemble film stills presented in succession, or photographs that could be assembled as a flicker book. There is a clear intimation of animation in works such as *Orange Car Crash 14 Times* (1963). The differing registration of the various repetitions of the same image lead the viewer to read them as distinct, extracts from a narrative sequence depicting the aftermath of a collision. A car has been totalled, but a light is pulsating: the car's indicators flickering, perhaps, or the lights of a nearby emergency vehicle illuminating the scene. A lighter patch at the left of each image waxes and wanes; is smoke emitting from the bonnet in waves? In other paintings, such as *Green Car Crash (Green Burning Car I)* (1963), the repeated images overlap, filling the canvas; the effect is reminiscent of film stock getting jammed in the gate, the image legible but vibrating, blank areas of the canvas reading as the snapping or burning through of the celluloid.

The closest that Warhol came to making a film of a car crash was his 1966 work *Since*, a feature-length, largely improvised drama based on the assassination of John F. Kennedy. Kennedy's car did not crash following the shooting (it was driven directly to a hospital), but the incident in Dallas brought together, in a spectacular and now mythic fashion, an automobile and the desecration of human bodies. Whereas Warhol's Jackie Kennedy screen prints are acts of mourning, *Since* is frantic, anarchic. As J. J. Murphy writes of the film,

> It's almost as if the death of the president becomes directly related to the sense of chaos that seems to exist among the participants on set. […] There is no attempt at realism. A large, crumpled sheet of red construction paper becomes blood. A banana substitutes for a gun. The couch in the Factory [Warhol's studio] serves as a car. Rather than evoking sadness, *Since* is actually quite comedic.[41]

In contrast, Bruce Conner's *REPORT* (1967) offers a more serious engagement with the assassination. In the first half of the thirteen-minute film, the soundtrack presents an account, narrated by news reporters, of the motorcade being attacked. This is accompanied by a limited array of visual material: looped footage of the president's car passing by; an illegible flicker of alternating black and white frames; a black screen; footage of a rifle being carried over someone's head; Jackie Kennedy climbing into the back of a car; countdown leader. In the second half of the film, which is slightly shorter than the first, we have looped backwards in time; the audio is of a news report about the Kennedys travelling on a state visit. The visuals accompanying this account are dense, complex: footage of the president and his wife meeting members of the public, getting out of aeroplanes and so on is intercut with a bullfight, an advertisement for a fridge, a rocket taking off, the Statue of Liberty, an atomic bomb mushroom cloud, footage from *Frankenstein* (Whale, 1931) … [42] The imagery of commercial television is chopped into snippets, shuffled, the banal intermixed with the horrific. Even though a car crash is not depicted in either *Since* or *REPORT*, both offer Pop takes on a famous historic incident of automobile-related tragedy, providing alternative models for registering the disruptive impact of such an event.

Conclusion

Although the images and soundtrack of Paolozzi's *The History of Nothing*, as Robin Spencer notes, may seem to be a 'random juxtaposition', there is some form and systematisation at play in the completed work.[43] Shapes match and rhyme across individual shots; particular collage elements (such as the mechanical butterfly design) reappear in different assemblages; stretches of soundtrack serve to provide coherence (however opaque) to particular sequences of images. Paolozzi evidently spent considerable time planning the film, as he produced both a set of notes about it, as well as a shooting script. Both were included in a forty-eight-page screen printed book called *Metafisikal Translations*, which was published in an edition of 100 in 1962, the same year as the film was made. Only one page in length, the shooting script consisted mainly of gestures at content: evocative phrases, allusions to a structure, the naming of some concrete objects. The relationship between the shooting script and the completed film is slight, but occasional links are present: a 'distorted lunatic cat' definitely appears, as do 'Robots aeroplanes ancient and modern'. One sentence of the script, however, seems to describe a significant moment of apocalyptic drama: 'MIDDLE SHOT Radial engine. Floral gears. Useful analogy military insignia transfer. Lagoon seen through cars windscreen. Aerial view of a city burning'.[44] Laocoön is mis-identified here as 'Lagoon' – but what is being described, in part, is the collision collage with which this essay opened. Reading this sentence in the script as narrative, as sequence, then the car-Laocoön collision results in devastation, a city on fire. This is not what transpires in the film: the next shot in the finished work is of a catalogue page of cogs and wheels. Or do these mechanical parts imply the car's disintegration, following the accident – a lesser but still significant type of cataclysm?

In the 1971 interview with Paolozzi and Ballard in which the two are asked about their interest in vehicular crashes, Paolozzi identifies a broader shared interest and approach:

> I think Ballard's subject-matter and mine touch at certain points. We're both involved with the encounter with machines, and we're both involved with forcing people to look and with preventing them from escaping from certain facts. I don't want to make prints that will help people to escape from the terrible world. I want to remind them.[45]

The History of Nothing may seem to bombard viewers with 'the terrible world'; its dominant tone is one of threat. A number of its images are sinister, unsettling; the music and sounds selected for the audio track are often

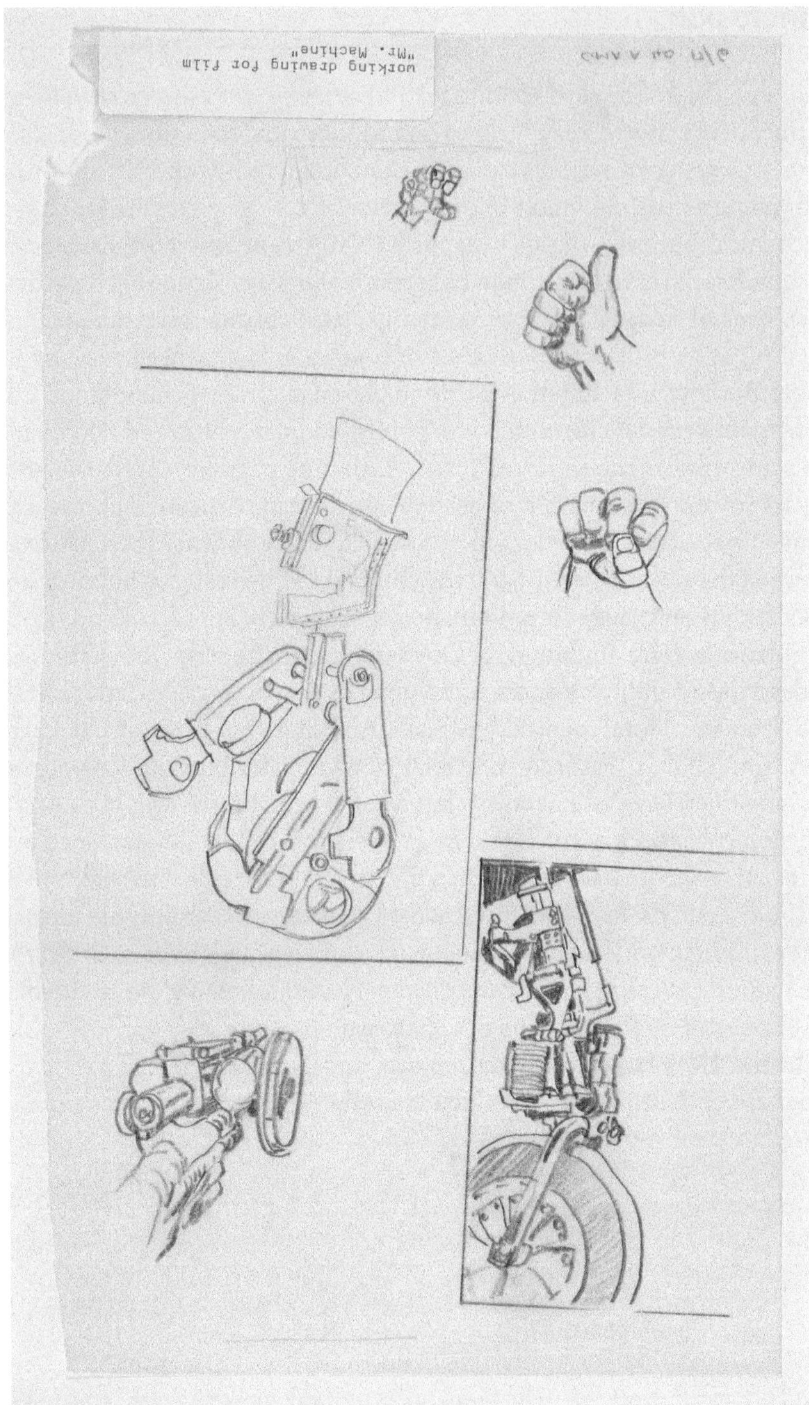

Figure 8.3 Eduardo Paolozzi, *Untitled [Mr Machine Working Drawing]* (ca 1974). National Galleries of Scotland. Source: © The Paolozzi Foundation, Licensed by DACS 2023.

abrasive. The film does contain brief moments of lightness, even whimsy: in one collage, for instance, two airline hostesses near the bottom of the stairs into a TWA aeroplane are met by a large, primitive automaton, whose name, Robert the Robot, appears printed on his form, roughly where his face might be. Such flashes are fleeting, however.

Paolozzi's 1971 film *Mr Machine*, made with the animators Peter Leake and Keith Griffiths and another significant work of Pop cinema, also slips swiftly from lightness into a darker mode. As Paolozzi stated in a 1983 talk at Middlesborough Art Gallery, the film 'drew inspiration from a small plastic toy bought in New York in the 60s – a golden age for American toys now sadly past'.[46] The five-minute black-and-white work brings to life drawings that the artist made of the toy (Figure 8.3), a simple mechanical man wearing a top hat. 'The mixture of mechanical and what I see as sinister perfection made an ideal motif for drawing', said Paolozzi; 'A story developed in which, by metaphor, Mr Machine destroys a city and civilisation – then destroys himself'.[47] Once again, Paolozzi teases out the dark underside of the commercial product; Pop's fascination with the potential for disaster inherent in advertising's promise of plenty resurfaces. What is especially notable, however – as this essay has demonstrated – is the frequency with which the automobile and its destruction has served as the focus of Pop's artists when they have engaged with this concern. Further, although these artists have forged vital interrogations of vehicular disaster using sculpture and screen printing, it is arguably through instances of Pop cinema that the mechanical, carnal, affective and symbolic ruptures caused by the car crash have been most deftly explored.

Notes

1 Diane Kirkpatrick, *Eduardo Paolozzi*, London: Studio Vista, 1970, p. 87.

2 Robin Spencer, 'Introduction: A Language for the Translation of Experience', in Spencer (ed.), *Eduardo Paolozzi: Writings and Interviews*, Oxford: Oxford University Press, 2000, p. 29.

3 Ibid., p. 31.

4 Kirkpatrick, op. cit., p. 92.

5 A fifth film was made but is no longer extant. Robin Spencer: 'After the exhibition *Parallel of Life and Art* in 1953, the artists, with Nigel Henderson and Peter Foldes, were awarded a grant of £50 (probably by the BFI) to make a film, which consisted of film-stock segments, clips from scientific films; some prints were dyed, and a soundtrack was added, but the film has since been lost'. See Spencer (ed.), op. cit., p. 344.

6 Lawrence Alloway, '"Pop art" since 1949', in Richard Kalina (ed.), *Lawrence Alloway: Imagining the Present: Context, Content and the Role of the Critic*, London and New York: Routledge, 2006, p. 81.

7 Ibid., p. 83.

8 Ibid., p. 82.

9 *Paolozzi*, dir: Louise Wardle, tx: 23:25 07/12/2000, BBC2 England, 35 mins.

10 Alloway, op. cit., p. 83.

11 Lawrence Alloway, 'The Development of British Pop', in Lucy Lippard (with contributions by Alloway, Nancy Marmer and Nicolas Calas), *Pop Art*, London: Thames and Hudson, 1970, 3rd ed., p. 36.

12 Ibid.

13 Daniel Herrmann, 'Eduardo Paolozzi: *Pop Art Redefined*', in Herrmann (ed.), *Eduardo Paolozzi*, London: Whitechapel Gallery, 2017, p. 9.

14 Ibid., p. 13.

15 Anne Massey, *The Independent Group: Modernism and Mass Culture in Britain, 1945–59*, Manchester and New York: Manchester University Press, 1995, p. 46.

16 For a detailed account of the history of *Bunk!* – both the original lecture and the subsequent screen print series – see John-Paul Stonard, 'The "Bunk" Collages of Eduardo Paolozzi', *The Burlington Magazine*, 150:1261 (April 2008), pp. 238–49.

17 Ed Halter, 'Pop and Cinema: Three Tendencies', in Darsie Alexander and Bartholomew Ryan (eds), *International Pop*, Minneapolis: Walker Art Center, 2015, p. 182. This essay is reprinted in this collection.

18 Graham Witham, 'Exhibitions', in David Robbins (ed.), *The Independent Group: Postwar Britain and the Aesthetics of Plenty*, Cambridge, MA, and London: MIT Press, 1990, p. 141.

19 Herrmann, op. cit., p. 9.

20 Ibid.

21 'Speculative Illustrations: Eduardo Paolozzi in conversation with J. G. Ballard and Frank Whitford', in Spencer (ed.), op. cit., p. 199.

22 See Stonard, op. cit., p. 242.

23 Kirkpatrick, op. cit., p. 75.

24 Ibid., p. 77.

25 Elly Thomas, '"Meccano Work": Eduardo Paolozzi's Kits', *Sculpture Journal*, 25:1 (2016), p. 108.

26 David Brittain, *The Jet Age Compendium: Eduardo Paolozzi at* Ambit, London: Four Corners Books, 2009, pp. 9–10.

27 Eduardo Paolozzi, 'The Unfilmed Scripts of Eduardo Paolozzi', *Ambit*, 50 (1972), p. 33.

28 See Spencer (ed.), op. cit., p. 196 for examples of these images. Paolozzi's *Conditional Probability Machine*, made in the same year as *Crash Head*, is worth noting here: a portfolio of twenty-four photogravures, it was divided into four sets of six prints. One set, titled 'Manikins for Destruction', featured images of vehicle crashes and crash test dummies.

29 Hal Foster has referred to *Crash* as a 'great Pop novel' and to Ballard as 'the best complement of Warhol in fiction': Foster, 'Death in America', *October*, 75 (Winter 1996), p. 48. For a sustained exploration of the relationship between *Crash* and Pop art, see Karen Beckman, 'Film Falls Apart: *Crash*, Semen, and Pop', *Grey Room*, 12 (Summer 2003), pp. 94–115.

30 J. G. Ballard, *The Atrocity Exhibition*, London: Fourth Estate, 2014, p. 153.

31 'Speculative Illustrations', op. cit., p. 201.

32 Ibid.
33 Ballard, op. cit., p. 157.
34 Thomas Crow, *Modern Art in the Common Culture*, New Haven: Yale University Press, 1996, p. 56.
35 Ibid., p. 61.
36 Ibid.
37 Ibid., p. 60.
38 Ibid., pp. 60–61.
39 Bradford R. Collins, 'Warhol's Modern Dance of Death: *Work* and *Text*', *American Art*, 30:2 (Summer 2016), p. 50.
40 Ibid., p. 52.
41 J. J. Murphy, *The Black Hole of the Camera: The Films of Andy Warhol*, Los Angeles: University of California Press, 2012, pp. 141–42.
42 For a sustained examination of Conner's *REPORT* and its use of (and commentary on) television, see Erica Levin, *The Channeled Image: Art and Media Politics after Television*, Chicago: The University of Chicago Press, 2022, pp. 25–58.
43 Spencer (ed.), op. cit., p. 97.
44 The shooting script appears in facsimile form in Spencer (ed.), ibid., p. 98.
45 'Speculative Illustrations', op. cit., p. 204.
46 'Eduardo Paolozzi – Invited Artist', in Spencer (ed.), op. cit., p. 231.
47 Ibid.

9

Wynn Chamberlain's *Brand X* (1970) and the Politics of the Generic

Kara Carmack

Throughout Wynn Chamberlain's film *Brand X* (1970), video artist Serge Boutourline periodically materialises to sell dirt. In his first appearance, accompanied by a psychedelic soundtrack, a hand cleans a white porcelain sink. Boutourline's voice-over softly asks the viewer: 'Is your house too clean? Did you know that, if your house is too clean, it may cause dangerous viruses to grow?' His instruction, 'use dirt', precedes the camera's cut to Boutourline pouring water out of a pure white teapot onto a pile of dirt spread across his bare legs because, so he explains, dirt is 'the only thing that can cause bacteria to grow'. Each time Boutourline speaks, the camera closely frames his heavily bearded face as his blue eyes implore the viewer to believe him, to buy what he is selling. The segment cuts from close-up pitches to product demonstrations: 'Dirt really works', he proclaims, rubbing moistened dirt variously across his stomach, chest and, finally, his face. 'Use dirt', he repeats.

This sardonic anti-commercial – one of many in the film – punctuates *Brand X*'s cycle of 'early morning masochistic game shows, voyeuristic talk shows, and fetishistic exercise programmes […] X-rated soap operas […] the sadistic late movie and crass closing sermon-for-this-day', as one reviewer described it.[1] Not naming a branded product – it is just dirt, not Dirt™ – the segment sells neither a unique material good nor a substance with monetary value. Dirt is free and widely available. However, Chamberlain shows that, if one deploys the semiotic language of ad men, then anything and everything can be commodified. Persuasive editing and sloganeering engender demand. Mimicking the subtle and not-so-subtle commercial practices of 1960s' advertising agencies, Chamberlain composes a sales pitch for an undesirable product that cannot be commercialised. An entire post-war economy was built on America's obsession with cleanliness, as evidenced by the abundance of print and televisual ads for bleaches, soaps and detergents, along with their attendant cleaning appliances such as vacuums, dishwashers and washing machines. Dirt, viruses and bacteria were to be eradicated, removed and feared as they metaphorically represented tensions over race, class, gender and war.[2] Paradoxically, in Chamberlain's televisual universe of *Brand X*, the polluted and the perverse are the order of the day.

Embedded in its socio-political and artistic moment, *Brand X* deploys the titular marketing strategy of 'Brand X' to denounce nearly all aspects of American culture that by the end of the decade had become increasingly codified, commercialised and branded. The term 'Brand X' originated in the middle of the twentieth century to refer to an unidentified, undesirable product that always fails to perform as well as a comparable name-brand product. It often stood in for a leading primary competitor; consumers can intuit that the 'Brand X' product in a Pepsi advertisement, for example, is Coca-Cola without the use of the latter's name and logo.[3] 'Brand X, the product that isn't supposed to work, is propaganda for the politics of joy and disorder', declared Chamberlain.[4] The salve to the country's anaemic and wearisome state by the late 1960s is not, in *Brand X*, rooted in wholesome, educational and rich content, but rather jubilant off-colour parody and taboo topics that revel in the inane and push society further into depravity.

Branding itself a 'Brand X', the film gleefully self-identifies as an inauthentic subpar competitor to the brands that had consolidated around Pop art, underground films and counter-cultural movements by the decade's end. Taking Chamberlain's title at face value, I argue that *Brand X* is an acerbic rejoinder to the pervasive politics and aesthetics of Pop, film, liberal and conservative ideologies and advertising's so-called 'Creative Revolution' that borrowed aesthetic strategies from the art and film scenes, through what I call the politics of the generic. Although generic products would not reach their heyday until the 1970s in the United States, *Brand X* traffics in the generic's crass aesthetic, lower quality and namelessness to tackle, like Chamberlain's fellow American Pop artists, critical discourses surrounding the rapid expansion of what journalist Vance Packard called 'hidden persuasion' in his 1957 bestselling book warning of the advertising industry's subliminal tactics for manipulating consumers.[5] But unlike other Pop moving image works that sardonically engage with post-war consumption, advertising and television, such as Robert Downey's *Putney Swope* (1969) and later Ann Magnuson and Tom Rubnitz's *Made for TV* (1984), *Brand X* eschews the brand in favour of its disparaged inverse.

T. T. V.

Brand X begins, as a day of television-watching does, with turning on the set. In the opening sequence, Taylor Mead – playing the role of a studio executive of the fictional T. T. V. station who is at once a producer and a consumer of televisual content – lays across the floor in front of a small TV in his cramped, disorderly apartment. The room, as Chamberlain pointedly describes, 'is a vortex of printed, scribbled, painted, photographic information [and] is a metaphor of the counter-culture, which we commend as an alternative'.[6] The camera slowly zooms toward the flickering screen as Mead reaches for one of the set's knobs. He watches a sequence of figures who scream at the viewer and at one another undisturbed, even a little bored. He then waves an antenna in the air like an orchestra conductor, gesturing to not only network studios' power to control production and dissemination, but also to the fiction of consumer power – that there is choice in what one watches. Once Mead changes the TV channel, he arrives at the same content (screaming) only with a different set of actors. The channel has changed, the people have changed, yet the fundamentally mindless content persists. As this realisation dawns on Mead's studio executive, fear and horror replace curiosity at the ridiculous, distasteful product he has perversely created.

This brief narrative arc that collapses producer and consumer into one figure epitomises a well-known provocation put forth by Newton N. Minow, the chairman of the Federal Communications Commission. Speaking at the National Association of Broadcasters' convention in 1961, Minow challenged the broadcasters to sit in front of their television sets 'and stay there, for a day, without a book, without a magazine, without a newspaper […] Keep your eyes glued to that set until the station signs off. I can assure you that what you will observe is a vast wasteland'.[7] Minow described television as a bleak landscape overrun by easily digestible and predictable content. 'You will see a procession of game shows, formula comedies about totally unbelievable families', he warned, as well as 'blood and thunder, mayhem, violence, sadism, murder, western bad men, western good men, private eyes, gangsters, more violence, and cartoons'.[8] Perhaps the most offensive were the endless commercials – 'many screaming, cajoling, and offending' – which *Brand X* seemingly delights in during its opening minutes.[9]

Brand X recreates and compresses a day of televisual programming into an absurdist, frenzied, hallucinatory experience. Commercials for improbable and taboo products like sweat, drugs and sex interrupt the flow of the film's programmes that include the 'What's My Sex?' game show, sponsored by a battery-operated vibrator company generically named Stimulator,

Tally Brown's daytime talk show parody 'Boys Talk' and a Johnny Carson-style show hosted by Taylor Mead, called 'The Tomorrow Show'.[10] The wide-ranging content paired with Chamberlain's cadre of counter-cultural icons – film stars Candy Darling and Ultra Violet, activist Abbie Hoffman, musician Jimi Hendrix and poet Anne Waldman – speak to the interconnected fields of American political activism and the arts in the late 1960s and their intersection with commercial mass media. With many of the actors repeatedly appearing in multiple roles, the dizzying array of programmes concludes with an irreverent late-night televangelical sermon delivered by a priest-playing Mead, followed by a shot of the American flag overlaid with the music of 'The Star-Spangled Banner'.

Mead's initial character is, in part, a cipher for the viewer. Audience members watch through the eyes of Mead's proprietor of and subscriber to T. T. V. the vast wasteland of programming that he has put on the air. The character is also an avatar for Chamberlain himself, who was inspired to make *Brand X* after a severe snowstorm trapped him and his wife Sally in their Staatsburg, New York, cottage for an entire weekend.[11] With nowhere to go and nothing to do, Chamberlain was forced to watch endless hours of banal and superficial content that left him feeling 'dismayed by the conservatism of mainstream culture, as embodied by TV', yet he soon transformed from bored TV viewer to the producer of his own sequence of inane TV programming in *Brand X*.[12] Indeed, *The Cornell Daily Sun* described the film as 'a TV producer's nightmares, or wet dreams, or hallucinations'.[13] Chamberlain and Mead, trapped variously in front of their television sets eight years after Minow's plea for culturally healthy programming, assemble an onslaught of vacuous content of the type against which Minow had railed.

Pop Art and the Politics of the Generic

By the time Chamberlain – then best-known for his Pop paintings of nude members of New York's creative underground and as producer of Charles Ludlam's off-off-Broadway play *Conquest of the Universe, or When Queens Collide* (1967) – filmed *Brand X* in 1969, the idea of the brand had spilled far beyond the edges of the domain of advertising. The New Left, the underground film scene and Pop art had coalesced around mutually acknowledged aesthetics and manufactured their own brandable cultures. The counter-cultural movement sold itself through psychedelic graphics, long hair and gender-bending flowy clothing that diametrically opposed the aesthetic of the straights' coiffed hair, clean-cut attire and conservative politics.

The form and content of 'underground film' had become a brand by the end of the decade, distinguished from that of the mainstream. In 1967, Sheldon Renan observed: 'The press [...] picked up the underground appellation because it made good copy. Exhibitors found more people would come to see "underground films" than would come to see something called "avant-garde" or "independent". *Underground film* has thus been absorbed into the national vocabulary'.[14] American Pop artists famously embraced the phenomenon of name-brand consolidation and unequivocally heralded its rise. Ed Ruscha emphasised the bold graphic recognizable design of Standard gas station signs. Jasper Johns fastidiously reproduced Ballantine Ale labels on his cast bronze beer cans and Tom Wesselmann dotted his still-life works with identifiable logos of products such as 7-Up, Café Bustelo and Camel. The distinction between advertising and fine art blurred as the 1960s wore on. Campbell's soup, for example, commissioned and sold Andy Warhol's *Souper Dress* (1966–67). Pop art thus became actual advertising for commercially made products, but also for itself and the celebrity artists behind it. The flat, colourful and boldly graphic representational style of the Pop artists became so easily identifiable in the American media landscape as a counter-point to Abstract Expressionism that, as Thomas Crow has demonstrated, everyone from an art director at *Esquire* to the rock band The Who appropriated it and thereby infused it back into the popular vernacular.[15] Pop turned itself into its own familiar, seemingly differentiated brand.

Chamberlain's film questions the brand cultures pervading all sectors of American life, including his own field of Pop. Across the country, sophisticated marketing campaigns competed to build brand differentiation and customer loyalty in a crowded field of post-war consumer standardised goods. The dilemma for ad men, as celebrated ad agency president David Ogilvy observed, was that there 'really isn't any significance between the various brands of whiskey or the various cigarettes or the various brands of beer'.[16] It was thus up to advertising agencies to conceive of and market a successful brand that was more than an image or a product, one that could elicit 'a character or personality that may be more important for the over-all status (and sales) of the brand than many technical facts about the product'.[17] In organising consumers' perceptions of brands, the imagery, according to ad consultant Irving S. White, 'provides the emotional and sensual qualities which distinguish a brand from the general product-class and help the consumer discriminate from brand to brand'.[18] Within the common class of Pop art, each artist necessarily had to differentiate themselves from one another, like soap and beer companies did. Warhol stopped painting comic strip characters after seeing Roy Lichtenstein's 1962 solo exhibition at

Castelli Gallery, for example, as the two resultant products were too similar for the art market.[19]

Chamberlain reframes the phenomenon of the brand in *Brand X* by embracing its foil of Brand X and deconstructing brand equity and his fellow Pop artists' embrace of name-brands. Compare, for example, *Brand X* with Andy Warhol's Cadence commercials (1965) and Fred Mogubgub's *The Great Society* (1967) that likewise focus on branding and television commercials. In one of Warhol's stark black-and-white Cadence ads commissioned by the ad agency Foote, Cone & Belding, actress Sunny Harnett prominently holds a bottle of the minimally packaged laxatives with its bold black name-brand letters emblazoned across its light background. Formally similar to Warhol's short Screen Tests – like Lou Reed drinking a bottle of Coca-Cola for the artist's unrelenting camera in 1966 – the commercial merges Warhol's recognizable branded aesthetic with Cadence's. Mogubgub's film flashes name-brand products like Anacin, Quaker Oats and Newport cigarettes across the screen to the tune of 'The Battle Hymn of the Republic', a cheeky wink at a great American society built on conspicuous consumption. Warhol's and Mogubgub's works participate within and manage the sign-system of American branding, while Chamberlain's film imagines alternatives by rejoicing in the generic nature of dirt, sweat and sex.

Chamberlain's film differs from Warhol's and Mogubgub's works not only in content and ideology but also in form, which is especially evident when contextualising *Brand X* alongside other contemporaneous underground films concerned with television's rising ubiquity in America, such as Warhol's *Soap Opera* (1964–65).[20] *Soap Opera* interrupts cinematic time with commercials but does not capture the structural pacing of TV time. Warhol intercuts his soap opera parody with actual commercials produced by Lester Perskey; they are readymades plucked out of their televisual context to be reused and recycled in film. The result, as Lynn Spigel observes, is that '[b]ecause the scenes are shot with a static camera, bad lighting, and no sound (and most segments have almost no editing), the soap opera portions of the film seem entirely banal when compared to the commercials'.[21] Warhol's film underscores the sophistication of 1960s commercials that many believed demonstrated more technical innovation and creative daring than the bland programmes.[22] Chamberlain's project, however, argues for no distinction across commercials and content. The formal and conceptual absurdity of the commercials bleeds across the programmes – jockstrap and Stimulator promos pair with the 'What's My Sex?' gameshow, for example – and thus emphasise the capitalist bedrock of the medium, built on an erasure of difference between entertainment and advertisements.

The modest attempts to apply a televisual structure to film in *Soap Opera* maintain a keen distinction between ad time and content. Such films become, then, *about* TV, but not *of* it.

In contrast, Chamberlain coerces film to act televisually and television to act cinematically. He experimented with the widescreen ratio and cinematography to simulate that of TV. He recalls of his experimentation: 'TV shaped mats were tried to create a distinction between the scene shots and shots p.o.v. tube front. They looked corny. Special footage for station breaks was shot, but after the first screenings these were eliminated because the breaks made people nervous [...] as though they needed a ham sandwich or a Fresca. This gave us an insight into the power of the TV format'.[23] *Brand X* may therefore be read as an experiment in the possibilities and limits of film and TV when attempting to bridge the two forms. 'We were impressed by TV's ability to compress information and deliver simultaneously on many levels – a device usually reserved for poetry', continues Chamberlain. 'We use this and visual frontality to make our point about TV, and we combine these with an overall structure of cutting and scoring which is cinematic in its building of movements, its compression of time and meanings – its welding of the disjointed sequences of TV into a continuous whole'.[24] *Brand X* wavers between the cinematic and televisual, manifesting a discomfiting experience.

By the late 1960s, viewers had increasingly become accustomed to watching film on television, which inverted the movie-going experience.[25] Viewers look toward light radiating out of a screen when watching film on TV, rather than looking with the light streaming from a projector. Additionally, the quality and format undergo shifts from one medium to the other. As Renan observes,

> Television is like film, but it's not film. When a viewer sees a film he is seeing an image made up of light moderated by shadow, and the texture is of thousands and thousands of tiny grains, usually imperceptible. When he watches television he is seeing an image made up of fluorescent light, and the texture is of hundreds of visible horizontal lines. The quality of image is different. The quality of the television image is of immediacy, and never of spectacle (film); of flow, and never of stability (film). Films are frequently run on television, but then their effect is not of film, but of television.[26]

Conversely, television is never shown on film, which accounts for the discomfort that viewers felt at Chamberlain's attempt at 'station breaks' during the first few screenings of *Brand X*. The unstable, immediate image of TV uncomfortably mixes with the stability and spectacle of film in Chamberlain's project. *Brand X* even makes fun of this media clash by including a parody of late-night melodramatic black-and-white b-movies with *Down on Your Ole Plantation*, featuring Taylor Mead, Sally Kirkland and Tally Brown. To watch a film on TV is to watch TV, not film; to watch TV on film is to watch film, not TV. By confusing and conflating the two, Chamberlain posits a new experiential and sensorial way of seeing and viewing both.

In so doing, *Brand X* wades into the discourses of underground film, the expectations of cinema and its uneasy relationship with fine art. Chamberlain notes:

> There is a certain flatness to the style of photography and camera movement in *Brand X*, thereby leaving the film open to attack by critics who espouse the fashionable standards of art film criticism. Our purpose was to imitate the flatness of the TV image, a style that seems almost simple-minded (until you think about it) like a comic strip, or like Matisse. A style in visual images which is common currency wherever people watch TV.[27]

The 'art film criticism' of the underground film scene and auteur theory propagated in the pages of *Cahiers du Cinéma* and *Film Culture* developed concurrently with the ubiquity of television. Ed Halter has observed: 'As television became the dominant medium of mass entertainment, movies assumed a position of cultural legitimacy formerly held exclusively by the more traditional arts'.[28] Television, then, remained in the realm of the popular arts, and its ubiquity and accessibility functioned to bolster film's status as a high art form – a distinction which *Brand X* troubles in its decided embrace of TV and attempt to marry it with cinema.

For Chamberlain, the flatness of his photography, the film's high-quality production and vivid colours, as well as the pop culture content pushed *Brand X* outside of underground film conventions, even though the film was uneasily labelled as such. Bobby Abrams in *Crawdaddy* called it 'the best underground film I've ever seen', but then warned readers: 'Don't get scared by the label "underground"; it's a label that's meant to be inclusive, not exclusive'.[29] Abrams soothed his readers' worries over the potential inscrutability associated with the term 'underground': 'This film deals with us – a generation brought up on television and dope, revolutions and driver's ed'.[30] He located something new in the film: 'It's the application of Fellini to content. Whereas the Italian filmmakers who came to prominence in the sixties concerned themselves more with style [...] and whereas the early underground filmmakers rarely created a satisfactory entity, we now have a filmmaker who can handle poetry as texture, poetry as style and poetry as meaning'.[31] Jonas Mekas also struggled to identify *Brand X* as strictly underground: 'It's neither Ozu nor Jack Smith nor Jerry Joffen. It's completely somewhere else'.[32] *Brand X* challenged even the brand that had codified around underground cinema by the late 1960s. It transposed the aesthetics and content of the popular medium of television into the reified underground film catalogue, breaking through the high-low threshold and forcing 'underground film' to contend with the form and content of TV.

Just as artists and directors mined the advertising industry's aesthetics and methods, ad men were paying close attention to the popularisation and consolidation of Pop art, underground film and the counter-culture. As Thomas Frank demonstrates in *The Conquest of Cool*, marketing executives in the 1960s began to abandon established practices – the show-and-tell format, products as solutions to problems and hard-sell testimonials – in favour of the soft-sell that privileged concept over function.[33] Critic Parker Tyler argued that television studios had by 1969 become the most 'loyal customers for independent film products [...] which screen them privately for the sake of borrowing tricks from them [...]. Not in the "imaginative" works shown on TV are the best montage and technical effects to be seen, but in the commercials that intersperse these works'.[34] The reciprocal gaze between the mainstream and the underground resulted in a tug-of-war between the two over the aesthetics of youth culture, aesthetic experimentation and individualist non-conformity.

The formal and conceptual approach in Chamberlain's commercials comments directly on the rise of this so-called 'Creative Revolution'. Hip advertising – pairing wit and humour with minimalist design elements – paradoxically proposed to cure mid-century conformity by liberating the masses through capitalist consumption. *Brand X* lays bare the psychologically manipulative tactics deployed by such ad agencies. In its multiple advertisements for 'balling', *Brand X* shows a white heterosexual couple having sex on the back of a sleek red Triumph convertible driving through lush countryside.[35] In one of these ads, the woman lays on her back and splays her legs wide in the air as a man gyrates against her and kisses her neck. A soft voice-over encourages viewers to '[l]oosen up. Get rid of nervous tension. And release the painful pressure on your nerves'. The camera cuts to a view of their bodies from above, particularly the man's toned ass, as the voice instructs us, 'Leave the dumb tight-assed world behind [...]. Try balling. It keeps you young-looking longer. Tones your skin in minutes. And keeps you fresh and soft. Let yourself go anywhere anytime. Balling. It can be fun'.[36] The commercial strips away the euphemism and innuendo that characterises soft-sell car commercials (and those for other products marketed to men). While a hip consumer and hip advertisers might identify with the free expression of love, Chamberlain returns us to the hard-sell. But, rather than selling a commercially-made product, Chamberlain's ad wittingly sells an act – sex – but also a cultural identity rooted in virility and sexual liberation in a brand-identification strategy championed by the Creative Revolution.

In manipulating the semiotic systems of advertising, politics and the dominating artistic trends of the decade, *Brand X* positions itself as the generic other to mid-century America's complex visual field. Its strategy aligns with the contradictory 'Brand X' products that entered the market in the 1960s, when the ubiquitous 'Brand X' paradoxically became a name-brand itself after marketing executives realised that it possessed valuable name-brand recognition. Around 1960, 'Brand X' cigarettes hit the market and its slogan – 'For the Man Who is Satisfied with Nothing Less than Second Best' – capitalised on the term's association with inferiority and poor quality.[37] Politically and aesthetically speaking, *Brand X* brands itself with an X. It always makes the wrong choice, revelling in the punishment for doing so, while striking out on its own to find new liberatory possibilities outside of the dominating brand cultures of the era.

The Revolution Will Not Be Televised

Throughout the 1960s, Americans witnessed national and international events in a way unlike any other generation before: flooded into the private sanctity of their homes. They saw the brutal realities of the America-Vietnam War; race riots in Watts, Newark and Detroit; student protests; and assassinations of movement leaders. The decade's early idealism crumbled as the disaffected youth took to the streets in protest and picked up cameras and pens to not only enact social change, but to produce and circulate counter-narratives to the mainstream media. Gil Scott-Heron's protest song 'The Revolution Will Not be Televised' speaks to the partiality of the mass media, its unwillingness and inability to participate in revolutionary aims because that would mean it would need to self-destruct entirely. News, advertising and politics, so Scott-Heron warns, are not separate, but powerful interlocking systems of hegemonic power that uphold systemic violence and inequity. Likewise wrestling with the relationship between activism and the mass media, *Brand X* offers its own politics of the generic as a new route to cultural and political freedom.

The media's importance to the rebellious anti-racist, anti-capitalist, anti-war and pro-drug movements of the era cannot be overstated. 'You can't be a revolutionary today without a television set! It's as important as a gun', declared activist Jerry Rubin in 1970.[38] A co-founder along with activist Abbie Hoffman and satirist Paul Krassner of the Youth International Party (later known as the Yippies), Rubin acknowledges that, by the end of the decade, television had become a battleground on which the counter-culture waged war against the status quo. The 1960s youth culture was, after all, the first generation raised on TV sets. Consequently, they became exceptionally media savvy and recognised the medium as a socio-political tool wielded by hegemonic forces.

Chamberlain's adoption of the televisual in *Brand X* acknowledges the medium's dominant role in the fraught political landscape of the 1960s, underscored by Yippie agitator Abbie Hoffman's turn as a cop in *Brand X's* 'Money Report'.[39] Hoffman lodges a scathing critique of the intersection of violence, money and racism in the American policing system that he had opposed for years. He introduces himself to the viewer as Loren while sitting on a toilet inside a white-tiled bathroom. A soundtrack of obnoxious gastric noises accompanies his account of coming home 'every night after a hard day of clubbing' – a description not of dancing at a club, but of beating unarmed people on the streets: 'hippies, pinkos, commies, a housewife'. 'I love my money. I bring it home and store it in my bathtub and in the sink', he proclaims. Hoffman's obsession with cleanliness starkly contrasts with Boutourline's praise of dirt. As he explains, 'I keep it here because it's the cleanest place in the house. It's white. And I don't think you could ever have a bathroom that's too white. White's my favourite colour'.[40] State power is rooted not only in violence, but in funding (legal: federal, state and local; and illegal: bribes) and its allegiance to whiteness. Stripping off the uniform, he climbs naked into the bathtub filled with money and continues to narrate his love of capital. However, out of uniform, Hoffman's character falters. The anti-cop anarchist play-acting a racist pig pages through a copy of the recently published *The Bust Book* – a cheap booklet circulated among youth activists and protesters, Black Panthers and student radicals as something of a survival kit against excessive police force (Figure 9.1). The segment ends with him setting money on fire while singing 'America (My Country, 'Tis of Thee)'.[41]

In his 1968 book *Revolution for the Hell of It*, Hoffman advocated for 'advertisement[s] for revolution', which included the clever camera-friendly spectacles of the Yippies.[42] Hoffman's framing of revolution in televisual terms likens activist efforts to commercials, the figure against

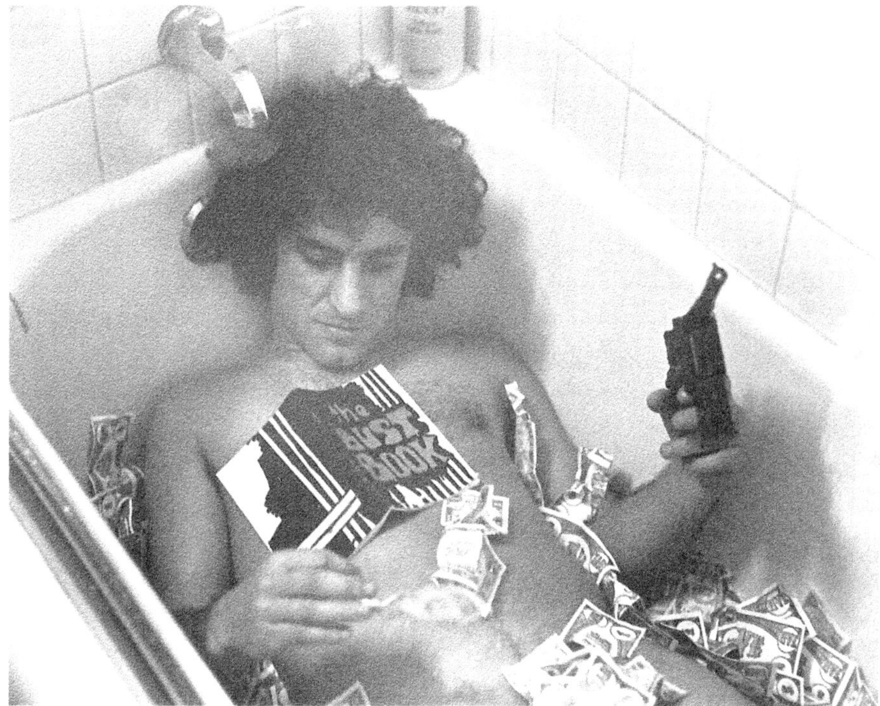

Figure 9.1 Abbie Hoffman in *Brand X*, publicity still. Source: Courtesy of Sam Chamberlain.

the ground of the status quo, or TV programmes. On the polemical media attention given to the state-inflicted violence upon unarmed protestors that unfolded in Chicago after the Yippies attempted to nominate a pig for the Democratic Presidential nominee, Hoffman posits: 'The rhetoric of the [Chicago] Convention was allotted the fifty minutes of the hour, we were given the ten or less usually reserved for the commercials. *We were an advertisement for the revolution.* We were a high degree of involvement played out against the dull field of establishment rhetoric'.[43] However, as Todd Gitlin and David Joselit have shown, there remained a fundamental tension between the goals of the counter-culture's revolutionary actions and the reality governing American mainstream media that could, and would, subsume the message into its broader flow and, in turn, nullify it.[44] As Joselit argues, 'Yippies captured a mass audience by starring in advertisements for revolution, but in maintaining television's opposition between figure and ground they failed to challenge the industry's struc-ture, and consequently insured their own recuperation'.[45] The content itself may be temporarily altered to make space for the politics and per-formance of oppositional radicals such as Hoffman (the figure), but the medium's fundamental form and thrust, the mechanics driving it forward (the ground), remain stubbornly unchanged.

On T. T. V., the ground of the 'establishment rhetoric' is entirely absent, as the whole absurd televisual experience hovers at the level of the figure. In other words, that which is disruptive is not diluted and absorbed back into a hegemonic master narrative. Rather, the disorderly, unsettling and rebellious, or the figure, comprise the entirety of *Brand X's* T. T. V. Outside of the strictures of conventional network TV, Chamberlain constructs a paradoxical eighty-plus minute commercial for overthrowing oppressive power structures, but there is no ground to be found. Indeed, the appearance of the Yippie slogan 'Abandon the Creeping Meatball' later in the film – a phrase signalling society's swelling conformity – across scenes from the late-night parody 'The Tomorrow Show' and another advertisement for balling reinforces the ideological and conceptual groundlessness of *Brand X*.[46] If the talk show gestures toward the trite and conservative and if the balling commercial represents the youthful free love counter-cultural movement, the phrase takes on a pointed critique against the conformism of both. In *Brand X*, a revolutionary stance must throw off the strictures of both to liberate itself from the figure-ground dichotomy and to resist the inevitable codification and stagnation of the cause. In *Brand X*, the revolution comes in the form of the dirty and the under-performing generic.

In addition to interrogating the limits and possibilities of revolutionary politics on television, *Brand X* parodies mainstream politics' exploitation of mass media. TV became increasingly central to American politics throughout the decade. In 1960, television had been then-presidential candidate Richard Nixon's downfall in the debate against the charismatic John F. Kennedy. In the lead up to his 1968 presidential bid, Nixon hired a team of media men to shape and manipulate his TV appearances. Pioneering lively and live-broadcast press conferences to generate suspense and contrive interest on the campaign trail, Nixon and his team exploited the relationship between politics, entertainment and advertising. The president was, after all, a commodity to be sold to the American people, like soap and corn flakes. Like the Yippies' TV-ready actions, such press appearances became emblematic of what Daniel J. Boorstin in the 1960s called 'pseudo-events', defined as those that are artificially created for the sole purpose of media coverage.[47] As Rubin also articulated in 1970, '[t]he media does not report "news", it creates it. An event happens when it goes on TV and becomes myth'.[48] The ascent of pseudo-events in the 1960s corresponded to the rise of network broadcasting; they are pre-planned and exist only to be reported by the press, with an ambiguous relationship to any sort of underlying reality.

Chamberlain, having witnessed the rising importance of television to politicians and the resultant inauguration of Nixon earlier in the year, stages a presidential press conference in *Brand X*, which inflates the spuriousness of such pseudo-events. Mead appears as an incompetent Nixon-like president, accompanied by Sally Kirkland as a bubble-blowing 'Plastic Pat', at a faux presidential press conference staged in front of a crowd of energetic and irreverent reporters – the mood more akin to a concert than an official government event.[49] Standing behind a podium in front of an American flag, Kirkland and Mead expertly weave together fact and fiction. Kirkland's distracted disinterest hits at Pat Nixon's repudiation of politics in favour of the traditional housewife role. Kirkland portrays her as a yo-yo, with a yo-yo, unperturbed and blissfully ignorant of real issues. Mead's Nixon is confused, jovial and politically incorrect. 'Here's how we're going to deal with India', he says. 'Give the Taj Mahal to Mr Carvel of Carvel ice cream. Take away their dope and give them candy. Replace incense with underarm deodorant. Kill their cows and [...] in short, drain the Ganges'. When asked by musician Jimi Hendrix, playing a reporter in the press pool, if Mead has ever been stoned (obviously a drug reference), Mead responds, 'in Venezuela', a coded reference to a 1958 attack on Nixon in Venezuela during a South American tour.

There is no substance, no important information shared by Mead's President. Mead's empty and entertaining performance in front of a bank of cameras meant to attract voters suggests that perhaps television, more than any other factor, had made Nixon the President of the United States. While other Pop artists such as James Rosenquist and Tom Wesselmann were interested in the politician-as-brand and their frozen iconicity, Chamberlain engages with the machinery that propagates the system itself. The hyperbole, self-aggrandisement and volley of dialogue between the podium and the press pool participate in the drama of soap operas, game shows and commercials – the empty, vapid and meaningless flow of television cycling around and around and around. As Joe Ginnis reminds us in his book *The Selling of the President 1968*, published the same year that Chamberlain directed *Brand X*, '[o]n television it matters less that [the politician] does not have ideas. His personality is what the viewers want to share. He need be neither statesman nor crusader; he must only show up on time'.[50] It seems that Mead, Kirkland and Hoffman can, at least, do that, too.

Scott-Heron's song concludes with a political exhortation packaged in a metaphor of broadcast television: he contends that the revolution will be live and not a familiar rerun. He entreats activists to hit the streets, to leave the home and the television set behind – to shift their position from passive spectators to active participants. To wage the battle *through* the screen only means that the revolution will be co-opted by the capitalist systems of oppression and will not, in turn, lead to real change. Similarly, *Brand X* contends with the futility of intervening in the mass media, which will only absorb the opposition into its very fabric and reframe it as entertainment. By contrast, *Brand X* imagines a different, and perhaps more honest, media ecosystem that repudiates at every possible turn any presumption of authenticity and possibility of radical change. If the branded forms of politics, goods, identities, art and film have failed the people, then the solution is to champion the bad and generic in the live revolution.

The Movie for People

'As we know it, dirt is essentially disorder', wrote anthropologist Mary Douglas in 1966.[51] 'Our idea of dirt is compounded of two things, care for hygiene and respect for conventions'.[52] *Brand X* openly scorns post-war American concerns over social and bodily hygiene and respect for convention in celebrating the polluted, the corrupt and the foul through the concept of Brand X. Labelled a 'tacky, vulgar, hilarious' movie in a *New York Times* review, the film is not only at once a counter-cultural product, Pop art and an underground film, but also equally a critique of their pretensions alongside those of the conservative mainstream.[53] In so doing, *Brand X* implicates them all as participating in a contaminated sign-system and posits an alternative.

Brand X debuted at New York City's Elgin Theater in May 1970 to much acclaim and spent several years playing on college campuses across the country. The film's poster borrows counter-cultural iconography: from the hippie figure smoking marijuana to bold graphic text in block red letters (Figure 9.2). Its subtitle, 'The movie for people', seems to posit the project as a populist film. But, the 'the' is missing: it is not a movie for *the* people, it is simply a movie for people. Even the subtitle skewers its own purported counter-cultural messaging. Chamberlain imagined a 'new nation of people who can take care of themselves and are tired of the no nos imposed on them by the dying culture [...]. Anyone can join, and if you're uptight, we hope this film will liberate you through laughter'.[54] Through the traumatic social upheavals of the decade's turn, Chamberlain and his cast and crew produced a riotous and hellish tour through the wasteland of not only television, but also the broader socio-economic and political systems devastating the nation. Finding an uneasy affinity with the counter-cultural movements

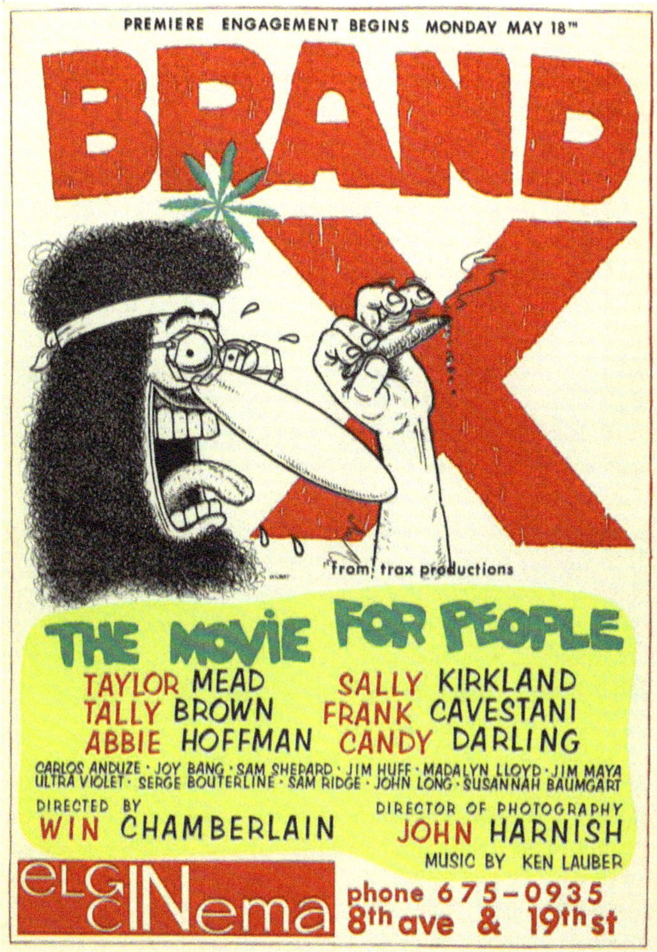

Figure 9.2 Gilbert Shelton, *Brand X* poster, 1970. Source: Courtesy of Sam Chamberlain.

of the era, the film, in the end, even sidesteps the branding that had consolidated around such efforts by cutting up, cutting us up and interrogating the role of media and brand cultures in the American capitalist political systems. Revelling in the unwanted and the failed, *Brand X* offers its own brand of satirical Brand X politics and aesthetics that rejoices in futility and exalts in the perversity of the disaffected.

Acknowledgements

I extend my sincere appreciation to the editors of this volume and Ariel Evans for their generative feedback on this essay.

Notes

1 Lewis Nightingale, 'Movie in Review: One of the Best Things on TV', *The Cornell Daily Sun*, 4 December 1970, p. 6.
2 Dianne Harris, *Little White Houses: How the Postwar Home Constructed Race in America*, Minneapolis: University of Minnesota Press, 2013; Suellen Hoy, *Chasing Dirt: The American Pursuit of Cleanliness*, New York and Oxford: Oxford University Press, 1995; and Carl A. Zimring, *Clean and White: A History of Environmental Racism in the United States*, New York: New York University Press, 2017.
3 The 'Brand X' era ended in the early 1970s, when the Federal Trade Commission began to support explicit brand comparisons. See Thomas E. Barry and Roger L. Tremblay, 'Comparative Advertising: Perspectives and Issues', *Journal of Advertising*, 4:4 (1975), pp. 15–20; William L. Wilkie and Paul W. Farris, 'Comparison Advertising: Problems and Potential', *Journal of Marketing*, 39 (October 1975), pp. 7–15.
4 Wynn Chamberlain, 'On *Brand X*', *Brand X* press kit, Browne Popular Culture Library, Bowling Green State University, Bowling Green, Ohio.
5 Vance Packard, *The Hidden Persuaders*, New York: Pocket Books, 1957.
6 Chamberlain, op. cit. This description obliquely references the long-standing division between high and low culture that defined modernism in the eyes of critics such as Clement Greenberg, who disparaged popular entertainment.
7 Newton N. Minow, 'Television and the Public Interest', address to the National Association of Broadcasters, Washington, DC, 9 May 1961.
8 Ibid.
9 Ibid.
10 'What's My Sex?' is an obvious play on gameshows such as *The Dating Game* and *The Newlywed Game* that reinforced heterosexual couplings and traditional expressions of gender identity. Brown's show riffs on Virginia Graham's wildly popular early-morning syndicated show *Girl Talk*.
11 Likely the 8–10 February 1969 nor'easter.
12 Wynn Chamberlain, 'Notes from the Director', *Brand X* Movie, http://www.brandx-movie.com/brandx12.html.
13 Nightingale, op. cit.
14 Sheldon Renan, *An Introduction to the American Underground Film*, New York: E. P. Dutton, 1967, p. 23.
15 Thomas Crow, 'The Absconded Subject of Pop', *RES: Anthropology and Aesthetics*, 55/56 (Spring-Autumn 2009), pp. 5–20.
16 David Ogilvy, quoted in Packard, op. cit., p. 17.
17 Burleigh B. Gardner and Sidney J. Levy, 'The Product and the Brand', *Harvard Business Review* (March-April 1955), pp. 33–39.
18 Irving S. White, 'The Functions of Advertising in Our Culture', *Journal of Marketing*, 24:1 (1959), pp. 8–14.
19 Andy Warhol and Pat Hackett, *POPism: The Warhol Sixties*, New York: Harcourt, 1980, p. 22.
20 One might also consider films in an international context, such as Andrzej Kostenko and Witold Leszczynski's *Rewizja osobista* (1972). [Editorial note: For more on this film, see David Crowley's essay in this volume.]

21 Lynn Spigel, *TV by Design: Modern Art and the Rise of Network Television*, Chicago: University of Chicago Press, 2008, p. 252.

22 Richard Goldstein likewise observed that 'nowhere has the underground had such a profound effect as in advertising [...] As a result, most prime-time programming now serves as a lull between commercials, where the real "action" is'. 'And Now a Word from Our Sensors', *New York*, 23 June 1969, p. 54. See also Cynthia B. Meyers, 'The Best Thing on TV: 1960s US Television Commercials', in Bo Florin, Nico de Klerk and Patrick Vonderau (eds), *Films that Sell: Moving Pictures and Advertising*, London: Palgrave, 2016, pp. 173–93.

23 Chamberlain, 'On *Brand X*', op. cit.

24 Ibid.

25 In the late 1940s, television networks began negotiations with Hollywood studios, but it was not until a decade later that movies began to regularly appear on primetime schedules. Barbara Moore, Marvin R. Bensman and Jim Van Dyke, *Prime-Time Television: A Concise History*, Westport: Praeger, 2006.

26 Renan, op. cit., pp. 240–41.

27 Chamberlain, 'On *Brand X*', op. cit.

28 Ed Halter, 'Pop Cinema: Three Tendencies', in Darsie Alexander and Bartholomew Ryan (eds), *International Pop*, Minneapolis: Walker Art Center, 2015, p. 182. Halter's essay is reprinted in this volume.

29 Bobby Abrams review, published in *Crawdaddy*, 21 May 1970, in *Brand X* press kit, op. cit.

30 Ibid.

31 Ibid.

32 Jonas Mekas, 'Movie Journal', *Village Voice*, 14 May 1970, in *Brand X* press kit, op. cit.

33 Thomas Frank, *The Conquest of Cool: Business Culture, Counterculture, and the Rise of Hip Consumerism*, Chicago: University of Chicago Press, 1997, p. 231. See also Aniko Bodroghkozy, *Groove Tube: Sixties Television and the Youth Rebellion*, Durham, NC: Duke University Press, 2001.

34 Parker Tyler, *Underground Film: A Critical History*, New York: Grove Press, 1969, p. 196. *Time* magazine observed the same: 'The men who make television commercials [...] regularly rent big batches of avant-garde films and ransack them for ideas'. 'Art of Light & Lunacy: The New Underground Films', *Time*, 17 February 1967, p. 94.

35 'Balling' appeared in songs of the time, including Frank Zappa's 'Absolutely Free' (1968) and Little Richard's 'Rip It Up' (1957).

36 References for the balling commercials range from the Beatles' song 'Why Don't We Do It in The Road?' to Bertolt Brecht's writings – 'The world has always been ruled by badly fucked people', as summarised by Chamberlain. The ad suggests that, if the world is going to fuck us and watch (as the news cycle did during the police violence at the 1968 National Democratic Convention), then we might as well enjoy it. Chamberlain, 'On *Brand X*', op. cit.

37 Robert Alden, 'Advertising: Cigarette Brand X Being Marketed Here', *New York Times*, 18 October 1960, p. 63.

38 Jerry Rubin, *Do It! Scenarios of the Revolution*, New York: Ballantine Books, 1970, p. 108.

39 At the time of his appearance in *Brand X*, Hoffman was awaiting the start of the much-anticipated trial of the Chicago 8, who were blamed for the violence at the 1968

Democratic National Convention in Chicago, when unarmed protestors clashed with the police and the National Guard following a Yippie media stunt.

40 Hoffman's use of racist rhetoric recalls the 1968 Kerner Commission findings that the 1967 riots in predominantly Black communities were the result of police brutality and institutional racism across all sectors of American life.

41 The money burning nods to his days as a member of the San Francisco Diggers, a community-action group of activists and theatrical actors who believed in a free economy and were notorious for setting money ablaze.

42 Abbie Hoffman, *Revolution for the Hell of It*, New York: Dial Press, 1968, p. 134.

43 Ibid, pp. 133–34.

44 Todd Gitlin, *The Whole World Is Watching: Mass Media in the Making and Unmaking of the New Left*, Berkeley: University of California Press, 1980; David Joselit, *Feedback: Television against Democracy*, Cambridge, MA: MIT Press, 2007, p. 122.

45 Joselit, op. cit., p. 122.

46 The phrase – a play on Jean Shepherd's article 'The Night People vs. Creeping Meatballism', *Mad Magazine* (April 1957) – appears in Hoffman's and Rubin's 1968 Yippie manifesto.

47 Daniel J. Boorstin, *The Image: A Guide to Pseudo-Events in America* (1961), repr., New York: Atheneum, 1987, p. 11.

48 Rubin, op. cit., p. 107.

49 The press repeatedly referred to Nixon's wife as 'Plastic Pat', and the *New York Times* once described her as 'a paper doll, a Barbie doll – plastic, antiseptic, unalive'. Judith Viorst, 'Pat Nixon Is the Ultimate Good Sport', *The New York Times*, 13 September 1970, SM13.

50 Joe Ginnis, *The Selling of the President 1968* (1969), repr., New York: Pocket Books, 1974, p. 22.

51 Mary Douglas, *Purity and Danger: An Analysis of Concepts of Pollution and Taboo* (1966), repr., New York: Routledge, 2001, p. 2.

52 Ibid, p. 7.

53 Vincent Canby, 'Ah, Youth! Ah, Sex! Ah, Revolution!', *New York Times*, 14 June 1970, p. 97.

54 Chamberlain, 'On *Brand X*', op. cit.

10

The *Other* Children of Marx and Coca-Cola: Pop Cinema in Eastern Europe[1]

David Crowley

In March 1969, the Dziga Vertov Group, the French film collective named after the pioneering Soviet filmmaker and cinema theorist, went to the Czechoslovak Socialist Republic. Filming in secret, Jean-Luc Godard, Jean-Pierre Gorin and a Czech documentary team shot on the streets of Prague and Bratislava and pointed their 16mm camera at Czech TV broadcasts on the television in their hotel room. The resulting work, *Pravda* (1969), is an essay film. Discontinuous clips shot *in situ*, short vignettes performed for the camera (a wineglass overflows, a pin-up photo is pulled from a pocket) and shots of the Czech media are accompanied by an invented dialogue between Vladimir and Rosa (that is, between Vladimir Ilyich Lenin and Rosa Luxemburg), written by the filmmakers. It is as if Lenin has been resurrected to judge the achievements of his followers in socialist Czechoslovakia. In the film voice-over, Lenin wonders where he is:

> This must be a country already thrust into the world of modern economy [...]

> A Western country.

> Yes, we are in the West:
> in the fields, advertising for large American companies.

> [...]

> The young workers like the Beatles a lot, and the government lets them wear their hair long. It must be Yugoslavia.

> No, it's Czechoslovakia. Full of historic Western traditions. On Sundays, many workers would rather wash their cars than have sex.

When he comes to recognise the world to which he has been transported, Lenin delivers a long and puritanical lecture on the corruption of Marxism-Leninism in the Socialist Republic of Czechoslovakia.

The Dziga Vertov Group were in Czechoslovakia in the aftermath of the repression of the Prague Spring. Warsaw Pact troops had invaded the country seven months earlier to put down the reform movement which had threatened the Communist Party of Czechoslovakia's monopoly on power. March 1969 – when they were filming – saw anti-Soviet protests in Prague (during which Aeroflot offices were destroyed) and in other Czechoslovak towns and cities. After the relatively free rein of political thought during the Prague Spring, full censorship was re-imposed in the same month, too. But none of this drew the attention of the filmmakers. They were rather more interested in the influence of America on Czechoslovakia than that of the Soviet Union.

Given the Dziga Vertov Group's avowal of what is sometimes called 'French Maoism',[2] it is not surprising that *Pravda* highlights the politics of 'convergence' during the Cold War, namely the growing similarities of Soviet-socialist and capitalist systems: capitalist societies increasingly depended on state planning to achieve complex modernisation projects, while Eastern European societies employed market mechanisms to improve the quality and supply of consumer goods. In his book *The Revolution of Everyday Life* (1967), Raoul Vaneigem writes:

> The cultural détente between East and West is not accidental! On the one hand, **homo consomator** buys a bottle of whiskey and as a free gift the lie that accompanies it. On the other, Communist buys ideology and gets a free gift, a bottle of vodka. Paradoxically, Soviet and capitalist regimes are taking a common path, the first thanks to their economy of production, the second thanks to their economy of consumption.[3]

That West and East came to look alike and that goods have corrupting social effects was an argument made frequently by the radical left at the end of the 1960s.

Cold War competition between East and West after Nikita Khrushchev took the reins of power in Moscow did much to produce the impression of convergence. Famously, the Soviet leader's promise made at the Twenty-Second Congress of the Communist Party of the Soviet Union in 1961 to 'overtake the West' was to be judged by many measures, not least the quality and supply of housing, leisure and consumer goods. What followed was a stop-start world: throughout the Bloc, promises were made and occasional boosts in production achieved; crisis would then follow. Nevertheless, the

1960s and 1970s saw the growth of 'socialist consumerism' across Eastern Europe,[4] a phenomenon found largely in the realm of images rather than things. One of the defining features of the post-Stalin years was the steady creep of commercial imagery into what one art historian at the time called the 'ikonosfera' (iconosphere) of socialism, much of it from the West.[5] Eastern Bloc distributors made arrangements to screen many of the most popular products of the American and Western European film industries in their cinemas.[6] Popular magazines increasingly featured advertising and fashion spreads, sometimes borrowed from western glossies.

Contemporary commentators, and historians since, have often equated what is sometimes called 'Refrigerator Socialism' with pacification. In the new 'contract' between state and society that was drawn up in the late 1950s (and, specifically, after the repression of the Hungarian Uprising in autumn of 1956), citizens were asked to accept communist rule in exchange for improved standards of living, measured in material terms. Failure to meet its side of the deal has been given as one reason for the widespread rejection of communist authority in the 1980s. Moreover, there was a discrepancy between ideology and practice. For instance, Eastern Bloc states equated the USA with imperialism, and yet socialist societies were undergoing a deep Americanisation from below, in the growing embrace by the young of pop music and fashion from the end of the 1960s onwards. And to channel these unruly desires, Eastern Bloc states created fashion houses and boutiques, issued rock albums and so on.

The merits of such arguments have been much debated since the end of communist rule in Eastern Europe,[7] but one face of socialist consumerism which is yet to be thoroughly analysed is the critical response it provoked, particularly in Moscow's satellites and the former Yugoslavia – those states where it was most advanced. One can track critiques of socialist consumerism from different quarters in the 1960s and 1970s. Reformist intellectuals published articles and books about the alienating effects of modern life, often inspired by their reading of 'early' Marx, as well as existentialist and Frankfurt School thinkers; others saw a threat to 'high' art in the march of popular culture.[8] In the 'underground', hippies living in the Eastern Bloc eschewed materialism and advocated communal ways of living; and groupuscules of young radicals even sought to revive the spirit of revolution, sometimes by engaging in subversive acts or by championing Mao or Che.[9] To this list of doubting voices one might add a handful of works of Pop cinema in Eastern Europe which took consumerism as a central theme.

Not a singular or coherent genre or the subject of comprehensive scholarship in the way that, say, Czech and Polish New Wave cinema has been, the label of 'Pop Cinema' in Eastern Europe might describe a number of films which seem to address popular culture using its own symbols and techniques.[10] Like their counterparts elsewhere, Pop films in the East demonstrate an interest in the media, in celebrity and in consumerism. In addition, they expressed the distinct consciousness in Eastern Europe and Yugoslavia of working with visual material that had been created elsewhere, specifically in the West. In what follows, I have singled out three 'Pop' movies, all of which had kinship with the works of Godard, albeit from before his Dziga Vertov Group phase. Indeed, Godard seems to have been a touchstone in Yugoslavia and the People's Republics of Eastern Europe in the 1960s and 1970s. His films were screened and reviewed, and books and articles were written celebrating his explicitly political films – even *La Chinoise* (1967), a strident and unambiguous critique of the Soviet Union, enjoyed critical approval.[11] In his 1970 book on the French director, Polish film critic Konrad Eberhardt characterised Godard's mid-1960s films as a critique of the effects of the mass image, a phenomenon that he associated with the widespread Americanisation of culture on both sides of what he called the 'great divide':

> The mass media attempts to absorb everything: art, philosophies, ideologies of the great divide, the secrets of the human psyche, love, imagination, and social conflicts. It gives an answer to absolutely every single question. It offers everything to the consumer in a fragment, in a nutshell, at an affordable price. A giant supermarket in place of a museum [...] Godard carries out his critique [...] of this gigantic superstore of values by specific means: not by rejecting them outright but by exploiting them to the point of absurdity [...] Generally speaking, the trick he uses is to alternate poignantly real, authentic moments with constructed situations in a deliberately primitive, artificial, schematic way.[12]

In a number of Godard's films, such as *Two or Three Things I Know About Her* (*2 ou 3 choses que je sais d'elle*, 1967) and *La Chinoise*, these 'constructed situations' took on a collage form: comic-strip frames, historical documents, as well as print advertisements to puncture the narrative flow. These inserts are a form of montage but, unlike the celebrated works of the Soviet avant-garde, the technique was not overtly dialectical, nor was it employed to drive narrative. These films employ visual non sequiturs that are much closer to collage than montage. This, as Angela Delle Vacche has shown in her discussion of Godard's *Pierrot Le Fou* (1965), is where their 'Pop' credentials lie.[13] Other forms of estrangement in *Pierrot Le Fou* include ventriloquism

in the famous party scene in which the pretentious conversation of the rev-
ellers is entirely derived from the discourses of advertising.[14] All of this has
usually been understood as experiments with distanciation, in a manner
that updated Brecht by pointing to the anomie of modern consumer societies. For a small number of Eastern European filmmakers in the late 1960s
and early 1970s, Godard's 'Pop' techniques provided the means for critical
reflection on the forms and effects of socialist consumerism.

Marx Factor

Personal Search (*Rewizja Osobista*, 1973) tells the story of the arrival of a
group of Polish travellers – a mother and son accompanied by a cousin
bearing a strong resemblance to Brigitte Bardot – at a customs office on a
border post between Poland and, strangely, Switzerland.[15] Driving a FIAT
sports car, these travellers have come from the West accompanied by a
cornucopia of consumer goods – luxury foods, chic clothes and glittering
trinkets (Figure 10.1). To cross the border into a world where such minor

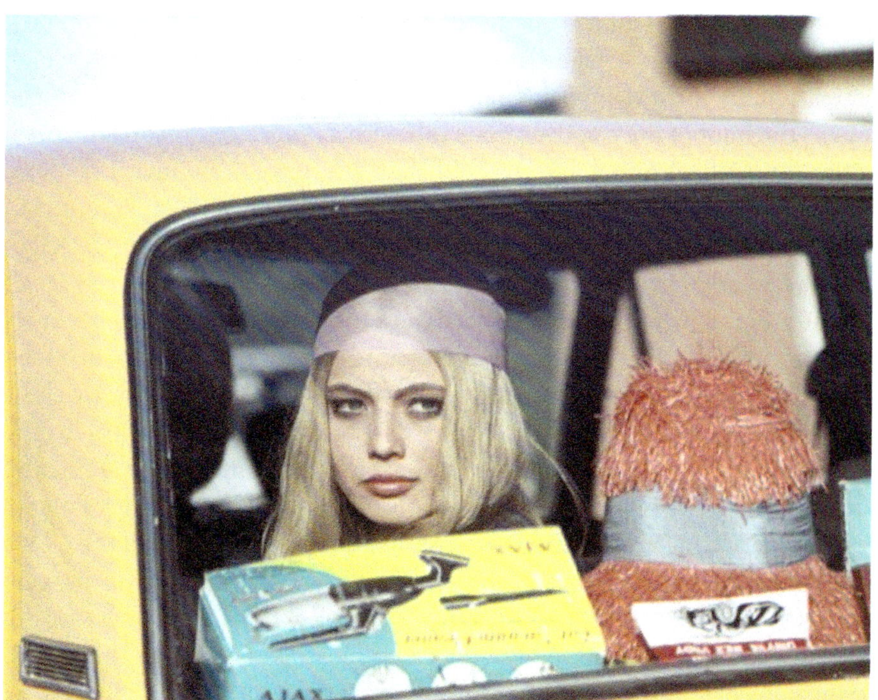

Figure 10.1 *Personal Search* (*Rewizja Osobista*, Andrzej Kostenko and Witold Leszczyński,
1973).

luxuries are in short supply, they have to strip these things of their exchange values: in other words, they have to turn commodities into personal possessions. Therefore, they divest the products of their glossy packaging and scuff them to give them a patina of use before packing them into their car. The opening titles roll over a bonfire of discarded consumer packaging.

But their labours are insufficient: the customs officer and his young colleague suspect the returnees of smuggling. The film then turns into a psychological drama; a tense battle between officialdom and the prosperous travellers fought with flirtation, hollow flattery, veiled threats and bribes. In an inflationary cycle which starts with a plastic cigarette lighter and culminates in the sexual 'gift' of her niece to the younger guard, the mother seeks to avoid the scandal that would follow from a 'personal search'. This cycle is only ended by the arrival of her high-ranking husband in his official car. He is a well-connected official in the Polish People's Republic. It is at this point that we understand that these imports from the West constitute the special privileges of the ruling classes in the classless society. From then on, the film moves towards its dramatic climax, the destruction of the car and its precious contents.

The most striking cinematic innovation in Witold Leszczyński and Andrzej Kostenko's film – made for the Łódź-based Wytwórnia Filmów Fabularnych Studio – takes the form of television advertisements which unexpectedly intrude into the narrative. When the young customs official opens the boot of the car, the screen fills with a French television advertisement for 'Collant Soleil' hosiery and then another for an 'invisible' 'huit' brassiere filmed on a Mediterranean beach. The footage is apparently an answer to his question 'What is this?' asked when he fingers the packages of underwear which fill her suitcase. Later, a bottle of Cointreau, the French aperitif shared by the customs officials and their unwilling guests, becomes the magic elixir at the heart of a thirty-second commercial from French television, filmed in the style of a James Bond movie. In this way, the tense chess game between the officials and the tourists is broken – momentarily – by the clichéd suspense provided by this mini-espionage drama. These are hardly conventional uses of montage, particularly in the context of socialist Poland. In his classic conceptualisation, Eisenstein in the Soviet Union of the 1920s and 1930s had argued that montage was 'dialectical', capable of marking the clash between the forces of progress and reaction shaping the world. Leszczyński and Kostenko's movie has far closer kinship with the abrupt transitions of Godard's 'collage' films.

The French ads are not the film's only lessons in consumer aesthetics. The cinematography also reproduces many of the clichés of advertising. Early on in *Personal Search*, a long tracking shot follows the young woman through the countryside at dawn to bathe *au naturel*. At the end, this 'Eve' catches the glance of the camera/viewer in the mirror – this is the male gaze *avant la lettre*. In another shot, the juice of a freshly-peeled orange is dripped onto her lips while she sleeps. Conflating sexual and consumer desire, both scenes could have been taken from a primer on advertising written on Madison Avenue in the 1960s. But, of course, they were not. These scenes were filmed in a country – the Polish People's Republic – that had declared its commitment to the liberation of its citizens from alienation. The seductive but hollow French advertisements and the vigilant operations of a customs post guarding the entrance to the socialist world *should*, according to the official creed of Marxist-Leninism, articulate the sharp differences between West and East. But Poland was undergoing a consumer revolution. A new leadership which took power in 1970 had promised a 'Second Poland' (*Druga Polska*): one which would benefit from high productivity and ready supplies of consumer goods (but, in the event, also racked up foreign debt to pay for these boons). The film ends by passing sharp judgment on the regime, highlighting the material luxuries which the elite enjoyed, as well as the ambiguous phenomenon of socialist consumerism.

The label 'Second Poland' pointed – inadvertently – to the phantasmagorical aspect of a 'new' Poland made in the image of Western modernity. In its pursuit of growth, the People's Republic was to become a double, a simulacrum of countries in the West. Made at the time when First Secretary Edward Gierek was formulating his ambitious vision for the country, *Personal Search* seems to anticipate this emerging programme of simulation. In a moment of high filmic tension, the car which has delivered the trio to Poland attracts the attention of the eagle-eyed customs officer. It is a new, 'bahama' yellow FIAT Mille Cinquecento (and the camera, like his gaze, lingers over the car's glittering marques). It seems that the trio are attempting to import a new foreign car, an illegal act. The nature of this offence is, however, rendered ambiguous by the official love affair that the communist authorities in Eastern Europe conducted with FIAT. In 1965, the Polish government – like the Kremlin one year earlier – had signed the first of a series of deals with the Italian car manufacturer to make copies of its products under license in Warsaw. Gierek accelerated the policy by establishing new factories in Tychy and Bielsko-Biała to manufacture FIAT's cars in large numbers. Owning a FIAT was not only a legitimate ideal in the Second Poland: it was a 'socialist achievement'. So why smuggle one across the border?

Although it addressed a new approach to the management of the socialist economy, Kostenko and Leszczyński's film sustained a long-standing distrust of the fetishistic hold of consumer goods on their users. This was a Marxist conception which fuelled the anti-state socialist *and* anti-capitalist reflexes of some intellectuals in the East in the 1960s. This was not, however, explicitly declared in the film. Instead, *Personal Search* took an ambivalent approach to commodity aesthetics, one which mirrored – and, in effect, highlighted – the ambivalence of the Polish authorities. So ambivalent was its interpretation that, according to one recent analysis of the movie by Justyna Jaworska, it was far easier for contemporary critics to dismiss it as a poor or incoherent film than engage with the unsettling image of socialism that it advanced.[16] Perhaps only in retrospect did it become clear how perceptive *Personal Search* was in its critique of socialist consumerism.

Return to Prague

Pravda, like all Dziga Vertov Group products, is preoccupied with the language and operations of film. It comes as no surprise then that, when working in Prague in 1969, the French filmmakers turned their attention, albeit briefly, to the work and role of Eastern European directors, too. In *Pravda*, the Group takes those filmmakers who seem closest to their own interests and practices to task. A still from the most famous scene in Yugoslav director Dušan Makavejev's *Love Affair, or the Case of the Missing Switchboard Operator* (*Ljubavni slučaj ili tragedija službenice P. T. T.*, 1967) appears. 'Flashing' an image of the central character Isabella lying naked with a black cat on her buttocks, Godard and his colleagues treat this notorious scene in Makavejev's filmic exploration of sex like one of the many pin-ups which appear periodically on screen in *Pravda*. Věra Chytilová, the Czech feminist director of *Daisies* (*Sedmikrásky*, 1967), also appears before the camera, in a scene filmed in an editing suite. She is accused by the voiceover of 'Westernism in Action'.[17] This was a cheap shot: in *Daisies* (a film that Godard is reported to have later dismissed as a 'non-political fantasy'[18]) 'Westernism' in socialist Czechoslovakia was precisely one of Chytilová's concerns.

In *Daisies*, two young women – sharing the same name, Marie, and seemingly the same persona – embark on a spree of gluttony in Prague, funded by the gullible old men who expect (but never receive) sexual favours in return (Figure 10.2). In fact, the two women only seem interested in food, albeit not necessarily in eating. Although the film does not have a clear narrative structure, it reaches a crescendo in an excessive and spectacular destruction of a banquet. The two women dance on a table laid with luxurious food and

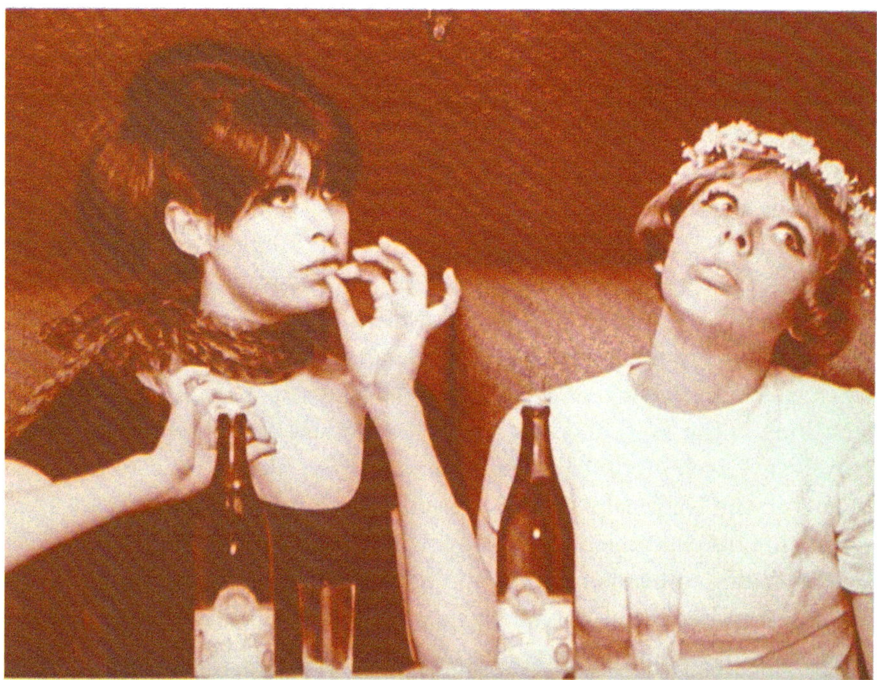

Figure 10.2 *Daisies* (Věra Chytilová, 1967).

alcohol, destroying everything under their stiletto heels. In between these bouts of excess, the young women sunbathe on the banks of the Vltava and play games in the bedroom. Some of Chytilová's techniques seem to be directly drawn from Godard's movies: sound and images are often discontinuous; still images are cut into the action, sometimes appearing so briefly that they barely register; and scenes are shot with coloured filters.

Chytilová's embrace of collage is important, too. The idea that all actions should point to a radiant future made narrative clarity a requirement of all Soviet films, at least until the 1970s. Of course, Czech New Wave cinema had already shaken off its Soviet shackles in the 1960s. But Chytilová's use of collage also eschews the *Bildungsroman* narrative structures of films made by contemporaries such as Jiři Menzel (*Closely Observed Trains / Ostře sledované vlaky*, 1965, for instance). That an individual should confront the absurdity of the world or forge his or her own fate was a motivating idea after Stalinism and shaped many of the most celebrated New Wave movies and documentaries made in Czechoslovakia in the 1960s. Chytilová's Maries confront their world in the most absurd ways. But far from encouraging the viewer to empathise with the tribulations of their lives, the director works to inhibit our identification with them. Choreographed by the soundtrack, their actions are exaggerated, comic even. As a reviewer writing in *Film Quarterly* in 1968 observed, '[i]t seems that the greedy little creatures are specimens of the capitalistic (or, for that matter, socialist) drive for acquisition, the rage for appropriation; the connoting factor that they are "schnorrers" or "spongers" brings in the idea of social or economic parasitism.'[19] Might these two girls in their fashionable dresses, and with their voracious and insatiable appetites, their amorality, their selfishness, their gluttony, be Chytilová's way of passing judgment on the consumer spectacle? After all, in one scene they run out of food and eat advertisements on the pages of glossy German and French magazines. They seem to take advertising literally at its word when it says: 'Eat Me'. This might be reason to interpret *Daisies* as a critique of the West and its capacity to produce anomie through excess. However, Czech commentators understood the film in local terms. One deputy in the National Assembly, for instance, protested the waste of food during the film's production 'at a time when our farmers with great difficulties are trying to overcome the problems of our agricultural production.'[20] Indeed, the Czech viewer would be justified in asking: just whose meal was being destroyed here? One reading is that the girls reveal and destroy the privileges which the gerontocratic elite in Socialist Czechoslovakia had reserved for itself. The deployment of food in Chytilová's movie is significant: in spoiling and toying with it, these young women announce their lack of interest in questions of need – a central plank of Marxist ideology. Indeed, the focus of their desires is on luxury, whether in the form of a groaning table or Western European advertising. But rather than issue a call for frugality, their actions set out to exhaust it. In so doing, they make an excess of what already surely seemed excessive.

Wake up Lenin

In the image economy of Eastern Europe of the 1960s, the number and sophistication of advertisements for products and services grew, usually disproportionately in relation to things, to commodities. But, of course, they joined other political advertisements and brands in the 'ikonosfera' of socialism. The party-state dressed its cities with monumental portraits of unblinking leaders and muscular heroes, as well as ringing slogans and posters. During red letter days in the calendar, streets would be decorated with temporary propaganda. In terms of the Cold War polarities, communist ideologues liked to contrast the uplifting effects of these city ornaments with the tawdry interests of commerce.[21] Often this imagery has been discussed by critics of communist rule in Eastern Europe in terms of its invisibility, at least in the sense that ordinary passers-by were so habituated to these slogans and portraits that they did not register their messages. But in the early 1970s young artists in Eastern Europe were, so it seems, alert to the mass imagery of communist rule, producing a kind of local variant of Pop art which was dubbed 'Sots Art'.[22] A compression of two terms – Sots Realism and Pop art – the term was coined by the Russian duo Vitaly Komar and Alexander Melamid to describe their own artworks in 1972. In this year they began creating works that treated the mass slogans and political images that formed a ubiquitous backdrop to life in the Soviet Union as art. Sots Art often directed attention to the manipulation of desire in propaganda, even if it framed these utopian images with dark irony.

Yugoslav film-maker Dušan Makavejev produced something like a Sots Art movie when, in 1971, he made *WR: Mysteries of the Organism* (*W. R. – Misterije organizma*). A funny and irreverent film essay, *WR* discovers Pop imagery in revolutionary politics. Like other counter-cultural products of the day, the film is an attempt to fuse Marx with Freud or, to put it another way, to insert a sexual revolution into a political one. It is in part comic, in part sensational. And, like all the films discussed in this essay, it is a collage. It combines a documentary on the life and work of psychoanalyst Wilhelm Reich; footage of Tuli Kupferberg from The Fugs wielding a gun in New York (Figure 10.3) and of Jackie Curtis, a genderqueer performer and member of Warhol's entourage; and footage of the activities of the 'plaster casters', famous for making moulds of the penises of rock stars. A kind of allegorical fictional love affair between Vladimir Ilyich, a celebrity ice-dancer who represents the Soviet Union around the world, and Milena, a combination of Yugoslav partisan and sexual revolutionary, threads its way through these documentary episodes. The film jumps back and forth between the Socialist Federal Republic of Yugoslavia and the USA, not to draw sharp contrasts but to create something like a kind of network of associations and contradictions: one idea appears only to be put in doubt by another. For instance, an attempt by Milena and a worker to arrest the passage of a Mercedes car with an improvised barricade during which her comrade protests loudly and violently about the privileges that the elite has reserved for itself ('fine food, fashion and Marx Factor'), is followed abruptly by a mobile shot of Jackie Curtis – Milena's double in New York – accompanied by the jaunty soundtrack of a radio advertisement for Maybelline cosmetics.

Makavejev has described the film as a 'personal' response to Reich's ideas. Reich, a protégé of Freud, had traced deep-seated sexual content in Nazi propaganda. In his book *The Mass Psychology of Fascism* (1933/1945),

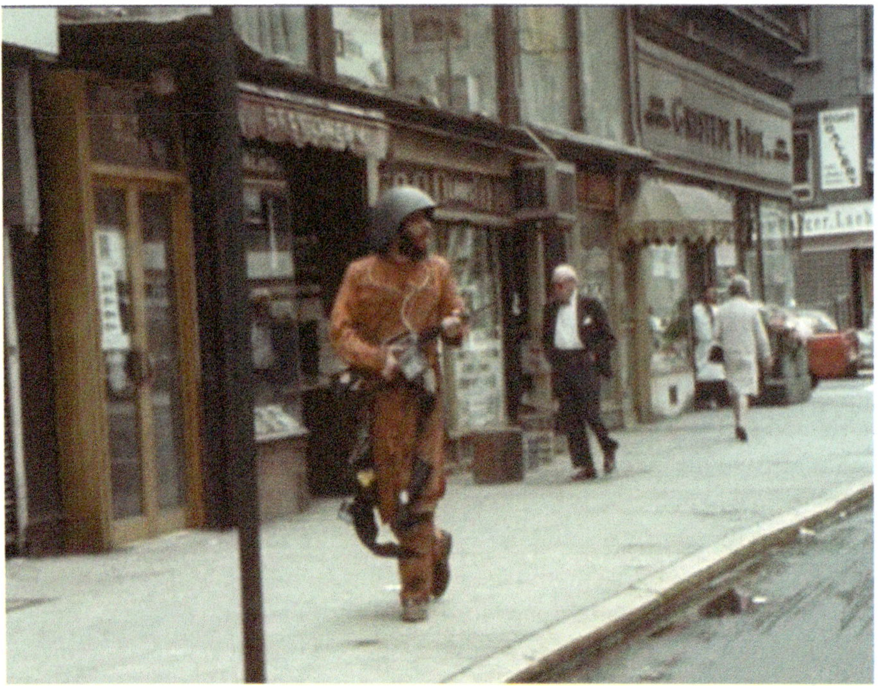

Figure 10.3 *WR: Mysteries of the Organism* (Dušan Makavejev, 1971).

Reich had argued that part of the appeal of Nazism in Germany derived from its ability to channel repressed sexuality. This is discussed in a scene in Makavejev's film where a notorious image of Hitler, surrounded by seemingly adoring Austrian schoolgirls in 1939, appears. But his interest is not in Hitler but in Lenin. Makavajev seems to transfer Reich's thesis about fascism to Soviet and Yugoslav communism: when Milena – a libertine – first sees Lenin's name-sake, the ice-skater, she ripples with pleasure. Hers is not, however, an individual fantasy but a collective one. The idea that Lenin – or his spirit – might still be alive and come back to cure the errors of his successors in the Soviet Union or that he might be a guiding force in Tito's Yugoslavia was a recurring theme in propaganda. After his death in 1924, he was regularly conjured up by those who claimed to be his successors. The 'Leninist spirit' was invoked at every crisis in the communist world as a kind of energising, restorative force. When the disaster of Stalinism was revealed by Nikita Khrushchev, for instance, loyal Soviet citizens were encouraged to 'return to Lenin'. Lenin was even issued a subpoena in Prague in 1968, as Warsaw Pact tanks rolled into the city. Sardonic graffiti appeared on the city's walls calling for the Bolshevik leader to revive: 'Wake up Lenin, Brezhnev's gone mad'. Gallows humour to be sure, but the idea that Lenin was only sleeping was not an entirely ironic one. After the death of the Bolshevik leader, a scheme was hatched by the faithful to ensure that he would be brought back to life one day. Embalming his body was just the first step in a complete programme of rejuvenation: 'Our duty, our task, consists in bringing back to life *all* who have died … '[23]

Both Godard's *Pravda* and Makavejev's *WR: Mysteries of the Organism* conjure up the ghost of Lenin. In the Yugoslav film, Vladimir Ilyich, the ice-dancer, not only shares Lenin's name, but he also shares his words and re-enacts his gestures. He is a man made in the image of another. Walking with Milena by a river, for instance, he climbs on to the deck of a wrecked boat to deliver a famous passage in which Lenin admitted to Gorky that beauty triggered violent thoughts and actions:

> Nothing is better than Beethoven's *Appassionata*. Amazing, superhuman music! I think with perhaps naïve pride: look what miracles man can perform. But I cannot listen to music often, it affects my nerves. It makes me want to say sweet nothings, to pat the heads of people who, in a filthy hell, create such beauty. But today we must not pat heads, or we'll get our hand bitten off. We've got to hit heads without mercy, though in the ideal we are against doing violence to people.

Milena's response to these words is to embrace her lover, an action which is met by violence (and ultimately her death). This scene is immediately followed by footage from Mikhail Chiaureli's film *The Vow* (*Klyatva*, 1946), featuring an actor portraying Stalin as benevolent patriarch who realises his predecessor's vision. Beauty is followed by violence: Lenin is followed by Stalin. As Milena had announced in a rousing speech earlier in the film, 'Socialism cannot exclude human pleasures from its programme. Free love was where the Revolution failed'.

In making a claim for *Personal Search, Daisies* and *WR* as expressions of 'Pop cinema' on the Eastern side of the Cold War divide, it is worth considering what was held in common in the East and in the West and what was not. Chytilová's movie does not, for instance, express the coolness that characterised so much Pop art in the West in the 1960s – an ironic or disinterested engagement with consumerism and mass media images. Instead, all three films engage with desire, the appetite for things and for sensations. And with their interest in sexual liberation, they also trace the contours of a feminist politics of female pleasure. Chytilová's film was, for instance, remarkably aligned, albeit unknowingly, with the writings of Germaine Greer published in London a few years later. 'Ultimately the greatest service a woman can do to her community is to be happy', Greer wrote; 'the degree of revolt and irresponsibility which she must manifest to acquire happiness is the only sure indication of the way things must change if there is to be any point in continuing to be a woman at all'.[24] These words might well have been spoken by Milena, Makavejev's sexual and political revolutionary. While organised feminist politics was not to take shape in Eastern Europe until the later part of the 1970s, all three works addressed – in a critical fashion – the transactional uses of sexuality in consumerism.

Another difference between the cool surfaces of Western Pop and these films was the excessive and, in some cases, violent fate of objects of desire. Revolutionary violence is a key theme of Makevejev's movie, as already noted. Leszczyński and Kostenko's film ends with the destruction of the precious commodities that have been smuggled into Poland. The boy who travelled to the border with his mother and sister dowses their FIAT Mille Cinquecento in petrol and sets it alight. The camera then lingers on the burning labels and packages that had formed its cargo before a final abrupt cut back to a French TV advertisement. This may be a 'bonfire of the vanities', but there is little in the scene to suggest that this sacrifice is made to atone for sins against socialism. Similarly, the highpoint of the two Maries' bacchanalian adventure in Chytilová's *Daisies* is the destruction of a banquet. While the meaning attached by Makevajev to the outpouring of violence is more or less clear (a symptom of the repressive nature of Soviet style socialism), the destructive climax in both the Czech and Polish movies is wilfully ambivalent, lacking any clear sense of disapproval or come-uppance. In the moral economy of socialism, where the meaning of images and actions could be judged against an ideological framework provided by Marxist Leninism, they offered exceptional commentaries on the strange and somewhat ambiguous phenomenon of socialist consumerism.

Notes

1 This talk was written for a symposium on 'Global Pop' at Tate Modern, London, in 2013. It has been revised for publication here. In undertaking that task, I thank the editors of this volume for their insightful guidance.

2 Man-tat Terence Leung, 'Struggling between Two Fronts: Godard, Dziga Vertov Group and the Ethical Predicaments of Post-1968 French Maoism', *Cinéma & Cie: International Film Studies Journal*, 18:30 (Spring 2018), pp. 21–40.

3 Raoul Vaneigem, *The Revolution of Everyday Life*, trans. John Fullerton and Paul Sieveking, London: Rising Free Collective, 1979, p. 36.

4 See David Crowley and Susan E. Reid (eds), 'Introduction', in *Pleasures in Socialism: Leisure and Luxury in the Eastern Bloc*, Evanstown: Northwestern University Press, 2010, pp. 3–53; Patrick Hyder Patterson, *Bought and Sold: Living and Losing the Good*

Life in Socialist Yugoslavia, Ithaca: Cornell University Press, 2012; Paulina Bren and Mary Neuberger, *Communism Unwrapped: Consumption in Cold War Eastern Europe*, Oxford: Oxford University Press, 2012.

5 Mieczysław Porębski, *Ikonosfera*, Warsaw: Panstwowy Instytut Wydawniczy, 1972.

6 See Dina Iordanova, *Cinema of the Other Europe: The Industry and Artistry of East Central European Film*, London: Wallflower Press, 2003, p. 28.

7 This argument is developed with considerable subtlety in Alexei Yurchak, *Everything Was Forever Until It Was No More*, Princeton: Princeton University Press, 2005.

8 See, for instance, Jerzy Kossak, *Dylematy kultury masowej*, Warsaw: Wydawnictwa Artystyczne i Filmowe, 1966. For a good survey of the reception of Frankfurt School thinking in Yugoslavia, see Marjan Ivković, 'Praxis Philosophy's "Older Sister": The Reception of Critical Theory in the Former Yugoslavia', *ZPTh: Zeitschrift für Politische Theorie*, 8:2 (2017), pp. 272–80.

9 See Juliane Fürst, *Flowers through the Concrete: Explorations in Soviet Hippieland*, Oxford: Oxford University Press, 2021.

10 See Łukasz Ronduda and Barbara Piwowarska (eds), *Polish New Wave: The History of a Phenomenon That Never Existed*, Warsaw: Adam Mickiewicz Institute / CSM Zamek Ujazdowski, 2008.

11 Károly Nemes, *Jean-Luc Godard*, Budapest: Magyar Filmtudományi Intézet és Filmarchívum / Népművelési Propaganda Iroda, 1979; Konrad Eberhardt, *Jean-Luc Godard*, Warsaw: Wydawnictwa Artystyczne i Filmowe, 1970.

12 Eberhardt, op. cit., pp. 92–93.

13 Angela Delle Vache, 'Jean-Luc Godard's *Pierrot le Fou*: Cinema as Collage against Painting', in *Cinema and Painting: How Art is Used in Film*, Austin: Texas University Press, 1996, pp. 107–34.

14 For a thoughtful analysis of Godard's deployment of the visual languages of advertising in *Pierrot Le Fou*, see Daniel Yacavone, 'Jean Luc Godard and Roy Lichtenstein: Originality, Reflexivity and the Re-Presented image', *FORUM: University of Edinburgh Postgraduate Journal of Culture and the Arts*, 1 (Autumn 2005), pp. 1–11.

15 For a thorough reading of the film, which examines its scenography and cinematography as well as the reasons why it was not well understood by critics at the time of its release, see Justyna Jaworska, '"Piękne widoki panowie stąd macie": Co widać w *Rewizji osobistej*?' *Pleograf: Kwartalnik Akademii Polskiego Filmu*, 2 (2017) available at https://akademiapolskiegofilmu.pl/pl/historia-polskiego-filmu/pleograf/kinofilia/8/piekne-widoki-panowie-stad-macie-co-widac-w-rewizji-osobistej/597.

16 Ibid.

17 This was one of a number of points of connection and encounter between Godard and Chytilová in their long careers. See Iveta Jusová and Dan Reyes, 'Between Two Waves: Věra Chytilová and Jean-Luc Godard', *Studies in Eastern European Cinema*, 1 (2019), pp. 22–38.

18 Godard, as cited by Peter Hames, *The Czechoslovak New Wave*, Oakland: University of California Press, 1985, p. 5.

19 Claire Clouzot, 'Daisies by Vera Chytilova', *Film Quarterly*, 21:3 (Spring 1968), p. 36.

20 Josef Škvorecký, *All the Bright Young Men and Women: A Personal History of the Czech Cinema*, trans. Michael Schonberg, Toronto: Peter Martin Associates, 1971, p. 110.

21 Ignacy Witz, 'Nasz Plakat', in *Przechadzki po warszawskich wystawach 1945–1968*, Warsaw: Wyd. Lit., 1972, p. 53.
22 See Carter Ratcliff, *Komar & Melamid*, New York: Abbeville Press, 1988.
23 Nikolai Federov, as cited in John Gray, *The Immortalization Commission: The Strange Quest to Defeat Death*, Harmondsworth: Penguin, 2011, p. 159.
24 Germaine Greer, *The Female Eunuch*, London: MacGibbon & Kee, 1970, p. 282.

11

'Mouthpiece of the Dictatorship': Television and the Domestic Sphere in Brazilian Women's 'Pop Cinema', 1972–77

Gillian Sneed

In a 1968 acrylic painting titled *Transposição 1* (*Transposition 1*), Brazilian artist Wanda Pimentel (1943–2019) depicts a domestic interior with simplified outlined shapes and flat planes of red, white and green (Figure 11.1). At the bottom right, we see a woman's white legs at the edge of a rectangular sofa, the toes of a lone foot sloping upward. They point toward the slanted ruffled line of a green curtain, parting to reveal a red wall peeking out from behind. The curtain (seen from the side) transforms into a green floor (seen from above) that meets the corner of another red wall above. At the bottom of this wall is a black electricity socket with a short wiggly cord connecting it to a television set. The image on the screen is a replica of this same domestic interior, which is repeated again and again within each successively smaller screen.

Pimentel's *Transposição 1* is part of her *Envolvimento* (*Entanglement*) series (1968–69), scenes depicting a woman's feet and legs inside colourful domestic interiors replete with geometrically-rendered furnishings, patterned rugs, women's clothing and shoes, kitchen stovetops and dishware, and feminised household objects (an iron, a sewing machine, a hairdryer and a make-up kit). *Transposição 1* reflects on the act of watching television, a private leisure activity that takes place in the home. Despite its subject-matter of relaxation, the composition's jarring use of the complementary colours of red and green, the flattening of space and the merging of perspectives result in a sense of tension and compression. The recursiveness of the vertiginous *mise en abyme* motif results in an image that functions to question representation itself, both pictorial and televisual. It thus also interrogates reality as one sees and experiences it.

In Pimentel's works, one's gaze is sometimes positioned as that of the artist, such that the viewer becomes her surrogate, seeing domestic space

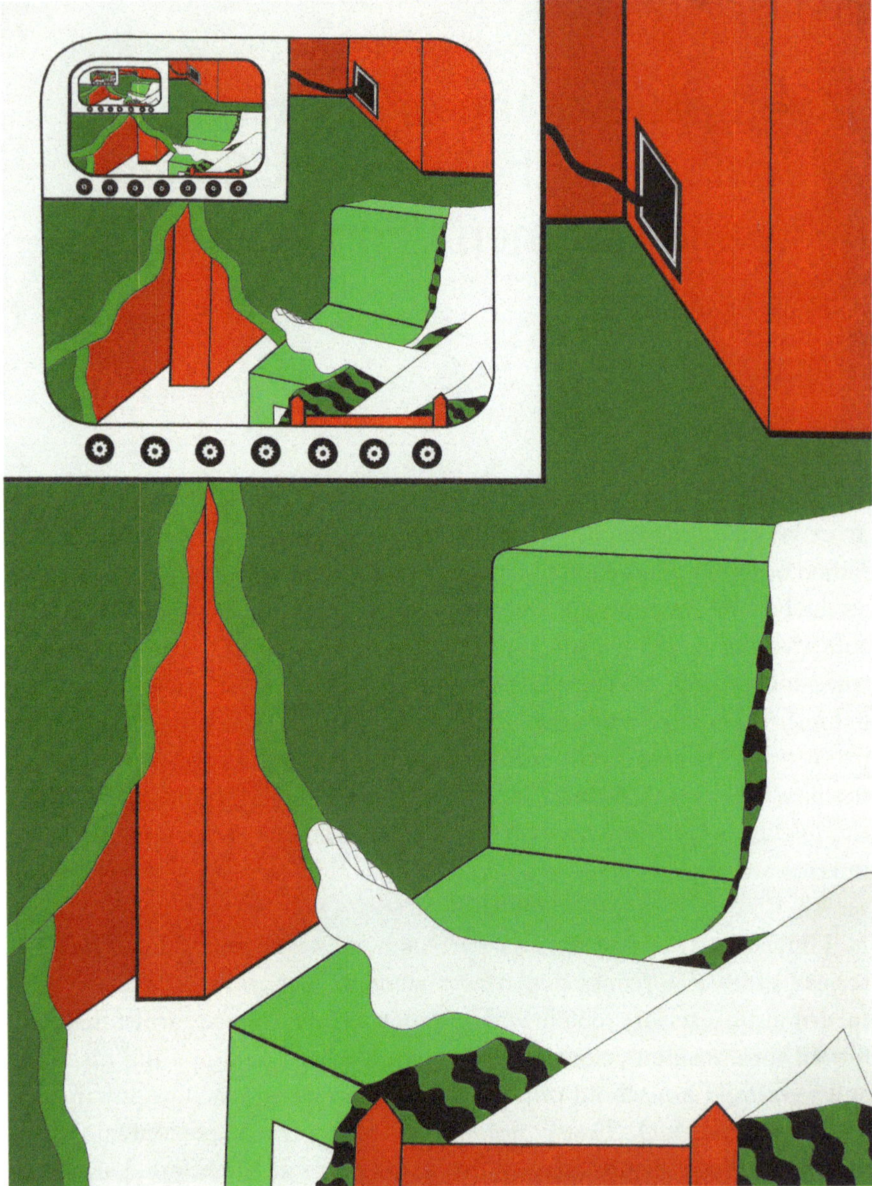

Figure 11.1 Wanda Pimentel, *Transposição 1* (*Transposition 1*), from the series *Envolvimento* (*Entanglement*), 1968. Vinyl paint on canvas, 51³/₁₆ × 38¹/₄ in. (130 × 97.2 cm). Source: Gilberto Chateaubriand, © MAM/RJ Collection.

from her viewpoint.[1] This imbues her images with a personal, feminised subjectivity. In *Transposição 1*, the legs depicted may or may not be those of the artist, but the intimate depiction of a woman's body parts within domestic space raises associations with women's roles within the home.

The artwork's framing of the image as a screen within a screen within a screen (*ad infinitum*), reminds the viewer of forms of visual and physical containment, particularly the ways in which women have been traditionally confined to the home, especially in the 1950s and 1960s in Brazil.

Pimentel's work was associated with international Pop art trends, although at the time in Brazil the term 'Pop art' was contested. In Brazil, it was negatively associated with the Global North and US cultural interventionist policies in the country, and it was seen as too apolitical of an art form.[2] To differentiate local art made in a Pop aesthetic from Euro-American Pop art, Brazilian artists defined a new style, which they called *Nova Figuração* (New Figuration). This movement paralleled international Pop in its foregrounding of figuration and its interests in the mass media, consumerism, quotidian experience and merging of high and low, but it was more critical in its tone. Pimentel's paintings align with *Nova Figuração* in their visual style and exploration of the numbing effects of the mass media and consumerism within daily life. Significantly, her reflections on these themes come from a particularly gendered perspective. Although feminism was not broadly accepted in the Brazilian art world of the time, the considerations of gender roles and women's experiences and subjectivities in her work, and others like it, merit interpretations rooted in feminism.[3]

New perspectives on both Pop art in Brazil and women's roles within it have recently begun to be elaborated, particularly in the scholarship of art historians Claudia Calirman and Giulia Lamoni, and in the exhibitions *International Pop* at the Walker Art Center (2015) and *The World Goes Pop* at Tate Modern (2015–16). However, the main focus of this research has been on painting and assemblage, thus foreclosing an in-depth examination of the relationships between the moving image and Pop art in Brazil and women's contributions to both.[4] Furthermore, while curators William Kaizen and Ed Halter have separately attempted to define a corpus of Pop films, they have largely focused on US and European traditions, neglecting those in Latin America.[5] A further accounting is needed of the relationship between experimental film and video art in Brazil and their relationship to international Pop art trends.

This essay aims to address these gaps by examining several examples of Brazilian experimental film and video artwork of the 1970s, made by or about women artists. I argue that these works can be considered exponents of what Kaizen terms 'Pop cinema' – moving image works in film and video – related to broader international Pop art. By analysing several works of Pop cinema by Brazilian women artists (and one by a man about a woman artist), I demonstrate that women played a central role in pioneering Pop cinema in Brazil. Using a feminist interpretive approach – even for work by women who did not identify as feminists – I argue that Brazilian women's Pop cinema functioned as an alternative to the typically masculinist iterations of Pop cinema across the Americas and in Europe.[6] This is particularly true in the ways in which their works undermine mass media representations of stereotypical gender roles or of women as commodified sex objects. I also show how these Pop cinema works adopt exaggeration and excess as strategies to critique television's infiltration in the domestic sphere as a propaganda and surveillance apparatus of the Brazilian military dictatorship then in power (1964–85).

First, I consider works that explore the relationship between television and the feminised domestic sphere through a Pop aesthetic, including Antonio Carlos da Fontoura's experimental documentary film *Wanda Pimentel* (1972) about the titular artist whose work is described at the opening of this essay. I also consider artist Lygia Pape's experimental film *Wampirou* (1973) and artist Sonia Andrade's video *Untitled* (1975), which both reflect on the function of television in the domestic sphere and its relationship to women's roles within that same space. Then, I examine Andrade's video *Untitled* (1977) and Pape's film *Eat Me* (1975), which appropriate the visual language of advertising to critique televisual representations of women ironically and subversively, as well as the relationship of both to socio-political hegemonies under the oppressive Brazilian military dictatorship.

Wanda Pimentel (1972)

The first work under consideration, *Wanda Pimentel*, was filmed by director Antonio Carlos da Fontoura. It is the only work discussed in this essay by a man or by a filmmaker (rather than a visual artist), but it is included here because it attempts to capture Pimentel's artistic subjectivity by recreating her painted domestic scenes using staged live tableaux intercut with still images of her paintings. The six-minute, 35mm experimental documentary opens with a shot of a bathroom sink set against yellow plaid wallpaper, with tubes of lipstick, bobby pins, shaving implements and a hairdryer littering the counter. An audio of the roar of the blowing hairdryer overlays this opening shot and is continuous with the next one, in which the camera pans from left to right across the wallpaper toward a bathroom mirror. In the mirror's reflection, we catch our first partial glimpse of the face of a woman – Pimentel herself – whose hand grips the hairdryer as she waves it over her head. The shot then cuts to a close-up shot of a painting by the artist, depicting yellow stripes and a woman's white bent leg, angled at the knee, beside an open drawer of a red dresser, with a yellow brassiere dangling out of it. This cuts to a close-up shot of a painting by the artist of a red desk fan. Next, we see a live-action shot of Pimentel's calves, as she runs an electric razor up and down them. The device's buzzing sound dominates the audio.

This intercutting between close-up images of the artist's paintings and scenes of the artist inside her home enacting daily activities continues. In one live-action shot, both of her feet appear perched on the edge of her bathtub near the faucets as she sprays her legs with a handheld shower head. In another, the bathroom faucet is left running. The audio of the running water continues after a cut to a shot of a painting depicting a room in reds and greens with a white sink overflowing with water. We see a live-action close-up of a steaming iron followed by the still of a painting of a sewing machine paired with the audio of the machine's clicking rhythm. Images of paintings of clothes hanging in a closet are overlaid with the sounds of a television advertisement. The camera pans across the products lining the top shelf of Pimentel's refrigerator – among them Real brand butter, Peixe brand ketchup, Maguary passion fruit juice and Hellman's Mayonnaise – and it later documents her using a blender to make a smoothie, set to the machine's whirring noise.

Prior to making this film, director Antonio Carlos da Fontoura was best-known for his feature-length narrative films *Copacabana me engana* (*Copacabana Tricks Me*, 1968) and *Rainha diaba* (*Devil Queen*, 1973), as well as an earlier documentary from 1966 about the male Brazilian *Nova Figuração* artists Rubens Gerchman, Roberto Magalhães and Antonio Dias, titled *Ver Ouvir* (*See Listen*), which won first prize at the Festival Brasilia and Bienal de Arte Jovem de Paris.[7] Both *Wanda Pimentel* and *Ver Ouvir* before it easily correspond to William Kaizen's Pop cinema category of documentary films about Pop artists that explore 'the consumption of popular culture and [its] effects […] on everyday life'.[8]

Wanda Pimentel also demonstrates elements of another category of Pop cinema outlined by Kaizen, one he labels 'collage films', or films that contain 'readymade images taken from the world of pop culture'.[9] This collage sensibility is most evident in *Wanda Pimentel* in a sequence of tableaux depicting televisions. The film opens with a shot of a television positioned on a table in front of one of Pimentel's paintings. The television plays a black-and-white superhero cartoon, in which we see a close-up of two eyes, accompanied by the show's bombastic dialogue.[10] The film then cuts to a shot of another painting by Pimentel, which the camera pans up on, coming to rest on the image of a red ashtray filled with two smoky cigarettes. This is backed by the audio of a cigarette advertisement from the real television set in the previous shot. The film cuts to a shot of Pimentel, seen from above, who is positioned in front of the television set, while leaning her arm on the table and flipping through fashion magazines, a smoking cigarette posed on an ashtray positioned between her body and the television. The audio is an advertisement playing the dramatic lilt of the violin solo from *The Godfather* theme song, accompanied by an announcer's deep masculine voice selling flowers. As the advertisement audio continues, the film cuts to a close-up shot of Pimentel's *Transposição 1*, described in this essay's introduction, focusing on the painting's successively smaller televisions within a television. As a collage film, *Wanda Pimentel* dispenses with narrative and approaches pop culture as a sort of flow of information.[11] It also juxtaposes different kinds of images from daily life scenes and television and advertising imagery with mass-produced products, such as the branded products in Pimentel's refrigerator. The overlay of televisual imagery and advertising audio with moving and still images advances the sense of a perpetual stream of mass media being pumped into the home.

It is important to remember that this film and the others mentioned in this essay were made against the backdrop of the country's repressive military dictatorship, inaugurated via a military coup in 1964, which understood the potential of television to prop up the regime. The dictatorship saw television as a useful communication tool for transmitting and managing political information, encouraging a sense of national unity across the country's disparate geographic regions and expanding the consumer economy through advertising.[12] These goals were achieved largely via the state-backed Globo Television Network, a television broadcasting company viewed by most Brazilians at the time as a 'mouthpiece of the dictatorship'.[13] Because of this, the image of the television appeared as a repeated trope in Brazilian art and moving image works of the 1960s and 1970s, as a way to resist the government's manipulation of information and to contest state power.[14] Because television was a medium that enabled overt and more subtle forms of state propaganda and ideologies to encroach on the private space of the home, it was a particularly apt subject for women artists, like Pimentel, who may have been eager to comment on the dual oppressions of authoritarianism and patriarchy within the domestic sphere.

Ultimately, *Wanda Pimentel* emphasises television as an integral part of domestic space. It also reflects on a woman's experience within that space, particularly in response to the artist's paintings which document her own body inside her home and the specific activities she undertook in that space: bodily maintenance, household chores and leisure and relaxation.

Fontoura claims that he was inspired to make the film by his desire to cinematically enter into what he describes as 'feminine loneliness, using only images and noise, without narration or testimonies'.[15] Thus, the film represents a man's attempt at interpreting a woman's sensibilities and experiences, albeit one made in collaboration with the artist. Whether Fontoura's interpretation is accurate or biased is open to question, although the film's gaze is decidedly more voyeuristic (that of an outsider peeping in) than the gaze in the paintings (that of a female subject representing her own body or the body of another woman).[16] In any case, both Pimentel's paintings and Fontoura's film explore the relationship of televisions to domestic space and, in particular, to the ways in which television infiltrates it. This situation is acutely emphasised with the shot of the cartoon eyes peering out of the television screen, which could be read as a cipher for the ways in which the military dictatorship, then entering its harshest phase, invaded the private space of the home through its modes of surveillance.

Wampirou (1973)

Lygia Pape (1927–2004) was another important artist who contributed to Pop cinema in Brazil. Best known for her role in the development of Brazil's Neoconcrete art movement in the early 1960s, Pape became interested in film when she began collaborating with Brazilian Cinema Novo filmmakers by designing the opening and closing credits for their films.[17] Eventually she began making her own short experimental films between 1967 and 1975. A year after Fontoura directed *Wanda Pimentel*, Pape directed a silent nineteen-minute super-8 film titled *Wampirou*.[18]

The film stars the artist Antonio Manuel, appearing as a bearded and long-haired vampire named 'Wamp' who aimlessly wanders the modern city of Rio de Janeiro, clad in a black cape.[19] Throughout the campy, low-budget, surreal narrative – which also features Pape and fellow artist Lygia Clark as actors – Wamp engages in various over-the-top activities, including sucking his own blood and the blood of others, attending a holy last supper and participating in extravagant liturgical and sexual rituals. He also performs quotidian activities such as lazily lying in bed and watching television, reading comic books and enjoying a refreshing Coca-Cola. Later, he appears in a suit as an artist meeting with an art dealer (played by artist Jackson Ribeiro). The dealer scares Wamp away with a cross and then robs a safe containing the markers of his identity: his cloak and his vampire teeth dentures. Upon returning home, Wamp pierces a woman's neck with an electric drill and cuts her with a saw. Her eyes turn red, and her mouth fills with blood. The film ends with a title card reading in bold red letters: 'Sangue é Vida, Doe Sangue' (Blood is Life, Give Blood).

Pape first showed the film in *Expo-Projeção* (*Expo-Projection*), an exhibition of sound art, slide projections and experimental films by artists, curated by art historian Aracy Amaral in São Paulo in June 1973. The film was closely aligned with a Brazilian cult genre of underground filmmaking known as 'marginal' or 'udigrudi' cinema.[20] Other udigrudi directors, including José Mojica Marins and Ivan Cardoso, experimented with the horror genre. The sub-genre of kitsch udigrudi horror came to be known as 'terrir', a Portuguese portmanteau of the words 'terror' and 'rir' (to laugh), and represented a combination of horror tropes, elements of the sexy *chanchada* comedy and melodrama, as well as parodies of Brazilian stereotypes.[21] Some film historians have concluded that the terrir genre was a form of satire intended to critique life under the military dictatorship.[22] Ivan Cardoso's low-budget terrir film *Nosferato no Brasil* (*Nosferatu in Brazil*, 1970) appears to have been an influence on Pape's *Wampirou*; they share narrative and aesthetic elements. Another term for underground films such as these is 'sub-z', extremely low-budget films featuring non-actors and deviant themes, which are also closely aligned with Pop cinema.[23] Like sub-z films, *Wampirou* indulges in low production values, homemade costumes and amateur actors; it riffs on conventional horror plots, while also referencing the art world and udigrudi cinema. Similarly, in its combining of genre codes and use of pastiche and irony to reveal hypocrisies in mainstream society, it engages camp sensibilities – which, as Halter and Kaizen have argued, are also associated with Pop cinema.[24]

One of the main ways in which Brazilian Pop differed from its counterparts in the Global North is that it was more overtly politicised. Brazilian Pop artists and filmmakers sought to address Latin American social realities and to critique consumer capitalism, which they saw as an influx of US corporate economic interventionism in the country and collaboration with the oppressive dictatorship.[25] From this perspective, *Wampirou* can also be interpreted as a politicised critique of the Brazilian state. In Brazil, the image of the vampire has been interpreted as a metaphor for the plundering of underdeveloped countries by neocolonial capitalist interests.[26] The character of Wamp thus becomes an allegory of political repression and surveillance, both of Brazilian citizens under the regime and of artists within a capitalist art market controlled by the Global North.

Wampirou can also be interpreted as a critique of the mass media's and consumer culture's intrusion into the private space of the home.

This is particularly evident in a scene that starts with Wamp lying in his bed, reading comic books and watching television, and ends with an erotically charged sexual fantasy. As he lies in bed, wrapped in floral blankets, above him on the wall hangs a painting depicting a nude woman's spread legs and genitalia. He smokes a cigar, sips Coca-Cola from a straw and removes his vampire dentures before falling asleep while watching Woody Woodpecker and Andy Panda cartoons on a black-and-white television. As he sleeps, a dream sequence depicts a semi-nude female vampire reclining on a bed, wrapped in black leather and writhing erotically. An androgynous vampire with blood dripping from his mouth appears wearing only a cape and his underwear. He sits on the bed, turns his head to the side and bites his own arm. Then he straddles the reclining woman and bites her breast. The camera focuses on drops of blood dripping on his skin. Then, looking at the camera, he shoots himself in the forehead. Wamp awakes from his dream, startled. With its US cartoons and comic books, the scene underscores the pervasiveness of US pop culture within Brazilian domestic spaces. Like Fontoura's film about Wanda Pimentel, *Wampirou* prominently features a ubiquitous international mass-produced food brand – Coca-Cola – alluding to the omnipresence of US products in Brazil and their widespread delivery into the hands of Brazilian consumers.[27]

The film also flirts with non-normative depictions of gender and sexuality. The dream sequence's gender-bending androgynous character, its explicit eroticism and its depiction of female sexual desire function to undermine state censorship of sex and nudity on television.[28] Even so, Pape did not label herself or her works as 'feminist', a refusal that was probably due to a number of factors, including Brazilian conceptions of feminism being doctrinaire, aggressive and a form of US imperialism.[29] While the over-the-top erotic performance and sexual sadism in the dream sequence demonstrate a kind of campy exaggeration common to udigrudi cinema, they also gesture toward a Pop aesthetic that works to critique television's infiltration of the home as an apparatus of state.

Untitled (1975)

Video artist Sonia Andrade (1935–2022) also addresses the penetration of television in the domestic sphere in her eight-minute black-and-white Portapak video *Sem Título* (*Untitled*, 1975).[30] The video opens with a shot of the artist recorded from a fixed vantage point as she sits at a table in a closed-in terrace, preparing to eat a traditional Brazilian meal: a plate of black beans, bread and guaraná soda. She faces the camera, framed so that we see the table, her seated upper body and a television placed directly behind her. Andrade begins to carefully ladle beans from a large pot into her bowl, tearing some bread and pouring herself a glass of the beverage.

While these actions unfold, the television behind her, tuned into the Globo Television Network, broadcasts an episode of the US television series *Tarzan*, dubbed into Portuguese, and the Brazilian commercials that accompany it. At first, the artist scoops the food into her mouth calmly, almost monotonously. But after a few minutes, she starts shovelling it in more aggressively. She doles out more beans from the pot and tears more bread with increased frenzy; then she begins to dribble the food on her head, pour it down her shirt and wipe it on her face and clothes. Eventually, she begins propelling the beans towards the camera, where they explosively impact a clear plastic surface placed between herself and the lens. This screen becomes increasingly clogged with beans until it goes black (see Figures 11.2–7).

Andrade is associated with a group of artists in Rio de Janeiro known as the 'pioneers of video art', who helped introduce the medium to the country in the early-to-mid-1970s.[31] Andrade shot *Untitled* in one continuous take, due to a lack of editing equipment, so that her actions unfold in 'real' time. The black-and-white video differentiates *Untitled* from Fontoura's and Pape's use of colour film and their bright Pop aesthetic. It also has a low resolution – a by-product of the limitations of video technology at the time – which casts a darker mood over the artist's frantic gestures, despite her silly antics. But while video's inherent qualities (grey tones, poor image quality, static framing and lack of editing) lend *Untitled* a bleak, documentary sensibility not normally associated with the exuberance of a Pop aesthetic, the work still can be considered Pop cinema, especially in its depiction of the interactions between the mass media and quotidian life.[32]

The television broadcast of *Tarzan* in the video's background (which acts as a screen within a screen, much like the televisual *mise en abyme* in Pimentel's *Transposição 1*) and its artificially dubbed soundtrack engage with a complex echo system of transnational media exchange. The pacing and timing of Andrade's live actions occur in concert with the rising tension in the television episode's plot, and the images and sounds in the television show have an impact on her performance. Although Andrade has stated that her inclusion of that particular show was not intentional, it is still worthy of analysis, both for its striking relationship to her performance and for what it reveals about the mass media in Brazil at the time.

Tarzan was a late 1960s US television series re-broadcast in Brazil in the 1970s. The titular character is an educated white man who has grown tired

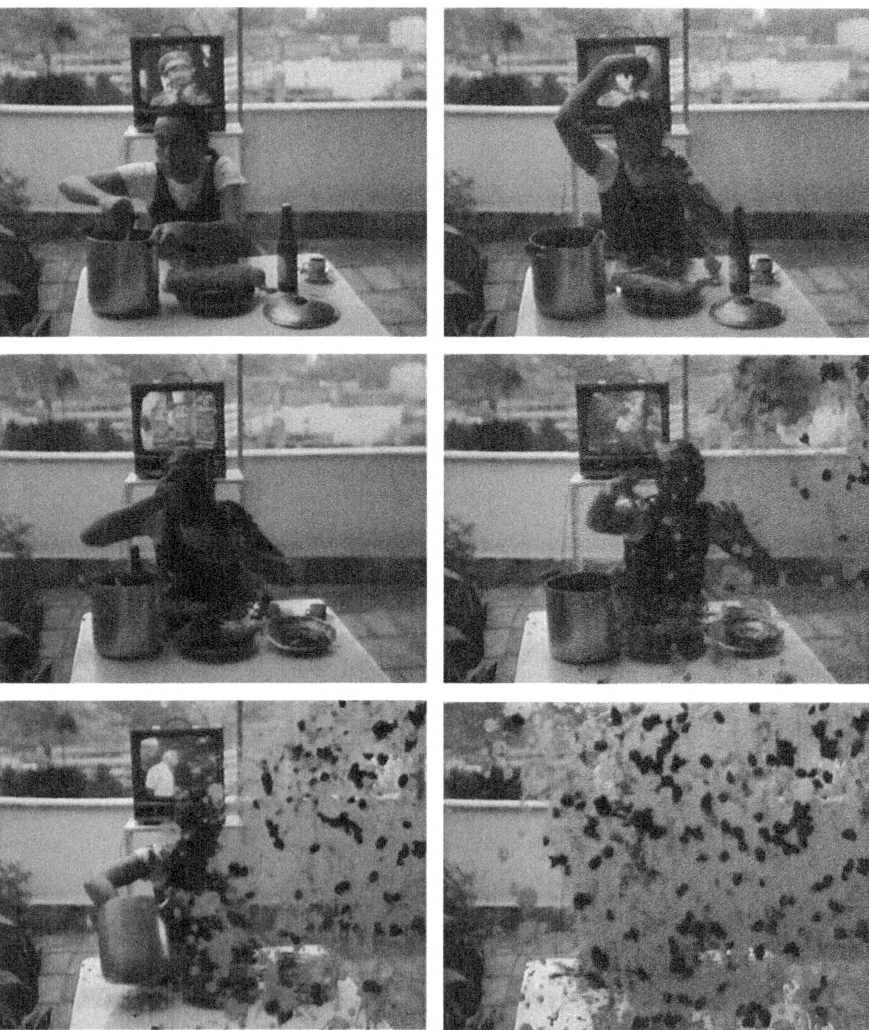

Figures 11.2–7 Sonia Andrade, *Sem Título* (*Untitled*, 1975). Black-and-white video with sound. 8 minutes, 47 seconds. Source: Courtesy of the artist.

of civilisation and has returned to the 'jungle' where he grew up to keep his home safe from poachers and other wrong-doers – largely 'coloniser'-types such as unscrupulous land developers, thieving traders, zealous missionaries and corrupt military and police. He is assisted by his chimpanzee, named Cheetah, and a local, brown-skinned orphan boy named Jai. The particular episode of *Tarzan* featured in *Untitled*, titled 'Voice of Elephant', tells the story of the wrongful accusation of Jai's elephant Tanto for the murder of an imperial bureaucrat, a cover-up for the real culprits – a tribal chief colluding with a thieving trader – and the elephant's subsequent 'trial' among the tribal elders, for which Jai procures a lawyer to 'defend' the animal. Andrade's bean performance is punctuated with the show's soundtrack of the chimp's incessant wailing, creating an unnerving connection between what is occurring onscreen and the artist's startling outburst with the beans.

As the *Tarzan* episode unfolds behind Andrade, it is interrupted at one point by the flashy Globo Television Network logo announcing a commercial break. The advertisements that occur in the interlude include spots for a hair product, soup (with a mother feeding her son) and a dance club featuring 'sexy' dancers. After returning from the commercial break, a new *Tarzan* sequence plays, in which Jai introduces a British colonial judge, wearing a suit and ascot, to the strapping Tarzan, clad in nothing but a loin cloth. Andrade's beans slowly accumulate on the screen in front of her, before completely blocking our view of the background and the television. The juxtaposition of Andrade's actions with the scenes on screen behind her exemplify the ways in which found footage can be used in film to produce ironic tension.[33] As such, Andrade's bean outburst appears to physically resist and cancel out what is going on in the television episode behind her.

The irony underscored by Andrade's inclusion of *Tarzan* in the background is that a show intended for US audiences about the inhabitants of an unspecified 'exotic jungle' (which could easily be a stand-in for the Amazon) was being broadcast in Brazil. Its appearance not only attests to the pervasiveness of US television programming in the country, but also reveals how US representations of 'exotic Others' were consumed by Brazilian audiences. The show represents a mid-1960s counter-culture utopian 'white-saviour' fantasy of a 'civilised' man (Tarzan) returning to the wild to fight imperialist wrong-doers, generically reflecting the US New Left's interest in anti-imperialism and resistance to authoritarianism. However, within the context of Brazil, that message was lost: it was distributed on the Globo Television Network, which was complicit in supporting the dictatorship. Andrade's bean outburst appears to physically resist and cancel out the kinds of imperialist, 'primitivising' representations of the encounter between 'civilised' and 'primitive' societies depicted in the show.

Thus, Andrade's inclusion of *Tarzan* and Globo advertisements can be interpreted on one level as a political critique of the state's mass media and its association with US economic interventionism in Brazil. Indeed, as mentioned above, Brazilian iterations of Pop art tended to engage in more political critique than the Pop art of their counterparts in the US and Europe.[34] As the dictatorship became increasingly hostile toward free speech, especially on television, Brazilian artists also sought out video art as an analogous medium that afforded covert modes for expressing subversive speech that resisted this censorship.[35] From another perspective, *Untitled* and its inclusion of television programming also work to undermine stereotyped mass media representations of women. Although Andrade has refuted any alignment of her art practice with feminism, *Untitled* merits a feminist interpretation because of its exploration of the themes of domesticity, traditional gender roles and media representations of women.[36] Andrade's positioning of her own body against televised images of masculinity creates a forceful contrast between media representations of archetypal men (powerful militarised elites or muscle-bound symbols of virility) situated in public spaces and the artist as a frustrated housewife, confined to the home where she eats alone. It echoes Pimentel's representations of a woman, isolated in her home, watching television. Andrade's initial consumption and later refusal to eat the beans function as a rejection of both 'the national' and the stereotyped gendered and primitivising tropes portrayed on the television behind her. Furthermore, the advertisements that appear on the television in the background also depict the ways in which advertisers use women to sell products, emphasising their value in society as either sex objects (dancers in a club) or domestic homemakers (a mother cooking soup for a child).

In the end, Andrade refuses to ingest the beans or to internalise the images on the television behind her. By launching the beans at the screen, she physically rejects the consumerism of television ads and imported US media images and reveals that television is far from transparent. This was especially true in Brazil in the 1970s, where the Globo Television Network moulded the public's interpretation of the content it delivered.

Untitled (1977)

Andrade further explored the theme of women's roles in the home and their representations on television in a later untitled work from 1977. In this short black-and-white video, we see a television monitor sitting on a counter, accompanied by the sound of piano music, which then shifts to elevator music. The artist's face appears 'inside' the monitor, as she picks up a piece of dental floss and begins to playfully floss her teeth. Next, she pulls out a tube of toothpaste, and as if displaying it as a product for sale in a commercial, she neatly squeezes some onto a toothbrush. In reality, she is actually physically occupying the space behind a fake screen, a hoax that is revealed when her hand gestures slightly exceed the boundaries of the monitor. She brushes her teeth in an exaggerated manner, and when she is done, she lifts a cup of water to her mouth, sips it, swishes it extravagantly and spits it out.

She does this several times, before shaking her head, wiping her mouth with a towel and capping the toothpaste tube. Staring at the camera, she smiles a wide, saccharine grin (Figures 11.8–13).

Untitled (1977) is a caricature of an actual toothpaste commercial that Andrade had seen and thus functions as an indictment of the superficial images used to sell products on television.[37] It also recalls a 1976 advertisement for Telefunken brand television sets, in which a smiling woman appears on the screen of a monitor placed on a counter, which I suggest may have been another source for the work. Given its origins in actual

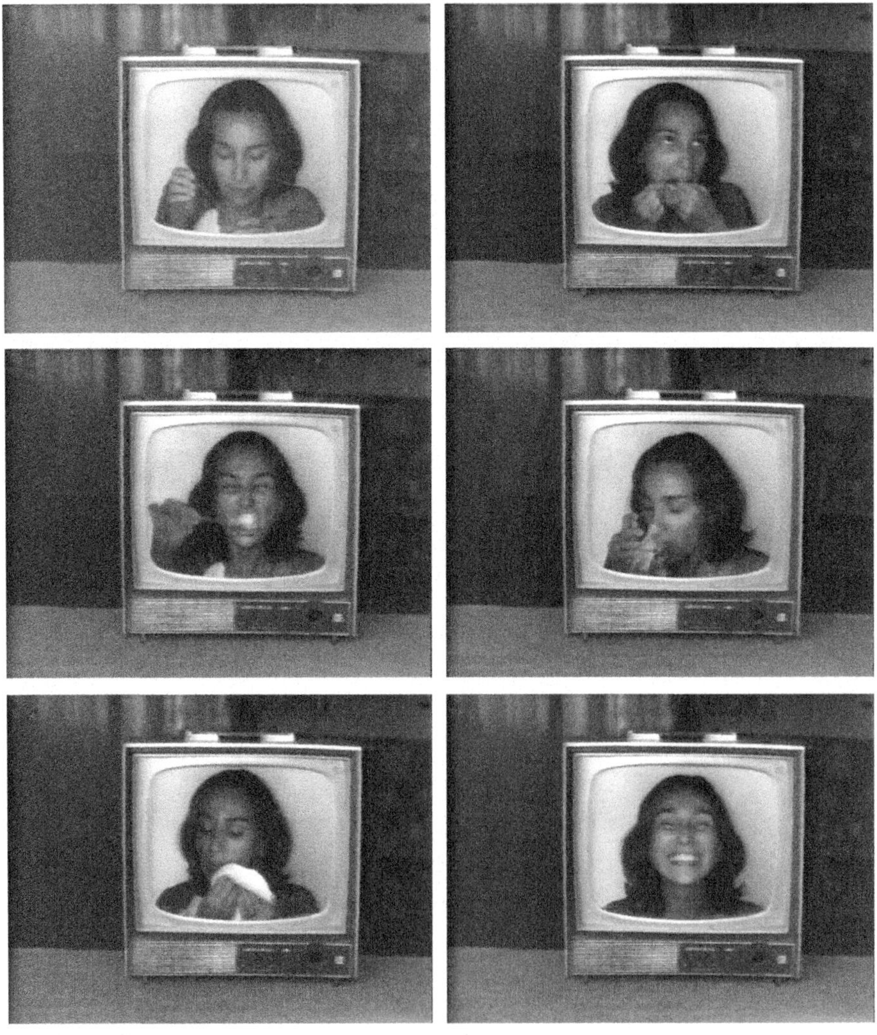

Figures 11.8–13 Sonia Andrade, *Sem Título* (*Untitled*, 1977). Black-and-white video with sound. 2 minutes, 24 seconds. Source: Courtesy of the artist.

commercials, *Untitled* exemplifies a combination of Pop cinema strategies, including films that depict popular culture consumerism and its effects on everyday life as well as sub-z movies, which appropriate directly from television and movie genres as readymades.[38] *Untitled* also seems to reference, but does not actually play, Brazilian pop music. Specifically, it is reminiscent of the lyrics of two songs on Tom Zé's Tropicália-era album, *Grande Liquidaçao* (*Big Clearance Sale*, 1968): 'Parque Industrial' (Industrial Park) and 'Catequismo, Crème Dental e Eu' (Catechism, Toothpaste and Me). The lyrics of the former song – 'we have the bottled smile / it comes ready-made and catalogued / just heat and reuse' – mock consumerism and 'pre-packaged identities',[39] while the latter song compares consumer capitalism to a bourgeois religion indoctrinating the public to buy personal hygiene products such as toothpaste.[40] In keeping with other works of Brazilian Pop, *Untitled* is thus stridently critical, repudiating the phony representations of happiness in advertising. It epitomises art historian Simone Osthoff's observation that early Brazilian video artists 'viewed television – structured by advertising – as superficial, intellectually empty, and ultimately as a weapon in the capitalist manipulation of consumers'.[41]

Yet, *Untitled* (1977) is more than just a critique of television. Like the earlier beans video (*Untitled*, 1975), it also addresses gender in its ironic subversions of televisual representations of women. In the beans video, Andrade's incorporation of actual advertisements for a hair product, a dance club and soup creates a critical distance that exposes their underlying ideologies around beauty standards for women, sexual objectification and domestic roles. By contrast, in *Untitled* (1977), Andrade parodies a commercial with her own body, satirising how advertising exploits images of beautiful, carefree women to sell products, by physically appropriating advertising modalities to reformulate its messaging. *Untitled* (1977) also implies that women, as the custodians of the domestic sphere, are the primary consumers of advertising, underscoring the fact that in the 1970s the default viewer of ads for household goods in Brazil was the housewife, who viewed commercials approximately every twelve minutes in the intervals of her beloved telenovelas.[42] For the many Brazilian middle-class women who were relegated to the home and its demands for maintenance, television represented their only conduit to the public sphere.

Ultimately, in *Untitled* (1977) Andrade depicts her own physical enclosure within the televisual monitor by 'appearing' onscreen as if it were a pre-recorded broadcast, while we are actually witnessing a 'live' performance: her 'real' body is framed by a fake monitor that visually contains it. But, in the end, the 'live' performance is just a recording as well, appearing on another monitor, the one on which we watch the video (thus becoming another televisual *mise en abyme*, as in Pimentel's *Transposição 1*). Andrade mobilises an unruly performance that literally cannot be contained inside the apparatus, exceeding its frame, to symbolically disrupt television's ideological messaging. By appropriating and transforming advertising's visual language, she also undercuts its depictions of beauty standards for women.

Eat Me: A Gula ou a Luxúria? (1975)

Lygia Pape uses a similar strategy of appropriating from advertising in her 1975 experimental film *Eat Me: A Gula ou a Luxúria?* (*Eat Me: Gluttony or Lust*). The nine-minute, 16mm colour film opens with a close-up of a man's mouth, moustached and painted with lipstick, as he sensually sucks and expels a red jewel with his tongue. The soundtrack of a moaning female voice accompanies this sequence as the jewel turns blue. Next, we see a woman's lips erotically sucking on a sausage, before returning to the male mouth as he expels the blue jewel and swirls saliva around his mouth with his tongue. Shots of the male and female mouths performing different movements evoking sex acts and eating alternate with increasing speed while off-screen voices rhythmically chant the phrase 'a gula ou a luxúria' (gluttony or lust) in different languages. The woman's moaning culminates in an orgasmic scream, which was an appropriated audio sample of Yoko Ono screaming taken from a Plastic Ono Band album.[43] The audio of a television advertisement for 'Cook Ladles' abruptly interrupts this shrieking, with a female voice intoning the words: 'bean soup; beans without soup, beans with soup; always Cook Ladles'.

Eat Me exhibits several characteristics of Pop cinema. It not only includes a collage technique in its use of found audio taken from pop music and advertising, but also in its production values it epitomises Halter's description of Pop cinema as appropriating the procedures and methods of the mass media.[44] The film's high production quality and tightly controlled framing and pace recall the aesthetic of television, which the film appropriates in order to challenge its logic. It also boasts a bright Pop colour palette facilitated by the high-grade 16mm film stock, which also emphasises its associations with colour television.[45] Furthermore, its professional lighting is cool and controlled, producing an affected sparkle on the juicy wet lips and jewels that conjures an advertising aesthetic. The framing of the mouths in *Eat Me* is tightly cropped and standardised, calling attention to the screen; the rhythm and timing of its cuts, determined by the artist according to a mathematical system, is regimented.[46] Thus, *Eat Me*'s satirical appropriation of advertising and marketing strategies can be interpreted as a critique of the dictatorship's collusion with mass media entities such as the Globo Network and their US economic interests.

Pape's critiques in *Eat Me* also challenge television's representations of normative gender and sexuality. While Pape explicitly claimed that she did not intend *Eat Me* as a feminist work, it still demonstrates the ways in which Pop artworks by Brazilian women occupy what Giulia Lamoni has described as 'a zone of tension between the questioning of gender relations and female subjectivities [...] and a critical appropriation of a variety of languages [such] as those of the media – especially cinema [and] television'.[47] This tension is evidenced in *Eat Me* in the film's pulsating wave of female moaning, alluding to an orgasm, which culminates in the appropriated audio of an actual advertisement for ladles, thus referencing representations of women on television and the ways in which eroticism is used to sell products. The film's saturated colours also lend it a sensuality that mimics advertising and underscores what one critic described as 'the use of eroticism as a vehicle of consumption'.[48]

In 1976, *Eat Me* was included in an eponymous installation at the now-defunct Global Art Gallery in São Paulo. Owned by the Globo Television Network, the gallery was dedicated to supporting emerging Brazilian artists. Globo Television promoted the gallery's exhibitions during its primetime national broadcasts, right before the most competitive time slot of the eight o'clock telenovela.[49] For her exhibition's promotional spot, Pape created a thirty-second video using footage from *Eat Me*, depicting 'a frankly pornographic mouth', which was broadcast on the network.[50] By creating a commercial with elements from the film, Pape hijacked the television waves.[51] Her subversion of the national broadcast circuits as a critique of the ways in which ads exploited lust to sell products, exemplifies Halter's observation that many Pop cinema artists 'began taking over [...] media channels themselves'.[52] This was even more radical when considering that Pape did this on the Globo Network, the official communication arm of the dictatorship.[53]

Conclusion

According to Kaizen, very few women filmmakers were associated with Pop cinema in Euro-American contexts, and when they did appear in films by male filmmakers, they were 'typically depicted as commodified figures of desire'.[54] By contrast, as I have shown here, in Brazil women were at the forefront of pioneering Pop cinema, especially because it provided an apt platform for exploring women's roles in the domestic sphere and representations in the mass media. Rather than ambiguously reproducing mass media stereotypes of women, Brazilian women Pop cinema filmmakers explicitly critiqued these images through parody, satire and camp. Brazilian Pop cinema was more political than its counterparts in the Global North, and Brazilian filmmakers used the appropriation of various mass media forms (movies, television shows and advertising) to critique state control of the media and the complicity of the regime with US socio-economic interventions in the country, such as its promotion of US-style consumerism and consumer products. The image of the television itself served as a cipher for the public/private divide, a device through which information and ideologies flowed from the public, politicised sphere into the private domestic space of the home, which was also coded as 'feminine' – structures which these artists sought to disrupt and dismantle.

Notes

1 Claudia Calirman, *Dissident Practices: Brazilian Women Artists, 1960s–2020s*, Durham: Duke University Press, 2023, p. 25.

2 Claudia Calirman, 'Pop and Politics in Brazilian Art', in Darsie Alexander and Bartholomew Ryan (eds), *International Pop*, Minneapolis: Walker Art Center, 2015, p. 124. This attitude in Brazil contrasted with how US Pop was received in Europe, especially in West Germany, where it was seen as a radical and progressive movement of the New Left that questioned and critiqued the orthodoxies of postwar consumer capitalism. Andreas Huyssen, 'The Cultural Politics of Pop: Reception and Critique of US Pop Art in the Federal Republic of Germany', *New German Critique*, 4 (Winter 1975), pp. 77–97.

3 Feminism was not widely accepted at the time, because it was associated with US imperialism and because the Catholic Church, the Brazilian dictatorship and the radical Left all rejected it. Heloísa Buarque de Hollanda, 'Gender Studies: Rough Notes from a Very Local Perspective', *Journal of Latin American Cultural Studies*, 11:3 (December 2002), pp. 321–31; Simone Osthoff, 'De musas a autoras: Mulheres, arte e tecnologia no Brasil', *Ars*, 8:15 (2010), pp. 75–78; Roberta Barros, *Elogio ao toque: Ou como falar de arte feminista à brasileira*, Rio de Janeiro: Relacionarte Marketing e Produções Culturais, 2016; and Calirman, *Dissident Practices*, op. cit., pp. 29–31.

4 Claudia Calirman's *Dissident Practices* (op. cit.) addresses video art by Sonia Andrade, Anna Bella Geiger, Anna Maria Maiolino and Letícia Parente, as well as Lygia Pape's film *Eat Me: Gluttony or Lust?*, but not as works of Pop art. Giulia Lamoni does not address cinema as Pop art, but she does address Brazilian women's video art. Lamoni, 'Unfolding the "Present": Some Notes on Brazilian Pop', in Jessica Morgan

and Flavia Frigeri (eds), *The World Goes Pop*, New Haven: Yale University Press, 2015, p. 71.

5 William Kaizen, 'Notes on Pop Cinema', in *Pop Cinema: Art and Film in the US and UK, 1950s–1970s*, Philadelphia: International House Philadelphia, 2011, pp. 11–30. Ed Halter mentions Brazilian Cinema Novo in Brazil in relationship to Pop cinema trends of the 1960s, but it was actually Brazilian udigrudi cinema that was more influential on what I discuss as Brazilian Pop cinema in this essay. Ed Halter, 'Pop and Cinema: Three Tendencies', in Alexander Darsie and Bartholomew Ryan (eds), op. cit., pp. 181–93.

6 Although Brazilian men also created what could be considered Pop cinema – including Ivan Cardoso, Antonio Dias, Rogério Sganzerla and Júlio Bressane – I do not analyse their works because they did not explore women's roles in the domestic sphere nor the gendered address of television and advertising within that realm. Some of the few exceptions to the lack of women in European Pop cinema include the Catalan filmmakers Eugènia Balcells and Joan Rabascall.

7 Rodrigo Murat, *Antonio Carlos da Fontoura: Espelho da alma*, São Paulo: Imprensa Oficial, 2008, pp. 45–48. *Ver Ouvir* was similar to British filmmaker Ken Russell's classic 1962 BBC Pop film *Pop Goes the Easel*, about British Pop artists. Ed Halter, 'Pop and Cinema', op. cit., p. 188. On *Ver Ouvir*, see Sergio B. Martins, *Constructing an Avant-Garde: Art in Brazil, 1949–1979*, Cambridge, MA: MIT Press, 2013, pp. 81–82.

8 Kaizen, op. cit., p. 16.

9 Ibid.

10 The onscreen cartoon's audio consists of a man's voice intoning the words in Portuguese: 'We need more strength, let's see, push with ease'. All translations by the author, unless otherwise noted.

11 Kaizen, op. cit., pp. 13, 20.

12 Joseph Straubhaar, 'Telenovelas in Brazil: From Traveling Scripts to a Genre and Photo-Format both National and Transnational', in Tasha Oren and Sharon Shahaf (eds), *Global Television Formats: Understanding Television Across Borders*, New York: Routledge, 2012, p. 140.

13 Tania Cantrell Rosas-Moreno, *News and Novela in Brazilian Media: Fact, Fiction, and National Identity*, Lanham: Lexington Books, 2014, p. 22.

14 Lidia Santos, *Tropical Kitsch: Mass Media in Latin American Art and Literature*, Princeton: Markus Wiener Publishers, 2006, p. 167.

15 Fontoura, quoted in Murat, op. cit., p. 45.

16 The film *Wanda Pimentel* was also commissioned by a man, artist and gallerist Vitor Arruda, possibly Pimentel's gallerist at the time, as a form of promotion. Murat, op. cit., pp. 45–48.

17 Lygia Pape, 'Filmes', in Afonso Henrique Neto (ed.), *Arte Brasileira Contemporânea: Lygia Pape*, Rio de Janeiro: Funarte, 1983, pp. 43–44.

18 'Wampirou' is a combination of the words 'wampire' (vampire) and 'louco' (crazy), which was meant to imply the idea of a vampire who 'went nuts'. Lygia Pape, 'My Work in Marginal Cinema', in Susan Fisher Sterling, Berta Sichel and Franklin Espath Pedroso (eds), *Virgen Territory: Women, Gender, and History in Contemporary Brazilian Art*, Washington DC: National Museum of Women in the Arts, 2001, p. 91.

19 Although the programme materials described the film as set in 'a city of the [Brazilian] interior', according to Paula Pape, it was actually filmed in Rio de Janeiro near Jardim

Botânico and Lapa. Paula Pape, as cited in Vanessa Machado, *Lygia Pape: Espaços de rupture*, unpubl. PhD diss., University of São Paulo, 2008, p. 142, n. 69.

20 'Udigrudi' was a mocking way of pronouncing 'underground' in Portuguese.

21 Randal Johnson and Robert Stam, *Brazilian Cinema*, New York: Columbia University Press, 1995, p. 405.

22 Mariana Baltar, 'Weeping Reality: Melodramatic Imagination in Contemporary Brazilian Documentary', in Darlene J. Sadlier (ed.), *Latin American Melodrama: Passion, Pathos, and Entertainment*, Urbana: University of Illinois Press, 2009, p. 132.

23 Kaizen, op. cit., p. 16.

24 Ibid., pp. 24–25; Halter, op. cit., p. 190.

25 Calirman, 'Pop and Politics in Brazilian Art', op. cit., p. 120.

26 Calirman, '*Marginália* in Brazil's "Stone-Throwing Age"', *Art Journal*, 1:78 (Spring 2019), p. 63.

27 Coke appeared in a variety of Pop artworks across the Americas during the period. These include Andy Warhol's *Green Coca-Cola Bottles* (1962), Marisol Escobar's *Love* (1962), Antonio Caro's *Colombia* (1977) and Cildo Mereiles' conceptual project *Insertions into Ideological Circuits: Coca-Cola Project* (1970).

28 A censorship decree had been passed in January 1970 (the same year that *Wampirou* was filmed), prohibiting television programming that was offensive to moral decency, specifically targeting nudity and sex. Elena Shtromberg, *Art Systems: Brazil and the 1970s*, Austin: University of Texas Press, 2016, pp. 8, 44.

29 Sonia E. Alvarez, 'Women's Movements and Gender Politics in the Brazilian Transition', in Jane S. Jaquette (ed.), *The Women's Movement in Latin America: Feminism and the Transition to Democracy*, Boston: Unwin Hyman, 1989, pp. 21, 62.

30 *Untitled (Beans)* is the second vignette in a series of eight short videos, performed and directed by the artist and shot by videographer Jom Tob Azulay.

31 Although the Sony Portapak was available to a handful of US artists as early as 1965, few Brazilian artists were initially able to purchase the device due to the expense. Video art emerged in Brazil due to external stimulation from the US, in the form of an invitation to curator Walter Zanini for Brazilian artists to participate in an exhibition titled *Video Art* at the ICA-Philadelphia. In response, Anna Bella Geiger began making video artworks with her art students, including Sonia Andrade, using a borrowed Portapak camera from an acquaintance named Jom Tob Azulay. See Arlindo Machado (ed.), *Made in Brazil: Three Decades of Brazilian Video*, São Paulo: Itaú Cultural, 2007.

32 Kaizen, op. cit., p. 12.

33 Ibid., p. 21.

34 Calirman, 'Pop and Politics in Brazilian Art', op. cit., p. 120.

35 Shtromberg, op. cit., pp. 102–4.

36 Sonia Andrade, interview with the author, 27 July 2015, Rio de Janeiro.

37 Shtromberg, op. cit., p. 115.

38 Kaizen, op. cit., p. 17.

39 Shtromberg, op. cit., p. 115, n. 87; p. 188.

40 Christopher Dunn, *Brutality Garden: Tropicália and the Emergence of a Brazilian Counterculture*, Chapel Hill: The University of North Carolina Press, 2014, p. 106.

41 Osthoff, op. cit., p. 83.

42 Shtromberg, op. cit., p. 112.

43 Pape, 'My Work in Marginal Cinema', op. cit., p. 91.

44 Kaizen, op. cit., p. 17; Halter, op. cit., pp. 188, 190.

45 Colour television was first introduced in Brazil in 1972, although it was not widely available until 1978. Albert Abramson, *The History of Television, 1942–2000*, Jefferson: McFarland, 2008, pp. 37–76, 105–21; Michèle Mattelart and Armand Mattelart, *The Carnival of Images: Brazilian Television Fiction*, New York: Bergin & Garvey, 1990, p. 21.

46 Pape, 'My Work in Marginal Cinema', op. cit., p. 91.

47 Glória Ferreira, 'Irreverence and Marginality', in Iria Candela (ed.), *Lygia Pape: A Multitude of Forms*, New York: The Metropolitan Museum of Art/Yale University Press, 2017, p. 50; Lamoni, op. cit., p. 71.

48 'Mulher-Objeto: Da fome ao sexo, da gula a luxuria', *Ultima Hora* (São Paulo), 12 May 1976, n. p.

49 Cacilda M. Rêgo, 'Novelas, Novelinhas, Novelões: The Evolution of the (Tele)Novelas in Brazil', *Global Media Journal*, 2 (2003), http://www.globalmediajournal.com/open-access/novelas-novelinhas-noveles-the-evolution-of-thetelenovela-in-brazil.pdf.

50 Lygia Pape interviewed by Angélica de Moraes, in Candela (ed.), op. cit., p. 44; see also Calirman, *Dissident Practices*, op. cit., p. 53.

51 Pape, 'Explicação do Tema', in 'A Mulher na Iconografia de Massa', unpublished text, October 1977, Rio de Janeiro, Funarte Foundation Archives, pp. 8–9.

52 Halter, op. cit., p. 188.

53 Unsurprisingly, the *Eat Me* film and the Global Art Gallery exhibition were both eventually censored. Pape explains that the film was 'read as pornography by the censors' and banned from cinemas for three years. Pape, 'My Work in Marginal Cinema', op. cit., p. 91. For a more detailed account of this episode, see Gillian Sneed, 'Sex, Satire, and Censorship: Lygia Pape's *Eat Me: Gluttony or Lust*, 1975–1976', *Revista de História da Arte*, 15 (2020), pp. 65–85. This parallels the work of women artists in other non-Western countries during the 1970s, who similarly confronted sexualised interactions with consumer products and ran into censorship issues. One salient example is the performance and film series by Polish artist Natalia LL titled *Consumer Art* (1972–75), which parodied the conflation of sex and consumption as a 'forbidden' spectacle in Soviet-era Poland. See Alfred Weidinger, Nathalie Hoyos and Rainald Schumacher (eds.), *Natalia LL: The Mysterious World*, Vienna: Verlag für Moderne Kunst, 2022.

54 Kaizen, op. cit., p. 27.

12

'Manhandle the Merchandise': Michael Snow's *Breakfast (Table Top Dolly)* (1976)

Jon Davies

Italian filmmaker Elio Petri's *Un tranquillo posto di campagna* (*A Quiet Place in the Country*, 1968) draws explicit connections between the aesthetic, the financial, the libidinal and the metaphysical realms. In it, a tempestuous expressionist painter, Leonardo Ferri (Franco Nero) – his work in the film made by the American Pop artist Jim Dine – moves to a country villa in search of inspiration and tranquillity. However, he quickly becomes sexually obsessed with the spirit haunting the house: a beautiful young countess, Wanda, who was killed during the war and whom he discovers to have also been a raging nymphomaniac. Ferri suffers from hallucinations and nightmares throughout the film, and his own artistic output becomes a tormenting force in his psychodrama. *Un tranquillo posto* opens in the ultramodern Milan apartment that Ferri shares with Flavia (Vanessa Redgrave), his lover and agent. Wearing only a loincloth, the handsome artist is bound in heavy rope, seated in a chair on a kind of stage. He is silent as he watches Flavia enter the room listing all the latest 'pop', absurdly high-tech gadgets she has purchased: 'an underwater television for scuba diving, an electric toothbrush, a transistor refrigerator, an electric knife sharpener, an erotic electromagnet ... ' She teases him with a knife, bites him and finally plugs in all these shiny new appliances, which now surround the bound artist, tauntingly, their motors aggressively running. Ferri escapes from his constraints only to be stabbed by Flavia before waking up from the nightmare in a panic. This sequence sets the stage for the artist's reduced power in the face of a technocratic consumer society; it is choreographed like a performance art piece – for example, a Happening. However, it is Ferri's subconscious – in crafting the horrific dream – that is the powerful artist, while Ferri himself is depicted as subjugated and victimised by the consumer products and by the woman who purchased them: Flavia, who we soon learn is also in control of his artwork sales and finances.

Some of the critical reception of Pop Art in the United States in the early 1960s focused on the artists' perceived lack of agency in their work, cast in similarly gendered terms. Some, like James Rosenquist and Andy Warhol, had trained as commercial artists and replicated the looks or techniques of industrial processes that bore no trace of the artist's unique hand. Peter Selz's 1963 essay 'The Flaccid Art' in *Partisan Review* is one of the most explicit critiques: he dismisses Pop artists as having nothing to say, claiming that their works are merely limp transcriptions of reality, an unimaginative and passive acceptance of things as they are. This decadent torpor is in sharp contrast to the heroic existential wrestling and moral seriousness of the Abstract Expressionists. If the Ab Ex painter is a 'great man' and noble in spirit, the Pop artist just smiles at the TV and says, as Selz puts it: 'Great, man!' He explains, 'Now that the generation of the Fifties has come of age, it is not really surprising to see that some of its members have chosen to paint the world just as they are told to see it, on its own terms. Far from protesting the banal and chauvinistic manifestations of our popular culture, the Pop painters positively wallow in them. "Great, man!"' Real men transform the world, Pop artists are happy to merely mimic it. He continues, 'The striking abundance of food offered us by this art is suggestive. Pies, ice cream sodas, coke, hamburgers, roast beef, canned soups – often triple life size – would seem to cater to infantile personalities capable only of ingesting, not of digesting nor of interpreting.'[1] Pop art is easy, cowardly and conformist; it is 'effete' (and we know precisely what that means). These critiques cast masculine activity against feminine passivity, shaping against reflecting, and contestation against appreciation. Selz again: '[T]he blatant Americanism of the subject matter – packaged foods, flags, juke boxes, slot machines, Sunday comics, mammiferous nudes – may be seen as a willful regression.'[2] Pop's temporality is nostalgically backwards rather than progressive. Liking[3] America's booming consumer culture is seen as particularly egregious in that it seemed to embody all the country's spiritual ills: think of Bruce Conner juxtaposing news of John F. Kennedy's assassination with footage of a refrigerator door magically swinging open to reveal its bounty in his film *REPORT* (1966). A fully stocked fridge might provide nourishment, but it was far from the icon needed to lead us through the tumult and revolutions of the 1960s.

The objects that Pop artists such as Warhol and Tom Wesselmann depicted were often resolutely domestic: cans of Campbell's soup, bottles of 7-Up. It was typically women who purchased these items in the supermarket, put them away in the kitchen and then laboured to transform them into appealing meals for their families in the woman's realm of the home.

These products also became the sustenance of Pop artists.[4] As in a *vanitas*, the pathos of Pop lies in how the most seductive appearances cannot hide the reality of age, death and rot: the reality of the imminent obsolescence of these dazzling objects – and, by extension, ours as mortal human beings – is always front and centre.[5] Food products such as a quart of milk or an orange have particularly brief life-spans, but even the least perishable goods risk going out of style – and not only out of date – at a moment's notice. In Warhol's universe, the 'disaster' afflicts Mrs McCarthy and Mrs Brown more than the can of tuna (*Tunafish Disaster*, 1963), and every Superstar runs the risk of falling out of the cinematic spotlight once they cease to be sufficiently entertaining to maintain Warhol's interest.[6] His term 'leftovers'[7] for all those left on the cutting-room floor neatly encapsulates how American culture cherishes the fresh and new, only to pivot to disdain when the patina of novelty wears off. An ethos of queer camp like Warhol's, however, loves the pathos-laden 'leftover', whether commodity or person, and invests them with creative potential.

When considering the interface and potential relationships between Pop art and cinema, the first image that came to this author's mind was the exploding modernist house that provides the climax to Michelangelo Antonioni's nod to 1960s radicalism in *Zabriskie Point* (1970). Following the initial spectacular explosions of the hillside house, the strains of Pink Floyd arise as Antonioni lovingly revels in the destruction in slow-motion. We see a large rack of clothes, a TV set – with flowers on top – and a refrigerator full of food all blow up, each of these explosions followed by shots capturing the majestic flight of the destroyed goods through the air: for example, the refrigerator explosion unleashes fruit, a raw chicken, a box of Special K cereal, a loaf of Wonder Bread and other comestibles-turned-debris. The final set-piece destroys vast bookshelves – an embodiment of humanity's accumulated knowledge as transcribed onto the printed page – before the music cuts out and the quiet of the desert returns. It is an experience of the technological sublime, with immense visual pleasure mined from staging cinematic pyrotechnics within a blank landscape.

Curator Mark Francis includes Antonioni's film in the final, post-1968 'Helter Skelter' phase of Pop alongside the Rolling Stones in his Phaidon volume on the movement.[8] With Antonioni's climactic 'pop' as a catalyst, we can look back and find a shadow history of Pop that was arguably always present, but which became more and more prominent as the late 1960s curdled into the 1970s and beyond. This is a Pop inflected with practices of defilement, a Pop which occasionally shades into the Destruction in Art movement that coalesced around Gustav Metzger's writings from the late 1950s and the legendary Destruction in Art Symposium in London in 1966. Scholar Kristine Stiles writes of this movement: '[D]estruction in art introduced destructive processes into artistic vocabulary in order to collapse means, subject matter and affect into a unified expression for the purpose of commenting directly on destruction in life'.[9] Notably, as early as 1962, Warhol was painting torn – ruined – Campbell's soup cans (see, for example, *Small Torn Campbell's Soup Can [Pepper Pot]*, 1962) alongside the pristine consumer-ready versions that lined the walls in their first exhibition at the Ferus Gallery in Los Angeles that year. He seemed to understand that a destroyed object is even more libidinally and visually potent than an intact one; just think of the power of the crumpled vehicles and human bodies in his car crash or suicide 'Death and Disaster' paintings. Pop was arguably as much engaged in the desecration and deterioration of objects as it was in their sanctification and celebration.[10]

While Pop in the United States was largely the terrain of painters and sculptors, its confluence with practices of destruction is particularly well-suited to the cinema; a time-based medium allows for actions to be done to people or to things – and for those actions to be recorded for posterity – for an art of verbs rather than nouns. Thinking cinematically about 'pop' as a verb also allows us to reconsider consumer goods not as iconic, branded images, but as organic material with limited lifespans, what artist and theorist Hito Steyerl might call 'things like you and me'.[11] Used as artistic material that changes over time, these objects open themselves up to provide viewers haptic and visual pleasures and receive their libidinal investments. Scholar Mikhail Iampolski argues that cinema has a privileged relationship to destruction due to the medium's capacity to repeat: 'Film in a sense immortalizes the moment of destruction, transforming it into its own brand of monument. […] This eternally protracted moment of destruction resembles the sadistic Freudian compulsion to repeat, in which iconoclasm imperceptibly turns into a new fetishism'.[12] The *Zabriskie Point* house explosion, of course, repeats the scene a dozen times from multiple different angles, slowing it down in order to fetishise it and revel in the orgasmic release of years of pent-up and anxious political energies.

When considering the active verb 'to destroy' as it interfaces with Pop, we must be cautious not to replicate critics' valuation of masculine activity and transformation, and their concomitant dismissal of feminine passivity and 'liking' of the given. To help us navigate these dynamics, I will focus on a decidedly 'minor' film by the late Canadian artist-filmmaker Michael Snow, *Breakfast (Table Top Dolly)* (1976), which intersects with a number of his other works in being animated by explicitly sexual energies, processes, structures and ways of looking. Because the libidinal is so tangibly present in Snow's oeuvre, it provides ways of working through how creation and destruction, activity and passivity in Pop are shaped by gender, desire and power. Snow's *Breakfast* is not usually seen as a (late) work in the lineage of Pop or of Destruction but rather as a footnote within his lauded structural film practice.[13] Here, in the showdown between a modified 16mm camera and a breakfast table, Snow compresses a potent forcefield of ideas.

***

> 'The destructive character knows only one watchword: make room. And only one activity: clearing away. […] For destroying rejuvenates, because it clears away the traces of our own age; it cheers, because everything cleared away means to the destroyer a complete reduction, indeed a rooting out, of his own condition'. – Walter Benjamin[14]

Breakfast (Table Top Dolly) is one of Snow's least critically discussed films; it was shot in 1972 and then put aside until he finished it in 1976. Scholar Regina Cornwell sees it as introducing a new camera movement into Snow's venerable cinematic corpus. She writes: 'It is a kind of comedy without characters, where objects are taken over by the camera's actions […] slowly mov[ing] into space'.[15] This is not an optical zoom as in his canonical *Wavelength* (1967), however, which does not require the camera to physically move into the scene that it is turned on – which means that *Wavelength* is more about the structural limits of the lens rather than those of the camera as a whole machine – but instead a tracking shot where the camera forcefully imposes itself onto the scene in front of it. Here, the camera does not just look but rather touches. As it moves closer and closer towards the breakfast table, it soon becomes apparent that it is actively transforming the set and props, as a piece of Plexiglas in front of the camera gradually presses the table setting and food against a wall (Figures 12.1–3). Cornwell concludes that *Breakfast* 'comes as a break from the seriousness and growing academicism of certain film directions from the mid-sixties onward which emphasized self-questioning, exploring or examining, among other things, the fixed and moved camera. […] On one level […] *Breakfast* literally drives the problem into the wall', declaring it over.[16] Snow would return to the problem of the camera after Cornwell was writing, however, in his much-debated *Presents* (1981), as we will see below.

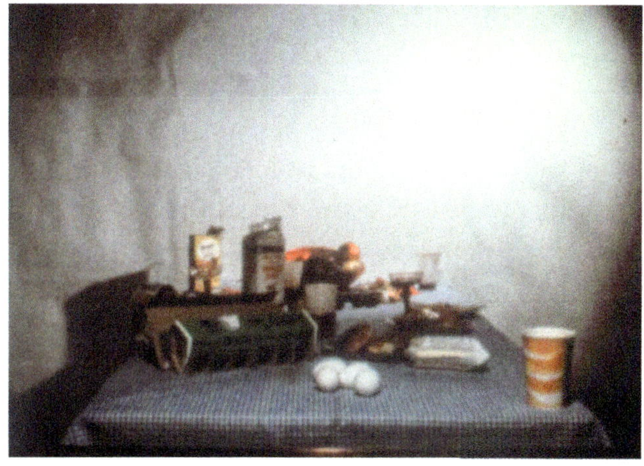

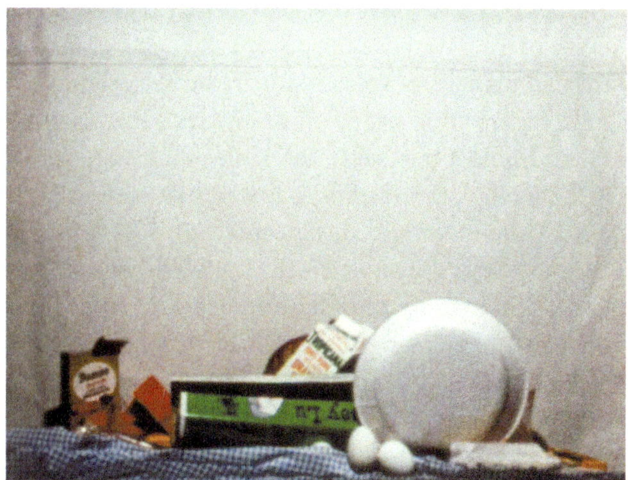

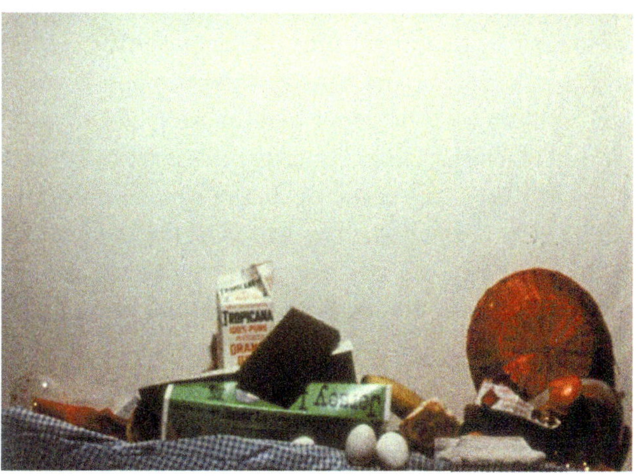

Figures 12.1–3 *Breakfast (Table Top Dolly)* (Michael Snow, 1976), stills from a 16mm film, 15 minutes, colour, sound. Source: Courtesy of Michael Snow.

The breakfast scene is crudely set up, somewhat lurking in the shadows; it lacks the bright lighting and careful styling of advertising photography. The objects are not seductive; they are simply there. Despite the paper backdrop that resembles the one used in photographer Thomas' studio in Antonioni's film *Blow-Up* (1966), the setup suggests a child's science experiment or a low-budget screen test rather than a work of film art. The composition includes eggs and an egg carton, a number of plastic cups and goblets, a Tropicana orange juice carton, a wicker basket of fruit, sticks of butter and a box of sugar. A milk carton and some buns become recognizable as the camera makes its slow progress forward. It takes some time to realise that this is happening: the scene before us seems to *twitch*, and it is unclear as to what physical forces the goods are being subjected. The blue-and-white gingham tablecloth starts to move like an ocean tide, and we realise that the perspective is fluctuating because the objects are being shifted, jostling into each other. The first casualty is a plastic cup in the foreground, which falls off the table; a milk carton soon drops off on the left. The orange juice carton topples over, and liquid pours over the table: things are certainly getting messy now. A paper plate starts bending upwards like a semaphore or a rising sun. Entropy has taken over, and unexpected surprises result. The camera's motion and the motion of the objects – the latter interrupted by moments of stasis – create a heightened sense of tension. Now the eggs are in a vise-like grip and under threat of breaking; they crack but do not burst. More objects fall off the table or lurch back and forth as they buckle under the pressure; the orange juice carton seems to slowly wave at us. At this point, it looks like an assemblage with a banana from the fruit bowl now prominent – widening as it is squished by the Plexi – joined by two eggs is creating a joke phallus. We are next mooned by two puffy buns pressed against the Plexi. The composition stays the same, but the objects now trapped between the Plexi wielded by the camera and the paper behind are bloating desperately. The tension is relieved when the camera quickly pulls back and the stressed composition falls apart. The titles come up as the camera climaxes by moving quickly back and forth through the space in a last penetrative hurrah, almost like a weightlifter shaking their muscles out after a heavy lift.

Snow transforms a three-dimensional, sculptural breakfast setting into a messy two-dimensional collage, or if one imagines the eggs (a nod to egg tempera?), juice and milk as pigments, perhaps a painting. Critic Jonathan Rosenbaum calls it a 'hoot' (although Snow himself does not find the film particularly funny) 'about the conversion of a painterly still life of groceries into gooey garbage by an advancing camera.'[17] Filmmaker Mike Hoolboom notes that *Breakfast* literalises a 'flattened' perspective, referencing the history of representational painting as a process of transforming three dimensions into two.[18] Snow has suggested that painting genres are useful for thinking about his films:[19] if *La Région Centrale* (1971) is the ultimate landscape, *Breakfast* is an attack on the still life. While a classic Dutch still life painting, for example, reminds viewers of their own mortality through depicting impossibly succulent fruit, fish and fowl that will be fresh for only a fraction of the time that the painting will exist in the world, Snow here accelerates the life-spans of these goods – making use of Pop's sped-up sense of chronology, ever attuned to the ephemerality of attention and the rapid turnover of trends – to hasten their demise through the vise-like movement of the camera with its Plexi press attached. If we focus on one element such as the Tropicana orange juice carton, we begin with an iconic image familiar from a TV advertisement, a brand that connotes health, vitality and starting the day out right, only for it to be revealed for the base matter that it really is – simply the juice derived from squeezing oranges flooding onto the table and floor – before becoming an image again, up against the wall. Instead of assisting in constructing a deceptive commercial image, Snow's camera becomes a tool for defamiliarisation and destruction by exposing the foodstuffs' material innards. The consumer goods here stop being products (exchange value) and become matter (use value) through being poked, prodded and squeezed by the physical force of the camera apparatus. Rosenbaum notes how in both *Breakfast* and *Presents*, a key scene of which *Breakfast* foreshadows and sketches,[20] 'by using things, you use them up at the same time'. Snow responds, 'It flattens it on the screen [...] you *do* feel that things are resistant – they break and squeeze and squash'.[21] Warhol has employed a similar vocabulary of 'using up':

Warhol: Well, it has to be something like the idea that, uh, uh… that all Pop artists aren't homosexual. And it really doesn't… you know… And everybody should be a machine, and everybody should be, uh, like…

Swenson: I don't understand the business about – if all Pop artists are not homosexual, then what does this have to do with being a machine?

Warhol: Well, I think everybody should like everybody.

Swenson: You mean you should like both men and women?

Warhol: Yeah.

Swenson: Yeah? Sexually and in every other way?

Warhol: Yeah.

Swenson: And that's what Pop Art's about?

Warhol: Yeah, it's liking things.

Swenson: And liking things is being like a machine?

Warhol: Yeah. Well, because you do the same thing every time. You do the same thing over and over again. And you do the same…

Swenson: You mean sex?
Warhol: Yeah, and everything you do.
John: Without any discrimination?
Warhol: Yeah. And you use things up, like, you use people up.
Swenson: And you approve of it?
Warhol: Yes. [*laughing*] Because it's all a fantasy ...[22]

Warhol aspired for everyone to be a machine because Pop is about liking things, and machines like everything; machines are bisexual (or rather pansexual) in liking everything, which means that every artist who uses a camera should be similarly open-minded. The camera eye is democratic, it 'likes' everything that is put in front of it. Snow's modified camera here does not have a preference for milk over juice or eggs over bread, it applies the same 'like', the same physical force to everything in front of it – it is 'flattening' on multiple levels. Liking things is using them up – eating food is the best example – and we repeat this every single day; when a camera does it, by contrast, it generates a great deal of visual rather than gastronomic pleasure.

We hardly need Warhol to bring matters sexual into Snow's oeuvre: libidinal forces are never far away in his work, and often tangible directly on the surface of his moving and still images and objects. Snow's interest in sex is the source for the structural shape of certain of his films; however, as he cautions, sex is not the only way of thinking about them. He has claimed that his films have 'a kind of sexual form – because they're orgasmic in a way. I think they're very sexy films myself'.[23] In an interview with scholar Scott MacDonald, he explains that 'the shape is climactic. *Wavelength* literally "cums" at the end: the last thing you see is liquid [...] the whole thing is sexual'.[24] (*Breakfast*, by contrast, hardly results in orgasm; it is rather more of a protracted edging.) He understands that the camera's gaze undertakes acts of penetration.

The pressing process that generates *Breakfast* can be seen as akin to print-making, a practice that Snow once explicitly compared to the act of fucking. In *Projection*, a 1970 lithograph produced at the Nova Scotia College of Art and Design, Snow depicts a man grasping his erection against one of his iconic Walking Woman forms. The text at the bottom of the print is highly revealing, drawing a direct parallel between print as a medium and 'projection' as a cinematic and psychoanalytic process. Indeed, it seems to anticipate 1970s feminist film theory:

TITLE. EXCUSE. EXPLANATION. ENDORSEMENT. RATIONALIZATION. EQUIVALENT. ANALYSIS. DEFENSE. EXTENSION. COMMENTARY

(SUB-TITLE) – – – – <u>PROJECTION</u>. OF A FRAME FROM A 1964 FILM TO A 1970 LITHOGRAPHIC PRINT. PRESENT FUCKS PAST. WHITE INKS BLACK PAPER. (LIGHT FUCKS DARKNESS. WET FUCKS DRY. SOFT FUCKS HARD.) MALE CHAUVINIST PRINT. THE ___KING WOMAN MEATS HER MAKER. A SYMBOL-MINDED EXAMPLE. CUNTLESS PRICK. PRINTS = FAKE FUCK. ENLARGEMENT ART. HARD-ON/CUT-OUT. D+ [?] PRESENCE MAKES ABSENCE. TOKEN POKIN'. FLAT FUCK. ART OF LOVE. MUSEPOSED PRINTERCOURSE. 16 MM. 8″. 5′. 18″ × 13½″. 24 × 20″-LAY.

In *Breakfast*, the camera is trying to eat breakfast, but it does not have a mouth, nor a digestive system or anus, so it fucks what is in front of it instead. Snow's formidable libido almost parodies those critiques of Pop art as passive rather than active.[25] While it would be easy to see this scene as a meal set for a nuclear family – the food likely purchased and prepared by a woman – only to be destroyed by a phallic male gaze, I wonder what other meanings we can glean from it. *Le petit-déjeuner, c'est nous?* The buns are a leading player here, plainly evoking buttocks, a body part that transcends gender without evading eroticisation. What if instead of fucking what is in front of it, the camera sucks instead? In an interview with Rosenbaum, Snow claims: 'I used to think sometimes of the camera as being something that sucked as opposed to shot'.[26] Here we have the polymorphous perversity that Warhol outlined, but put in more concretely carnal terms: the camera does not just 'like' whatever is put in front of it, but also derives pleasure in fucking and sucking, both penetrating and receiving, being 'active' and 'passive'. As a kind of rejoinder to *Breakfast*, I like to imagine Snow's lustful camera meeting its match in the kitchen implements aggressively wielded by feminist artist Martha Rosler in her contemporary video work *Semiotics of the Kitchen* (1975). As Rosler stabs the air with a fork and hammers the countertop with a tenderiser, we can find not only an attack on women's confinement to the domestic sphere, but perhaps a wild new erotics being enacted as well. If the camera can fuck and suck, surely a blender or meat grinder can, too?

With these dynamics in mind, *Breakfast* unexpectedly links into debates over the objectification of women in Snow's work that developed over the course of the 1970s. Looking only at Snow's filmography, it could initially be written off as a mere test run for the most striking sequence in the feature-length *Presents*. However, broadening our examination to include his work in sculpture and in photography from the early to mid-1970s, we find many parallels to *Breakfast*, including some of the works criticised for their objectifying depiction of women. If we foreground the gendered implications of destroying a bountiful breakfast table, then *Breakfast* can even be seen as a hinge between still-life works such as the slideshows *Sink* (1970) and *A Casing Shelved* (1970), which focus on the masculine space of the studio and the physical labour of the male artist,[27] and formally similar works that use women's bodies to investigate questions of flatness, depth and perception. One example that resonates with the Plexi press in *Breakfast* is *Crouch Leap Land* (1970), in which viewers must squat down in order to see three serial photographs of a nude woman shot from below (through a Plexi floor) – thus putting you in the photographer's POV – as she performs, Muybridge-style, the titular actions.[28]

The soundtrack of *Breakfast* consists largely of crashing and banging noises and occasionally low men's voices on an unintelligible radio.[29] Legible language only exists in the title card – which announces our two clashing forces: BREAKFAST and (TABLE-TOP DOLLY)[30] – and in the product packaging on screen. The focus on words in the visible brand names such as Dairylea milk, Tropicana 100% Pure Pasteurized Orange Juice, Domino Dots sugar and Jersey Lu eggs connect the film back to Snow's friend Hollis Frampton's practice of collecting words found in the environment, which ended up as an archive for his masterpiece, the hour-long film *Zorns Lemma* (1970). The visualisation of language in the brand names also links the film to the major cinematic project that was occupying Snow at that time. In 1972, Snow was in the middle of his three years of work on his four-and-a-half-hour opus *Rameau's Nephew by Diderot (Thanx to Dennis Young) by Wilma Schoen* (1972–74), an encyclopaedic mosaic of performed scenes demonstrating various sound and image dynamics. The film has many Pop moments, from its celebration of an Italian tin of mints with the brand name 'MENTAL' to the 'Laughing Chair' sequence, which introduces maniacal laughter on the soundtrack and identifies the source as a yellow chair with a microphone pointed towards it. There is also a magi-cally roving 'Voice' that seems to come from a coffee cup before moving to speak as a light fixture, a pen and finally a piece of cheese. Rather than fol-lowing a predetermined concept or gestalt as in films such as Snow's break-through *Wavelength*, *Rameau's Nephew* uses actors, a script, sets and props for a series of skits playing in different ways with the relationship between language and meaning. Rosenbaum notes that the destruction of a table in the 'Hotel' sequence anticipates the acts of destruction to come in future Snow films.[31] The smashing of the green table occurs in order to prove that the table actually exists; what this means, in the world of *Rameau's Nephew*, is demonstrating that 'table' has a material depth and is not just a word or idea. Destruction proves that what was destroyed was tangibly real. The fact that it is a sculptor, Royden Rabinowitch, who destroys the table, was likely not lost on Snow; this is the vocation that would be most concerned about the status of physical matter, and perhaps about cinema's capacity for dematerialised illusion, turning three-dimensional objects into two-dimensional images.

So can *Breakfast* also be seen as Snow's attempt to make coffee cups speak, to find out what inanimate objects like them might say?[32] Like a confession extracted under pressure, Snow squeezes meaning from the commodities laid out in front of him, a last gasp before they 'pop'. The way in which they respond to the stress is out of his control, a chance operation dependent on physics. The camera shapes reality, disrupts decorum, destroys things. The camera turns food into art, three dimensions into two, signs into stuff. Critic Aldo Pellegrini wrote in 1961: 'Objects break down or are destroyed according to the internal laws of the materials that compose them: their destruction reveals the secret of their fundamental structure. [...] When an object is destroyed its material virtuality [essence] is released. That is why every act of destruction means an attack on decency, in so far as it presents us with the complete nakedness of the matter'.[33] Notorious Vienna Aktionist Otto Muehl wrote in the 1966 text 'Supermarket':

> walk through the supermarket and manhandle
> the merchandise. direct service. don't place
> a plane before reality and
> paint on it: walk right through it and
> dismember things.
> [...]
> establish a furniture factory for the serial production
> of home furnishing, reliefs,
> sculptures made of plastic and everything is inflatable;
> or even better, begin with the
> killings immediately.
> make plans not to build cities,
> but to blow them up and to level the mountains.
> everything is merchandise that is looked at as such.
> everything is real that is looked at as reality.
> everything is art that is looked at as art.
> everything is a fit for everything else, everything can be substituted
> and mixed.
> no more style; instead, the art of cooking.
> after all, everyone wants to find some grub.[34]

With its slow, creeping camera movement, Snow's methodically-driven destruction may seem miles away from that of artists like Muehl – whose performances enacted ritualistic violence and sexual transgression – or the Puerto Rican Rafael Montañez Ortiz, another key figure in 1960s Destruction in Art. Montañez Ortiz viciously attacked pieces of furniture such as armchairs until they were mere craters of textile, stuffing, wood and springs; mutilated pianos and chickens in concerts; and turned the violence on himself in his notorious 1966 *Self-Destruction*.[35] Snow instead tasks the modified camera with enacting the destruction rather than using the expressive physical force of his own performing body; *Breakfast* is machine-like, logical and controlled – politely Canadian – rather than unleashing the wild *id*. However, if we turn to *Presents*, we see how entropy, the irrational, the libidinal and, perhaps, the demonic, can ensnare even Snow.

In a second interview with Rosenbaum, about the much-maligned *Presents*, Snow claims:

> Fundamentally, it's about creation and destruction. There has to be something that has to be chopped off, something that has to be smashed or flattened. How do you make these films? Where does that come from? It has to be gouged out of the ground. There's a lot of violence involved. Some of these things are not explicitly stated, but they're kind of bubbling in *Presents*.[36]

Meanwhile, scholar Bart Testa writes that on a certain level *Presents* is 'a low-comic joke on the notion of penetrating filmic space'.[37] The film is divided into three parts, and each has received its share of critical attention. Testa calls it Snow's most 'critically abused' film,[38] although this is perhaps not surprising, as Snow explicitly sought to enter debates around the male gaze with a provocation. The feminist critiques, led by Teresa De Lauretis, focused largely on the opening sequence, featuring the image of a nude woman reclining in bed, which is stretched and squashed by analogue video technology.[39] The next section garnered plaudits for its daring: we are presented with a domestic interior and slowly realise that what seems like camera movement is actually the opposite: the set has been constructed to be moved – and it breaks apart in the process – by heavy machinery (specifically, forklifts) while the camera remains in a stationary position. This middle section culminates in a six-minute scene where the camera not only moves but physically imposes itself into and rams through the set, menacing the actors and destroying the furniture in a far more chaotic scene of destruction than in *Breakfast*. Snow recalls:

> [D]estroying a set is a creative act in a sense, because flattening is a two-dimensionalizing, and so on. But it's the reverse of making the set, which involved even more violence, because most of that stuff is

wood, it had to come from somewhere [that is, from trees], and it was all hacked and hammered and sawed. I mean, which end is which? It has a lot to do with power. And that gets involved with the fact that there's a machinery for looking – the film itself [...] The part where the set moves is literally a role (and 'roll') reversal on the relationship of the camera to the subject.[40]

While this sequence germinated in the camera movement in *Breakfast*, what is fascinating here is that it is not only the camera that attacks the set but Snow himself, manning it from a motorised wheelchair. His description of the anarchic scene has a sexual charge to it:

I drove the dolly in that section, and I had a whole course in mind – where I was going to go, what speed, and so on. But I couldn't really rehearse it, because I'd smash everything […] And the first thing that happened was, the top of the table came off – which is fabulous. I think it's really beautiful. But it scared the shit out of me, and I didn't know what to do after that. I had to keep on plowing.[41]

I am amused by this vision of the structural filmmaker as a runaway vehicle, or more precisely by the image of a lusty male artist whose first impulse when plan A fails is to just 'keep on plowing'. The word 'plowing' is appropriately polyvalent: in Canada we 'plow' snow (Snow), but farmers 'plow' the fields that produce food for the breakfast table; it also, of course, is a euphemism for fucking. Snow told MacDonald, meanwhile: 'The film is involved with [...] the unfortunate truth that in order to make something, you have to destroy something else, or at least change its form. And that crisscrosses with the sexual themes in some ways, but again, it doesn't attribute any one way of making to one gender or the other'.[42] In my hazy memory, the destruction of the *Presents* set was ecstatic, Dionysian. Perhaps this was due to the influence of critics and scholars who refer to the camera as 'an avenging movie monster' invading the space 'in an orgy of slapstick destruction'.[43] Rewatching it now, I am struck by how pathetic it is. There is no mastery here. The camera/chair moves very awkwardly, squeaking and creaking – not so much 'plowing' as stumbling to and fro. A moment where it seems that Snow might accelerate into the woman's rear is chastely redirected towards a table instead. The pieces of furniture reveal themselves as replicas – they were made to collapse more easily, even though it takes multiple strikes to do so.[44] The most satisfying 'pop' is when the 16mm film camera attacks the TV set, cinema's great rival. (The sequence ends when the camera escapes through a wall.)[45]

Critics' suggestions that the objects in *Breakfast* and *Presents* are as or even more animated than human characters provide another salient connection between these Snow films and Pop. Cornwell's view of *Breakfast* as a 'comedy without characters' is echoed in Stuart Liebman's article on *Presents*, where he suggests that 'the bumbling, awkward performers are so shaken [by the moving set] that they have no "stage presence" while the conspicuously artificial props become emphatic presences in the pictures as they swing and crash wildly'.[46] If Snow's films are primarily discussed through the lenses of formalism or sexual politics, a turn to metaphysics may initially appear surprising; that said, it is striking how often the figure of the ghost popped up in my research. Speaking with Rosenbaum, Snow reminds us that 'there *is* something to do with death in the taking of photographs. The images live on another level now, but they really are, in the other terms, ghosts'.[47] Describing his *A Casing Shelved*, a single 35mm slide of a full shelving unit that is projected along with an audiotape of Snow describing its contents and what we see, he diagnoses the sense of disassociation that the work generates by confessing: 'It's like there's a ghost of me in front of the image of the shelves looking at them'.[48] Liebman's analysis of *Presents* turns on the 'ghost in the machine' that is Snow himself, operating the 'plowing' camera, reflected as a spectre in the Plexi. The Plexi takes up the full screen, a 'surrogate lens'[49] picking up reflections of the set and glare, not just of Snow (the Plexi's relationship to the camera lens is arguably like that of a shadow to a body). For Liebman, the destruction in *Presents* – and by extension *Breakfast* – is exerted by an 'invisible force', even if we might glimpse the mechanics of it in the Plexi. When Liebman catches sight of it, the ghost metaphors fly: 'The camera swings left toward a blue chair and a spectral image appears superimposed over the scene. The apparition lasts for only a few seconds, but it is legible: the head and shoulders of a man, wrapped as if he was a mummy. His eyes peer intently'. He continues: 'It is as if the camera was suddenly possessed by a mad analytic impulse which led it to destroy the integrity and coherence of the scene in order to find a hidden essence. Or, alternatively, it is as if a crazed will to form was guiding the camera's frenzied effort to impose some new meaning on the objects of the scene'. He suggests that Snow's image here is not an intentional declaration of authorship or self-reflexive gesture but that, judging from Snow's comments, he 'lost his "presence of mind" […] "Snow" is projected onto the space of the film as, literally and metaphorically, a ghost in a machine […] The filmmaker is not the source of his text's meaning; like the image and the story, he is an effect'.[50]

I would like to close by rewinding back to the late 1960s and to another striking nightmare sequence from Petri's *Un tranquillo posto di campagna*.

Facing a creative block, the painter, Ferri, can no longer work in the city and demands a change of scenery; an inexplicable force draws him to a dusty old villa near Venice. His first night in the country house, Ferri has a vivid nightmare of the villa coming to life; the camera careens through the estate before we see the large studio space that he recently set up go about destroying itself. We watch a table full of bottles of paint first tremble before tipping over and being up-ended by an invisible force, crashing to the floor with buckets of pigment sloshing left and right. His worktables, chairs and large painting stretchers fall onto the floor – again, seemingly of their own volition – and smash into shards. When Ferri, utterly panicked, wakes up from his nightmare, he opens the door to find his studio completely destroyed, just as he had dreamt. He is unable to accept that, despite his delusions of grandeur, he is simply a producer of commodities within a market. Critic Pasquale Iannone points out that Ferri's self-image as an artist is antiquatedly romantic; he claims that the countess' 'ghostly presence comes to represent a vital eroticism that the painter wants to somehow recapture – a task that Petri sees as doomed to failure in a consumerist society'.[51] Here a powerful poltergeist swoops in to usurp the artist's hand – taking over the artist's creative-destructive role – the spectre violently wielding the paints for its own unknowable supernatural purposes. The artist can only stand by and survey the destruction.

Notes

1   Peter Selz, 'The Flaccid Art' (1963), in Steve Henry Madoff (ed.), *Pop Art: A Critical History*, Berkeley: University of California Press, 1997, p. 86. See also the opinions of many of the participants, including Selz, Hilton Kramer and Leo Steinberg in 'A Symposium on Pop Art' (*Arts* magazine, 1963), reprinted in Madoff, pp. 65–81.

2   Selz, op. cit., p. 86.

3   See Jonathan Flatley, *Like Andy Warhol*, Chicago: The University of Chicago Press, 2017, which brilliantly analyses 'liking' and 'likeness' as key to Warhol's expansive mode of affective engagement with the world and its things.

4   See Cécile Whiting, *A Taste for Pop: Pop Art, Gender, and Consumer Culture*, Cambridge: Cambridge University Press, 1997.

5   See Sara Doris, 'Pop Art, Obsolescence, and Camp', in Doris, *Pop Art and the Contest over American Culture*, Cambridge: Cambridge University Press, 2007.

6   For more on the *Tunafish Disaster* series, see Thomas Crow, 'Saturday Disasters: Trace and Reference in Early Warhol', *Art in America*, 75:5 (1987), pp. 128–36.

7   See 'Why I Love Leftovers', in Andy Warhol, *The Philosophy of Andy Warhol (From A to B and Back Again)*, London: Harcourt Brace Jovanovich, 1975, pp. 93–94.

8   Mark Francis (ed.), *Pop*, London: Phaidon, 2005, pp. 186–87.

9 Kristine Stiles, 'The Story of the Destruction in Art Symposium and the "DIAS Affect"' (2005), in Sven Spieker (ed.), *Destruction*, London: Whitechapel Gallery; Cambridge, MA: The MIT Press, 2017, p. 105.

10 Looking back to Robert Rauschenberg's 'Combines', each collaged element was wrested from its original source through an act of destruction – a comic strip cut from a newspaper, for example – before being reconstituted in a new constellation. Claes Oldenburg's soft sculptures provide another example of deterioration or, more accurately, *collapse* as an approach to consumer goods, as if they have undergone a form of hollowing out or putrefaction.

11 Hito Steyerl, 'A Thing Like You and Me', *e-flux journal*, 15 (2010), https://www.e-flux.com/journal/15/61298/a-thing-like-you-and-me/.

12 Mikhail Iampolski, 'In the Shadows of Monuments: Notes on Iconoclasm and Time' (1995), in Spieker (ed.), *Destruction*, op. cit., p. 179.

13 On the relationship – or lack of it – of Snow's wider body of work to Pop, see James King, *Michael Snow: Lives and Works*, Toronto: Dundurn, 2019, pp. 115–26. While his Walking Woman works of the 1960s were received in the context of Pop, Snow and several commentators have suggested that he was more interested in disseminating his own figure into the visual landscape than drawing on popular culture for his work.

14 Walter Benjamin, 'The Destructive Character' (1931), in Spieker (ed.), *Destruction*, op. cit., p. 33.

15 Regina Cornwell, *The Films and Photographs of Michael Snow*, Toronto: Peter Martin Associates, 1980, p. 86.

16 Ibid, pp. 86–87.

17 Jonathan Rosenbaum, 'The "Presents" of Michael Snow', *Film Comment*, 17:3 (1981), p. 35.

18 Mike Hoolboom, 'Michael Snow's *Seated Figures*', *Millennium Film Journal*, 22 (1989–90), p. 32.

19 Michael Snow, 'The Camera and the Spectator: Michael Snow in Discussion with John Du Cane', *The Collected Writings of Michael Snow*, Waterloo, ON: Wilfrid Laurier University Press, 1994, p. 88: 'I guess the fastest way to get to talking about it is still to divide things into landscapes, still life, portraits, figure compositions, things like that'.

20 *Breakfast* also anticipates *Egg* (1985), a hologram of Snow breaking an egg that hovers over a real frying pan. See King, op. cit., pp. 211–12.

21 Rosenbaum, 'Presents', op. cit., p. 37. This vocabulary of squeezing and squashing echoes that of classical animation, which was seen as investing bodies and objects with an uncanny malleability. Snow uses force to animate the objects before him.

22 Jennifer Sichel (ed.), '"What is Pop Art?" A Revised Transcript of Gene Swenson's 1963 Interview with Andy Warhol', *Oxford Art Journal*, 41:1 (2018), p. 88. Sichel notes that 'John' is either Warhol's boyfriend John Giorno or John Wieners, both poets.

23 Snow, 'The Camera and the Spectator', op. cit., p. 89.

24 Scott MacDonald, 'Michael Snow', in MacDonald, *A Critical Cinema 2: Interviews with Independent Filmmakers*, Berkeley: University of California Press, 1992, p. 64. King, op. cit., writes that one possible interpretation of *Wavelength* is that 'the film re-enacts sexual intercourse in that the slowly moving zoom represents the phallus heading into a tight small space that denotes the vagina' (p. 132).

25 Snow once told an interviewer: 'I've been extremely active sexually. I've been involved in a lot of happiness and pleasure that way, but I've also caused a lot of trouble. […] I was extremely horny, and if I was attracted to someone I would simply try to go to bed with them' (quoted in King, op. cit., pp. 147–48).

26 Rosenbaum, 'Presents', op. cit., p. 38.

27 Always attuned to word play, can we see the 'Synch Sound' sequence in *Rameau's Nephew* and the 35mm slideshow depicting the vicissitudes of his studio sink in *Sink* as Snow foreshadowing the labour required to clean up the mess he and his camera will make in *Breakfast*? Cleaning up the destroyed breakfast table here can be seen as both domestic work and as akin to the cleanup that follows a painting session, each gendered differently. For more on *Sink*, see King, op. cit., pp. 163–65.

28 Cornwell, op. cit., writes that this triptych 'anticipates a later film work, *Two Sides to Every Story* (1974), in which the viewing situation is isomorphic with its making. It is as if in some way, in illusion, the woman were pressing on the camera through the plexiglass, impressing her image on it. As voyeurism always has more to do with the subject than the object, this work reflects back on the viewers, their responses…' (p. 40).

29 Cornwell claims the film's sound is of 'dishwashing' and the radio (op. cit., p. 86); the louder noises that I heard could have been effects of the print or projection. It is available on 16mm from the Canadian Filmmakers Distribution Centre.

30 The name 'dolly' for the mechanism that smoothly allows a camera to track also feminises the apparatus.

31 Rosenbaum, 'Presents', op. cit., p. 37.

32 Perhaps it was in homage to *Breakfast* that Snow began referring to his musical ensemble CCMC not as the Canadian Creative Music Collective but instead as Crushed Cookies Make Crumbs.

33 Aldo Pellegrini, 'Foundation for an Aesthetic of Destruction' (1961), in Spieker (ed.), *Destruction*, op. cit., p. 72.

34 Otto Muehl, 'Supermarket' (1966), in Spieker (ed.), *Destruction*, op. cit., pp. 100–1.

35 See *Rafael Montañez Ortiz: Years of the Warrior 1960, Years of the Psyche 1988*, New York: El Museo del Barrio and Exit Art, 1988. Some of Muehl's Aktionist performances can be seen in the films of Kurt Kren.

36 Jonathan Rosenbaum, 'Snowbound: A Dialogue with a Dialogue', *Afterimage*, 11 (Winter 1982–83), https://jonathanrosenbaum.net/2020/01/snowbound-a-dialogue-with-a-dialogue/.

37 Bart Testa, 'An Axiomatic Cinema: Michael's [sic] Snow's Films', in Jim Shedden (ed.), *Presence and Absence: The Films of Michael Snow, 1956–1991*, Toronto: Art Gallery of Ontario and Alfred A. Knopf Canada, 1995, p. 57.

38 Ibid, p. 47.

39 See Teresa De Lauretis, 'Snow on the Oedipal Stage', *Screen*, 22:3 (1981), pp. 25–40.

40 Rosenbaum 'Snowbound', op. cit.

41 Rosenbaum, 'Presents', op. cit., p. 37.

42 MacDonald, 'Michael Snow', op. cit., p. 73.

43 Rosenbaum, 'Presents', op. cit., p. 36.

44 Artist Robin Collyer recalls building the moving set as well as constructing the 'crushable furniture'; he very generously provided me with behind-the-scenes photographs.

45 The camera escapes into the street, transitioning us to the third and longest part of the film: a panoply of about 2,000 brief shots recorded by Snow with a hand-held camera, of a vast range of subjects, with each fleeting shot paired with a beat on a snare drum.

46 Stuart Liebman, 'The Presents of Michael Snow', *Millennium Film Journal*, 12 (1982–83), p. 103.

47 Rosenbaum, 'Presents', op. cit., p. 38.

48 Snow, 'The Camera and the Spectator', op. cit., p. 91.

49 Rosenbaum, 'Presents', op. cit., p. 36.

50 Liebman, 'The Presents of Michael Snow', op. cit., pp. 104–5.

51 Pasquale Iannone, '*Un tranquillo posto di campagna/A Quiet Place in the Country*', *Senses of Cinema*, 67 (2013), https://www.sensesofcinema.com/2013/uncategorized/un-tranquillo-posto-di-campagnaa-quiet-day-in-the-country/.

Appendix: A Pop Cinema Filmography

This filmography has been divided into broad categories covering non-fiction films, documentaries about Pop artists, narrative fiction films and non-narrative experimental works. The list is by no means exhaustive and could have been formulated in alternative ways (by decade, country and so on). It should be approached as a preliminary mapping promoting exploration by researchers, and also as an outline sketch requiring further shading and colour.

Non-Fiction Films

- *O Dreamland* (Lindsay Anderson, UK, 1953)
- *Jazz of Lights* (Ian Hugo, USA, 1955)
- *Mama Don't Allow* (Karel Reisz and Tony Richardson, UK, 1956)
- *Nice Time* (Alain Tanner and Claude Goretta, UK, 1957)
- *La Chant de la Styrene* (*The Song of Styrene*, Alain Resnais, France, 1958)
- *Broadway by Light* (William Klein, USA/France, 1958)
- *Where Did Our Love Go?* (Warren Sonbert, USA, 1966)
- *--- ------* (aka *The Rock and Roll Film*) (Thom Andersen and Malcolm Brodwick, USA, 1966–67)
- *Tonite Let's All Make Love in London* (Peter Whitehead, UK, 1967)
- *La dialectique peut-elle casser des briques?* (*Can Dialectics Break Bricks?*, René Viénet, France, 1973)
- *La Société du Spectacle* (*The Society of the Spectacle*, Guy Debord, France, 1974)
- *Get Out of the Car* (Thom Andersen, USA, 2010)

Non-Fiction Films about Pop Artists

- *Pop Goes the Easel* (Ken Russell, UK, 1962)
- *Andy Warhol* (Marie Menken, USA, 1965)
- *Andy Warhol's Silver Flotations* (Willard Maas, USA, 1966)
- *Superartist* (Juan Drago and Bruce Talbot, USA, 1967)
- *Love's Presentation* (James Scott, UK, 1967)
- *Richard Hamilton* (James Scott and Richard Hamilton, UK, 1969)
- *The Great Ice Cream Robbery: Claes Oldenburg* (James Scott and Claes Oldenburg, UK, 1970)
- *Andy Warhol* (Lana Jokel, USA, 1973)
- *David Hockney's Diary* (Christian Blackwood and Michael Blackwood, USA, 1978)
- *Jim Dine, London* (Michael Blackwood, USA, 1978)
- *Edward Ruscha* (Geoffrey Hayden, UK, 1979)
- *Roy Lichtenstein* (Geoffrey Haydon, UK, 1979)

Narrative Fiction Films

- *The Girl Can't Help It* (Frank Tashlin, USA, 1956)
- *The Golden Record* aka *The Golden Disk* (Don Sharp, UK, 1958)
- *Expresso Bongo* (Val Guest, UK, 1959)
- *Pillow Talk* (Michael Gordon, USA, 1959)
- *Breathless* (*À Bout de Souffle*) (Jean-Luc Godard, France, 1960)
- *A Hard Day's Night* (Richard Lester, UK, 1964)
- *Une Femme est Une Femme* (*A Woman is a Woman*, Jean-Luc Godard, France, 1961)
- *Blood and Black Lace* (Mario Bava, Italy, 1964)
- *The Planet of the Vampires* (Mario Bava, Italy, 1965)
- *Pierrot Le Fou* (Jean-Luc Godard, France, 1965)
- *The 10ᵗʰ Victim* (*La decima vittima*, Elio Petri, Italy, 1965)
- *Batman* (Leslie H. Martinson, USA, 1966)
- *Daisies* (*Sedmikrásky*, Věra Chytilová, Czechoslovakia, 1966)
- *Made in the USA* (Jean-Luc Godard, France, 1966)
- *Modesty Blaise* (Joseph Losey, UK, 1966)
- *Qui êtes-vous, Polly Maggoo?* (*Who are You, Polly Magoo?*) (William Klein, France, 1966)
- *Who Wants to Kill Jessie?* (*Kdo chce zabít Jessii?*, Václav Vorlíček, Czechoslovakia, 1966)

- *Black Lizard* (Kinji Fukasaku, Japan, 1967)
- *La Chinoise* (Jean-Luc Godard, France, 1967)
- *Jeu de Massacre* (*The Killing Game*) (Alain Jessua, France, 1967)
- *Deux ou trois choses que je sais d'elle* (*Two or Three Things I Know About Her*) (Jean-Luc Godard, France, 1967)
- *Barbarella* (Roger Vadim, France/Italy, 1968)
- *Danger: Diabolik* (*Diabolik*, Mario Bava, Italy/France, 1968)
- *The Green Slime* (Kinji Fukasaku, Japan, 1968)
- *Satanik* (Piero Vivarelli, Italy/Spain, 1968)
- *Yellow Submarine* (George Dunning, UK, 1968)
- *Erotissimo* (Gérard Pirès, France/Italy, 1968)
- *The Laughing Woman* (*Femina Ridens*, Piero Schivazappa, Italy, 1969)
- *Mr. Freedom* (William Klein, France, 1969)
- *Putney Swope* (Robert Downey, USA, 1969)
- *Brand X* (Wynn Chamberlain, USA, 1970)
- *Personal Search* (*Rewizja osobista*, Andrzej Kostenko and Witold Leszczyński, Poland, 1972)
- *Funeral Parade of Roses* (Toshio Matsumoto, Japan, 1971)
- *Tout va bien* (titled *All's Well* for US release and *Just Great* for international release, Jean-Luc Godard and Jean-Pierre Gorin, France, 1972)
- *Daddy* (Peter Whitehead and Niki de Saint Phalle, UK/France, 1973)
- *Suspiria* (Dario Argento, Italy, 1977)
- *Pepi, Luci, Bom y otras chicas del montón* (*Pepi, Luci, Bom and Other Girls Like Mom*, Pedro Almodóvar, Spain, 1980)
- *Breathless* (Jim McBride, USA, 1982)

Non-Narrative Films

- *Rose Hobart* (Joseph Cornell, USA, 1936)
- *Puce Moment* (Kenneth Anger, USA, 1947)
- *A Tub Named Desire* (George and Mike Kuchar, USA, 1956)
- *The Naked and the Nude* (George and Mike Kuchar, USA, 1958)
- *A MOVIE* (Bruce Conner, USA, 1958)
- *A La Mode* (Stan VanDerBeek, USA, 1959)
- *Science Friction* (Stan VanDerBeek, USA, 1959)
- *I was a Teenage Rumpot* (George and Mike Kuchar, USA, 1960)
- *Very Nice, Very Nice* (Arthur Lipsett, Canada, 1961)
- *COSMIC RAY* (Bruce Conner, USA, 1962)
- *History of Nothing* (Eduardo Paolozzi, UK, 1962)

- *A–Z* (Manfred Kuttner, Germany, 1963)
- *Flaming Creatures* (Jack Smith, USA, 1963)
- *Lust for Ecstasy* (George and Mike Kuchar, USA, 1963)
- *Pussy on a Hot Tin Roof* (George and Mike Kuchar, USA, 1963)
- *The Queen of Sheba Meets the Atom Man* (Ron Rice, USA, 1963/82)
- *REPORT* (Bruce Conner, 1963–67)
- *Scorpio Rising* (Kenneth Anger, USA, 1963)
- *Shopper's Market* (John Vicario, USA, 1963)
- *Television Assassination* (Bruce Conner, USA, 1963–64/1995)
- *21–87* (Arthur Lipsett, Canada, 1964)
- *Empire* (Andy Warhol, USA, 1964)
- *Free Fall* (Arthur Lipsett, Canada, 1964)
- *Harlot* (Andy Warhol, USA, 1964)
- *KISS KISS KISS* (Tadanori Yokoo, Japan, 1964)
- *Mario Banana (No. 1)* (Andy Warhol, USA, 1964)
- *Patriotism* (Joyce Wieland, USA, 1964)
- *Soap Opera* (Andy Warhol, USA, 1964)
- *Tokuten Eizo Anthology no. 1* (Tadanori Yokoo, Japan, 1964)
- *Vivian* (Bruce Conner, USA, 1964)
- *Cadence Commercial* (Andy Warhol, USA, 1965)
- *Corruption of the Damned* (George Kuchar, USA, 1965)
- *Filmmontagen I–III* (Peter Roehr, Germany, 1965)
- *Kachi Kachi Yama* (Tadanori Yokoo, Japan, 1965)
- *Kakafon Kakkoon* (Eduardo Paolozzi, UK, 1965)
- *Kustom Kar Kommandos* (Kenneth Anger, USA, 1965)
- *Melting* (Thom Andersen, USA, 1965)
- *Now* (Santiago Álvarez, Cuba, 1965)
- *O Dem Watermelons* (Robert Nelson, USA, 1965)
- *Sins of the Fleshapoids* (Mike Kuchar, USA, 1965)
- *Achoo Mr. Kerrooshev* (Stan VanDerBeek, USA, 1966)
- *All My Life* (Bruce Baillie, USA, 1966)
- *Breakaway* (Bruce Conner, USA, 1966)
- *Flik Flak* (Jeff Keen, UK, 1966)
- *Hold Me While I'm Naked* (George Kuchar, USA, 1966)
- *The Pop Show* (Fred Mogubgub, USA, 1966)
- *Screen Test [ST245]: Nico (Hershey)* (Andy Warhol, USA, 1966)
- *Screen Test [ST269]: Lou Reed (Coke)* (Andy Warhol, USA, 1966)
- *Screen Test [ST270]: Lou Reed (Hershey)* (Andy Warhol, USA, 1966)
- *Cineblatz* (Jeff Keen, UK, 1967)
- *The Great Society* (Fred Mogubgub, USA, 1967)

- *Jimmy James and The Vagabonds* (Peter Whitehead, UK, 1967)
- *Marvo Movie* (Jeff Keen, UK, 1967)
- *When I Was Young* (Peter Whitehead, UK, 1967)
- *Airborn* (Chas Wyndham, USA, 1968)
- *American Time Capsule* (Chuck Braverman, USA, 1968)
- *Filmtract no. 1968* (Jean-Luc Godard and Gerrard Fromanger, France, 1968)
- *Meatdaze* (Jeff Keen, UK, 1968)
- *The Movie Orgy* (Joe Dante, UK, 1968)
- *L. B. J.* (Santiago Álvarez, Cuba, 1968)
- *MARILYN TIMES FIVE* (Bruce Conner, USA, 1968–72)
- *Rockflow* (Robert Cowan, USA, 1968)
- *Underground Sundae (Schrafft's Commercial)* (Andy Warhol, USA, 1968)
- *White Lite* (Jeff Keen, UK, 1968)
- *Camembert Martial Extra-Doux (Extra-Soft Martial Camembert,* Martial Raysse, France, 1969)
- *Carrots and Peas* (Hollis Frampton, USA, 1969)
- *Lemon* (Hollis Frampton, USA, 1969)
- *NEW LEFT NOTE* (Saul Levine, USA, 1969/1982)
- *ABID* (Pramod Pati, India, 1970)
- *Pravda* (Dziga Vertov Group, France, 1970)
- *Link* (Derek Boshier, UK, 1970)
- *Three Landscapes* (Roy Lichtenstein, USA, 1970)
- *COMMERCIAL WAR* (Keiichi Tanaami, Japan, 1971)
- *GOOD-BY MARILYN* (Keiichi Tanaami, Japan, 1971)
- *GOOD-BY ELVIS and USA* (Keiichi Tanaami, Japan, 1971)
- *Metastasis* (Toshio Matsumoto, Japan, 1971)
- *Schick Aftershave Commercial* (Dziga Vertov Group, France, 1971)
- *WR: Mysteries of the Organism* (Dušan Makavejev, Yugoslavia/West Germany, 1971)
- *The Selling of New York* (Nam June Paik, USA, 1972)
- *Consumer Art* (Natalia LL, Poland, 1972–75)
- *Frank Film* (Frank and Caroline Mouris, USA, 1973)
- *Mona Lisa* (Toshio Matsumoto, Japan, 1973)
- *Oh Yoko!* (Keiichi Tanaami, Japan, 1973)
- *The Politics of Perception* (Kirk Tougas, Canada, 1973)
- *Andy Warhol: Re-Production* (Toshio Matsumoto, Japan, 1974)
- *Bio Dop* (Joan Rabascall and Benet Rossell, Spain, 1974)
- *Metro-Goldwyn-Mayer* (Jack Goldstein, USA, 1975)
- *Semiotics of the Kitchen* (Martha Rosler, USA, 1975)

- *Breakfast (Table-Top Dolly)* (Michael Snow, Canada, 1976)
- *Rocky* (Paul McCarthy, USA, 1976)
- *Learn Where the Meat Comes From* (Suzanne Lacey, USA, 1976)
- *Boy Meets Girl* (Eugènia Balcells, Spain, 1978)
- *Technology/Transformation: Wonder Woman* (Dara Birnbaum, USA, 1978–79)
- *Wild Gunman* (Craig Baldwin, USA, 1978)
- *Kiss The Girls: Make them Cry* (Dara Birnbaum, USA, 1979)
- *PM Magazine/Acid Rock* (Dara Birnbaum, USA, 1979)
- *Kojak/Wang* (Dara Birnbaum, USA, 1980)
- *General Hospital/Olympic Women Speed Skating* (Dara Birnbaum, USA, 1980)
- *Remy/Grand Central: Trains and Boats and Planes* (Dara Birnbaum, USA, 1980)
- *The Critic Laughs* (Richard Hamilton, UK, 1980)
- *Watching the Press, Reading the Media* (Antonio Muntadas, USA, 1981)
- *Andy Warhol Eating a Hamburger* [part of *66 Scenes from America*] (Jørgen Leth, Denmark, 1982)
- *Credits* (Antonio Muntadas, USA, 1984)
- *Death Valley Days* (Gorilla Tapes, UK, 1984)
- *Made for TV* (Anne Magnuson and Tom Rubnitz, USA, 1984)
- *Absence of Satan* (George Barber, UK, 1985)
- *Global Taste: A Meal in Three Courses* (Martha Rosler, USA, 1985)
- *I'm Not The Girl Who Misses Much* (Pipilotti Rist, Switzerland,1986)
- *Production Notes: Fast Food for Thought* (Jason Simon, USA, 1986)
- *Undercover… Me!* (Tom Rubnitz, USA, 1988)
- *1001 Colours Andy Never Thought Of* (George Barber, UK, 1989)
- *Pickle Surprise* (Tom Rubnitz, USA, 1989)
- *Strawberry Shortcut* (Tom Rubnitz, USA, 1989)
- *Bossy Burger* (Paul McCarthy, USA, 1991)
- *Hovis Ad* (George Barber, UK, 1994)
- *SCHWEPpeS AD* (George Barber, UK, 1995)
- *Altair* (Lewis Klahr, USA, 1995)
- *2001 Colours Andy Never Thought of* (George Barber, UK, 1996)
- *Suspension* (Anthony Discenza, USA, 1997)
- *Pony Glass* (Lewis Klahr, USA, 1998)
- *December 3, 1998 – 12:03–01:17 A.M.* (Anthony Discenza, USA, 1998)
- *pulse pharma phantasm* (Les LeVeque, USA, 2002)
- *Mouse Heaven* (Kenneth Anger, USA, 2004)
- *Light is Waiting* (Michael Robinson, USA, 2007)

- *Following Your Heart Can Lead to Wonderful Things* (George Barber, UK, 2008)
- *Hold Me Now* (Michael Robinson, USA, 2008)
- *The Dark Krystle* (Michael Robinson, USA, 2013)
- *The Rapture* (Michael Fleming, USA, 2015)
- *Sixty-Six* (Lewis Klahr, USA, 2015)

Index

EU Authorised Representative:

Easy Access System Europe Mustamäe tee 50, 10621 Tallinn, Estonia

gpsr.requests@easproject.com

Printed and bound by CPI Group (UK) Ltd, Croydon, CR0 4YY

03/06/2026

02126131-0001